The Tamil Separatist War in Sri Lanka

The complex and long-drawn war between the Sri Lankan government and the Liberation Tigers of Tamil Ealam (LTTE) ended with the defeat of the Tigers in 2009. This book provides a military history of the conflict in tracing its evolution from a battle between a ragtag guerrilla force and a mainly ceremonial army to one between an organised guerrilla force with semi-conventional capability and a state military apparatus that had morphed into a large and potent force with modern armour, aircraft and naval vessels. Using a wide range of sources, this book offers an incisive analysis of the progress and conclusion of one of the longest and most destructive wars in modern South Asia.

Comprehensive and accessible, the volume will be of great interest to scholars and researchers of modern South Asia, especially Sri Lanka, military history, politics, defence and strategic studies, as well as the general reader.

Channa Wickremesekera is an independent scholar and obtained his PhD from Monash University, Australia. He is the author of *Best Black Troops in the World* (2002) and *Kandy at War* (2004).

The Tamil Separatist War in Sri Lanka

Channa Wickremesekera

Routledge
Taylor & Francis Group

LONDON AND NEW YORK

First published 2016
by Routledge
2 Park Square, Milton Park, Abingdon, Oxon OX14 4RN

and by Routledge
711 Third Avenue, New York, NY 10017

Routledge is an imprint of the Taylor & Francis Group, an informa business

© 2016 Channa Wickremesekera

The right of Channa Wickremesekera to be identified as author of this work has been asserted by him in accordance with sections 77 and 78 of the Copyright, Designs and Patents Act 1988.

All rights reserved. No part of this book may be reprinted or reproduced or utilised in any form or by any electronic, mechanical, or other means, now known or hereafter invented, including photocopying and recording, or in any information storage or retrieval system, without permission in writing from the publishers.

Trademark notice: Product or corporate names may be trademarks or registered trademarks, and are used only for identification and explanation without intent to infringe.

British Library Cataloguing-in-Publication Data
A catalogue record for this book is available from the British Library

Library of Congress Cataloging-in-Publication Data
A catalog record has been requested for this book

ISBN: 978-1-138-18311-7 (hbk)
ISBN: 978-1-315-64605-3 (ebk)

Typeset in Galliard
by Apex CoVantage, LLC

To Victor Melder,
without whose generosity this book would
have never been written

Contents

Acknowledgements	ix
Maps	x
Introduction	1
1 From assassins to guerrillas: the birth of the Tamil rebellion	6
2 Learning to fight: the Sri Lankan military	28
3 The first showdown: 'Operation Liberation'	48
4 The IPKF interlude and the Tigers' return	63
5 The army on the offensive	85
6 The rise of the Sea Tigers and the battle for Kilali	100
7 A new regime, a new war	112
8 The problem of the Wanni	127
9 The East in ferment	148

10 The rise and fall of the Unceasing Waves	157
11 The peace that failed and the reconquest of the East	173
12 The rolling up of the Wanni	196
13 The last retreat of the Tamil Tigers	211
Conclusion	233
Bibliography	238
Index	267

Acknowledgements

My thanks go to Kaushik Roy for giving me the opportunity to write this book and to Victor Melder for allowing me to use the vast resources of his library.

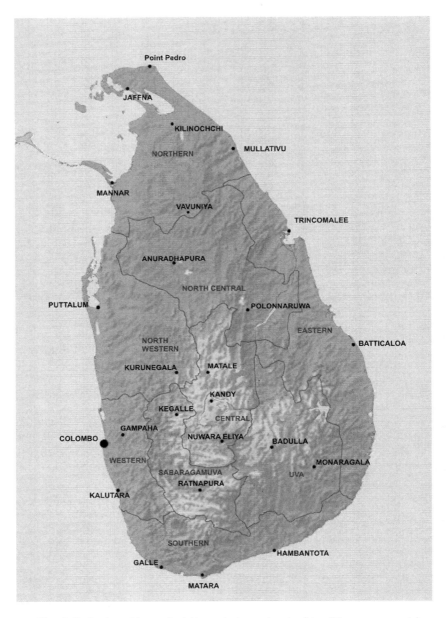

Map 1 Sri Lanka, with provincial boundaries and main cities (Maps not to scale)
All maps are by the author.

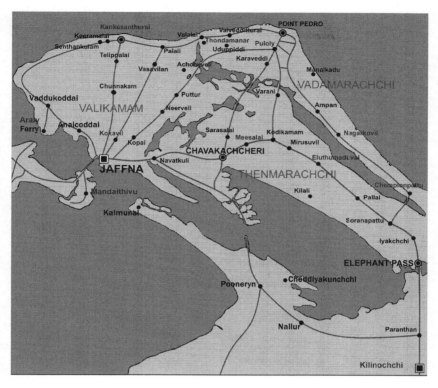

Map 2 Jaffna Peninsula (Maps not to scale)

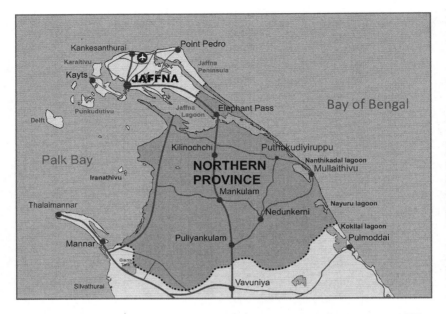

Map 3 Area under LTTE control at the start of the Wanni Offensive in 2007 (Maps not to scale)

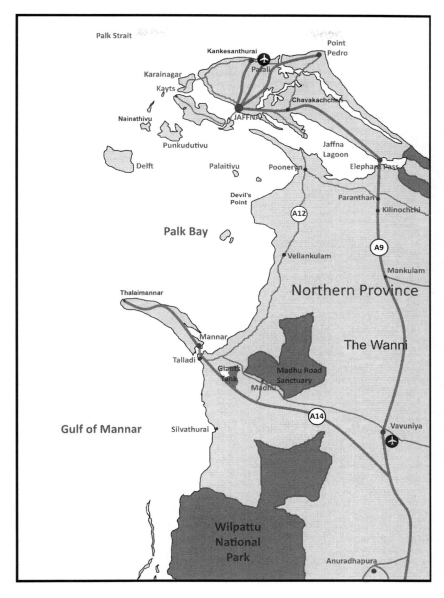

Map 4 Jaffna and North-western Wanni, the scene of heavy fighting in 2007–08 (Maps not to scale)

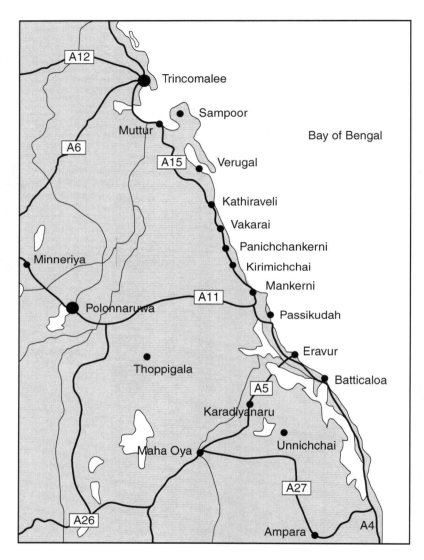

Map 5 The Eastern coastline and the interior (Maps not to scale)

Introduction

On May 19 2009, the long civil war in Sri Lanka finally came to an end. The Sri Lankan armed forces that had been steadily encroaching on the Tamil Tigers' de facto state for more than three years eventually cornered the Tiger leadership and wiped them out. The war that had cost more than 100,000 lives and billions of rupees was finally over.

The crushing of the Tamil Tigers by the Sri Lankan Security Forces is a rare event in the history of counter-insurgency. The insurgency that had dragged on for nearly three decades and one that had frequently been dismissed as an 'unwinnable war' had ended with the government forces annihilating the insurgents. The defeat of the LTTE was complete. Reportedly, the top three rungs of leadership were wiped out along with almost the entire hard core of the cadres. Thousands of captured or surrendered LTTE cadres were being carefully screened to detect any hard core sympathisers among them. To date, there is no indication that any leader of note had escaped.

For a war of such a long and tortuous course and such a complete conclusion, the war between the Tamil Tigers and the government forces in Sri Lanka has attracted little attention from students of military history. To date, only three full-length monographs, C. A. Chandraprema's *Gota's War the Crushing of Tamil Tiger Terrorism in Sri Lanka*,[1] Paul Moorcraft's *The Total Destruction of Tamil Tigers* and Ahmed S. Hashim's *When Counterinsurgency Wins: Sri Lanka's Defeat of the Tamil Tigers*,[2] have been written on the military aspects of the conflict. One may also include H.L.D. Mendis's *Assignment Peace*,[3] which while being supremely informative suffers terribly from a lack of objectivity and an analytical touch, not to mention the depressingly ponderous style to be ranked as a 'study' of the conflict. There is indeed a more substantial literature on different aspects of the war, such as Narayan Swamy's biography of Prabhakaran, several monographs by Rohan Gunaratna and a

2 Introduction

growing literature on the Indian Peace Keeping Force's involvement in Sri Lanka. Edgar O'Ballance's *Cyanide War*[4] is one of the earliest attempts at writing a narrative history of the war even though it covers the conflict only up to the end of the Indian involvement, while Tom Marks produced several articles on the first phase of the war based on first-hand observations in the war zone. There are also a number of memoirs written by former soldiers and officers and studies by academics and military analysts on different aspects of the military conflict. The arrival of the World Wide Web has also provided scope for a considerable amount of writing by professional and amateur 'analysts'. However, the works of Chandraprema, Moorcraft and Hashim remain the only substantial efforts to cover the entire war.

This book aims to contribute to this meagre literature. Like the other major works on the war, it too will trace the evolution of this long, brutal yet fascinating war, but it will be a different 'history' from the ones compiled by Chandraprema, Moorcraft and Hashim. The work of Chandraprema is primarily a biography of the former secretary to the Ministry of Defence, and due to this very objective, it falls short of being a history of the war. The works of Moorcraft and Hashim while being far more professional and objective in their approach than *Gota's War* tend to be more preoccupied with the last phase of the war than the conflict as a whole. This is not difficult to appreciate. Many students of the conflict in Sri Lanka have been impressed by the crushing nature of the defeat handed to the LTTE at the end of it. In popular imagination and also in the eyes of many students and analysts of the war, this phase of the war has become the most important and often the only important phase of the entire conflict. The total crushing victory over the Tigers obtained at the end of this phase banished everything else that happened before to the margins of the history of the military conflict. What seems to matter is the defeat of the Tigers, and the causes of this are sought mainly in the way the war was led and conducted during the last phase. There is little attempt to view the last phase as the climax of a developing and evolving conflict. What happened before 2006 is largely treated as skirmishes before the main battle.

However, a study of the war that focuses mainly on the final stage of the conflict overlooks aspects of the war that were crucial to its evolution and conclusion. It was during the phases of the war prior to that which commenced in 2006 that the LTTE rose to prominence, first as a guerrilla organisation and then as a semi-conventional army, reaching its zenith in the triumphant campaigns of 1999–2000. The enemy the Sri Lankan forces defeated in 2006–09 had already reached the end of its limits in semi-conventional warfare and was in no shape for a grand showdown. The consolidation of their power over 'fortress Wanni', the territory over which they were forced to fight the last campaign, had taken place long before the war recommenced in 2006, and the Tigers' predicament in the Wanni owed much to the necessity of defending this territory as a territorial power. The Sri Lankan Security Forces too reached the dominance they possessed in 2006–09 thanks to not only the unwavering focus on final victory and novel battlefield tactics but also the lessons learned from the disappointments and frustrations in the 1990s. A close study of these developments is necessary in understanding why the military conflict continued and ended the way it did.

This book aims at presenting a comprehensive, coherent narrative and analyses of the key military events of the entire war. These events are treated chronologically as well as thematically in an attempt to enable the reader to understand the evolution of the war from a conflict between a ragtag guerrilla outfit and a ceremonial government force into a major military contest between a rebel army with semi-conventional capabilities and Sri Lankan Security Forces that eventually succeeded in crushing the rebels completely. It is a history that follows the big events and campaigns of the war, explaining and interpreting their contribution to the evolution of the military conflict, particularly from a tactical and strategic perspective. It aims to provide a narrative framework for understanding the progress of the conflict and its major signposts. Combined with the analyses of key strategic and tactical issues, it is hoped that the book will enable the reader to obtain a broader and more comprehensive understanding of the military dimension of one of the most destructive and savage conflicts in modern South Asia.

Sources

As mentioned earlier, apart from the works of Chandraprema, Moorcraft and Hashim, there is a fairly substantial literature on different aspects of the war. Besides those already alluded to, there is also a massive volume of writing by amateurs and professionals on the Internet and newspapers. These include the various situation reports and analyses by professional organisations such as Jane's and numerous blog sites. Like all modern wars, much of the war was 'reported' rather than studied.

4 Introduction

These writings, while demonstrating the dire need for more serious studies, have also functioned as the sources for this book. Along with the memoirs and studies, the reader will also find copious reference to newspaper reports and articles which form the largest body of writing on the war. Using such sources is always problematic. Many of the writers depended on their own sources on the ground and there is always a possibility that the writer may have exaggerated, omitted or even created information to suit their agenda, to dramatise and to excite. Still, despite their potential to manipulate facts, such reports also remain the most voluminous source of information on the war and they also remain, in spite of all the hearsay, drama and propaganda, valuable and sometimes the only sources of information on certain aspects of the war. Many writers such as Iqbal Athas and Rohan Gunasekera had reliable informants on the ground, and for many military operations, they remain the primary published sources. Their expertise was recognised by respectable journals and organisations such as Jane's and the *Asian Defence Review*. The insights of analyst Dharmaratnam Sivram (Taraki) are unsurpassed. Any serious work on the history of the war needs to consult them while being mindful of their limitations. The lack of focus on the earlier phases of the war also stems partly from the difficulties associated with accessing and in some cases a lack of awareness of these sources, particularly reports and similar publications relating to the period before the publication of online newspapers.

However, unlike Moorcraft and Chandraprema, I have not used any interviews with participants. This is due to a number of reasons. There is the obvious logistical problem of interviewing people who are in another country. Unless cleared by the highest authorities in the Ministry of Defence, many officers are also not willing to speak about their experiences, and what they are willing to say after clearance is very likely to provide a skewed view of the conflict as the views of many of the surviving participants who are from the Sri Lankan military are likely to be coloured by the continuing controversies surrounding the end of the war. Apart from being able to claim that one has 'inside information', there is very limited merit in speaking to people who are deeply conscious of the impact of their words on their own image – and security. I have spoken to participants at the lower levels of the military hierarchy, but these sources have expressed a wish to remain anonymous. I have refrained from using their information as I am not a great believer in the use of unnamed sources.

Notes

1 C. A. Chandraprema, *Gota's War: the Crushing of Tamil Tiger Terrorism in Sri Lanka*, (Ranjan Wijeratne Foundation: Colombo, 2012).
2 Paul Moorcraft, *Total Destruction of the Tamil Tigers: The Rare Victory of Sri Lanka's Long War* (Pen and Sword Military: Barnsley, England, 2012); Ahmed S. Hashim, *When Counterinsurgency Wins: Sri Lanka's Defeat of the Tamil Tigers* (University of Pennsylvania Press: Philadelphia, 2013).
3 L.M.H. Mendis, *Assignment Peace: in the Name of the Motherland*, (Author publication: Colombo, 2009).
4 Edgar O'Ballance, *The Cyanide War: Tamil Insurrection in Sri Lanka 1973–88*, (Brassey's: London, 1990).

Chapter 1

From assassins to guerrillas
The birth of the Tamil rebellion

The Tamils are not the Chechens of South Asia. There is no long tradition of a fierce sense of independence tenaciously defended. Nor are they like the Kurds, a minority maintaining its identity in the face of centuries of conquest, displacement and discrimination. Tamils in Sri Lanka are a minority fighting majority domination which is of relatively recent origin. The reasons for this lie in the Tamils' unique experience as people in Sri Lanka.

Today Tamils are the dominant ethnic group in the Northern Province of Sri Lanka. They share the Eastern Province with the Sinhalese and the Muslims, the former being the majority community in the island. The Tamil influx into the Eastern Province is of more recent origin, but the heartland of Tamil rebellion, the northern Jaffna Peninsula, has been home to them for centuries.

On a map, the Jaffna Peninsula appears like a patchwork of small landmasses at the northern tip of Sri Lanka, separated by fingers of water. The three main segments in this collage are Vadamarachchi, Thenmarachchi and Valikamam. Of these, Valikamam is the most populous, with the capital of the Northern Province, Jaffna, and its suburbs occupying its south-western corner. The waters that surround the landmasses are branches of the Jaffna lagoon, which spread inland, fanning into a landscape of mudflats and mangroves. The land is almost completely flat with no mountains, rivers or lakes to break its general evenness and contiguity except the swampy lagoon. The peninsula itself is connected to the mainland at its south-eastern end by a slender strip of land. To the west of this isthmus, at Elephant Pass, the main highway from the south crosses the shallow sea, linking the peninsula with the mainland. Between the peninsula and the mainland lies the Jaffna – or Kilali – lagoon, an expanse of shallow water with a maximum depth of about three metres. A string of eight islands to the immediate west of the peninsula completes the geography of the northern end of the island.

The mainland immediately below the peninsula is sparsely populated and relatively flat, but unlike the peninsula it is irrigated by a number of rivers and dotted with numerous man-made irrigation tanks, some of vast proportions. On the east, the coast is broken by several inlets, while on the west the coast caves in to form the Gulf of Mannar. The islet of Mannar off the north-west coast of the island forms part of a chain of reefs, the remnants of a land bridge that connected Sri Lanka with the neighbouring subcontinent millions of years ago.

The predominance of the Tamils in this part of the island dates back centuries. It is a story of migration, conquest and survival.

A little history

When Sri Lanka (then known as Ceylon) gained independence from Britain in 1948, the Jaffna Peninsula and the adjacent mainland had long established itself as a predominantly Tamil region. Tamils had begun migrating from the neighbouring South India centuries ago, arriving as traders and adventurers. Tamil domination of the region, however, began with invasions. From the tenth to the thirteenth centuries, the armies of the Chola and Pandyan kings of South India overran the North, pushing the Sinhalese kingdoms southwards, leading to the emergence of a Tamil kingdom in the North. By the fourteenth century, it extended over the greater part of the northern plains on the mainland, swallowing much of what was once the kingdom of Anuradhapura. With the entrenchment of Tamil rule in the North, the eastern seaboard also became gradually populated by Tamil communities, Sinhala settlements in the East retreating to the interior, under the shadow of the central highlands.[1] From the north, Jaffna cast covetous eyes on the southern kingdoms, struggling to recover from the loss of their seats of power to the North. Invasions of the south ended in failure, but the kingdom of Jaffna remained strong, looming as a potential predator to the North. Then in 1449, a new ambitious king from the kingdom of Kotte, in the south, Parakramabahu VI (1415–67), made a bid for the overlordship of the entire island, sending an army to conquer Jaffna. The North fell to the conquering army, and for the first time in two centuries, a ruler of a Sinhala kingdom claimed overlordship over the North. But it was short-lived. Upon the death of Parakramabahu VI, Jaffna reverted to its former independence while the Sinhala polity fractured into several kingdoms and chieftaincies.

8   From assassins to guerrillas

The Jaffna kingdom retained its autonomy from the southern Sinhalese rulers until the early seventeenth century, now a mere shadow of its greatness in the fourteenth century, but still surviving as an independent kingdom. This was put to an end by the advent of European colonial powers. The Portuguese had begun establishing themselves in the coastal regions of Sri Lanka in the sixteenth century, and after several attempts, they finally brought Jaffna under their control in 1618. The peninsula now became part of the Portuguese Indian Empire with a separate administration based in Mannar. From the Portuguese, Jaffna passed over to the Dutch, who succeeded them in 1658. Jaffna became a British possession in 1796 when the British took over Dutch-administered territory in the island.

While Jaffna lost its independence and passed from one European master to another, the Sinhalese fought a long but losing battle against European encroachment. The seat of Sinhala power had shifted to Kandy in the central hills in the late sixteenth century, where, among the rugged Kandyan hills, the Sinhalese fought off repeated attempts by the Portuguese and the Dutch to bring it to heel. The British finally succeeded where the Portuguese and the Dutch had failed, conquering Kandy in 1815 and becoming the first power to rule the entire island in nearly four centuries.

Thus, from the thirteenth century the ethno-political geography of the island was dominated by two distinct regions: the Tamil region in the north and the Sinhala region in the south. They also developed into distinct cultural regions – the Tamil region based on the Tamil language and Hindu religion and the Sinhala region based on Sinhala language and Buddhism. They were also more or less politically independent of each other. The integration of the Tamil North into the maritime dominions of the Portuguese and the Dutch ended the independence of the Tamils but still kept them separate from the rule of the Sinhalese in the south, whose main seat of power had now shifted to Kandy in the central hills. The eastern coast at this time seems to have accepted Kandyan overlordship. But the separation of the North was firmly established. Even in the East, the Tamil language and culture predominated with the majority of the population being either ethnic Tamil or Tamil-speaking Muslims. The British conquest of the whole island in 1796 did not bring an end to this. Sinhala Buddhist and Tamil Hindu cultures maintained their dominance in their respective heartlands regardless of British hegemony over the island. Indeed, the British were making a tacit acknowledgement of this reality when they divided the whole island into five administrative provinces demarcating the Tamil-dominated North and the East as the Northern and Eastern Provinces.

However, this does not mean that Tamils and Sinhalese were separated from each other as peoples. Far from it. Tamil-speaking communities were part and parcel of the society outside the North and the East with considerable numbers of them engaged in trade and commercial activities in and around ports. Sinhala kings and members of the royal families frequently intermarried with South Indian princely families. The last dynasty of Kandyan kings was of South Indian descent, and their rule led to the emergence of a strong Tamil presence in the town of Kandy.[2] The British had also inducted a large number of labourers from South India into their tea and coffee plantations in the central highlands, and they formed a substantial Tamil population among the Sinhalese in former Kandyan territories. During British rule, many Tamils and Sinhalese from the upper strata of society came to enjoy the advantages of an English education and they interacted freely with each other. There were also thriving Tamil business communities in many parts of the island. These Tamils, however, lived among the Sinhalese with the tacit acceptance of the primacy of the Sinhalese as the majority community and Buddhism as the dominant religion. For the members of the elite, ethnicity hardly mattered. They were largely deracinated, having more in common with each other than their ethnic communities. But it was different with Tamils in the North. There they enjoyed the position of cultural dominance in a region outside the influence of the Sinhalese. Under British rule, even the dominance of the Sinhala culture in areas outside the North and the East did not feel overbearing without any corresponding political clout. Sinhala language and culture predominated, but it was the British who ruled, a fact driven home by the use of English as the language of administration.

This changed with independence in 1948. Now, with independent Sri Lanka having to elect governments by majority vote, Tamils for the first time faced the real possibility of being ruled by a government dominated by the Sinhalese. This should not have caused much anxiety had the deracinated elite who took over from the British hat stuck to their cosmopolitan ways in conducting the politics of post-independent Sri Lanka – or Ceylon as it was known then. But the leaders of new Ceylon found the lure of political power too hard to resist. And the reality of coming to power through majority votes in a land of different ethnic groups that still thought largely in pre-industrial terms of caste, ethnicity and religion made communal politics very attractive. Island wide, there were simply more Sinhalese than Tamils and more Buddhists than Hindus, Christians and Muslims. And in the North and the East, the Tamils outnumbered other communities.

Therefore, instead of focusing on building a national identity that every ethnic group in the island could lay a claim to, the leaders of independent Ceylon resorted to using communal sentiment to ride to power. It was easy and cheap, in more ways than one. So when SWRD Bandaranayake had the opportunity to tilt at national political power by pandering to the wishes of the Buddhist clergy, he grabbed it by both hands, promising to make Sinhalese the official language. His party came to power with a powerful mandate in the 1956 elections, and the new prime minister went about delivering on his promise. It was a ridiculous policy that forced Tamils to learn Sinhalese in order to get jobs in the government. Predictably, the Tamils who were the majority in the North and the East voiced their opposition to the decision, seeing it, quite understandably, as an attempt to marginalise them in the new nation. Their resentment was only exacerbated by the failure to negotiate a settlement with the government. Attempts by Sri Lankan governments to redress Tamil grievances through a measure of power sharing in 1958 and 1965 were stymied by the increasingly powerful lobby of Sinhala nationalists led by Buddhist monks.[3] This made many Tamils feel that the Sri Lankan government had little interest in going against the strident voices of the Sinhala nationalists.

Their protests had initially been peaceful, the usual demonstrations and sit-ins. They tried it in 1958 and 1961, the latter an exceptionally successful satyagraha which attracted widespread support from the Tamils in Jaffna and Batticaloa in the Eastern Province. The Sri Lankan government's response, however, was stern. The protesters were treated like contemptible upstarts. And to remind them of their place the military was called in, and the satyagrahis were handled with harshness, sometimes even with brutality.[4] The resistance gradually petered out. The sit-ins had galvanised the people in the North into action but achieved little more than ensuring that the government remained firm in its stance.

By the early 1970s, the increasing ineffectualness of the tactics of the old guard of Tamil political leadership was beginning to frustrate the youth. The old leaders were too steeped in traditional methods of persuasion. Sit-ins and petitions did not work with a government that seemed too closely bound to the majority community. They needed something more imaginative – and powerful.

The rise of Tamil militancy

That alternative was provided by growing militancy, led by a number of militant youth organisations that had sprouted in the late 1960s and early 1970s. The Liberation Tigers of Tamil Ealam or LTTE, which was to gain notoriety later as a ruthless and powerful Tamil guerrilla group, was one of them. It began its life as the Tamil New Tigers (TNT) formed by Velupillai Prabhakaran, a youth from Velvetithurai in Vadamarachchi in Jaffna. The TNT and another group under a youth called Nadarajah Thangathurai were the two leading militant groups at the time. Both were committed to armed struggle as a means of fighting Sinhalese hegemony.

Under pressure from these groups, the main Tamil political party, the Tamil United Front (TUF), changed its name to Tamil United Liberation Front (TULF) and gave vent to the rising militancy by passing a resolution at its congress in Vadukkodai in May 1976, calling for a separate state of 'Tamil Ealam' as the solution to the Tamils' marginalisation in Sri Lanka.[5] The militants' demands were becoming more extreme and influencing the politics of mainstream parties. Then, in a further sign of warning to the government, the Tamils voted overwhelmingly for the TULF's platform of separation at the general election in July 1977. The TULF won 18 out of the 24 seats they contested in the North and the East, including all the seats in the Northern Province, the Tamil heartland. Separation was no longer something that only the militants and the politicians wanted. It now had the endorsement of the Tamil masses as well.

But by then, the militant youth had gone one step further. Around midday on Friday, July 27 1975, three young men shot dead Alfred Duraiappah, the mayor of Jaffna, as he arrived at the *Kovil* at Ponnalai in Jaffna for his customary Sunday prayer.[6] The victim was carefully chosen. A member of the ruling Sri Lanka Freedom Party (SLFP), the mayor was seen as a government stooge, a sell-out who had betrayed his people for the crumbs from the government's table. The rebel youth had finally declared war on the Sri Lankan state.

The militants' violence now followed a familiar trajectory: terrorist attacks followed by guerrilla-style operations. Duraiappah's murder was followed by more killings. These included police officers as well as informers.[7] Gradually, the attacks extended to police stations and Security Forces' details. The operations were carried out by small groups of young men often arriving on bicycles and were aimed at keeping the Security Forces on their toes and seizing weapons. By now there were several armed groups leading the charge against the Sri Lankan state. These were the Liberation Tigers of Tamil Ealam (LTTE), Tamil Ealam Liberation Organisation (TELO), People's Liberation Organisation of Thamilealam (PLOTE), Ealam People's Revolutionary Liberation Front

(EPRLF) and Ealam Revolutionary Organisation of Students (EROS). Velupillai Prabhakaran had renamed the Tamil New Tigers the LTTE in 1976, while TELO had originated from a group of militants around two leaders, Nadrajah Thangathurai and Selvarajah Yogachandran or 'Kuttimani' in 1979. The PLOTE under Uma Maheswaran was the result of a split within the LTTE. Uma quarrelled with Prabhakran in 1978 and formed a separate group. EROS had also emerged in the 1970s while the EPRLF was an offshoot of the EROS.

Soon violence reached alarming heights. In July 1983, the LTTE staged a well-coordinated ambush at Tinneveli in Jaffna, wiping out an army patrol, killing 13 soldiers. The haul of weapons was also rich: a dozen SLRs, a shotgun and a small pile of ammunition. It was the biggest single loss suffered by Sri Lankan Security Forces in the war against Tamil militants to date.[8]

The ambush led to widespread anti-Tamil rioting in Colombo and several other cities. Hundreds of Tamils were killed, thousands of Tamil-owned residences and businesses burned and looted and thousands of Tamils made homeless. In many places, the riots were well organised and often the police and the military stood by idly without stopping the violence and in some cases even took part in it.

A lull descended on the North after the riots. Then in August 1984, violence broke out in a sustained spell, making the sporadic bloodletting prior to July 1983 appear like a Sunday outing. A string of landmine attacks took a heavy toll on the lives of Security Forces. The victims included Colonel A. Ariyapperuma, the commander of the Sri Lankan army's northern command, who was killed by a landmine explosion at Tellipillai in Jaffna on November 19. The attacks on police stations also began to occur with greater frequency, the most daring being the attacks on Chavakachcheri and Jaffna police stations. The former, occurring on the afternoon of November 23 1984, reduced the police station to rubble, killing 24 policemen.[9] The attack on the Jaffna police station, less than a mile from the Jaffna Fort, took place on April 10 1985 and caused extensive damage to the buildings.[10] On May 10, the Mannar police station too suffered a particularly serious assault. The attack flattened the police station and killed five policemen while four were reported 'captured'.[11] On January 19 1985, in another shocking attack the militants blew up the Yal Devi train from Jaffna to Colombo as it was pulling out of Murunkandi, south of Kilinochchi, under heavy military escort, leaving 39 dead, 28 of them soldiers.[12] A few weeks later, on February 13, a band of militants also attacked the Kokilai army camp; the attackers were dressed in military-style uniforms and wearing night vision goggles.[13] The assault failed, but it demonstrated that the guerrillas were now confident enough to take on army camps. In the months that followed, the militants pressed their offensive, attacking more Security Forces camps all over the North, including the Karainnagar and Gurunagar camps on the peninsula and Kokavil and Kilinochchi camps in the mainland.[14]

But bigger blows were on the way. Early in the morning on May 14, a group of about 20 LTTE guerrillas hijacked a bus from the Puttalam depot and drove to Anuradhapura, a city sacred to Buddhists. When they arrived at the Central Bus Stand, the place was already filling with people bound for work. The men in the bus opened fire at the people at the bus stand. The bus then drove slowly through the streets, the guerrillas firing away at the fleeing people, making its way to the sacred Sri Maha Bodhi, where they continued their killing before hijacking another bus and speeding back towards Puttalam. On the way, they fired at the Nocchiyagama police station, and when they arrived at the Wilpattu National Park, they shot dead 24 of the employees and forced one to be their guide. At the end of the rampage, 148 people lay dead, including 120 killed at the Sri Maha Bodhi. The latter included three monks and two nuns. Over a hundred were injured.[15]

Finally in June 1985 under India's patronage, five militant groups agreed to a ceasefire with the Sri Lankan government. Talks were arranged in Thimpu. But the talks came to nothing, and by the end of the year, the ceasefire was in tatters. The war recommenced with a vengeance.

Mother India

The situation the Sri Lankan Security Forces found themselves in late 1985 owed much to the events in July 1983. The mobs in Colombo and other cities, while 'punishing' Tamils by burning and looting Tamil properties and killing defenceless Tamils, had also fuelled the anger and insecurity of a people. Hitherto, many Tamils outside the North and the East had remained somewhat aloof from the militancy and the militants were treated with tolerance and even with some apprehension. But after the riots, few Tamils in Sri Lanka felt secure under a Sinhalese-dominated government, and almost overnight, the militants turned into saviours, defenders of the dignity and lives of the Tamils. Tamil youth who had been smarting from the indignities of July 1983 now naturally turned to the militants as an avenue of revenge and hope. Within days of the riots, thousands of eager Tamil men and boys were seeking enlistment with the militant groups.

14   From assassins to guerrillas

But having thousands of eager recruits does not make an army. They need training, weapons and money. These came from across the seas, from neighbouring India.

A mere 22 miles of shallow sea separates Tamil Nadu, the Tamil majority state in South India, from Jaffna. Across this narrow Palk Strait, the people of Tamil Nadu and Jaffna have shared a culture and language for centuries. Visitors from India instantly recognised the similarity, a Bombay journalist quipping in 1984 that 'one may be pardoned for mistaking Jaffna for a medium-sized town in Tamil Nadu' before going on to observe rather pointedly that although Jaffna's body was in Sri Lanka its soul was in Tamil Nadu.[16] There was much truth in this. Jaffna Tamils looked up to South India for cultural nourishment, idolising South Indian movie stars and following subcontinental fashions and trends closely. Even the informal economy of Jaffna was closely tied to Tamil Nadu; towns such as Velvetithurai were the bustling centres of smuggling between Sri Lanka and India. Many Tamils regularly travelled back and forth between Jaffna and the cities in Tamil Nadu for business and pleasure; it was not uncommon for Jaffna youths to dart across the sea to South India to catch a late-night Tamil movie and return home in the morning.[17] For many Tamils in the North, India was a closer home than Sri Lanka.

It was only natural then that the Tamil struggle in Jaffna aroused the sympathy of many Tamils in Tamil Nadu. Local politicians such as P. Nedumaran followed Tamil politics closely and showed a keen interest in the direction of the militants' struggle. Understandably, Tamil Nadu evolved as a safe haven for Tamil militants from an early time. Guerrilla leaders such as Prabhakaran frequently crossed over to Tamil Nadu to evade arrest while wounded militants were shifted there for medical attention. When the army came down heavily on the militants, it was to Tamil Nadu that many militant leaders fled. There, in camps set up in Tiruchirapalli and Madurai, they underwent training, under the guidance of some retired Indian officers who spoke Tamil.[18]

Still, until July 1983, South India was merely a convenient 'rear base'. But after the riots in 1983, India came to play a bigger role in the Tamil struggle. Now it became a source of training, weapons, money and patronage at the highest levels of the Indian administration. The Tamil insurgency now became part of India's strategic considerations.

The island's proximity and the cultural ties between Tamil Nadu and the Northern Province of Sri Lanka meant that events in Sri Lanka and Sri Lanka's strategic decisions would be closely monitored by India now led by Indira Gandhi. After the victory of the United National Party in

Sri Lankan elections in 1977 under J. R. Jayawardena, who had a reputation as a friend of the West, this scrutiny became closer. India, with its close relationship with the Soviet Union, was predictably irked by the Jayawardena regime's pro-Western stance within the Non Aligned Movement highlighted by Sri Lanka's support for Britain in the Falklands War. Western countries were also pouring money into Sri Lanka's development projects, extending their influence over the island. These concerns grew when India began to suspect that Sri Lanka was favouring an American consortium for the contract for repairing and restoring the WW II vintage oil tanks in Trincomalee to an American firm. America was a strong supporter of India's traditional rival Pakistan, and an American foothold in Trincomalee which was one of the finest natural harbours in the world was too much for India to stomach. Last but not least, the central government could not ignore the public opinion in Tamil Nadu, which was firmly behind the Tamils in Sri Lanka.[19]

Increasingly resentful of Sri Lanka's cosying up to the West, India was keen to show its tiny neighbour that it was not free to ignore India's interests in the region. The riots in July 1983 made it imperative. The disturbances drove tens of thousands of Sri Lankan Tamils to Tamil Nadu, bringing with them horror stories that incensed public opinion in South India. The situation in Sri Lanka was threatening to become a problem for India itself, something which India could not ignore anymore. India had to put its foot down, hard and fast, and the boot was provided by the militants.

India's intelligence organ, the Research and Analysis Wing (RAW), soon began making overtures to the militants. And it could not have been better timed. As refugees from the riots arrived in Jaffna with tales of horror, the militants' ranks were swelling with angry young men, eager young men impatient to get back at the state they held responsible for humiliating and murdering their people. The militants accepted the Indian offer. Soon boatloads of young Tamils were leaving for training in India, braving the choppy seas in little rickety boats to learn what the Indians had to offer.

By September–October 1983, training had begun in earnest. In South India, training camps had sprouted in the districts of Tiruchirapalli, Madurai, Thanjavur and Madras, while in the north they were established at Dehradun, near New Delhi and also in Uttar Pradesh. Some of the camps in the South were run by the guerrilla groups themselves while the authorities turned a blind eye to them. For example, PLOTE maintained a number of camps in Thanjavur while the LTTE established a camp in Madurai. Others were run by RAW itself, providing instructors,

16 From assassins to guerrillas

many of whom were retired Indian army officers.[20] The recruits were trained in a range of guerrilla skills, including the use of weapons such as assault rifles, mortars and rocket launchers and in reading maps and handling explosives.[21] They were also put through gruelling physical drills to condition them to the rigours of combat. The Indians also provided the armed groups with an assortment of weapons, which included SLRs, RPGs, AK-47s, sub machine guns and light machine guns.[22]

By 1987, India is said to have trained thousands of militants. Upon completion of their course, the trained militants were brought down to Madras by bus, from where they were put on boats and returned to Jaffna. PLOTE is even said to have trained a few Sinhalese.[23]

Indian training boosted the morale and battle readiness of the militants. However, not everybody was satisfied. According to Anton Balasingham, the LTTE's theoretician, LTTE leader Prabhakaran was disappointed with the level of Indian support. The Indians clearly did not want the militants to acquire a limited effectiveness. They were trained in the use of small arms that would have helped them to fight the Sri Lankan military to a standstill, not in modern sophisticated weapons systems that would have enabled them to defeat their enemy decisively.[24] It was a grudge that Prabhakaran would bear for a long time.

Frustrated by the Indians' chicanery, the LTTE began exploring alternative avenues for augmenting their arsenal. The problem however was that while the Indians were offering their meagre supplies free of charge independent procurement of weapons required a substantial treasury. This problem was solved by the generosity of M. G. Ramachandran or MGR, the actor-politician in Tamil Nadu. MGR gave the LTTE 2 million rupees, a precious financial windfall that raised the rebel group's stocks considerably. Anton Balasingham would later recognise this as 'the cornerstone of the development of the LTTE'.[25] The Tigers now had the money to purchase the arms they felt they were denied by India.

With plenty of spending money, Prabhakaran now set his sights on developing his own arms procuring establishment. This was set up under K. Pathmanathan – or K.P. as he came to be known – who travelled the world, shopping in arms bazaars of Asia, Europe and the Middle East. A shipping line was established for the purpose. The first consignment of arms arrived in South India without the knowledge of the Indians in 1984. The weapons were promptly dispatched to Sri Lanka by boat.[26]

Soon word began to seep out about the many camps that trained militants on Indian soil. In March 1986, the *South* magazine even went so far as to publish detailed list of camps in India.[27] As the existence of the camps became public knowledge, the Sri Lankan government requested India to close them down, but India repeatedly denied their existence. There were no terrorist camps in India, the Indian government said firmly. There were only refugee camps. Indian Prime Minister Rajiv Gandhi even went so far as to invite journalists to visit India and check for themselves.[28]

As the militants became more established on the peninsula, they opened camps on Sri Lankan soil itself. In July 1985, a reporter from Colombo watched about 75 LTTE guerrilla trainees going through mock battles in their camp on the outskirts of Jaffna. An EPRLF leader told the same reporter that their recruits were trained for 10–14 weeks before they were considered fit to 'face the enemy'.[29] Another journalist from the south of Sri Lanka watched around 175 LTTE recruits going through a rigorous drill that included scaling walls, creeping under barbed wire with weapons in hand and taking part in 'mock commando style assaults'. The training grounds were a public park only 5 miles from the Jaffna city centre.[30] The jungles deep in the Wanni also provided ideal grounds for building the rebel army. A journalist of the Associated Press was treated to the spectacle of about 150 recruits going through a 'gruelling three and a half hour workout' in one such camp. Ominously, most were teenagers, some as young as 12. The commander of the camp explained that the recruits were trained for six months. He claimed there were three Tiger camps in the Wanni, training about 400 cadres, the one visited by the journalist being the largest.[31]

Along with their training, the militants also began to intensify the campaign against suspected informants in an effort to bring the population into line. The first half of 1984 alone saw at least 40 assassinations of suspected informants by militants. The victims' bodies were usually tied to lamp posts with placards announcing their treacherous activities.[32]

While the informants perished, the militants' ranks were expanding rapidly. According to the analyst the late Dharmaratnam Sivaram, the total number of militants who had basic military training before July 1983 was 800. In 1984–85, this had grown to 44,800. According to Sivaram, PLOTE had the largest number at that time, with 6,000 cadres under training in its camps in South India and around 12,000 cadres in the camps in the north of Sri Lanka. TELO had 4,000 cadres under training in its camps in South India and 2,000 in the North-east. EPRLF had about 7,000, including 1,500 girls, in South India and the North-east. The LTTE had fewer than 3,000 cadres and EROS 1,800 cadres. The balance belonged to the smaller militant groups.[33] This appears to be a very extravagant estimate, but what is important

18 From assassins to guerrillas

is that the militant numbers were growing. Besides, Sivaram's numbers only relate to those who received training, not necessarily those who were armed.

The new rulers of the North

By mid-1986, a major shift had also taken place in the power alignment among the militant groups. In April 1985, the long-standing rivalry between the TELO and the LTTE erupted into violence. Using a street clash between its cadres and TELO men, the LTTE launched a lightning strike on the TELO on April 29 1986. Tiger cadres pounced on all the TELO camps and hideouts in the Jaffna Peninsula, ruthlessly gunning down their rivals. Some were killed while sleeping, others while they were having lunch. The TELO leader Sri Sabaratnam escaped and went into hiding, but the Tigers tracked him down and killed him on May 7. Not stopping at murdering their rivals, the LTTE went on to make a telling example of its brutality to anyone daring to question its primacy. Some of the victims were piled up at junctions and burnt in public. At least one was thrust into a car and exploded, while one TELO cadre was allegedly shot in the leg and dragged through the streets of Jaffna to find out the whereabouts of their leader. Sabaratnam's bullet-riddled body was displayed at the Jaffna bus station to demonstrate to the population the end of the TELO.[34] 'Like mad dogs they killed our men,' a survivor recalled in dismay.[35] Another TELO spokesman was more prophetic. 'If this continues,' he warned, 'they are going to create a cemetery, not a country.'[36]

Within a week, TELO had ceased to exist in all but name. Other small groups of militants were quickly absorbed into the LTTE.[37] In October, the LTTE ordered the PLOTE to leave Jaffna. Impotent before the almighty Tigers, the group agreed but not before their Jaffna commander was brutally murdered by the Tigers.[38] Of the other groups, the EPRLF too came in for a brutal crackdown in December 1986, and having lost a number of its cadres and much of its arsenal in Jaffna, they retreated to Batticaloa where lay their main base.[39] EROS alone established a working relationship with the LTTE. Hereafter, it will be referred to as the LTTE.

The siege

By the end of 1986, the insurgency had taken a turn for the worse for the government. The Security Forces held on to their camps in the

Jaffna Fort, Palali and a few other places, but venturing beyond the perimeters of these had become dangerous. Rebel bunkers ringed the camps, almost taunting the men inside. From behind the walls of empty houses or piles of sandbags, young Tigers watched the enemy, clutching their rifles and keeping a few grenades on stand-by. Roadblocks built of burnt-out cars, old tyres, and sandbags plugged the approaches to the army camps. In some places, even walls had been constructed across the roads.[40] Whenever a patrol tried to probe the siege, the sentries alerted the LTTE main forces, who rushed to the place and attacked the enemy patrol with grenades and gunfire.[41] Soldiers were not completely secure inside their bases either. Mortars descended on the camps regularly, keeping the troops on their toes. Occasionally, a lucky strike would kill and maim. The fort was a favourite target of the militants, a few mortars finding their way within its walls almost every night. An officer quipped that mortar fire was so frequent that they fell like rain.[42]

Outside Jaffna too, the Tigers were tightening their grip. In the Wanni, the vast hinterland on either side of the A9, the main trunk road from Kandy to Jaffna, they held supreme. The army was already too stretched in the northern peninsula and parts of the east to occupy the ground in the Wanni in strength. On the long A9 highway, there were only two outposts between Vavuniya and Mankulam and only the small post guarding the TV and radio transmitter at Kokavil between Mankulam and Kilinochchi. On the road from Mankulam to Mullaithivu, there was only a small camp manned by an engineering squadron at Oddusudan. There was virtually no military presence between Vavuniya and Mannar. This allowed a vast area in the Northern Province to go under the control of the Tigers. As in the peninsula, the army was capable of holding out in their camps. But outside their camps, on the long, jungle-fringed roads, they were highly vulnerable to guerrilla attacks. The troops usually travelled these roads in large convoys, sometimes of dozens of vehicles with air cover. Still, the guerrillas could launch well-coordinated attacks that took a heavy toll on the soldiers. One such attack took place at Kokavil on the Vavuniya Kilinochchi road on April 2 1986 when the Tigers sprang a well-organised ambush on a military convoy including trucks and armoured cars, killing seven soldiers and wounding 15.[43]

And to make matters worse, the Tigers also brought the war to the South. A large Tamil population lived outside the North and the East, especially in Colombo, and the Tigers had, over the years, inducted a number of their operatives into the city. Now they went to work in devastating fashion. On May 3, a bomb exploded aboard Air Lanka flight UL512, breaking the aircraft into two and killing 21 people, including

20   From assassins to guerrillas

13 foreigners. The explosives had been hidden in a container with meat, vegetables and fruits destined for Mali. The explosion was to occur in mid-air, but a 45-minute delay resulted in the bomb ripping through the aircraft while passengers were still boarding.[44] On May 7 1986, a parcel bomb ripped through the Central Telegraph Office in the fort area in Colombo, killing 11 and injuring more than a hundred. The colonial-era building suffered severe damage, with its wooden upper floor collapsing.[45] A few weeks later on May 29, another bomb blew up a lorry parked inside Ceylon Cold stores warehouse at Slave Island in Colombo, killing nine and injuring several more. The number of casualties would have been much higher had there not been a delayed lunch break.[46]

The East

The Eastern Province was an integral part of the territory the militants were fighting for, part of the 'Traditional Homeland' of the Tamils. But the troubles started slowly there, the East remaining relatively calm well after the 1983 riots while the North simmered and boiled. This changed with the intensification of violence in August 1984, the war quickly spreading to areas outside the Jaffna Peninsula. A landmine had killed six soldiers in Mannar on August 11. By the end of 1984, the rebel 'offensive' had spread to the East too, the landmine announcing its arrival in deadly fashion.

However, launching the struggle for Tamil Ealam in the East was different from waging the separatist war in the North. The Eastern Province is a far more complex region than the Jaffna Peninsula and the northern mainland. It is geographically more extensive with a long coastline. Its eastern boundary is the coast that extends all the way south from the southern banks of the Kokilai lagoon in the north to the eastern end of the Hambantota district. It is relatively narrow, embracing mainly the immediate fertile hinterland of this coastal belt, except near Batticaloa where it spills deeper inland up to the central foothills. The province is divided into three districts: Trincomalee, Batticaloa and Ampara.

The geographical features of the province favoured the guerrillas. In particular, the extensive coastline with numerous inlets and harbours made it easier for them to feed men and material into the province. The area north-west of Trincomalee harbour and the mainland to the west of the Batticaloa lagoon up to the border with Polonnaruwa was also thickly forested and sparsely populated, ideal country to set up bases. Western Batticaloa, in particular, provided a perfect sanctuary for guerrilla activity with vast forested tracts, dominated by the 712-foot high Thoppigala rock and populated mainly by Tamils. The province also had a long border with Sinhala-dominated districts of Anuradhapura, Polonnaruwa and Hambantota, which made them vulnerable to guerrilla infiltrations and attacks. Through Badulla, which had a large number of ethnic Tamil estate workers, inroads could be also made into the hill country.

However, it was the demographic factor which made things complicated. Ethnically, the population is dominated by Tamils and Muslims, the former making up about 40 per cent and the latter 37 per cent. The Sinhalese form a large minority with about 21 per cent. The ethnic composition of the population of the Eastern Province has undergone significant changes over the past few centuries. During the time of the Anuradhapura and Polonnaruwa kingdoms, the eastern seaboard and its hinterland was ruled by Sinhalese kings with a predominantly Sinhala population. However, as explained earlier, with the retreat of the Sinhalese kingdoms to the south in the thirteenth century, the eastern seaboard had come to be gradually settled by Tamil-speaking people. By the turn of the nineteenth century, the Tamilisation of the East was more or less complete. The 1901 census shows Tamils making up 55.83 per cent of the population of the province, while Muslims form 35.97 per cent. Sinhalese come a distant third with only 5.06 per cent. However, by 1963 the Sinhalese population had risen to 19.88 per cent with the Tamils making 45.03 and the Muslims 33.75 per cent. By 1981, nearly a quarter of the population was Sinhalese.

The influx of Sinhalese in the twentieth century was the result of several irrigation schemes undertaken by the Sri Lankan state after independence. The Gal Oya Scheme in 1956 dammed the Gal Oya River and opened up around 40,000 hectares in the Eastern Province for cultivation. It also brought in nearly 20,000 new colonists, the majority of them Sinhalese, to settle inside the western borders of the Batticaloa District, which changed the demographic proportions. Two other irrigation projects, the Allai-Kantalai Project and the Padaviya scheme in the 1950s and the 1960s, and the Gomarankadawela–Moraweva Projects in the 1970s and 1980s also resulted in the establishment of Sinhalese settlements, this time in the Trincomalee District. They were settled in lands in the north and south of Trincomalee District, forming corridors of Sinhala villages encompassing Kottiyar Bay. As a result of these settlements, the percentage of Sinhala settlers increased substantially. From a mere 4.2 per cent in 1946, the Sinhala population in Trincomalee had risen to nearly a third of the inhabitants in the district by 1981.[47]

22 From assassins to guerrillas

Such settlement schemes increased the ratio of Sinhalese settlers to Tamils and Muslims, altering the ethnic balance in the province. In 1958, the government carved out a third district in the East out of the Muslim majority areas in the South and the newly colonised western part to form the Ampara District. In Trincomalee too, a new AGA division of Seruvila was created out of the settlements, where the vast majority of the inhabitants were Sinhalese settlers from outside.[48]

It is unclear whether these colonisation schemes were originally strategic in aim. The alteration of the demography of the province and the positioning of the settlements seem to suggest so. However, what is very clear is that after the outbreak of the insurgency, the government found the Sinhalese settlers to be a valuable tool for undermining the separatists' strategy. Now Sinhala colonisation became clearly strategic in aim, the insertion of more Sinhalese settlements between the Eastern and Northern Provinces calculated to break the contiguity of Tamil settlements in the Eastern and Northern Provinces. Accordingly, a string of new Sinhalese settlements along the *Maanal Aru* (or Weli Oya as it was known in Sinhalese) was initiated, linking Padaviya with the Kokilai lagoon and the east coast. The Tamil villagers in these areas were gradually evicted after July 1983 in favour of the projected Sinhalese settlements. Just before Christmas 1984, the army asked several villages around Kokilai to be vacated within 24 hours.[49]

Around the same time, another settlement project was planned along the *Maduru Oya* in the Batticaloa District. This was aimed at introducing a Sinhalese element into the population in the Batticaloa District which was largely Muslim and Tamil. The coastal belt between the 40-kilometre long lagoon and the sea was heterogeneously Tamil and Muslim, while the large expanse on the mainland to the west across the lagoon was largely Tamil dominated.[50] The Batticaloa town, a thin strip of land 2–4 km long, was located on the coastal belt and also boasted a mixed Tamil and Muslim demography.[51] If successfully carried out, the Maduru Oya Project would have inserted Sinhalese settlers between the Batticaloa and Trincomalee districts, breaking the contiguity of the 'Tamil Homeland' even further. However, the project fell through when it received wide publicity. The few Tamil ministers in the government, including the powerful Saumyamurthi Thondaman, vehemently protested, pushing the government into a tight corner. In the aftermath of July riots, large-scale colonisation of Tamil-dominated areas was a very sensitive issue with India keeping a close eye on developments. The government backtracked, going so far as to arrest some of those responsible and removing the settlers. However, later, many of these settlers were found homes in the Weli Oya region.[52]

The establishment of this Sinhala 'buffer zone' – and the presence of other Sinhala colonists – set the tone for the separatist struggle and the fight against it in the Eastern Province. The Sinhalese settlers were an element missing from the war in the north. To the Tamil militants, the Sinhalese settlers were clearly the allies of the state, planted to frustrate their drive for independence. Therefore, in addition to attacking the Security Forces, a large part of the militants' strategy in the East involved the removal of these Sinhalese settlers. The execution of the strategy was ruthless and savage.

A savage cycle

The first to taste the militants' wrath were settlers in Dollar and Kent farms in Mullaithivu. These were originally two Tamil-owned business concerns. After the anti-Tamil riots in 1977, the two farms had been used to settle Tamil refugees of Indian origin from the plantations. Later, the two farms were bought by the Prisons Department and became a cornerstone of the government's policy of Sinhalese settlement in the area. The Tamil settlers in the farms were evicted in mid-1984 and several hundred Sinhalese ex-convicts were settled in them. It was alleged that the settlers became a source of much harassment to the Tamil villagers in the area, acting with impunity due to the backing of the army.[53]

During the early hours of November 30 1984, two busloads of heavily armed Tamil Tiger guerrillas descended on the two farms and shot and hacked all the males they could find. Altogether 62 including three jail guards were killed at Dollar Farm and 20 more at Kent Farm.[54] The butchery continued the following day when another group of Tigers descended on Nayaru and Kokilai, two villages of migrant Sinhala fishermen on the east coast south of Mullaithivu. When they finished, 59 fishermen lay dead, many of them killed in the most brutal fashion.[55]

The massacres ushered a period of insecurity for the Sinhalese villages on the frontier. As the Security Forces hastened to protect the villages with outposts and patrols, the guerrillas stepped up their attacks. In a scenario typical of a rural insurgency, the Security Forces held on to the towns and the main roads while the roads and tracks in the outlying areas became danger areas infested with mines. According to a naval officer in Trincomalee, all but one of the 40 military deaths that had occurred by September 1985 had been caused by landmines.[56] The toll steadily rose in the following years with the use of bigger and more powerful landmines by the Tigers. In September 1986, one literally ripped apart a Saracen APC near Mihindupura in the Trincomalee District,

24 From assassins to guerrillas

killing a lieutenant and six men.[57] And the attacks on civilians continued. In March 1986, a landmine explosion in Dehiwatte in Trincomalee District resulted in the death of 35 civilians and four soldiers.[58] Then on May 25, a group of militants entered Mahadivulweva near Anuradhapura and massacred 20 Sinhala settlers and set fire to 40 houses.[59] A wave of attacks on Sinhala settlements followed in June and July, leaving dozens dead and thousands homeless. The Security Forces did not escape the violence either. Ironically, the siege in the north had spared them from the landmine, but in the East the danger remained.

By mid-1985, Trincomalee was ringed by a number of guerrilla camps, even extending into the neighbouring Polonnaruwa district.[60] There were attacks even within the Polonnaruwa District.[61] To the north of Trincomalee, the guerrillas controlled a long stretch of the coastline that extended up to Kokilai and its immediate hinterland. The blowing up of the bridge that connected Nilaveli to Trincomalee limited the military's access to the area by land, forcing them to rely more on the navy. The control of the coast in this part of the island was of great strategic advantage to the guerrillas; it had many inlets which became safe havens for the rebel boats that plied men and material between the North and the East.

Further south, in the Batticaloa District too, the Security Forces maintained their hold on the towns, at least during daytime. However, the vast, largely forested hinterland to the north, west and the south belonged to the guerrillas. The Maha Oya–Chenkaladi road was almost totally cut off while the Polonnaruwa–Batticaloa road remained open but under threat. On September 7 1985, eight security personnel met their death on this highway when their jeep hit a landmine.[62] Even in the towns, the guerrillas could sometimes present remarkable opposition. For instance in September 1985, a large group of guerrillas estimated at well over a hundred attacked the police station at Eravur, killing seven constables.[63] However, such attacks were the exception rather than the norm.

Notes

1 *Sri Lanka's Eastern Province: Land, Development, Conflict*, International Crisis Group, Asia Report no.159, p. 3, http://www.genocidewatch. org/images/Sri_Lanka_08_10_15_Sri_Lanka_s_Eastern_Province_ Land,_Development,_Conflict.pdf
2 Lorna Srimathie Dewarajah, *The Kandyan Kingdom*, (Lake House: Colombo, 1972), pp. 35, 41 and 79.
3 David Little, *The Invention of Enmity*, (U. S. Institute of Peace: Washington, DC, 1994), pp. 68–74.

From assassins to guerrillas 25

4 S. Ponniah, *Satyagraha: the Freedom Movement of the Tamils in Ceylon*, (A. Kandiah: Jaffna, 1963), pp. 54–94.

5 T.D.S.A. Dissanayake, *War or Peace in Sri Lanka*, (popular Prakashan: Colombo, 1996), p. 268.

6 M. R. Narayan Swamy, *Inside and Elusive Mind*, (Konark Publishers: Delhi, 2003), p. 33.

7 M. R. Narayan Swamy, *Tigers of Lanka: from Boys to Guerrilas*, (Konark Publishers: Delhi, 1994), p. 58.

8 T.D.S.A. Dissanayake, *War or Peace in Sri Lanka*, (popular Prakashan: Colombo, 1996), pp. 34–6, Sarath Munasinghe, *A Soldier's Version*, (Author publication: Colombo, 2000), pp. 2–5.

9 Sri Lanka (Ceylon) News-Letter published by the High Commission of the Democratic Socialist Republic of Sri Lanka in Canberra, 12.10.84, p. 10.

10 *Ceylon Daily News*, 13.10.85, p. 14.

11 'A New Spiral of Violence', *Asiaweek*, 24.5.85.

12 'Yal-Devi Blast: Death Toll 39', *Sun*, 22.1.85, Aruna Kulatunga and Premalal Wijeratne, 'The Train Tragedy', *Sun*, 22.1.85.

13 Malinga Guneratna, *For a Sovereign State*, (Sarvodaya Book Publishing Services: Ratmalana, 1988), pp. 239–40.

14 L.M.H. Mendis, *Assignment Peace, in the name of the Motherland*, (Author publication: Nugegoda, Sri Lanka, 2009) p. 49, *Sri Lanka Army, '50 years on'-1949–1999*, (Sri Lanka Army: Colombo, Sri Lanka, 1999), p. 428. Sri Lanka Army erroneously dates this attack to 1984.

15 'Tamil Terrorists Kill 150, Wound 300 in Sacred City Attack', *Australian*, 15.5.85, 'Tamil Killings a Reprisal for Earlier Village Deaths', *Australian*, 15.5.85.

16 Quoted in S. Sivanayagam, *Sri Lanka: Witness to History, a Journalist's Memoirs 1930–2004*, (Sivayogam: London, 2005) p. 236.

17 Cyril Ranatunge, *Adventurous Journey, from Peace to War, Insurgency to Terrorism*, (Vijitha Yapa: Colombo, 2009), p. 75.

18 Narayan Swamy, *Inside and Elusive Mind*, p. 57.

19 Thomas A. Marks, 'Insurgency and Counterinsurgency', *Issues and Studies*, August 1986, pp. 92–5.

20 Rohan Gunaratna, *Indian Intervention in Sri Lanka: the Role of India's Intelligence Agencies*, (South Asian Network on Conflict Research, Colombo, 1993), pp. 39–43, Naryan Swamy, *Inside an Elusive Mind*, pp. 96–7.

21 Gunaratna, *Indian Intervention*, pp. 39–43.

22 Ibid., pp. 140 and 153.

23 'Top Secret Camp for Terrorists', *The Island*, 5.10.86, p. 9 and 15.

24 Anton Balasingham, *War and Peace: Armed Struggle and Peace Efforts of Liberation Tigers*, (Fairmax Publishing: Mitcham, 2004), p. 61.

25 Ibid., p. 62.

26 Narayan Swamy, *Inside an Elusive Mind*, pp. 108–10.

27 'Military Training in Tamil Nadu and India', *The Island*, 5.10.86, p. 9.

28 'Is Rajiv Gandhi Being Misled?' *The Island*, 5.10.86, p. 9.

29 Faizal Samath, 'Terrorist Training Camp at Jaffna', *The Island*, 14.7.85, pp. 1 and 2.

30 Dexter Cruez, 'Within the Jaws of the Tiger', *Weekend*, 26.10.86, p. 8.

26 From assassins to guerrillas

31 'Inside a Tiger Training Camp', *The Island*, 8.7.85.
32 Edgar O'Ballance, *Cyanide War*, the Tamil Insurrection in Sri Lanka 1973–88, (London: Brassey's, 1989), p. 39.
33 'Taraki' (D.Sivaram), 'The Cat a Bell and a Few Strategists', *Sunday Times*, 20.4.97, p. 7.
34 Narayan Swamy, *Inside an Elusive Mind*, pp. 135–6, *Broken Palmyra*, pp. 81–2, 'How the LTTE Destroyed the TELO', Illustrated Weekly of India, reproduced in *The Island*, 18.6.86, p. 6.
35 Jehan Hanif, 'Massacre in Jaffna: TELO Man Tells All', *The Island*, 14.9.86, p. 13.
36 The words are attributed to a TELO spokesman identified as 'Charles'. 'How the LTTE Destroyed the TELO', *Illustrated Weekly of India*, reproduced in *The Island*, 18.6.86, p. 6.
37 O'Ballance, *Cyanide War*, pp. 61–2.
38 Narayan Swamy, *Inside an Elusive Mind*, pp. 141–2.
39 Narayan Swamy, *Tigers of Lanka: From Boys to Guerrillas*, pp. 220–22.
40 S. Venkatnarayan, 'A visit to Jaffna', *The Island*, 15.2.87, p. 6.
41 Malini Parthasarathy, 'A Military and Political Misadventure', *Frontline*, May 31–June 13 1986, p. 19.
42 Iqbal Athas, 'The Fear of Living Dangerously', *Weekend*, 3.8.1986, p. 23 (11 and 23).
43 Humphrey Hawkesley, 'Tamil Guerrillas Kill 7 in Troop Convoy Ambush', *The Age*, 3.4.86; *Sri Lanka Situation Report*, Tamil Information Research Unit, Madras, 15.4.86, p. 2, and 15.5.86, p. 5.
44 Dissanayake, *War or Peace in Sri Lanka*, p. 71.
45 William de Alwis and Srimal Abeywardene, 'Eleven Killed by Bomb in CTO', *Ceylon Daily News*, http://www.dailynews.lk/2009/06/08/fea10.asp
46 Amal Jayasinghe and Sarath Malalasekera, 'Terrorist Blast Kills Nine at Cold Stores', *Ceylon Daily News*, 30.5.86, http://www.dailynews.lk/2009/06/10/fea09.asp
47 http://www.uthr.org/Reports/Report11/appendix2.htm. See also *Sri Lanka's Eastern Province: Land, Development, Conflict*, pp. 4–6.
48 http://www.uthr.org/Reports/Report11/appendix2.htm
49 http://www.uthr.org/SpecialReports/spreport5.htm#_Toc512569422
50 D.B.S. Jeyaraj, 'LTTE Ascendant in the East', *The Island*, 9.3.97, p. 13.
51 P.A. Ghosh, *Ethnic Conflict in Sri Lanka and Role of the Indian Peace Keeping Force*, http://books.google.com.au/books?id=YZscr75ijq8C&pg=PA131&lpg=PA131&dq=operation+checkmate+IPKF&source=bl&ots=0XZJyh-Run&sig=LSoPlhN80q_ayOqT_JmQF2lFVnc&hl=en&sa=X&ei=Ds-pT4S4H8uuiQfcvuWtAw&ved=0CFUQ6AEwAw#v=onepage&q=operation%20checkmate%20IPKF&f=false, p. 129.
52 See Guneratne, *For a Sovereign State*, Prabhakaran, chapter 22, T. Sabaratnam, Pirapaharan Phenomenon, Chapter 23, http://www.sangam.org/articles/view2/?uid=633 (last accessed 3.11.13)
53 http://www.uthr.org/SpecialReports/spreport5.htm
54 '84 Reported Slain as Guerrillas Raid Sri Lanka Farms', *Toronto Star*, 1.12.84.

From assassins to guerrillas 27

55 Sabaratnam, Pirapaharan Phenomenon, Chapter 23, 'Tamil Guerrillas Kill 57 Villagers', *Canberra Times*, 3.12.84.
56 Shekar Gupta, 'Terror Tactics', *India Today*, 15.10.85, p. 53. (50–56).
57 Iqbal Athas, 'The Grand Design', *Weekend*, 21.09.86, p. 8.
58 Michael Hamlyn, 'Tamils Step Up Attacks on Civilians: the Communal Conflict in Sri Lanka', *The Times*, 11.3.86. http://infoweb. newsbank.com.ezproxy.lib.monash.edu.au/iw-search/we/InfoWeb?p_ product=AUNB&p_theme=aggregated5&p_action=doc&p_docid= 0F90AB6C0643A541&p_docnum=193&p_queryname=1
59 'More Sinhalese Civilians Killed', *Saturday Review*, 31.5.86.
60 Norman Palihawadana, 'Terrorists Get Away with Jeeps from Mahaveli Maduru Oya Schemes', *Island*, 19.7.85.
61 For instance, in mid-May 1985, the police guard room near the Manampitiya bridge was attacked, leading to the death of two policemen. 'Manampitiya Police Guard Room Attacked-2 PCs Killed', *Island*, 21.5.85.
62 *Saturday Review*, 7.9.85.
63 'Terrorists Kill Two TULF Ex-MPs and Seven Policemen', *Ceylon Daily News*, 4.9.85, W.G. Gooneratne, 'Eravur OIC Bluffed the Terrorists', *Ceylon Daily News*, 7.9.85.

Chapter 2

Learning to fight
The Sri Lankan military

The Sri Lankan government first treated the escalating violence in the North as a police matter. But when the police came increasingly under pressure, the president J.R. Jayawardena decided to take matters seriously. When Police Inspector Guruswamy was shot down in Jaffna on July 1, the government imposed a state of emergency in the north.[1] A brigade of 1,500 soldiers was now dispatched to Jaffna under Brigadier Tissa Weeratunga. The brigadier was given express orders to 'eliminate in accordance with the laws of land the menace of terrorism in all its forms from the island and more especially from the Jaffna District' before December 31 1978.[2]

The army sent to the North was a quaint one. A few thousand strong and armed with outdated weapons, it soon found itself facing an enemy it was never trained to fight.

A new army for an old country

Until independence in 1948, Sri Lanka did not possess a standing army along Western lines. Before British conquest, wars in Sri Lanka were fought not by professional soldiers but by peasants who left their fields to fight for their kings and returned to their villages when the fighting was over – or when their food supplies ran out. The only professional fighters were foreign mercenaries who functioned more as palace guards and an elite body than as an army. The British, when they mastered the entire island, did not look favourably upon the Sinhalese or even the Tamils as potential recruits for their military establishment on the island. Therefore, the 'native' Ceylon Rifle Regiment maintained after British conquest came to compose largely of Malay soldiers. The unit was disbanded in 1874, but seven years later, the British raised a new unit called the Ceylon Light Infantry Volunteers (CLIV) which incorporated Europeans and Ceylonese within its ranks. In 1910, the CLIV was renamed the Ceylon Defence Force (CDF). During WW II, the CDF performed guard duties in the city of Colombo and manned the artillery at the harbour. Despite having a Ceylonese component in the CLIV and the CDF, the British ensured that their officer cadre were exclusively British. The natives, even the most Westernised, had no place as military leaders under their colonial masters.[3]

After 1948, the new government of Ceylon had the task of raising an army for its defence. It was modest in size and equipment. There was no great need for anything more than this; there was no conceivable enemy in the region, and even if there was one, a defence agreement with Britain ensured that the island's former colonial masters would come to its aid.[4] Naturally, the CDF came to form the nucleus of the new army. The first units to be raised were an artillery regiment, an infantry regiment (the Ceylon Light Infantry or CLI), a signals squadron, two engineering units, a service unit, a military police unit and a recruiting unit. The British, although they had given up the reigns as the rulers, still had a measure of influence in the running of post-independence Ceylon. The army was raised under close advice from the British military. A British officer was even appointed the first commander-in-chief. The soldiers were all equipped with discarded British hardware. The infantry carried .303 Lee Enfield rifles and a few Bren guns, while the artillery was equipped with a handful of 4.2 inch mortars and 3.6 inch anti-aircraft guns.[5]

The army evolves

In 1956, a new infantry unit, the Sinha Regiment, was formed. Another regiment, the Gemunu Watch, was added in 1962. An 'armoured regiment' was raised in 1955, a rather grandiose title for a unit whose 'armour' consisted of several Ferret Scout cars.[6] But later, a measure of greater respectability was added by the acquisition of a number of Saracen-armoured personnel carriers that the British army was happy to relieve themselves of as they withdrew from Singapore and Malaya.[7]

Thus for the first time, an independent Sri Lanka – or Ceylon – had a standing army, structured, trained and equipped after the Western fashion. As the size and the armament of the new army was not one that could intimidate any potential invader, the doctrine of the army shifted from preparing for a conventional confrontation to maintaining internal security. There was also focus on preparing for a long guerrilla campaign, something made fashionable by the eruption of guerrilla wars in many parts of the former European colonies in the 1950s and 1960s.

In the event of an invasion – which the military was not equipped to repel – the army was to retreat into the jungles and from there wage an irregular war to cripple the enemy.[8]

No invasion materialised, but there were a few internal disturbances in the 1950s and the 1960s to keep the little army busy. Thus, during a wave of strikes and ethnic unrest in the 1950s, the army 'aided the civil power' in facing the challenge of maintaining law and order as well as running essential services smoothly. In 1961, the military was also called in to keep order when the Federal Party launched the satyagraha in the North and the East. In the 1950s and 1960s, the army was also stationed in the North to thwart illegal Indian migrants from entering Sri Lanka.[9]

However, even though the army's fighting potential hardly changed until the early 1970s, there were other changes that boded ill for the future. This was the steady Sinhalisation of its ranks. The change in composition reflected political events. As explained earlier, since the mid-1950s communalism was beginning to play an important role in the political discourse of the island. The majority of the people being Sinhala, the state began to reflect the interests and sensibilities of the Sinhala people. The Sinhala Only Act in 1956 was a first step in the direction of Sinhalisation of the state, which ignored the multi-ethnic nature of the society that had gained independence from the British. And as the state institutions Sinhalised, the army began to gradually acquire the role of the armed forces of a Sinhala state, the Sinhalisation of the forces simply completing the organic link between the two. The percentage of Sinhalese commissioned officers in the Ceylon Light Infantry rose from 5 per cent in 1949–51 to 96 per cent in 1963–69, while the number of Tamils dropped from 18 per cent to 12 per cent. The percentage of Buddhists, who were almost exclusively Sinhalese, rose from 34 per cent in 1949–51 to 89 per cent in 1963–69, while Christians dropped from 59 per cent to 7 per cent. Somewhat similar trends were seen in the artillery as well.[10] After the few Tamil officers retired, few if any joined the army and the enlistment of Tamils in the ranks was reduced to a trickle. By the late 1970s, the army was almost exclusively Sinhalese.

There were other aspects that reflected and aided this process. The names of the new military units formed after 1956 – Sinha Regiment and Gemunu Watch – had a clear Sinhala nationalist flavour. The mascot of the CLI was the elephant Kandula named after the famous war elephant of King Dutugemunu who is credited with unifying the country by defeating the Tamil King Elara. After 1956, the words of command were also given in Sinhala. The growing parochialism was further aided by the discontinuation of sending officer cadets abroad for training.

Learning to fight   31

After independence, selected officer cadets were sent for training at Sandhurst, but this was discontinued in the late 1960s in favour of local training. The rising economic cost was the main reason behind this decision, but its impact was far-reaching. Not only did it deny the cadets an opportunity to train at the highest levels, but it also robbed them of the chance to experience and absorb the military culture of more professional military establishments.

The increasing Sinhalisation and the growing communal tensions also served to redefine the military's role. In the late 1950s, there were only two small military detachments stationed in the North, one at Palali and one in Mannar. The military presence in the North had come as a result of the Sinhala Tamil riots in 1958. This may not have been communally motivated as other units were placed in the western, southern and eastern parts of the island to quell civil unrest.[11] However, there were signs that military deployment in the North was beginning to acquire greater importance in the early 1960s. In 1963, the secretary to the Ministry of Defence N. Q. Dias reportedly wished to establish a greater military presence in the North by setting up a chain of army camps, 'all the way from Arippu, Maricchikatti, Pallai, and Thalvapadu in the Mannar District, through Pooneryn, Karainagar, Palely, Point Pedro and Elephant Pass in the Jaffna District, and on to Mullaithivu in the Vavuniya District and Trincomalee in the East'. He also wanted to set up a task force ostensibly to watch smugglers and illicit immigration but in reality to watch the Tamils in the North and prevent them from challenging the government's authority.[12] This was a reaction to the satyagraha agitation in 1961, where the Tamils protested vehemently against the government's Sinhala-only policy. The agitation was seen as a sign of things to come, an extraordinarily prescient view. Dias's proposal for the ring of camps was not implemented, but a task force was set up to curb illegal immigration, bringing a greater military presence to the North. The proposals show the conception of the army as an instrument to cow the Tamils, at least in some powerful sections of the government of the time.

First blood

Ironically, when the army finally had to put up a fight it was not against Tamils but against Sinhalese insurgents. In April 1971, the left wing JVP rose in revolt, launching an island-wide armed assault on the government. The insurgents were highly motivated young men and women, armed with somewhat primitive – yet deadly – weapons. And they were attempting a takeover of the government by launching simultaneous

32 Learning to fight

attacks on police stations across the island. For a while the army was stretched; lack of experience in handling an insurgency and the inadequacy of transport critically handicapped the soldiers. Still, after the initial shock the army was able to grab the initiative. The army's rifles and Bren guns were more than a match for the ill-aimed shotguns and home-made hand bombs of the enemy.[13] But the victory was not bought without cost. A number of officers and men were killed and wounded before the enemy could be brought to bay.[14]

The JVP insurrection provided the army with real operational experience for the first time, no matter how fleeting the fighting may have been. The army also gained materially from the assistance extended by foreign countries. Many countries felt sympathetic towards Sri Lanka in its hour of need and demonstrated this by sending weapons and equipment. During 1971 and 1972, Sri Lanka received over 30,000 rifles and semi-automatic rifles from China, while Australia also chipped in with 5,000 rifles. Russia donated 12 light mortars, Yugoslavia sent four pieces of 76mm mountain guns and China provided 30 pieces of 85 mm artillery. In 1972, the USSR also donated 10 BTR152 APCs, while Sri Lanka purchased 18 Ferret Scout cars from the UK to boost the existing fleet of Saracens and Ferrets. The UK also supplied several Saladin armoured cars.[15]

When the Tamil insurgency raised its head, the army was much better armed than it had ever been. Still, it was woefully backward in comparison with any modern army in terms of training and equipment. Although the donations and acquisitions in the wake of the 1971 insurgency had boosted the army's firepower, the arms and equipment the army received was what the countries that donated them thought Sri Lanka needed or what they could conveniently dispose of, not necessarily what the army needed. The armoured cars and the BTR 152s were not in production anymore, while the 85mm artillery pieces were of dubious usefulness in guerrilla warfare. Still, some of the equipment such as the light mortars, the mountain guns and the armoured personnel carriers did have a counter-guerrilla or counter-insurgency function. But generally, the equipment reflected the convenience of the donors rather than the wants of the recipients.

Moreover, these changes were more cosmetic than fundamental. In many ways, the army remained the same. It continued to recruit heavily from the Sinhalese community and made little effort to improve training. A gradual rearming of the infantry was taking place, but there was no uniformity; some units were armed with the Chinese T56 while others received SLRs from Australia while still others remained armed with the vintage .303s. The artillery remained the same while armour improved little beyond receiving a consignment of reconditioned armoured and Scout cars in the late 1970s.[16] Moreover, no major organisational or structural changes took place other than the division of the army into six area commands. Even this was done in a manner that ensured chaos rather than order in the case of an emergency, as all units under one area command were stationed in that area. It demonstrated a lackadaisical approach which smacked of complacence and a lack of vision.

The only innovative measure to come out was the formation of a commando unit in 1977. At first, this 'regiment' consisted of only a handful of men seconded from various units. Trained by members of the elite SAS, the commandos were divided into two groups of 20 men and officers each. One was an assault group, the other a sniper team. This however had little to do with preparation for the looming confrontation with the Tamil militants but was initiated as a safeguard for the tourism industry. The main focus of the commandos was the protection of the Katunayake International Airport. They were more rigorously trained than the regular soldiers but were mostly armed with only T56 assault rifles.[17]

If the army was inadequately prepared for war, the air force and the navy were in a worse state. When the JVP launched its uprising in 1971, the Sri Lankan 'air force' consisted of a fleet of ageing fixed wing aircraft and four helicopters. The fixed wing aircraft consisted of several De Haviland Herons and Doves, which were transport aircraft, about a dozen chipmunk trainers and jet provosts, while the helicopters were three Bell Jet rangers and one Hiller helicopter.[18] During the insurgency, the air force brought the jet provosts out of storage and armed them with Browning machineguns and rockets while the helicopters were provided with Bren guns to act as improvised gunships.[19] Although very rudimentary, these measures enabled the government forces to maintain their superiority against a lightly armed guerrilla group. But like the army, the air force too benefitted from the generosity of foreign countries in the wake of the 1971 uprising. The Russians provided six MiG-15s, one MiG-17 and two Ka-26 rescue helicopters. The British sent six Bell 47Gs armed with 7.62mm machine guns, which were immediately used against the JVP.[20] But after 1971, the air force joined the other forces in languishing in inactivity. The Bell 47Gs went into storage and the Bell Jet rangers were used to provide 'helitours', scenic flights for tourists.

Up to the insurrection in 1971, the navy possessed only two ageing frigates and about two dozen patrol crafts. Following the insurrection,

34 Learning to fight

Sri Lanka received two Shanghai class patrol craft from China. Three more were purchased the following year. Several patrol boats were also purchased from the Soviet Union.[21] Expansion beyond this was not seen necessary and financially unaffordable.

A different enemy

The Tamil insurgency had subsided after the imposition of the emergency in 1979. Content with the results, the government had recalled the army, maintaining only a token presence in the North. But the militants had only gone underground, and they returned to the fray in 1981. Now the army too returned. Tissa Weeratuga, now a major general and the commander of the army, was sent back North to complete the job which now seemed only half finished. An army brigade was now to be stationed permanently in Jaffna.[22] But this time they found an enemy somewhat different from the one they had scared off barely two years ago.

To be sure, the soldiers were far better equipped than the militants. The real problem for the army, however, was that it was geared to fight a more conventional enemy than the bomb-throwing and sniping Tamil militants. Even the JVP insurgents, although deadlier than the early Tamil militants, with all their amateurish enthusiasm, had been a more tangible enemy. They often came to attack in large groups and tried to capture territory and installations rather than harass the enemy. The Tamil militants were different; they operated in small groups, sometimes even individually or in pairs and relied on stealth, surprise and speed to achieve their objectives, which were killing of security personnel and informants and capture of weapons. They had no intention of taking over towns and establishing their authority – at least not yet.

In the sea, the situation was no less difficult. The tiny Sri Lankan navy possessed only a handful of patrol crafts for preventing the guerrillas from smuggling arms and men. The army commander in Jaffna in 1984, Brigadier Nalin Seneviratne, lamented that he had about 150 miles of coastline to protect and that if access from nearby countries could be sealed off the battle would be 80 per cent won.[23] But this was only wishful thinking as long as the Sri Lankan navy consisted of only a motley collection of patrol boats and ageing gunboats. The few Bell 206 helicopters were helpful, but not sufficient to cover the long stretches of coast.

But as the situation in the North began to deteriorate, the military began to look for ways to counter the challenge. One of the first steps was the appointment of Brigadier General Nalin Seneviratne, a tough, no-nonsense officer, to oversee the administration of Jaffna in March 1984.[24] The army's presence was also augmented. Immediately after the killing of the two soldiers in October 1981, the existing army detachments at Velvetithurai, Madagal and Elephant Pass had been brought up to the strength of a company in each place.[25] When the Tamil 'offensive' began in August 1984, the number of camps was also increased.[26] At the same time, recruitment was also stepped up. The army had stood at just over 11,000 in 1983, but with the outbreak of sustained violence in August 1984 the army embarked on a rapid expansion. The plan was to increase the numbers by 2,000 every two months. The training period was also cut down to eight weeks from three months to speed up the process.[27] The response to the army's call for recruits was positive, thousands of eager young men 'barely out of their teens' queuing up outside the army headquarters to enlist.[28] By 1985, the army had expanded to 16,000 and 30,000 in 1986. In 1987, it had grown further, standing at 40,000 men.[29]

The government also looked for new equipment and specialised training. They needed to boost the army's defence against the threat of landmines and explore more effective ways of carrying out surveillance and interception in the sea. This however was not easy to achieve. Sri Lanka in the early 1980s was no economic powerhouse, and sophisticated weapons and equipment were not quite within the means of such a struggling economy. A bigger problem was the lukewarm response from potential sources of help. In mid-1984, President Jayawardena visited China and the US seeking assistance but got little more than sympathy. Minister for National Security Lalith Athulathmudali also visited the US in January 1985, but apart from a promise to share and exchange information on terrorism, the US was not willing to provide much else.[30] One major reason was that the government's cause was not greatly appreciated by those who could help, especially in the aftermath of the riots in July 1983. The Sri Lankan military too did not seem in a fit state to receive aid. Vernon A. Walters, the roving US ambassador, is said to have even expressed the concern that the Sri Lankan army was on the verge of mutiny.[31] There was also the desire not to antagonise the regional power India, which clearly had a stake in the outcome of the struggle in Sri Lanka. In the context of the Cold War, with India developing close relations with the Soviet Union, the USA was not averse to cultivating Sri Lanka as an ally in the Indian Ocean, but the Americans were not willing to do that conspicuously.

Undaunted by the reluctance of the Western nations to help, the government sought arms and equipment from other sources that were willing to supply them without publicity. These included Italy, Israel, Yugoslavia, South Africa and South Korea.[32] China too loomed as a willing source of military aid. Military expenditure began to rise, as the embattled government scraped its coffers, obtaining 2 million rupees (US $ 875,000) by March 1985.[33] The cost would continue to grow in the future, becoming a severe burden on the struggling economy.

The military modernises

Predictably, the equipment purchased was of a modest nature. Immediately after the ambush in July 1983, several Shorland and Hotspur armoured personnel carriers were purchased to provide better protection against landmines and ambushes. Placed in a new armoured squadron under Major P. A. Karunatilleke, the APCs provided greater protection to the army's patrols in the North.[34] The army also began gradually arming its troops with the Chinese-made T56 assault rifle and RPGs to match the growing sophistication of the enemy.

In the second half of 1985, arms and equipment began to arrive in large quantities. These included 25 pounder artillery, light aircraft, helicopters, recoilless rifles, RPGs and large quantities of ammunition.[35] By mid-1985, two plane loads of mortars and RPGs had also arrived from Pakistan.[36] The army also received an unspecified number of Saladin armoured cars from Britain and new Buffel APCs from South Africa.[37] The latter vehicles with their mine-deflecting chassis boosted the confidence of the soldiers to some extent. Later, the electrical and mechanical engineers of the Sri Lankan army also started work on locally produced armoured vehicles based on a Japanese truck chassis and modelled on the Buffel. Called Unicorns, these APCs were an additional boon to the embattled soldiers.[38]

Although the army too was becoming bigger, there were still many drawbacks. There was still no one standard rifle for the infantrymen, many of the troops being armed with T56 assault rifles but carrying the Belgian FN FAL rifle and even a few Soviet-made AK47, a part of a stock received in 1971. The troops still lacked .transport. More and more Unicorn and Buffel APCs were entering service along with the existing fleet of Saracens, but this was still not sufficient. Civilian vehicles were still being commandeered for troop movements. 'Armour' still consisted of a fleet of Saladin armoured cars and Ferret Scout cars. Infantry units were allocated armour from this pool of armoured cars and APCs when operations were carried out. Still, there were some notable improvements. The army's firepower had been markedly enhanced by the addition of the 25 pounders to the ageing collection of 76mm and 85mm field guns. The infantry was also getting more streamlined with increased firepower. Each battalion was now split into several companies, each comprising four platoons of 30 men. The platoons were further broken into 10-man sections. Nine men in each section were armed with rifles, while the remaining soldier carried a light machine gun. One of the riflemen also carried a rocket launcher, usually a Chinese copy of the RPG-7. In some units, this was replaced by the West German Heckler and Koch Grenatenpistole 40mm grenade launcher or the South African-made Amscor six shot grenade launcher. Sometimes a 60mm mortar was included for added support. Thus armed, the Sri Lankan army now was a much formidable force than it was in the early 1980s.[39]

The air force also got new wings. When the war escalated in 1983, the Bell 47Gs were not in service anymore and the air force had to depend on its small fleet of Bell Jet rangers to carry out reconnaissance, transport and interception duties. Some of these were fitted with 70mm rocket pods on one side and .50 calibre machine gun pods on the other.[40] The government was also looking for a better helicopter to be used in surveillance and attack, but the lack of funds prevented them from obtaining dedicated gunships. They had to settle for the Bell 212. Two were purchased in 1984 and 12 more ordered. Nine of these were to be fitted with 50mm machine gun pods and rocket pods. The first two arrived in Sri Lanka in February 1985, while four more were delivered in July that year.[41] More significantly, several light aircraft, Siai Marchetti SF260 jet trainers, had also arrived in late 1985. These light planes, used in counter-insurgent warfare by several other countries, were capable of carrying 250-lb bombs, 70mm rocket pods and machine gun pods and could be used in ground-attack capacity.[42]

In the early to mid-1980s, the Sri Lankan navy also acquired more vessels in order to police this coastal belt. These were several coastal patrol craft and a number of Inshore Patrol Crafts which were produced by the Colombo Dockyards. In 1984, the navy also purchased six Israeli-built Dvora class patrol boats armed with 20mm cannon. The navy also acquired ten Cougar Class inshore patrol boats.[43]

Losing hearts and minds

While the numbers increased and the equipment upgraded, the strategy and tactics on the ground and in the sea were somewhat crude. After the spike in violence in August 1984, the military banned the use of private vehicles in Jaffna. They also launched large-scale cordon and

38 Learning to fight

search operations that were aimed at netting militants and their sympathisers. One of the earliest and biggest such operations took place between December 9 and 12 1984. Jaffna, Kilinochchi and Mullaithivu were placed under a 42-hour curfew and hundreds of soldiers supported by armoured vehicles ranged through the towns and villages, detaining over 700 youths and netting some weapons and documents.[44] According to a Tamil MP, the army usually surrounded a village early in the morning and ordered men in the age group of 18–35 to report at a designated place. The houses were then searched, and if any young men were found there, they were 'severely dealt with'. Those who went to the designated place were questioned and if found suspicious sent to Boosa in Galle for further detention and interrogation. By January 1985, Boosa had become host to some 800 such detainees.[45] In the sea, the government tried to overcome the challenge of inadequate resources by enforcing a harsh measure. In April 1984, a naval surveillance zone was also declared around Jaffna, where boats with outboard motors were banned. In November the same year, this zone was tightened by the declaration of a 'prohibited zone' that extended 100 metres into the sea. Entry to it was only with permission of the local police station. In November 1984, the government also banned all fishing off the northern coast.[46]

Along with such harsh measures came violent reprisals from the Security Forces. After the attack on a polling booth in May 1983, which resulted in the death of a soldier, the deceased soldier's colleagues went berserk, burning scores of houses and vehicles.[47] When two airmen were killed in Vavuniya on June 1 the same year, it was the air force's turn to go on the rampage, burning and destroying. One of their victims was the Gandiyam farm just 1.5 miles outside Vavuniya.[48] All these attacks were still directed more against property than people. That, however, changed dramatically with the ambush in Tinneveli in July 1983. Sri Lankan soldiers from the Madagal, Palaly and Velvetithurai camps broke out of the camps and went on a rampage, shooting civilians. Some officers struggled to maintain discipline but to no avail.[49]

As the violence escalated in 1984, so did the civilian toll. When an army truck was attacked with a car bomb in April 1984, the soldiers hit back with violence. According to the government agent of Jaffna, Devanesan Nesiah, the army shot dead about 50 people during the rampage.[50] After a landmine attack in Velvetithurai on August 5 1984, the forces went berserk, destroying houses and businesses, shooting people indiscriminately. A terrified Jaffna resident claimed that it was 'as if the soldiers had been given permission to fire at will' and that they were shooting at 'anything that moves'.[51] According to the

Velvetithurai Citizens Committee, sporadic rampages between August 4 and 9 destroyed 130 houses, 90 shops, four cars and six fishing boats while 29 boats were also confiscated by the navy.[52] Military detachments passing through the hostile countryside often left scenes of death and destruction in their wake. A group of foreign journalists driving through Atchuveli in Jaffna in mid-August 1984 met a convoy of armoured vehicles accompanying troops on foot, firing into deserted dwellings at random and setting them on fire.[53] When a landmine killed six soldiers in Mannar on the eleventh of the same month, the troops ran amok, burning more than 100 shops. A few months later, Mannar suffered again, this time in response to a landmine attack that killed a soldier and wounded six others near Jubilee Junction on the Mannar–Medawachchiya road. According to the Mannar District Citizens' Committee, the army went berserk, shooting civilians in homes and vehicles. Altogether 90 people were reportedly killed that day.[54]

The number of civilians killed in these terrible bouts of retribution is hard to estimate. The *Saturday Review*, relying largely on Citizens' Committees in the North who kept meticulous records on the details of the dead, claimed that 2,215 civilians were killed during 1985, while Rajan Hoole relying heavily on the records of the Citizens' Committees estimates the number of civilians killed by the armed forces in the North and the East between 1984 and 1987 to be around 7,000.[55] This was probably close to the truth. One unnamed government official went on to claim that the maximum number of people killed in a single attack since 1981 was around 75 or 100.[56] Such was the prevalence of casual military brutality. Violence on civilians became so commonplace that Western diplomats described Sri Lanka's tiny army as one of the most undisciplined in the world.[57] It was such observations that prompted General V. Walters, President Reagan's special envoy, to go so far as to warn President Jayawardena that his armed forces were 'running out of control'.[58]

These actions betrayed the lack of a sound counter-insurgency strategy. When the Tamil insurgency escalated, the Security Forces began to study counter-insurgency strategy, mainly with the help of British manuals. But the focus was on military aspects such as conducting ambushes, patrols and raids. The emphasis was on destroying the enemy in combat, not on separating the militants from the population. Even the combat instructions were sometimes offered by personnel with no experience or expertise.[59] A Western observer well versed in counter-insurgency warfare noted with disappointment that no attempt was being made to dominate areas in successive fashion, leading to a lopsided response.[60]

40 Learning to fight

However, as the conflict intensified, foreign expertise was sought to infuse greater professionalism into the Security Forces. Although the US effused to provide arms, their help came in a more subtle way. In May 1984, Sri Lanka announced that Israel has opened a 'special interest section' in Sri Lanka. The move was facilitated by the US, who allowed the Israeli interest section to function from the American Embassy in Colombo. The Israelis were from the internal security agency known as *Shin Bet*, and they were to help with counter-insurgency training for the Sri Lankan Security Forces.[61] The government denied that the foreigners were engaged in any combat but that they were only engaged as 'consultants' in training the local Security Forces in intelligence gathering.[62] President Jayawardena explained the decision to turn to Israel as necessitated by the need for foreign help in a context where little help was forthcoming.[63] Expertise with counter-insurgency came from other sources as well. Even though the British government was reluctant to provide direct military aid, it was, just like the US, prepared to be of use in other ways. Accordingly, they did not stand in the way of *the* British security firm, KMS services, which employed former Special Forces personnel, from offering its services to the Sri Lankan Security Forces. In 1984, a number of KMS personnel arrived in Sri Lanka to organise training for the Special Task Force. The Special Task Force, or the STF as it came to be known, was a paramilitary police force formed in 1983 to boost the Sri Lankan police in its operations against the militants. Initially, it had consisted of a handful of policemen, trained in the handling of military weapons by the army. Now this force was expanded with the help of foreign expertise. They were similarly armed to the regular army and operated mainly in sections of 12 men.[64]

The STF was deployed in the East, where it soon earned a reputation as a no-nonsense outfit. But the police commandos were still learning the ropes. Their approach to winning hearts and minds was still at its infancy and was marred by many missed opportunities as the commandos spent more time looking for the guerrillas than they did in trying to build a sound relationship with the locals who supported the rebels. They were also accused of systematic torture and casual brutality towards civilians. 'We can't go on the road without being threatened. We can't go to our shops, we have no freedom at all,' a man complained to a foreign journalist.[65]Reprisals could be swift and brutal. In May 1985, at least 40 Tamil civilians in Kalmunai in the Ampara District were gunned down, allegedly after being forced to dig their own graves. The police confirmed the killings by 'unidentified attackers', but the massacre was widely attributed to the STF.[66] The police commandos were often

Learning to fight 41

blamed for brutal, often casual murders of civilians, sometimes as casual as taking potshots at peasants from passing vehicles.[67]

However, as the war protracted and developed into an increasingly bloody and messy affair, some army units began experimenting with a more nuanced approach to the challenge posed by the militants, especially in the Eastern Province where the Security Forces were not confined to their camps. In Muttur in the Trincomalee District, the forces under the leadership of Major Mohan Rockwood, one of the very few Tamils in the army, carried out aggressive patrolling and positive engagement with the community, clearing parts of the area of guerrillas. Rockwood's A Company dominated the area assigned to them with patrols and ambushed and won the trust and support of the community by helping them rebuild their lives shattered by the war. Rockwood, a fluent speaker of both Sinhalese and Tamil, also encouraged his men to learn Tamil in order to deal with the civilians. As a result, they succeeded in killing a large number of guerrillas and clearing a substantial area of rebel influence.[68]

The army was also exploring ways to break the pattern of attrition on the ground. In early 1986, they began working on a 'tracker' team. Formed under the command of Major Gamini Hettiarachchi, this was simply a long-range reconnaissance team that conducted small group operations deep inside enemy territory. Originally comprising 2 officers and 38 men, they were based in Vavuniya and were equipped with specialised equipment such as sniper rifles and trained to live away from base for days. They impressed their commanders very quickly. In one operation, a team of four led by Captain Suresh Hashim landed by boat south of the Trincomalee Bay, and after lying in ambush for several days, they killed the Trincomalee rebel leader and escaped under heavy fire into a waiting helicopter, carrying the body of the slain rebel with them![69] The project was still at an experimental stage with numbers being small, but it showed that the military was beginning to think in new ways to undermine the enemy. The commando squadron, of which the tracker team was a part, was itself elevated to the level of a separate unit in March 1986.[70]

Such measures were, however, still in their infancy. The general approach of the Security Forces, especially in the North, was one of indifference to the requirements of counter-insurgency warfare and reliance on knee-jerk responses. The siege mentality was the inevitable outcome of this. With little done to win over the people in the North, naturally, the army faced an increasingly hostile population and a growing guerrilla army. The road bound soldiers could only expect more ambushes and attacks. They recoiled into their camps in frustration, leaving the peninsula to the enemy.

Air power – the double-edged sword

A particularly interesting feature of the military operations from 1986 onwards was the increased use of air power. With the army under siege in the North, it came to depend more and more on the air force for supplies and reinforcements. The air force also became a way of retaliating. As explained before, the SLAF received a considerable boost to its strike capacity with the acquisition of the Siai Marchettis and the Bell 212 and Bell 412 helicopters. It enabled the Security Forces to take the fight to the enemy without too much risk. The purchase of the Y-12s provided a valuable mode of transportation that was useful in supplying the beleaguered garrisons in the North.

An important aspect in the deployment of air power was the use of foreign helicopter pilots. While offering expertise to the STF, the KM Services also supplied the SLAF with helicopter pilots. Occasionally, if not frequently, they also took part in combat, playing the role of the gunners.[71]

The air force used its newly acquired Siai Marchetti jet trainers in a bombing attack for the first time in Kilinochchi in February 1986. A large force of guerrillas had surrounded Kilinochchi army camp, and the light aircraft were used to relieve pressure on the garrison.[72] The Siai Marchettis conducted their first run over Jaffna on February 19 1986, when five aircrafts carried out a raid on what was a suspected Tiger camp, which lasted nearly one hour.[73]

A particularly unique development was the 'Barrel bomber', a crude attempt to compensate for the lack of heavy bombers. These were simply AVRO aircraft converted to 'bombers'. The bombs were large metal 45 gallon drums filled with gelignite or sometimes flammable gas or rubber tubes. Sometimes they were also filled with explosives. Upon exploding, the flaming pieces of rubber burst out, sticking to the skins of anybody unfortunate to be in the vicinity.[74] It was a measure that smacked of ingenuity, desperation and total lack of regard for the conventions of modern war.

While the new aircraft and devices afforded the military new ways of responding to the enemy, their efficacy was questionable. What air power seemed to do was to take indiscriminate retaliation to another dimension. Unable to retaliate on the ground, the army called in the air force to do the job and the air force usually did what the army would have done on the ground had they been able to move out more freely. They fired at any suspicious movement, usually at any movement, joining the artillery that often responded to mortar fire by firing blindly in the direction of the fire. The trend was set from the very first bombing raid on Jaffna on February 19. Dubbed 'the first aerial attack in Sri Lanka since WW II' by the Jaffna-based *Saturday Review*, the bombs reportedly killed seven civilians and damaged several houses and a rice mill.[75] The following week, the same area was bombed again, this time by three planes supported by two helicopters. Three civilians were reported killed and five injured.[76]

This was a dangerous way to carry out counter-insurgency warfare, especially in Jaffna town which was essentially a built-up urban environment. Tigers operated in small groups in this urban setting, presenting very few discernible targets for the air force. The weapons in the aircrafts were also not the most accurate. The helicopters were cumbersome machines that were hard to manoeuvre and the ammunition, some of it made in India, was often unreliable as regards to accuracy. 'When fired at a target 200 meters away the rounds were hitting the grounds anywhere from 80 to 300 meters away and 20 meters to the left or right,' observed a British mercenary with contempt.[77] Such ammunition had an equal chance of hitting the target as well as bystanders, especially in built-up areas where the militants were often encountered. The rockets fired and bombs dropped by the Siai Marchettis were no more accurate. It was said derisively that the SLAF tried to bomb a guerrilla camp in a crowded market area four times during April and May 1987 and failed to hit the target each time, instead killing and wounding dozens of civilians.[78]

But the weapon that was most dangerous to the civilians was the 'barrel bomb,' developed in mid-1987. These were large metal 45-gallon drums filled with gelignite or sometimes flammable gas or rubber tubes. Sometimes they were also filled with explosives. Upon exploding, the flaming pieces of rubber burst out, sticking to the skins of anybody unfortunate to be in the vicinity.[79] They were dropped (or pushed – sometimes using feet) from a height of over 300 metres to stay out of range of the enemy fire, and having no ballistic stability whatsoever, they could hit anything within a wide radius of the target.[80] It was a danger not only to the foe but to the friend as well. 'If you look up you can see them twisting and turning as they fall,' said one army colonel to a journalist. 'Sometimes we ourselves are mortally afraid of where they're going to land.'[81]

The result was that the bombing and strafing by the helicopters and the light aircraft added to the woes of the civilians, joining the artillery fire from the camps. Scores were killed or wounded while leaving whole swathes of Jaffna in ruins. Just as the buildings in the fort were getting

44 Learning to fight

gradually pulverised by the militants, the area immediately around it was also getting worked over by the air force and the artillery. Lalith Athulathmudali himself admitted that the bombings had been inaccurate and suspended air attacks in March 1986.[82] But the perceived advantage afforded by the new weapons was too great for the government to resist for the sake of civilian casualties. Air strikes resumed later that month, bringing more death and destruction on the city.[83]

However, the increased firepower and air attacks did have some positive outcomes for the military. It boosted the morale of the soldiers. And sometimes when the guerrillas would be caught in the open the aircraft, it could give them a terrible mauling as a group of Tigers found during an attack on a military outpost at Thondamanaru in June 1986. A large group of Tigers made a bold attempt to overrun a small army outpost but were caught in relatively open scrubland by a helicopter gunship. The result was the death of at least a dozen guerrillas.[84]

Notes

1 *Emergency '79*, Movement for Inter Religious Justice and Equality, Colombo, 1980, p. 21.
2 Quoted in Sivanayagam, *Sri Lanka: Witness to History*, p. 186.
3 Donald L. Horowitz, *Coup Theories and Officers' Motives: Sri Lanka in Comparative Perspective*, (Princeton University Press: Princeton, NJ, 1980), p. 63.
4 Brian Blodgett, *Sri Lanka's Military: the Search for a Mission 1949–2004*, (Aventine Press: San Diego, CA, 2004), p. 25.
5 Blodgett, *Sri Lanka's Military*, pp. 26–8.
6 '1st Reconnaissance Regiment Sri Lanka Armoured Corps', *Army Magazine*, 30th Anniversary Issue October 10, 1979, p. 23.
7 *SL Army 50 years on*, p. 92.
8 Ibid., p. 167.
9 Blodgett, *Sri Lanka's Military*, p. 34.
10 Horowitz, *Coup Theories,* pp. 69–70.
11 Anton Muthukumaru, *The Military History of Ceylon – an Outline*, (Navrang: Delhi, 1987), p. 165, pp. 170–2.
12 Neville Jayaweera, 'Into the Turbulence of Jaffna: a Chapter Extracted from the Author's Unpublished Memoirs Titled "Dilemmas"', *The Island*, http://www.island.lk/2008/10/05/features2.html
13 The army's firepower had been boosted by the purchase of 990 semi-automatic rifles from Australia. Blodgett, *Sri Lanka's Military*, p. 53.
14 See A.C. Alles, *The J.V.P. 1969–1989*, (Lake House: Colombo, 1990), James Manor and Gerald Segal, 'Causes of Conflict: Sri Lanka and India Ocean Strategy', *Asian Survey*, 25, no. 12 (December 1985), pp. 1165–85. Also, Cyril Ranatunga, *Adventurous Journey*, pp. 40–53; *'71 Aprel Mathakayan*, 71 Sahodrathwa Sansadaya, Rajagiriya, 2006, pp. 51–75.
15 Blodgett, *Sri Lanka's Military*, pp. 68–9.

Learning to fight 45

16 *Sri Lanka Army*, p. 294.
17 Shamindra Ferdinando, 'Armless Veteran Speaks of War and Peace', *The Island*, 27.10.02, http://www.tamilcanadian.com/page.php?cat=130& id=1311
18 Blodgett, *Sri Lanka's Military*, pp. 56–7.
19 Ibid., pp. 72–4; Peter, Steinemann, 'The Sri Lanka Air Force', *Asian Defense Journal* Feb. 1993, pp. 54–56.
20 Blodgett, *Sri Lanka's Military*, pp. 72–6. At least, one MiG appears to have been used against the insurgents in the Anuradhapura district in late April or early May without much effect; *'71 Aprel Mathakayan*, p. 57.
21 Blodgett, *Sri Lanka's Military*, pp. 79–80.
22 T.D.S.A. Dissanayake, *War or Peace in Sri Lanka*, (popular Prakashan, Colombo, 1995), p. 28.
23 'Now, the Brigadier Speaks', *Saturday Review*, 25.8.84, p. 1.
24 'Army Officer for Jaffna', *Malaysian Straits Times*, 29.2.84.
25 *SL Army 50 Years On*, p. 347.
26 Suvendrinie Suguro, 'More Army Camps Planned', *Daily Observer*, 31.12.84.
27 Iqbal Athas, 'Sri Lanka Strengthens Defence Forces', *Jane's Defence Weekly*, v. 3, no. 2, (12.1.85), p. 45.
28 'Thousands Answer Army's Call', *Weekend*, 9.12.84, p. 1.
29 Blodgett, *Sri Lanka's Military*, p. 3.
30 'The Know-how to Combat Terrorism', *Sun*, 26.1.85.
31 Edgar O'Ballance, *The Cyanide War: the Tamil Insurrection in Sri Lanka 1973–88*, (Brassey's: London, 1990), p. 38.
32 Ibid., pp. 52–3.
33 Denzil Peiris, 'Colombo Rides the Tiger', *Weekend*, 3.3.85, pp. 6 and 22.
34 Mendis, *Assignment Peace*, p. 44, Blodgett, *Sri Lanka's Military*, p. 92.
35 The 25 pounders, recoilless rifles and RPGs came from Pakistan, while at least 15,000 small arms were reportedly bought from Singapore, Pakistan and China; V.G. Kulkarni, 'The Military Modernises to Meet Rebel Threat', *Far Eastern Economic Review*, 12.6.86, pp. 29–31.
36 Robert Karniol, 'Rocket Boost for Sri Lanka', *Jane's Defence Weekly*, 28.6.2000. The bulldozers that led the attack on Kokavil in May 1985 were stopped by RPGs, the first to be fired by the army in Sri Lanka. *Sri Lanka Army 50 Years On*, p. 428.
37 O'Ballance, *Cyanide War*, pp. 55 and 58. The Saladins were received in February 1985.
38 Blodgett, *Sri Lanka's Military*, p. 92.
39 Tom Marks, 'Counter Insurgency in Sri Lanka, Asia's Dirty Little War', *Soldier of Fortune*, Feb. 1987, p. 42; Blodgett, *Sri Lanka Military*, pp. 92–3.
40 Robert Craig Johnson, 'Tigers and Lions in Paradise: the Enduring Agony of the Civil War in Sri Lanka', http://worldatwar.net/chandelle/ v3/v3n3/articles/srilanka.html (23.10.10), Tom Cooper, 'Sri Lanka since 1971', Air Combat information Group, 2003, http://www.acig. org/artman/publish/article_336.shtml#top (23.10.10)
41 Steinemann, *Sri Lanka Air Force*, p. 58.
42 Johnson, 'Tigers and Lions in Paradise'.

46 Learning to fight

43 Blodgett, *Sri Lanka's Military*, pp. 102–3.
44 'Operation Search and Destroy Launched', *Weekend*, 9.12.84; O'Ballance, *Cyanide War*, p. 43.
45 'Siva Tells the Hindu – Jaffna Area a Prison', *Sun*, 21.1.85.
46 O'Ballance, *Cyanide War*, p. 36; Thomas A. Marks, 'Insurgency and Counterinsurgency', *Issues and Studies*, August 1986, pp. 82–3. (63–102).
47 Rajan Hoole (et al), *Broken Palmyrah: The Tamil Crisis in Sri Lanka, an Inside Account*, (Sri Lanka Studies Institute: Ratmalana, Colombo, 1992), p. 57.
48 Ibid., p. 59.
49 Munasinghe, *A Soldier's Version*, pp. 8–9.
50 'More Than 50 Killed in Tamil Violence', *Canberra Times*, 20.4.84.
51 William Claiborne, 'Tamils Hide in Fear as Troops Take Revenge', *The Age*, 15.8.84.
52 Velvetithurai, 'A Fishing Village Victim of Pogrom', *Financial Times*, 21.8.84, reproduced in S. Sivanayagam (ed), 'Tamil Information', (published for private circulation) Madras, v. 1, nos. 4 and 5 (1.9.84), p. 12.
53 S. Sivanayagam (ed), 'Tamil Information', 1.9.84, citing an article by Saeed Naqvi of the *Indian Express*, who was one of the journalists, pp. 16–17.
54 'Mannar Tragedy', *Saturday Review*, 22.12.84, p. 3.
55 'Bleeding Statistics', *Saturday Review*, 4.1.86, Rajan Hoole, 'Border Aggression and Civilian Massacres', *Colombo Telegraph*, 7.2.15, https://www.colombotelegraph.com/index.php/the-toll-1983-july-1987/
56 Don Mithuna, 'It Will Only Be a War of Attrition If They Seek a Military Way Out', *Weekend*, 17.11.85, p. 6.
57 Maryanne Weaver, 'Civil War Looms with Separatists', *The Australian*, 31.1.85.
58 O'Ballance, *Cyanide War*, p. 38. According to O'Ballance, it appeared in the *Times of India* of December 7, 1984.
59 Raj Vijayasiri, *A Critical Analysis of the Sri Lankan Government's Counter Insurgency Campaign*, (Master's Thesis, Fort Leavenworth: Texas, 1990), pp. 37–40.
60 Tom Marks, 'Winning the War in Sri Lanka', *The Island*, 2.6.86, p. 6.
61 O'Ballance, *Cyanide War*, p. 37.
62 Israeli, 'British Agents Helping Lankan Forces', *New Sunday Times*, 12.8.84.
63 'Sri Lanka "Forced" to Seek Israeli Help', *The Straits Times*, 3.7.84.
64 Phil Miller, *Britain's Dirty War against the Tamil People 1979–2009*, (International Human Rights Association: Bremen, 2015), pp. 12–15; Tom Marks, 'Sri Lanka's Special Forces', *Soldier of Fortune*, July 1988, pp. 34–5.
65 Steven Weisman, 'Terror on the Beach in Sri Lanka', *Sydney Morning Herald*, 12.2.85.
66 'Latest Anti Tamil Violence Claims 56', *The Australian*, 20.5.85; '59 Tamils Murdered', *Sun* 21.5.85.
67 *Broken Palmyrah*, p. 119.
68 Tom Marks, 'Counter-insurgency in Sri Lanka: Asia's Dirty Little War', *Soldier of Fortune*, February 1987, pp. 38–9.

69 Cyril Ranatunga, *Adventurous Journey*, p. 118.
70 *SL Army 50 Years On*, p. 391; Tim Smith, *Reluctant Mercenary: the Recollections of a British Ex-army Pilot in the Anti-terrorist War in Sri Lanka*, (The Book Guild: Sussex, UK, 2002), p. 217.
71 Phil Miller, *Britain's Dirty War against the Tamil People 1979–2009*, (International Human Rights Association: Bremen, 2015), pp. 12–15; Smith, *Reluctant Mercenary*.
72 O'Ballance, *Cyanide War*, p. 56.
73 'Jaffna Bombed', *Saturday Review*, 22.2.86, p. 1.
74 Thomas Abraham, 'Pounding Jaffna', *Frontline*, 2–15.3.91, p. 56 (56–57).
75 'Jaffna Bombed', *Saturday Review*, 22.2.86, p. 1.
76 'Death Rains from the Skies', *Saturday Review*, 1.3.86.
77 Smith, *Reluctant Mercenary*, p. 68.
78 *Broken Palmyrah*, p. 106.
79 Thomas Abraham, 'Pounding Jaffna', *Frontline*, 2–15.3.91, p. 56 (56–57).
80 Robert McDonald, 'Eyewitness in Jaffna', *Pacific Defense Reporter*, August, 1987, p. 26.
81 Julian West, 'Passage to Jaffna', *Asiaweek*, 8.3.91, reproduced in http://www.sangam.org/PIRABAKARAN/Part7.htm

> Even though West was writing in 1991 during Ealam War II, the above observations are valid for Ealam War I as well, considering that the same technology was being used.

82 Michael Hamlyn, 'Tamils Step Up Attacks on Civilians: the Communal Conflict in Sri Lanka', *The Times*, 11.3.86. http://infoweb.newsbank.com.ezproxy.lib.monash.edu.au/iw-search/we/InfoWeb?p_product=AUNB&p_theme=aggregated5&p_action=doc&p_docid=0F90AB6C0643A541&p_docnum=193&p_queryname=1 (5.12.10)
83 Humphrey Hawkesley, 'Sri Lanka Resumes Air Raids on Tamil Villages', *The Age*, 29.3.86.
84 Smith, *Reluctant Mercenary*, pp. 80–2.

Chapter 3

The first showdown
'Operation Liberation'

By late 1986, except the few military encampments, the entire Jaffna Peninsula was firmly under LTTE control. The Tigers tightened their grip on the populace, establishing their own administration in 'liberated' Jaffna. They levied their own taxes. They had also set up a court system to try criminals and antisocial elements.[1] Prabhakaran was still in South India at this time, but under the leadership of Kittu who was in charge in Jaffna, the Tigers meted out rough justice to those who disobeyed them. Many who were found guilty were executed and displayed tied to lamp posts. The Tigers were also intensifying their training and arms production. They established five main camps around Jaffna where new recruits were being trained. Quite alarmingly, an increasing number of them were boys, some in their early teens. Unlike in 1984/85, the Tigers were now struggling to meet the growing demands of their military commitments, having to rule the peninsula and besiege the military camps all on their own now.[2] The five camps were reportedly producing around 80 fighters every three months. By now, every graduate of Tiger training was also wearing a 'cyanide necklace', which simply consisted of a phial of cyanide hanging from a string around the neck.[3] The rebel cadre was expected to bite into the phial and commit suicide if faced with capture. In an effort to give their forces an aura of professionalism, the Tigers also began to confer regular military ranks on their cadres. Some of the regular cadres also wore military-style uniforms. From late 1985, the Tigers had also begun inducting women into their fighting ranks. They were formed into separate female units but initially placed under male command, the Mannar LTTE commander 'Lt. Colonel' Victor taking charge of them.[4]

The LTTE also stepped up arms procurements and production. By 1986, they had begun to manufacture home-made mortars and shells and even the ammunition for RPGs. The mortars were 50, 81, 90 and

155mm and had a cast iron or aluminium shell and black powder as the propellant.[5] In October 1986, Kittu boasted that the Tigers were producing around 25 mortars and 100 grenades daily.[6] 'We prefer our own mortars to the ones we have bought,' he claimed.[7] The mortars, some of which were as big as 155mm, had aluminium cases which, according to the army, caused shrapnel to explode into large pieces, causing horrible wounds to the soldiers.[8] A visiting Indian journalist, however, was not impressed by the Tigers' 'ordnance factory', dismissing it as 'nothing more than a junk shop'.[9] Such contempt for the home-grown technology of the rebels was justified to an extent by the performance of the products of these 'factories'. The mortars fired at the Jaffna Fort were frequently inaccurate, sometimes only about a third of those fired hitting the fort.[10] But it was sufficient to keep the soldiers cooped up and ducking for cover.

Moreover, the Tigers were also supplementing their crude arsenal with more sophisticated weapons. Now there were more rocket launchers around, usually the Soviet RPG-7. Tiger cadres were now carrying a variety of modern rifles, the commonest being the AK 47 and T56 with the occasional M16. By late 1986, they had also purchased a number of Browning .50 and .30 calibre machine guns. The former were mounted on pickup trucks for easy mobility.[11] These, along with the RPGs and the mortars, made up the rebels' heavy firepower.

The drift towards a showdown

By mid-1986, breaking the siege in Jaffna was becoming the main military focus of the government. The siege was proving too costly and the government was increasingly concerned about the loss of much of the North to rebel control. The acquisition of new weapons had also boosted the confidence of the Security Forces, making them eager to take the fight to the enemy. However, this posed a serious challenge from a counter-insurgency perspective. Pushing the rebels from their well-entrenched positions required large troop concentrations as well as the deployment of heavy firepower. This had dire implications for civilians and diplomatic relations with India. To be sure, the army had regularly lobbed shells into Jaffna without much regard for civilian life, but these actions were casual acts under the radar. A major operation to push the rebels back had the potential to attract unwanted attention.

Predictably, the first actions were tentative. Between May 1986 and March 1987, the Security Forces launched a series of probing attacks in strength, aimed at clearing areas around their camps in the North and

50 The first showdown

the East. In Jaffna, the mainland troops occupied Vasavilan Central College, where a small camp was set up. Kayts was also secure, strengthening the military's control over the western coast of the peninsula. On May 22 1986, Mandaithivu Island was brought under control to complete this hold.[12] The capture of Mandaithivu in particular enabled the air force to land supplies for Jaffna without too much hindrance from the guerrillas who used the island to snipe at troops in the Jaffna Fort.[13]

In February the following year, the troops also ventured out of the fort and captured the Jaffna telecommunications exchange and the buildings in the vicinity. These buildings were taken to deny the Tigers vantage points from which to harass the soldiers in the fort.[14] In March 1987 after constant sniping and mortar attacks, the troops moved out of Palaly to clear the area around the Kattuwan junction to the south of the Palaly air base and establish an outpost. An area of approximately 4 miles around the junction was declared cleared by the troops.[15] The forces also moved out of the Navatkuli camp to the Navatkuli junction to extend its perimeters after the Tigers pounded the camp with mortars for nearly 20 hours on March 7 and 8.[16]

In the Wanni and the East too, the army made inroads into rebel territory. In Mannar, troops moved south-east towards Uyilankulam and northwards towards Adampan and then towards Illuppukadavai further north. In Trincomalee, areas around Kurumbupiddy up to Pulmoddai and Yan Oya were reported completely cleared. In the Kilinochchi District, two military columns from Kilinochchi and Elephant Pass converged on Paranthan, securing the town and setting up roadblocks. Troops occupied government buildings in town, including the post office and the chemicals factory. In Batticaloa, troops ventured out of camps in Kokkadicholai and Vavunativu and destroyed several militant hideouts.[17]

These operations relieved some of the pressure on the troops. But the damage to the rebels was limited. There was very little resistance except in Jaffna. This was only to be expected. The guerrillas did not have the strength to meet a strong Security Forces contingent head-on except perhaps in the Jaffna Peninsula. Besides, the Security Forces gave the guerrillas plenty of warning about their designs. The fledgling military struggled with its transport, which relied heavily on the few transport aircraft and road bound transport. This meant that a troop build-up took considerable time, giving sufficient warning to the enemy of an impending operation. This probably explains the unusually light mortar fire reportedly experienced by the army during its advances.[18]

But by the beginning of 1987, there were also encouraging signs from across the Palk Straits. India was beginning to turn up the heat on the Tigers. After the rebels had fired into a crowd in Tamil Nadu on Diwali Day in November 1986, the Indian government clamped down on them. Since the failure of peace talks, the Indians had been waiting to do this. The Tigers had matched the Sri Lankan government in their reluctance to engage in a meaningful peace process, which exasperated the Indians who were trying to broker peace. Now they got their chance to serve the militants notice. On November 8, they raided the hideouts of five guerrilla groups in a state-wide crackdown, arresting militant leaders and confiscating a massive haul of weapons. Among the many arms and equipment captured were thousands of AK47, RPGs and several SAM-7 missiles.[19] The Tiger leaders were later released, but the weapons were lost forever. India was sending the militants a clear message: if you want to enjoy our hospitality, play by our rules.

Undaunted, the Tigers transferred whatever weapons that had eluded the Indians to their stronghold in northern Sri Lanka.[20] Prabhakaran himself returned to Jaffna in January 1987, after a sojourn of several years in India. They also responded to the government's offensives with ferocity. On February 7, the day the army began its probing operations, they struck in Aranthalawa in Ampara, killing 28 men, women and children, almost all of them brutally hacked to death.[21] On March 24, another village in the East, this time Serunuwara in Horowapotana, suffered the Tigers' wrath, losing 26 villagers.[22]

In the North, as usual, the newly captured areas were proving hard to hold on to. As usual, the Tigers simply focused their attacks on the newly established posts. The outposts around the Jaffna Fort in particular came in for some serious punishment. Early in the morning of March 23, the Tigers launched a sustained rocket and mortar barrage on the Jaffna Fort and its outposts. While the garrison in the fort was pinned down by this fire, a group of Tigers stormed the outpost at the entrance to the Pannai causeway, where six soldiers and three policemen were stationed. The initial confrontation killed a corporal and a militant, and soon the militants surrounded the outpost. A party sent to reinforce the outpost was ambushed, killing a sergeant and three soldiers. In the meantime, with their ammunition exhausted, the remaining soldiers and policemen surrendered to the Tigers.[23]

The military operations in the North were widely seen as a precursor to a large-scale offensive to capture the peninsula. Tension was running high in Jaffna in anticipation of an imminent assault. In Jaffna, Tigers were busy digging trenches and building bunkers. Buildings were being booby-trapped, and there were reports of bamboo stakes being driven to the ground in school playgrounds to counter landing by helicopter-borne

52 The first showdown

troops.[24] All the key LTTE leaders were called to Jaffna and the Tiger ranks in Jaffna were reinforced with troops from other areas.[25] Streets became deserted in Jaffna by 6 p.m. as people sought the refuge of their homes. Many homes now had bunkers and many residents spent the majority of their time at home in these dinghy dugouts.[26]

Then in a sudden gesture of goodwill, the government declared a ceasefire to cover the New Year period, April 11–20. But the Tigers responded with two gruesome attacks. On Good Friday, April 17, they stopped a convoy of civilian buses on their way to Trincomalee near the village of Aluth Oya on the Habarana–Trincomalee road and killed 127 of the passengers, many of whom were service personnel returning to duty after the New Year celebrations. Four days later, a massive car bomb exploded in the heart of Colombo at the Petah bus stand, killing 110 people and injuring over 300.[27]

Outraged by the massacres, Jayawardena finally unleashed his troops on Jaffna in May. 'Everybody told us, the government, you are doing nothing,' explained Lalith Athulathmudali, giving reasons for the decision. 'So we had to launch a crackdown on the terrorists.'[28] The 'crackdown' came on May 26 with the launching of 'Operation Liberation', the biggest military operation launched by Sri Lanka since independence.

Operation Liberation

The Vadamarachchi division of the Jaffna Peninsula is a thin strip of land that extends north-west from Elephant Pass. It flares into a broad, oblong area in the north-western end, making the strip look like a smaller version of the peninsula. The narrow part of Vadamarachchi is sparsely populated while the top end is home to the vast majority of the inhabitants, concentrated in an area roughly 7 miles long and 5 miles wide. It boasts of two sizeable towns, Point Pedro and Velvetithurai, the latter the hometown of the Tiger supremo Prabhakaran and, as explained earlier, a haven for smugglers.

The objective of 'Operation Liberation' was to seal off and capture this strip of land. Lalith Athulathmudali explained the focus on Vadamarachchi as driven by several strategic considerations. The area, he claimed, housed many of the ordnance factories of the Tigers and was also one of the main arms supply points.[29] It was also hoped that the military would be able to capture Prabhakaran. Military intelligence had noted that the Tiger chief was in Velvetithurai.[30] If they could net him, it would be a prize catch indeed and a promise of a swift end to the war. However, according to Gerry de Silva who was in overall command of Jaffna at the time, Vadamarachchi was chosen as the main theatre of operations because the president refused to allocate a brigade size force to hold and dominate the Jaffna municipal limits. Jayawardena was unconvinced that such a large force would be needed once 'carpet bombing' had reduced the area to rubble. The military top brass had to settle for Vadamarachchi as the second best option.[31]

Expecting an all-out assault on Jaffna town itself, the Tigers called their cadres to strengthen defences in Valikamam. The number of Tiger cadres preparing for battle in Jaffna at this time is hard to estimate. The Tigers claimed in early 1987 that they had 10,000 cadres, but the government played down the numbers, placing them at 1,500–2,000.[32] The commander of Jaffna Fort, Lieutenant Colonel Asoka Jayasinghe, believed that there were only about 300–400 Tigers in Jaffna city itself but that they could rely on additional cadres anytime.[33] The rebels no doubt inflated their numbers while the government downplayed them. The number of hard-core cadres was probably counted in their hundreds, but the number of young men and women armed or willing to fight would have been much higher.

Probing attacks by the army had begun days earlier. Air attacks on targets in the peninsula, especially in the Valikamam area, began immediately after the bomb blast in Pettah. From May 18, the army also made several forays from their bases in Palaly, Thondamanaru, Kurumbasiddy, Kadduvan and Navatkuli. The operation proper began on May 26. The military imposed a dawn curfew on the entire Jaffna Peninsula and followed it by dropping leaflets, warning the civilians to take shelter in designated safe havens: government buildings and temples. Then, two hours later, aircraft swooped on Tiger targets in Vadamarachchi and around Jaffna town.

The Sri Lankan air force marshalled an impressive assembly of aircraft for the operation. It was still a poor man's air force, but it was the biggest deployment of air power by Sri Lanka yet. Six Siai Marchettis functioned as ground-attack aircrafts while two helicopters were deployed as gunships. One BAC-748 (AVRO), two Y12s and one De Haviland Heron were used as improvised bombers. Two BAC-748s, two Y12s and one De Haviland Doves were employed as transports, ferrying goods and men. Eight helicopters also figured as troops carriers. Casualty evacuation also received high priority; one Y12 was devoted to that purpose.[34] This was the biggest array of aircraft ever assembled by the air force for a single operation.

On the ground, the deployment was no less remarkable. Sri Lanka was making its largest military effort since independence, deploying in

54 The first showdown

excess of 5,000 troops for the operation, organised in three brigades. Scores of armoured personnel carriers, armoured cars and jeeps mounted with recoilless rifles were pressed into service along with 25-pounder artillery and 120mm mortars. The army was deployed in three brigades, two of which took on Vadamarachchi. The First Brigade under Wijaya Wimalaratne moved out of Thondamanaru and moved eastwards along the coast, while the Third Brigade led by Denzil Kobbekaduwa moved parallel to it about 8 miles southwards to protect its flank. In the meantime, a group of commandos was dropped by helicopter in the south and south-west parts of Vadamarachchi as well as on the east coast of Vadamarachchi. Their role was to seal off the southern and western parts of Vadamarachchi and the east coast of the sector to prevent any militants from escaping. They immediately set up roadblocks in anticipation of a Tiger exodus, while the group dropped near the coast took position on the sand hills overlooking the beach at Manalkadu. In the meantime, the Second Brigade led by Gerry de Silva took on a diversionary role, making brief forays from the camps in Valikamam including the Jaffna Fort. The Jaffna foray was joined by two groups of commandos, numbering about 300 landed by sea.[35] To the south, another column – also part of the Second Brigade – advanced from Elephant Pass. It moved up to Iyakachchi and then on towards Sornampattu with the final goal being Chempionpattu on the Vada strip.[36] They were hoping to seal off the southern end of Vadamarachchi.

The column from Elephant Pass overcame initial resistance to achieve its objective. But the troops from the Jaffna Fort ran into difficulties within moments. They were confronted by Tigers led by the Jaffna commander Kittu, and after about two hours of fighting, the first column returned to the fort. A second team advanced about 700 metres and returned to base after a sharp fire fight. The rebels claimed to have foiled another foray towards Keerimalai from Kankesanthurai army camp and another attempt by troops to come out of their outpost in the cement corporation at the same location.[37] The Tigers hailed this as a success, but troops had achieved their objective: to keep the enemy guessing.

The real threat to the Tigers was the two main columns moving west–east in Vadamarachchi. The rebels had blasted the ridge at Thondamanaru earlier. The troops negotiated this obstacle with the help of the engineering regiment only to run into a thickly laid minefield. Here the army got bogged down, and for a while the advance seemed to hang in the balance as the landmines began to take a heavy toll, one killing eight members of the engineering regiment.[38] The leading company of the First Brigade lost about 90 per cent of its men within the first half hour. The command vehicle of the First Battalion of the Gajaba Regiment was also blown up; luckily for the commander, he was on foot at the time.[39] But the advance ground on, the First Brigade now moving along the coast while the Third Brigade moving astride the Thondamanaru–Uduppiddy road. But the advance was necessarily slow due to the threat of mines; at the end of the first day, the First Brigade managed to move barely two kilometres while the Third Brigade encamped for the night just a kilometre from Thondamanaru.[40]

But the breakthrough had been made. When it was evident that the army had broken through the mine barrier, the Tigers fell back, telling the civilians to run for cover. Their resistance, however, stiffened as the troops came closer to Velvetithurai. Here the army had to capture well-laid out rebel stronghold, ringed by bunkers and minefields. It was finally taken on May 28 at the cost of six soldiers being killed. Thereafter, the Tigers' resistance petered out as they concentrated on preserving their forces without further confrontation. In the South, the Second Brigade had seen lesser action, often moving ahead of the northern column. Uduppiddy had fallen to them on twenty-eighth and Nelliady soon after, the army establishing small camps at Uduppiddy Girls' School and Nelliady Madhya Maha Vidyalam before moving on towards their next big prize – Point Pedro. On June 1, the army approached Point Pedro, moving cross-country in three lines, breaking through fences, cutting barbed wire and scaling garden walls.[41] As they did, the troops cooped up in the Point Pedro army camp broke their shackles and ventured out to join up with their comrades.

By May 31, Vadamarachchi was declared under government control. New camps and bases were established in the captured area. Four camps were set up in Mulli, Puloly, Karaveddi and Nelliady.[42] Nearly 5,000 youths between the ages of 15 and 35 had been rounded up and awaited transportation to the detention camp at Boosa in Galle, where they were to be processed.

On June 4, a limited operation was launched to capture Atchuveli. But the army withdrew from the town a few days later. Brigadier Gerry De Silva who headed the operation gave the reason for the withdrawal as the concern for civilian casualties.[43]

With the Atchuveli Operation ended the much-awaited offensive. According to the government, the cessation of offensive operations was due to the completion of the first phase of the operation. But the truth was that further military activity was becoming increasingly difficult due to Indian pressure. Despite being peeved with the Tigers for their recalcitrance, India had also been wary of the Sri Lankan government's

56 The first showdown

commitment to a peaceful resolution of the conflict. After the crackdown on the Tigers in November, India had warned Sri Lanka not to take it as a go-ahead for an all-out offensive in the North.[44] Sri Lankan Security Forces' operations in early 1987 had met with firm rebuffs from India, and the outrageous actions of the LTTE in April had not made India any softer towards the Sri Lankan government. The launching of the Vadamarachchi offensive came to be seen with great alarm by Delhi, which saw it as the much talked about attempt to crush the militants for good. And as news of widespread destruction in Vadamarachchi and civilian casualties began to pour in, India issued protests. When they failed to stem the military advance, the Indian government sent a flotilla of fuel, food and medicines to Jaffna as a 'humanitarian gesture'. The Sri Lankan navy turned the flotilla back on June 3, but the following day India retaliated by sending five Antonov transport planes with relief supplies escorted by four Mirage fighters. The planes entered Sri Lankan airspace for a few minutes, dropping 22 tonnes of relief supplies. The message to the Sri Lankan government was clear. The military offensive would continue only at the risk of inviting further Indian interventions.

That ended the most ambitious military operation undertaken to date by the Sri Lankan army after independence. It had succeeded in bringing the entire Vadamarachchi area under government control. The military claimed to have killed about 200 guerrillas and wounded twice that number. They also claimed to have captured a large haul of arms and ammunition. These included four lorry loads of arms and ammunition abandoned by the retreating militants ahead of Point Pedro and several 120mm and 155 mortars mounted on trucks. Two small ammunition factories were also destroyed at Uduppiddy.[45] The army admitted to losing 39 killed and 150 wounded. Hundreds of youths were also arrested and sent into detention camps awaiting further investigations. But the prize catch was missing. Prabhakaran had vanished with some of his top lieutenants. It was later revealed that he had slipped out of the net when the troops approaching the area he was holed out in were delayed by booby traps.[46]

Vadamarachchi: the balance sheet

Operation Liberation was the first real showdown between the two sides, the result of the government's attempt to wrest the initiative from the enemy that was besieging the Security Forces. Whether it was intended as a decisive stroke to cripple the Tigers is unclear, but the progress of the operation and the Indian intervention reminded the Sri Lankan state of the military and diplomatic realities of such a bold venture. The Sri Lankan Security Forces, despite their superior firepower, lacked the ability to grind down what was essentially a guerrilla enemy. The Indian intervention showed that no major move against the rebels was possible without Indian backing.

To be sure, the operation placed the LTTE under immense pressure. Despite all their bragging, the Tigers did not have the resources to fight simultaneously on several fronts, and they were hopelessly outgunned when the Sri Lankan military chose to unleash its firepower freely as it did to a great extent in Vadamarachchi. True, the Tigers had the bulk of their heavy weapons in and around Jaffna town in anticipation of the major military thrust taking place there, but still a stronger concentration of firepower in the form of mortars and .50 calibre machine guns could have stood little chance against cannon and aerial bombing and strafing. As a civilian explained to a journalist, 'The firepower of the army was immense. You cannot stand up to shells with AK47s.'[47]

On the other hand, the Sri Lankan Security Forces also faced a number of challenges. Despite having control over large areas of the Jaffna Peninsula, the LTTE was still very much a lightly armed guerrilla outfit. The Tigers had few major bases or structures that could be targeted. The Sri Lankan Security Forces had deployed their biggest force to date in Vadamarachchi, but this was still not enough to prevent the rebels from dispersing and regrouping elsewhere. The navy in particular still did not possess enough vessels to patrol the coast effectively. The commandos, who were still in their infancy, were the best bet against intercepting escaping guerrillas, but their numbers were also small. As a result, even though the Security Forces claimed to have killed over 200 Tiger cadres, many more made good their escape. These included 300–350 top rebel cadres.[48]

Going after such an elusive foe had dire implications for the safety of civilians. Despite the boost to their firepower and the increase in numbers, the Sri Lankan Security Forces were still rather primitive in their capabilities. The SLAF had no means of carrying out precision bombing. The Siai Marchettis were wildly inaccurate; Lalith Athulathmudali himself had admitted that the previous year.[49] They were better suited to attacking ground targets in bush land rather than built-up areas. The helicopter gunships and the 'barrel bombers' were no more accurate. This was bad news for civilians whose abodes often stood in close proximity to the rebel bunkers.

Government sources gave the civilian casualties as a handful, while the Tigers claimed hundreds were killed and wounded.[50] The government,

58 The first showdown

no doubt, underplayed the extent of the harm to civilian life and property, while it was in the Tigers' interest to exaggerate them. Indian sources, often fed by pro-Tiger informants and with India's own interest in bringing the hostilities to an end in mind, also joined the chorus in accusing the military of causing heavy civilian casualties.

A Western journalist, one of the few independent observers in Jaffna at the time, found no evidence of 'carpet bombing' as claimed by some Tamil sources, but witnessed 'line after line of buildings beyond repair' in Velvetithurai, which had borne the brunt of the government's assault.[51] Point Pedro was in no better shape. 'Between the army camp and the inhabited area there lies a swathe of utter destruction,' observed another journalist. 'The main square is littered with rubble and whole buildings have collapsed.'[52]

The army attributed much of the destruction to the booby traps left by the retreating Tigers. There is no doubt these caused much damage. However, residents spoke of indiscriminate bombing and strafing by aircraft.[53] According to a foreign journalist present in Jaffna at the time, heavy mortars fired from the Jaffna Fort and naval gunfire caused civilian deaths and spread terror without warning. 'Within hours (of the leaflet drop) the downtown area was hit by heavy mortar fire and shells from a naval gunboat. The result was panic and confusion among the civilian population – one mortar that landed near the hospital killed a 12-year-old boy. A single small piece of shrapnel had hit him in the right side of his head.'[54]

The places of worship which were designated places of refuge did not escape the shelling and bombing either. One shell landing on Mariamman temple in Alvai is said to have killed 35 people and another bomb hitting the Sivan Kovil on KKS Road claimed 17 victims.[55] Eight people including women and children were reported killed by a shell at St James School while seven more were reportedly killed by a bomb at the Amman Kovil at Suthumalai.[56] Reports claimed up to 75 people being killed by shellfire and were burnt to death at Mathumari Amman temple at Alvai on May 29.[57]

Given the primitive means of carrying out air raids, it would have been a miracle if civilians had not been hurt. It was the inevitable outcome of a war fought on a shoestring. It also showed that the Sri Lankan Security Forces had a tough fight ahead if they were to widen the war to include Valikamam and Thenmarachchi. Taking the war into the more heavily built-up Valikamam in particular ran the risk of causing far more destruction than in Vadamarachchi without necessarily causing much damage to the enemy's forces. It also had the potential to alienate a population already much harassed by the conflict with dire consequences for future operations with the disaffected civilians swelling the ranks of the rebels. Furthermore, such a venture also had the potential to raise the casualties of the Security Forces considerably. The vast majority of the army's casualties in Vadamarachchi were caused by booby traps, and this threat loomed larger in the heavily built-up Valikamam.

Another problem faced by the army was that of occupying the area captured by them. The capture and occupation of Vadamarachchi showed the seriousness of this issue. At least 5,000 troops were required to take Vadamarachchi, and these were increasingly harassed by the guerrilla activities of the rebels. Soon after Operation Liberation ended, a landmine blew up a truck, bringing released detainees back to their homes, killing ten of the detainees and three soldiers.[58] An officer confided to a foreign journalist that 'some terrorists' had infiltrated the area considered cleared by the army.[59] The first major counterattack, however, came in Jaffna town. In the early hours of June 3, an improvised armoured truck laden with explosives approached the military post at the telecommunications building adjoining the Jaffna Fort. The truck was the spearhead of a devastating attack by a group of Tigers said to have numbered more than 50. The explosion brought down much of the building, killing three soldiers and wounding more than 40. The Tigers attacked the survivors furiously and the soldiers fought back with the aid of helicopters that sprayed the area with machine gunfire and rockets. By morning, the attackers had withdrawn, taking their dead and wounded with them. Among the booty captured by the rebels was one GPMG, seven Belgian-made FNGs, one AK grenade launcher and over a 1,000 rounds of ammunition.[60] Tigers claimed to have killed 22 soldiers, including a second lieutenant. More importantly, they also took captive three soldiers, their second such haul that year.[61] A much more powerful attack on July 5 saw the Tigers using suicide cadres for the first time. An explosives-laden truck driven by a cadre named Miller rammed into the army camp at Nelliaddy Central College, killing 17 and wounding over 30. They also captured a large haul of small arms and ammunition, including a mortar launcher. At least one Saladin armoured car was also destroyed.[62]

These experiences gave a taste of what would have come had the army tried to occupy the entire peninsula. The army had in excess of 40,000 troops at the time, but these numbers would have been fully stretched in the event of the occupation of the entire peninsula in the face of a population outraged by the destruction caused by the campaign and, therefore, even more supportive of the rebels than they had been before

60 The first showdown

the operation. Such a situation would have been ideal for a protracted guerrilla war. Even providing for an increase in recruitment on the back of the military success, this would have been a daunting task. Athulathmudali himself later admitted that it was questionable whether they had adequate forces to dominate Jaffna.[63]

Therefore, Operation Liberation, while giving the Tigers a jolt, also exposed some serious limitations in the Sri Lankan Security Forces. Despite the advances made in acquiring heavy firepower, training and increase in numbers, its ability to deliver the rebels a crushing blow was undermined by limitations in their means as well as the elusive nature of the enemy. Due to these factors, the Security Forces could go after the Tigers only at the risk of heavy casualties to themselves and civilians and by overstretching their resources without any great certainty of destroying the enemy's forces.

Finally, India's intervention pointed to the diplomatic pitfalls of making an all-out military effort to defeat the Tigers. Indian intervention demonstrated that even if the Sri Lankan Security Forces had a chance of achieving a decisive shift in the balance of power on the ground it was doomed to failure without India's support. It was true that India was more than irked by the LTTE's intransigence, but that did not mean that the Indian government was going to stand by while the Sri Lankan Security Forces crippled the Tamil rebellion, their bargaining tool. It demonstrated the complexity of the problem faced by the Sri Lankan Security Forces: fighting a war that was not limited to military operations.

Notes

1 Michael Hamlyn, 'Tiger Guerrillas Step into Rulers Role: Jaffna Tamils Prepare for Post-settlement Role in Sri Lanka', *The Times*, 18.9.86, http:// infoweb.newsbank.com.ezproxy.lib.monash.edu.au/iw-search/we/ InfoWeb?p_product=AUNB&p_theme=aggregated5&p_action=doc&p_ docid=0F90B42F18F127F6&p_docnum=333&p_queryname=1 (11.1.11), S. Venkatnarayan, 'A visit to Jaffna', *The Island*, 15.2.87, p. 6.
2 *Broken Palmyrah*, p. 78.
3 O'Ballance, *Cyanide War*, p. 66.
4 Adele Balasingham, *Women Fighters of Liberation Tigers*, (Thasan: Jaffna, 1993), pp. 17–35.
5 Rohan Guneratna, *War and Peace in Sri Lanka*, (Institute of Fundamental Studies: Colombo, 1987), p. 47.
6 Cruez, 'Within the Jaws'.
7 Jon Swain, 'Face to Face with the Guerrilla Commander: Cyanide Martyrs Bar Way to Peace', *Sunday Times*, 10. 8.86, reproduced in *Lanka Guardian*, 1.9.86, pp. 11–12.

The first showdown 61

8 'Inside Jaffna Fort: Battle of Nerves', *Ceylon Daily News*, 11.9.86, reproduced in *Saturday Review*, 20.9.86, p. 6.
9 S. Venkatnarayan, 'A Visit to Jaffna', *The Island*, 15.2.87, p. 6.
10 'Tigers Hold Troops as Captive Force', Reuters report, *Weekend*, 21.6.87, p. 11.
11 Guneratne, *War and Peace in Sri Lanka*, pp. 46–7; Marks, *Counterinsurgency in Sri Lanka*, p. 42.
12 'Sri Lanka: the Siege Within', *India Today*, June 15, 1989, p. 121; O'Ballance, *Cyanide War*, p. 63, Mendis, *Assignment Peace*, p. 52.
13 Tom Marks, 'Winning the War in Sri Lanka', *The Island*, 2.6.89, p. 6; Mendis, *Assignment Peace*, pp. 50–52.
14 'Security Forces Secure Large Areas', *Sunday Observer*, 15.2.87, p. 1; Mendis, *Assignment Peace*, pp. 57–8.
15 Iqbal Athas, 'Rendezvous in Madras to Receive seized Arms', *Weekend*, p. 7 (7 and 21).
16 Iqbal Athas, 'Peace through the Ballot?', *Weekend*, 15.03.87, p. 7.
17 'Security Forces Secure Large Areas', *Sunday Observer*, 15.2.87, p. 1; Mendis, *Assignment Peace*, pp. 57–8.
18 'Tigers at Bay', *The Economist*, 28.2.87, p. 28.
19 S.H. Venkatramani, 'Taming the Tigers', *India Today*, 30.11.1986, pp. 22–3; 'India Cracks the Whip', *Asiaweek*, 23.11.86, p. 33. The offices belonged to the LTTE, PLOT, EPRLF and EROS. The confiscated weapons and equipment were valued at Rs 40 crore. 'Operation Tiger: the Reasons behind', *The Island*, 7.12.86, p. 9 (courtesy *Amrita Bazaar Patrika*)
20 Jon Swain, 'Face to Face with the Guerrilla Commander: Cyanide Martyrs Bar Way to Peace', *Sunday Times*, 10. 8.86, reproduced in *Lanka Guardian*, 1.9.86, p. 11.
21 H.W. Abeypala, 'Black Saturday's Slaughter House', *Weekend*, 15.02.87, pp. 6 and 11.
22 Elmo Perera, 'Bloodlust of the Brutal Tigers', *Weekend*, 20.3.87, pp. 8 and 21.
23 Iqbal Athas, 'Bid to Internationalise Hostage Crisis by Tigers', *Weekend*, 29.3.87, p. 7 (7 & 23).
24 Athas, 'Rendezvous in Madras', p. 7.
25 *Broken Palmyrah*, p. 99.
26 Ibid., pp. 114–15.
27 O'Ballance, *Cyanide War*, p. 76.
28 'The Army Will Stay On', (Athulathmudali's interview with *India Today*'s Dilip Bob and S.V. Venkatramani), *Lanka Guardian*, 1.7.87, p. 9 (9–10).
29 'The Army Will Stay On', Athulathmudali's interview with *India Today*'s Dilip Bob and S.V. Venkatramani), *Lanka Guardian*, 1.7.87, p. 9 (9–10).
30 *Broken Palmyrah*, p. 125.
31 Gerry de Silva, *A Most Noble Profession*, p. 75.
32 S. Venkat Narayan, 'A visit to Jaffna', *The Island*, 15.2.87, p. 6.
33 'Tigers Hold Troops as Captive Force', *Weekend*, (Reuters Report) 21.6.87, p. 11.
34 Senaratne, *Sri Lanka Air Force*, p. 79.

62 The first showdown

35 Athas, 'The Vadamarachchi Landing', *Weekend*, 5.31.87; p. 6, O'Ballance, *Cyanide War*, p. 82.

36 Athas, 'The Vadamarachchi Landing', *Weekend*, 5.31.87, p. 6.

37 R.C., 'All Quiet on the Northern Front', *Saturday Review*, 30.5.87, p. 4; 'Tigers Hold Troops as Captive Force', *Weekend*, (Reuters Report) 21.6.87, p. 11.

38 'Operation Liberation Encircles Key LTTE Post', *Daily News*, 28.5.87, p. 1.

39 Chandraprema, *Gota's War*, (Vijitha Yapa: Colombo, 2012), pp. 163–4.

40 Tilak Senananayake, *Vadamarachchi Vimukthi Meheyuma*, (Godage Publishers: Colombo, 2004), p. 12 and 37.

41 'Vadamarachchi: The Missing Generation', p. 4.

42 Iqbal Athas, 'The Plot that Failed at the Airbase', *Weekend*, 21.06.87.

43 Derek Brown, 'Jaffna Reality – Two Strange Forms', *The Guardian*, 15.6.87, reproduced in the *Saturday Review*, 11.7.87, p. 4.

44 John Elliott, 'India Warns Sri Lanka of Offensive,' *Lanka Guardian*, 1.12.86, p. 3.

45 Mendis, *Assignment Peace*, pp. 67–9.

46 *Broken Palmyrah*, p. 125.

47 'Vadamarachchi Operation: The Missing Generation', *Saturday Review*, 20.6.87, p. 3.

48 Qadri Ismail, 'Military Option and Its Aftermath', *Sunday Times*, 7.6.87, p. 5.

49 Michael Hamlyn, 'Tamils Step Up Attacks on Sinhalese Villagers: the Communal Conflict in Sri Lanka', *The Times*, 11.3.86.

50 Lalith Athulathmudali claimed only 47 civilians had died according to the government's estimate, while the LTTE was giving a figure of 600. 'The Army Will Stay On', p. 9.

51 John Elliott, 'Battle for Tamil Hearts, Minds and Stomachs', *Financial Times*, 6.6.87, reproduced in Lanka Guardian, 15.6.87, p. 8.

52 Derek Brown, 'Jaffna Reality – Two Strange Forms', *The Guardian*, 15.6.87, reproduced in the *Saturday Review*, 11.7.87, p. 4.

53 John Elliott, 'Battle for Tamil Hearts, Minds and Stomachs', p. 8.

54 Robert McDonald, 'Eye Witness in Jaffna', p. 27.

55 *Broken Palmyrah*, pp. 127–8.

56 'Operation Blue Star', *Saturday Review*, 30.5.87, p. 1.

57 'The Day of the Lions (Jackals?)', *Saturday Review*, 6.6.87, p. 2; Vadamarachchi Operation, 'The Missing Generation', *Saturday Review*, 20.6.87, p. 3.

58 Iqbal Athas, 'The Post Vadamarachchi Crisis', *Weekend*, 14.6.87.

59 Derek Brown, 'Jaffna Reality – Two Strange Forms', *The Guardian*, 15.6.87, reproduced in the *Saturday Review*, 11.7.87, p. 4.

60 Iqbal Athas, 'How Operation Jellyfish Stung India's Flotilla at the Kutch', *Weekend*, 7.6.87, p. 23 (6 & 23)

61 'Telecom Soldiers Charred', *Saturday Review*, 6.6.87.

62 For the Nelliaddy attack, see Iqbal Athas, 'Tigers Explode Peace a Nelliady', *Weekend*, 12.07.87, p. 6 (6 and 11), D.B.S. Jeyaraj, 'Birth and Growth of the Black Tiger Suicide Squad', *The Island*, 13.7.97, p. 16.

63 Rohan Gunaratna, *Indian Intervention*, p. 178.

Chapter 4

The IPKF interlude and the Tigers' return

The Indian intervention ended the first phase of the war between the Tamil militants and the Sri Lankan Security Forces. It also led to the signing of the Indo-Lanka Accord, which brought the Indian Peace Keeping Force (IPKF) to Sri Lanka. Under the accord, the Sri Lankan government agreed to establish provincial councils as the unit of devolution. The accord was the result of discussions and negotiations between the Sri Lankan government and India since at least late 1985. After many frustrations, the Indians had withdrawn from mediating in February 1987. The Sri Lankan government's offensive in Jaffna allowed them to re-enter the process and persuade Colombo to accept their proposals based on the provincial council model that had been discussed before. The Tigers also agreed, albeit reluctantly.

The accord was signed on July 29, and Indian soldiers began arriving in Sri Lanka the following day. They came with a limited mandate – to supervise the handing over of weapons by the LTTE, to supervise the dismantling of Sri Lankan military camps established after May 1987, to separate the two warring parties and to help civilians displaced by the violence return to their homes.[1]

Initially, only one division, the Fifty-Fourth, arrived in Sri Lanka. They were received as heroes in Jaffna and the East. For a people traumatised by years of artillery and aerial bombardment, these men were indeed saviours. The Tamils felt – as they had often felt during the conflict – that the Indians were on their side, a feeling justified by India's very public sympathy for their plight and especially the giant neighbour's role in putting an end to the assault on Jaffna.

The end of the honeymoon

But the warmth of the Tamil people did not last very long. Soon the protectors became another enemy to fight against. The Indians found

64 The IPKF interlude

dealing with the LTTE challenging from the beginning. According to the Indo-Lanka Accord, the rebels were to surrender their weapons to the IPKF. The LTTE complied with this, but only up to a point. Even though the IPKF had estimated the Tigers to possess about 1,700 weapons when they arrived in Sri Lanka, only 488 weapons were handed over to them.[2] More problems followed soon. The Tigers wanted the lion's share of the proposed Interim Administrative Council and were opposed to the resettlement of Sinhalese refugees who had been displaced in the East. To assert and underline their primacy, they also began to eliminate their rivals. Events came to a head in September 1987. On September 16, a 26-year-old student Thileepan went on a hunger strike, demanding an end to Sinhala colonisation and speedy settlement of Tamil refugees. On September 26, he was dead. Then to make matters worse, on October 3, the Sri Lankan navy intercepted 17 Tiger cadres, including the regional commanders of Jaffna and Trincomalee. They were taken to the Palali airbase, and when the Sri Lankan authorities tried to take them down to Colombo for questioning, they committed suicide by biting into their cyanide capsules. Tigers unleashed a savage campaign of retribution. Eight soldiers held prisoner by them were killed, nearly 200 Sinhalese villagers massacred and thousands made homeless.[3] On October 8, the LTTE threw down the gauntlet to the IPKF by ambushing a patrol. All five soldiers were killed and their bodies burned with tyres around their necks.[4]

There seemed no alternative but to finish the job the Sri Lankan Security Forces had started in May. On October 9, the IPKF went on the offensive, launching an attack on Jaffna. Four columns, each of brigade strength, converged on Jaffna from four directions.[5] After a hard-fought campaign, the city was captured, and in the weeks that followed the IPKF extended its control over the peninsula. The Indians had done what the Sri Lankans had failed – or prevented from achieving.

The assault on Jaffna, however, demonstrated what might have awaited the Sri Lankan army had it ventured into Jaffna during Operation Liberation. Despite RAW reports that claimed Jaffna could be captured within 72 hours, the Indians required nearly two weeks to capture the town.[6] To be sure, the Indians were hampered by having only two under-strength divisions[7] which left them with little over 5,000 men to take on a guerrilla force estimated at 1,500–2,000.[8] Their hands were also tied by the restriction of the use of heavy artillery and air power. Of armour, there was little: only one squadron of three tanks and two companies of infantry fighting vehicles. They also had several heavy mortars to provide artillery support.[9] But the difficulty in capturing the town also owed a lot to the tenacious resistance of the LTTE. Rebel resistance, particularly booby traps, took a heavy toll of the Indian troops, while a daring commando raid on the Jaffna University ended in disaster with the Tigers ambushing the commandos and wiping them out.[10] The Tigers claimed they destroyed 21 Indian military vehicles and captured five along with a large haul of weapons and ammunitions that included bazookas, mortars, Bren guns, LMGs, SMGs, SLRs and 35,000 rounds. They admitted to losing only 43 fighters including seven female cadres but claimed to have killed over 300 of the enemy.[11] Indians admitted to losing 17 officers and 276 other ranks killed and 53 officers, 67 junior commissioned officers and 919 other ranks wounded. On top of these losses, the Indians also failed to prevent the rebel leadership and the bulk of their forces escaping the net. They slipped out of the peninsula into the vast expanse of the Wanni to fight another day.

A rural insurgency

For the next two years, the Indians focused on flushing the rebels out of their jungle bases. Now armed with heavy firepower and air support which included tanks, field artillery and dedicated helicopter gunships, they engaged in large-scale sweeps and cordon and search operations aimed at capturing guerrilla bases and isolating their leaders. In February–March 1988, the Indians used four brigades to sweep the North in Operation 'Vajra'. Operation Viraat–Trishul (April–June 1988) followed on the heels of Operation Vajra, ranging across the Northern Province from Mannar to Mullaithivu and Elephant Pass to Vavuniya.[12] 'Operation Checkmate' was carried out from May till the end of August 1988. The objective was to clear the Tigers' jungle hideouts in the Mullaithivu, Mannar and Vavuniya Districts ahead of the provincial councils elections. The Indian army moved deep into the Tigers' jungle refuges, especially in Mullaithivu around the Nittikaikulam tank where the troops could barely see through the dense scrub. The operation was hailed a success as the provincial elections were held without hindrance in the East.[13]

In the East, the Indians first sealed off the coastal belt using the navy and the air force before moving in on the hinterland.[14] This was followed by large sweeps as in the Wanni.[15] These produced mixed results. They succeeded in overrunning LTTE camps and destroying similar assets but failed to kill a large number of Tigers as they managed to slip through the net. In classic guerrilla style, the Tigers soon returned to their old haunts when the Indians returned to their camps. Occasionally, they also fought fiercely to buy time for their cadres to melt into the jungle. In March 1989, a patrol of Gurkhas ran into a strong Tiger concentration around the Nittikaikulam tank in Mullaithivu. The Gurkhas had to be extracted by sending reinforcements but with a loss of 15 killed and 30 injured. The Indians claimed to have killed 70 enemy cadres.[16] But as with the Sri Lankan army, it was the regular ambush that took a steady toll of the Jawans. On May 13 1989 in a particularly deadly attack, the Tigers killed an Indian major and 18 soldiers at Nedunkerni in the Mullaithivu District. Eleven more soldiers were wounded while the rebels helped themselves to a rich haul of small arms including two mortars.[17]

The IPKF had cornered the Tigers but they had not crushed them. The Indians struggled with some serious limitations in their campaign. At the initial stages of the war, the troops used the semi-automatic Belgian 7.62mm FN FAL assault rifles FNC, which were much inferior to the AK-47 and T56 used by the Tigers. The Indians also found the challenges of rural guerrilla warfare hard to negotiate. They often sent out large patrols that provided ideal targets for ambushes.[18] Unlike the Sri Lankan military, the IPKF had the services of the Mi25 helicopter gunships, which proved a great asset to their infantry. Still, even these flying fortresses found the thick jungle canopy of the Wanni, especially in the Mullaithivu area, hard to penetrate.[19]

The LTTE for their part stuck to their usual strategy of avoiding confrontation with enemy concentrations and bleeding the Indians dry with sporadic ambushes. Apart from their own arsenal of assault rifles, machineguns and mortars, they also used weapons taken from the IPKF. The Tigers also developed some effective devices of their own. These included the 'Arul' rifle grenade and the Jony mine. The latter in particular was to have a significant impact on the conduct of the war in the future. It was no more than a small wooden box with 3–400 grams of TNT or C4 that exploded from pressure. When it exploded, it blew off the foot of the person stepping on it. Many Indians lost their feet to it, and hundreds of Sri Lankan soldiers would also suffer a similar fate in the future.[20]

Despite the heavy losses, the IPKF fell short of completing the task of completely neutralising the LTTE as a military threat or in setting up an alternative political authority. Their stay in Sri Lanka had never been popular among the Sinhalese, and it had helped the radical Janatha Vmukthi Peramuna (JVP) launch a second rebellion against the government. With the South in the grip of savage violence, President Ranasinghe Premadasa decided to take the wind off the sails of his southern opponents. On June 1, 1989, Premadasa declared that he wished to see the IPKF withdrawn by the end of July 1989. The Indian government reacted strongly, saying that the time frame was not acceptable.[21] After hectic negotiations and tough talk on both sides, the Indians agreed to a token withdrawal to be followed by a high-level discussion to finalise details of the final pull-out. The real withdrawal of the IPKF began in 1990 and was complete by the end of March. On March 25 1990, the last of the Indian troops left Sri Lanka.[22] They left 1,115 dead. In comparison, India lost 1,047 troops in the war over Bangladesh.[23]

The government, LTTE and the TNA

While battling the Tigers, the Indians had also promoted what they thought would be a political alternative to the LTTE. The original intention was to form a multi-ethnic political alternative to the Tigers, but in the event it turned out to be little more than a coalition of three militant groups – EPRLF, remnants of TELO and ENDLF – who loathed the LTTE and supported the Indo-Lanka Accord.[24] It was known as the Three Stars' group and soon came to be seen as an Indian stooge by the pro-LTTE Tamils. Still, they had electoral success. In the November 1988 elections for the N-E provincial council, EPRLF won 36 of the 71 seats. In Jaffna, they were the only party allowed to contest and were elected unopposed.[25]

The cadres of the 'Three Stars' were drafted into a Citizen's Volunteer Force (CVF) as a regional police force. As the Sri Lankan government's demands for the withdrawal of the Indians became shriller, the EPRLF and its allies also began raising a paramilitary force called the Tamil National Army (TNA). They were to be the IPKF's replacement in the North and the East when the time came for the Indians to withdraw. The move had the blessings of the Indian government, and the IPKF issued the fledgling army with an arsenal of captured and brand new assault rifles and anti-tank weapons, including several Swedish Carl Gustav recoilless rifles.[26] By October, Vartharaja Perumal was talking of raising the TNA to 20,000 and also of establishing a 10,000-strong police force.[27]

While the Indians were busy setting up their proxy army, the Sri Lankan government moved closer to the LTTE. They declared a cease-fire against each other on June 28 1989.[28] The Sri Lankan government, however, went a step further, countering the Indians' patronage of the TNA by providing an assortment of small arms, ammunition and building materials to the LTTE.[29]

As the IPKF began withdrawing, the Tigers began moving into the districts vacated by them, setting off clashes between them and the

TNA. In November 1989, the IPKF moved out of Ampara District and Tigers immediately rushed in, sparking of violent confrontations with the TNA. The latter found it no match for the seasoned Tiger cadres, and by the end of the month the district was under LTTE control.[30] In Jaffna too, the Tigers pounced, their cadres attacking a TNA camp near Jaffna town and making away with a large haul of weapons after killing two dozen TNA members.[31] The TNA withdrew to Batticaloa. By the end of December 1989, Batticaloa too had fallen with scores of TNA's cadres killed.[32]

On March 1 1990 with the Tigers poised to take Trincomalee, an increasingly desperate chief minister of the North-east Provincial Council, Varatharaja Perumal, renamed the council national assembly of the Free and Sovereign Democratic Republic of Ealam.[33] But that was not sufficient to save him or his government. As the Tigers continued to close in on Trincomalee, the last bastion of his beleaguered government, Perumal, fled to India. The rest of EPRLF leadership along with hundreds of their supporters followed him into exile.[34]

By April 1990, the Tigers were in complete control of the Eastern Province. The defeat of the TNA had made them the de facto rulers of the North and the East again. It had also given them a rich haul of over 2,000 brand new assault rifles.[35] The rebel numbers had also grown. When they arrived in Sri Lanka, the IPKF estimated the LTTE's strength to be around 4,000. When they left, it had climbed to 10,000.[36]

The return of the Tigers

On page 72 of his book *War and Peace in Sri Lanka*, Rohan Gunaratna carries the picture of an LTTE guerrilla carrying an assault rifle, dressed in military-style webbing and smiling confidently at the journalist who is eagerly snapping his picture.[37] The 'guerrilla' is, in fact, a mere child, hardly bigger than the gun he is carrying. Yet he holds the gun with poise, like an experienced soldier.

Youth had been at the forefront of the Tamil militant movement. As a movement led by the youth, it was always possible that young men – and women – of a wide range of age groups would join the struggle. As the militants' ranks expanded, they were filled with young men and boys willing to fight. Initially, they were given non-military training, but this changed with the intensification of the conflict in the mid-1980s. Many of the rebel cadres who manned the bunkers around the army camps in the North were teenagers. A visiting journalist spoke to a few 17-year-old 'Tiger cubs' in early 1987 and found them full of enthusiasm. They also underlined the misery and despair that bred their zeal. One of the boys, Chandran, had left school in grade 9 to join the struggle. Six of his brothers had fled to France, where they lived as refugees. Another teen confided that his younger brother who was 14 was also in the rebel force.[38]

But as the demand for more cadres grew as a result of the confrontation with the IPKF, the LTTE began to depend more heavily on their younger recruits. According to Rohan Gunaratna, some of these boys were as young as nine.[39] The boys were integrated with other units. With the departure of the IPKF, child recruitment gathered momentum. A child carrying an assault rifle was not an object of curiosity anymore. It was fast becoming the hallmark of the LTTE. As the IPKF withdrawal approached, the TNA too was reportedly engaged in child recruitment.[40]

With the IPKF gone, the Tigers returned to the helm in the North and the East. They moved around in strength, collecting taxes and manning checkpoints, behaving like de facto rulers. Hooded men picked out collaborators who had worked with the IPKF. Ominously, the guerrilla army that was so harried by the IPKF was now posing as a conventional army, its cadres dressed in camouflaged uniforms.[41] The Sri Lankan Security Forces were confined to the barracks. They required the Tigers' permission to move out of their barracks.[42] To rub in the humiliation, the bunkers at the Point Pedro Police station even had a poster stuck on it, informing the men inside that they were to leave the premises only with the permission of the LTTE.[43]

The Tigers also set up a political organisation, the People's Front of Liberation Tigers (PFLT). It was a move made with the aim of contesting elections in future. Having taken over control of the North and the East by the force of arms, the rebels were keen to demonstrate that they had the support of the people as well.

In April 1990, the Tiger leader Velupillai Prabhakaran emerged from his jungle hideout to give a press conference in Jaffna. Calling the war against the IPKF 'a monumental event in the history of the world', the Tiger leader went on to declare the departure of the Indians ' a grand victory for our struggle'. The armed struggle was now becoming a political one, with the formation of the PFLT, he explained. But he warned the Tigers were not prepared to lay down their weapons or to give up the demand for a separate state. 'So far the Government has not offered a substantial alternative to Eelam,' he said. 'When an alternative is given to us, we will consider it.'[44]

Despite their aggressive stance, the Tiger theoretician Anton Balasingham was confident that Colombo would not resort to war. 'Sri Lanka

70 The IPKF interlude

cannot afford another war with the LTTE. It cannot have its record of human rights stained any further as it might interrupt the flow of foreign aid. The Sri Lankan army also cannot contain us. So the best way is to take a new approach to making peace with us,' he averred.[45]

The talks with the government foundered on the rebels' demand for the repealing of the Sixth Amendment to the constitution and the calling of fresh elections to the North-east Provincial Council and the government's demand that the Tigers lay down their arms.[46] The government was reluctant to repeal the Sixth Amendment due to the backlash it could invite from the southern electorate. By June 1990, there was every sign that the Tigers were preparing for war. Bunkers and sentry points were coming up in close proximity to military camps and police stations, including on the edge of the runway at Palali. Sensing the approach of something terrible, civilians were beginning to move out of the vicinity of military encampments.[47]

1990 — the Tigers' blitzkrieg

The war that everyone feared was inevitable finally broke out in June 1990. On June 11, using the arrest of an LTTE cadre in Batticaloa as a pretext, the Tigers launched simultaneous attacks on a number of police stations and army camps in the Batticaloa and Ampara districts. Along with the Kiran army camp, the army and police posts at Kalavanchikudi, Eravur, Vellaveli, Valachchenai, Kalkudah, Samanthurai, Kalmunai and Akkaraipattu were now besieged by large groups of armed rebels, forcing the surrender of about 600 policemen. The army camps at Kalavanchikudi and Kiran alone stood up to the Tigers' demands, while the troops in the Vellaveli and Kalmunai camps escaped captivity by being evacuated by sea. By the twelfth except for the Kalavanchikudi and Kiran camps the rebels were in control of the two districts.[48]

Soon the rebel onslaught moved northwards. In Trincomalee, the Uppuveli, Kinniya and Muttur police stations came under attack on June 12. Kinniya and Uppuveli were overrun while Muttur held out. Elsewhere in the Wanni, other military garrisons were also coming under attack now. Kokavil, Mankulam and Kilinochchi were threatened, while in the East, Mullaithivu too was surrounded. The camps held out, despite intense pressure. Further south, the Tigers also attacked police and security installations in Vavuniya town in an attempt to evict them from the area. In Mannar, the Thalladi garrison came under attack while the Tigers took over the Mannar town. The small army detachment at Thalaimannar evacuated to the navy detachment at the pier.[49] By the fourteenth, Jaffna too had erupted. The army garrisons in the Jaffna Fort and Palali were attacked and then besieged by large rebel force.

The Ealam War, interrupted by the intervention of the Indians, had recommenced. Whether the Tigers were aiming for a full-scale war or simply wanted to push and prod what they thought was a recalcitrant government is a moot point. But clearly their survival and recrudescence during the war with the Indians had imbued them with a confidence that induced them to take on the Sri Lankan Security Forces in an offensive that aimed at territorial control. The objective seemed to be to take the enemy by surprise and gain maximum ground before they could regroup.

The government hit back hard, sending nearly 3,000 troops including the STF commandos with artillery to batter through rebel barricades in the East. By June 19, all the police stations in the East had been recaptured and Kalavanchikudi and Kiran relieved.[50] In Trincomalee too, the Security Forces were gaining the upper hand, clearing the Trincomalee town and pushing northwards up to Nilaveli, recapturing Uppuveli on the way.[51] Further north in Weli Oya, the First Battalion Gajaba Regiment advanced up to Kokkuthuduwai and set up a base there and began operations to threaten the rebel bases in the surrounding jungle.[52] By June 24, the army had also begun operations in the Mannar District. Two battalions of the Vijayaba Regiment marched northwards from Puttalam, pushing back rebel groups barring their way. They crossed the Modaragam Aru and advanced up to Silvathurai which they reached on July 5.[53]

The police stations were recovered but not the police officers who had surrendered. A hint of their fate came when the troops fanned out in Trincomalee to reclaim areas captured by the rebels. In Kinniya and Uppuveli, they found the remains of over a dozen policemen massacred by the Tigers when they captured the police station on June 12.[54] The worst fears of the families of the missing men were realised when Piyaratne Ranaweera, one of the policemen that surrendered at Kalmunai, made his escape and reached the safety of government-controlled areas. Ranaweera related how the rebel cadres ordered the policemen to lie face down on the ground after removing their watches and wallets. Then, as the doomed men cowered in fear, the rebels walked up and down the line, shooting them in the head. The female cadres had laughed mockingly when the men shook with fear and had applauded when the bullets pierced their brains. Fortunately for Ranaweera, the bullet meant for him went through his ear lobe. He survived, but hundreds of others did not.[55] On July 21, an STF patrol in Tirukkovil found

72   The IPKF interlude

three mass graves with the remains of about 200 burnt bodies. The remains of belt buckles, shoes and number tags suggested that at least some of them belonged to the missing policemen.[56]

Jaffna and the Wanni

In Jaffna, a major operation was launched in September to relieve the garrison in the fort. The troops, ferried by sea and heli-dropped, first took hold of Kayts and Mandaithivu without much trouble.[57] On September 13, the soldiers finally crossed the lagoon in dinghies under covering fire from helicopter gunships and Siai Marchettis, losing dozens that were killed and wounded.[58] They fanned out to eject the rebels from their bunkers around the fort.[59] Having achieved this, the army withdrew all the troops from the fort. The Mandaithivu Island was also evacuated as the troops now redeployed in Kayts.[60] The government explained the evacuation as the result of their concern for the welfare of the Tamil people in Jaffna, but it is doubtful whether a government that until then had had little qualms about unleashing its firepower in the vicinity of the fort without much concern for civilians would have been motivated solely or even mainly by humanitarian concerns. What was a more likely motive was the avoidance of another costly siege.[61]

With the problem of defending the Jaffna Fort out of the way, the Security Forces now turned their attention to consolidating their main base in the peninsula: Palali. On October 17 1990, 'Operation Jayashakthi' expanded the Palali perimeter. A main supply route was also established between Kankesanthurai and Palali. Now ships could dock at the Kankesanthurai pier and aircraft could land at Palali out of range of rebel mortars. The troops also captured a substantial amount of arms and ammunition, including heavy mortars and Jonny mines. They also captured elaborately constructed bunker lines, some of which even ran through the Vasavilan school.[62]

In the Wanni, however, the Tigers were gaining the upper hand. When Ealam War II broke out, there were several military outposts in the Wanni, but Kokavil was perhaps the most isolated. It was set up to guard the television tower at Kokavil, located in the heart of Wanni between the other two military outposts in the region, Mankulam and Kilinochchi. On July 10 at dusk, the Tigers launched a major attack on the camp with mortars, RPGs and small arms. A major assault followed, and although this was beaten off, the garrison faced annihilation as their ammunition ran out. The commanding officer, Lt Aladeniya, bravely refused to withdraw, preferring to be with his men. By the

The IPKF interlude 73

following morning, it was all over. The Tigers had gained possession of the camp, killing more than 40 soldiers. A civilian waiter of the camp mess who arrived in Mankulam two days later with his pet dog was the only survivor.[63]

Immediately after the fall of Kokavil, the army withdrew the garrison at Kilinochchi which had been under siege for weeks. An expeditionary force was heli-dropped north of Kilinochchi on July 19, and after several days of fighting, they reached the besieged camp and evacuated the garrison.[64] This left only Mankulam in the Wanni heartland, garrisoned by 312 soldiers from the Vijayaba Infantry Regiment under Major Daulagala. The camp too had come under siege during the rebel offensive in June, but commandos heli-dropped on July 12 had relieved the pressure temporarily.[65] Now it remained isolated in the middle of the Wanni, a considerable distance from all the other military camps in the region. It had to be left as it was, surrounded by the enemy.

On Thursday, November 22 1990, the Tigers were ready to remove this last irritant from the Wanni heartland. They launched a ferocious attack at daybreak and succeeded in capturing much of the camp by the following night. Sometime between the twenty-fourth and the twenty-fifth, the survivors of the camp broke out of the cordon of rebels around the camp and trekked quietly and hopefully through the jungle in the direction of Vavuniya. The following morning, the twenty-fifth, they were attacked by a party of rebels searching for them, breaking up the group. By Sunday (twenty-fifth) evening, air force helicopters picked up about 60 of the survivors. More men were picked up in the next few days, while a handful also made it through the jungle all the way to Vavuniya. All in all, 117 of the original 312 reached safety. The official death toll was given as 32 confirmed killed while 163 were listed as 'missing'.[66] Tigers were said to have lost 62 cadres.[67]

With the Wanni under control, the rebels now moved to capitalise on their advantage by clearing the army from its periphery. To smoothen their way, they carried out two major terror attacks. On March 2 1991, a devastating bomb attack in Colombo killed the Deputy Defence Minister Ranjan Wijeratne. Wijeratne, the nemesis of the JVP, was also the linchpin of the government's efforts to cow the rebels. With him out of the way, the Tigers seem to have scored another advantage over the government, setting the stage for a renewed offensive to clear the Security Forces from the 'Tamil Homeland'.

Two months later, the rebel bombers struck again, this time in Tamil Nadu, South India. On May 21 1991, an LTTE suicide cadre blew herself up at an election rally in South India, killing the former Indian

Prime Minister Rajiv Gandhi. It was a pre-emptive strike. Indian general elections were scheduled to be held and Gandhi's Congress Party was emerging as the front-runner. Another term for Gandhi was bad news for Prabhakaran, who feared that he would send Indian troops again to battle his troops, the last thing he wanted when his forces held the upper hand in the North. He dealt with the perceived threat the only way he knew – by killing Gandhi.

While the assassination of Wijeratne may have given the rebels a strategic advantage, the killing of Rajiv Gandhi proved to be a serious error. The murder brought the wrath of India upon the Tigers. Since the outbreak of Ealam War, India had remained somewhat aloof, a role very different from its intervention in the first Ealam War and one that reflected how wary it had become of burning its hands once again. But the killing of Rajiv Gandhi changed this. The police raided LTTE hideouts in South India, capturing Tiger operatives and confiscating property. Soon after Gandhi's assassination, India also imposed a ban on the LTTE. This was the more immediate response. The murder also hardened India's attitude towards the Tigers in the long term with devastating results for the rebel group.

But for the moment, the Tigers were content that they had averted a potential immediate disaster. The real struggle was in the Wanni, where their cadres were battling to remove the remaining army footholds. But the task of clearing the periphery of the Wanni was proving to be more difficult and costlier than conquering its heart.

Slaughter at Silvathurai

Silvathurai is a small town on the west coast of Sri Lanka a few miles to the south of Mannar. It commands a stretch of the coast between Kudiramalai point and Arippu, which was vital for the Tigers' logistics runs between Sri Lanka and South India. The safest run between Tamil Nadu and Sri Lanka was the 'one that zig zags through the shifting sandbanks which make up the Adam's bridge between Thanushkodi and Thalaimannar. It is also safe when it is off season on the Point Calemere Jaffna run: when the sea was generally as calm as a pond. No seasoned boatman would want to try his luck on a sea that is not manageably tumultuous'.[68] The coast south of Mannar also had as its hinterland a sparsely populated and thickly forested part of the northern Puttalam district, especially the Wilpattu National Park. With the Mannar–Vavuniya road cut off, the rebels had unhindered passage between this part of the coast and their vast Wanni stronghold. Realising the significance of this

The IPKF interlude   75

stretch of coastline, in the wake of the outbreak of Ealam War II, the army had set up several mini camps at Silvathurai, Kokkupadayan and Kondachchi (the latter two to the north of Silvathurai) to neutralise it. These acted as satellite camps for the larger military base at Thalladi near the mainland end of the causeway that connected the Mannar Island with the mainland. In November 1990, in the wake of the expulsion of Muslims from Mannar, the army had also taken Mannar Island in what had turned out to be an almost bloodless operation.[69] On the western coast of the Wanni, these were the only army footholds.

In March 1991, the Tigers launched a ferocious assault on these camps. The attack was aimed at either removing the army presence or delivering a morale-sinking blow that would have limited the army's mobility along the coast and the hinterland. The curtailment of the army's presence would enable the rebels to gain control of the coastline between Kudiramalai and Arippu and boost their seaborne operations on the western coast. It would also strengthen their growing hold over the Wanni.[70]

In the event, however, the attacks turned out to be a costly failure. The 190-man garrison defended itself vigorously and, reinforced by sea, went on to repulse the assaults. The rebels suffered severely; some reports spoke of as many as 131 bodies of rebels being recovered from outside the camp perimeter along with over 50 automatic weapons. The army's own losses were also heavy; 23 soldiers killed and 56 wounded – 15 of them seriously – according to military sources.[71]

It was clear that the rebels had received a sound beating. But they were far from demoralised and their resources were still largely intact. Abandoning the idea of taking control of the north-western seaboard, they now cast their eyes on a much bigger prize to the North: the strategic base of Elephant Pass.

The 'final battle'

Elephant Pass is the name given to the causeway that connects the Jaffna Peninsula with the island landmass. The name is said to originate from Dutch colonial times when elephants were driven by the Dutch across this narrow passage to the peninsula to be sold at a fair. Its strategic importance arises from the fact that the only land route to Jaffna runs through this point. Recognising its significance, the army had maintained a presence at Elephant Pass after independence to curb illegal immigration.[72] As explained elsewhere, the garrison was augmented when the fighting escalated in the early 1980s. By 1991, the camp had been expanded to comprise a base camp and several mini camps guarding the perimeter. The camp now sprawled north–south across the lagoon. The southernmost satellite of the base, the Rest House camp, had been set up north of the Paranthan junction to obtain fresh water for the garrison.[73]

From the beginning of Ealam War II, the Tigers had been building up their strength around Elephant Pass in preparation for a major attack. The overrunning of the camp would deliver the strategic pass to the Tigers and enable them to communicate with their Wanni conquests with ease. It was to be a great blow, billed as the Final Battle for Ealam.

The onslaught came in the early hours of July 10. A massive barrage of mortars and rocket fire preceded waves of rebel cadres assailing the camp's perimeter. Again, the rebels' intention was to swamp the camp in a massive onslaught, where they deployed overwhelming firepower and numbers. But despite its ferocity, the initial attack failed to break through the camp's defences. For the next three days, the Tigers launched themselves ferociously at the camp, attacking it from the north and the south. Alarmingly, some of their outer defences began to crack under the assault. On the night of the eleventh, they succeeded in pushing the soldiers out of the army post at the old Paranthan Chemicals factory guest house on the southern perimeter of the camp.[74]

But the attacks had also cost the rebels dearly. After the assault on the thirteenth night alone, the army counted 59 bodies of Tigers lying around the camp perimeter.[75] Therefore, rather than battering the camp into submission, the rebels were now preparing to starve the soldiers out.[76] But the Tigers' designs were thwarted by an ambitious operation by the Security Forces. On July 14, they effected an amphibious landing at Vettilakerni across the neck of the peninsula. Despite heavy resistance, the relief force of nearly 8,000 soldiers cut their way overland to Elephant Pass. It was after nearly three weeks of intense fighting that the relief column finally managed to reach the beleaguered camp on August 3.[77] Thereafter, the troops fanned out to clear the surrounding area of rebels. It was almost another week before dust finally settled on the battle for Elephant Pass.

The changing character of the war

At the end of the battle for Elephant Pass, several key military realities of the new phase of the war emerged. The Tigers were evidently willing to give ground in the East, the rebels melting into the jungles after little more than token resistance. This was probably because they were not in great strength in the province in terms of numbers or heavy weapons. The siege of Kiran, which lasted just over a week, failed to batter into submission a garrison of 48 men without exceptionally strong fortifications. Only one soldier had died from the enemy firing, even though nearly 40 of them were wounded.[78] The rebels had obtained the surrender of the policemen through intimidation and were not in a position to force the submission of determined troops or to thwart the advance of well-armed troops on the offensive.

But in the North, where the rebels were in strength, they were demonstrating a capability to challenge the Security Forces in semi-conventional warfare, particularly in the Wanni. The capture of Kokavil and Mankulam showed a new disturbing potential of the Tigers to overrun military camps. In the 1980s, despite besieging many military encampments, the rebels had never come even close to overrunning them. But now they were able to overwhelm two camps within the space of six months, one of them with a sizeable garrison. The new-found prowess owed itself to several factors. The rebels were now deploying a firepower that they had not possessed in previous encounters with the army. The heavy mortar was now being used frequently and with increased effectiveness. At Mankulam, the rebels were also employing a new variety of the weapon, the Pasilan 2000. This heavy mortar with a range of 1 km carried 30 kg of explosives, and it had the power to smash through a four-inch thick concrete wall. Many buildings in the camp were also badly damaged as the Pasilans rained down.[79] At Kokavil, Silvathurai and Mankulam, the rebels also used a weapon they had previously used with some effectiveness against fortified places – the explosives-laden vehicle. At Kokavil and Silvathurai, the truck was stopped in its tracks by the fire from the defenders, but at Mankulam the vehicle driven by Mapanapillai Arasaratnam alias 'Lt. Col. Borg' succeeded in breaching the defences.[80] It was a crude but devastatingly effective tactic which was to haunt the Sri Lankan army for a long time to come.

However, the most disturbingly effective weapon unleashed was the human wave assaults by mostly teenage cadres. Many of the treble casualties in the battles in the North were teenagers. The majority of the 62 rebels killed at Mankulam were in this category, while many of the rebel dead at Silvathurai were described by defence sources as mere children 'no bigger than the weapons they carried'.[81] A large number of the nearly 3,000 cadres marshalled in the trenches before Elephant Pass were also young teenagers, including many young girls, the result of an intensive recruitment campaign in Jaffna. The Tigers had raised great enthusiasm for the battle among the youth in Jaffna, calling it the last battle to liberate the Tamil homeland. Many girls and boys, some said to be as young as 10 or 11 years, had joined. Girl guides had been assigned with the task of keeping the roads to Elephant Pass open during the battle.[82] These youngsters, now a regular part of the rebel outfit, were used to storm the defences after they had been battered by mortars and suicide trucks. This 'baby brigade' provided the Tigers with a potent new weapon – a large pool of expendable cadres who could be used to swamp the enemy's defences.

Such tactics, crude and brutal as they were, enabled the Tigers to undermine the advantage the Security Forces possessed in terms of fire-power. The deployment of anti-aircraft weapons also prevented the air force from making optimum use of their meagre resources. In the siege of Jaffna, the arsenal of heavy machine guns replenished with overseas purchases and captured TNA stocks kept the air force at bay, forcing them to drop supplies from a healthy distance above the fort. As a consequence, few of the supplies reached the besieged. In one airdrop, only three of the eight food parcels dropped fell into the fort and only cheese was edible in the parcels that were recovered![83] One parcel even came crashing through the roof of St Peter's Church, one-third mile away.[84] During the rescue mission in September, the rebels also claimed they shot down a Siai Marchetti air craft although the air force denied it. During the battle for Elephant Pass, the Tigers went a step further in their efforts to curtain the air force, deploying at least one powerful anti-aircraft cannon. It was able to target an aircraft at a range of 1,500 metres as opposed to the heavy machine guns which could only reach 600 metres.[85]

The assault and siege of Elephant Pass also showed the extent to which the rebels had matured as a semi-conventional force. They prepared meticulously for the assault. Apart from deploying the anti-aircraft weapon and mobilising thousands of cadres, they also dug an elaborate trench system around the perimeter of the camp, the frontlines of which were sometimes only 200 metres from the army's positions. The bunkers were in two tiers, the foremost manned only by observation posts during the day. The second line was where the main force gathered and was well constructed. The bunkers were dug into the roots of trees and scrub to mask them from aerial view and strengthened with railway sleepers, at least some of them reinforced with concrete to withstand artillery fire and aerial bombardment. The frontlines were connected to the rear by communication trenches. To mislead the military, the Tigers also set up decoy posts, with dummy mortars and soldiers.[86] The attack was entrusted to two main battle groups. The task of capturing the southern

The IPKF interlude 79

defences was allocated to rebel cadres from the Wanni led by Balraj, while the destruction of the northern defences fell to the lot of Bhanu with his troops from Jaffna.[87] The rebels also deployed the heaviest firepower they could muster. These consisted of mortars, including the vaunted Pasilans, RPGs and heavy machine guns. A fleet of tractors was assembled, beefed up by about five bulldozers, the former requisitioned from the civilians and the latter no doubt stolen and commandeered at various times from government agencies. All were armour plated. The Tigers had drafted hundreds of civilians into digging their tunnels and bunkers. During the siege, they were to remain at hand to evacuate casualties.[88]

Given such resourcefulness, it was mainly the government forces' air and naval superiority and their superior firepower that enabled them to prevent the rebel advances in the North from turning into an utter disaster. The Sri Lankan navy still had control of the sea and was able to ferry troops to relieve Jaffna Fort, Silvathurai and Elephant Pass. The navy gunboats were also able to blast rebel positions on the shore. Despite their best efforts to curtail the air force, the Tigers were unable to keep the ageing Bell helicopters and the Siai Marchettis from the sky. The Sri Lankan pilots matched the rebel commanders in their resourcefulness. Two daring helicopter rescue missions replenished the garrison at Jaffna Fort and evacuated casualties, relieving the pressure. At Silvathurai, the Siai Marchettis and Bell helicopters joined the fray gallantly, strafing and rocketing the rebel positions and blowing up their armoured vehicles. As many of the attacks took place in darkness and the rebels were creeping ever closer to the camp's perimeter, the air force had to carry out its missions with the utmost care. In an extraordinary improvisation, the airmen oriented their attacks on a little kerosene lamp lit in a pit dug in the middle of the camp. The flickering flame also guided them in their supply drops.[89] The attempt to crash through the camp's defences using an explosive-laden vehicle went awry when it was hit by an air strike and exploded before it reached the perimeter.[90] At Elephant Pass too, the air force made its presence felt, despite the rebel anti-aircraft fire preventing it from making low passes. Air strikes played a crucial role in disrupting supplies, which the Tigers later admitted was a serious handicap.[91] Significantly, the camps that fell to the rebels were the ones that were isolated and difficult to be supplied by air or sea.

Overall, the Security Forces still had superiority in firepower. The rebels' conventional arsenal of Pasilans, armoured bulldozers and tractors, despite making a strong impression, was not sufficient to dominate the battle for long. Their strength was sufficient to overwhelm small isolated

80 The IPKF interlude

garrisons but not larger camps that could be supplied by air and sea and, as at Elephant Pass, with its own artillery.

And still, the greatest strength of the rebels lay in their ability to wage guerrilla war. This had been brought home in no uncertain terms during the early days of the new phase of the war. On June 15, a commando team numbering nearly 50 was airlifted to Trincomalee to break the siege on Muttur. The men moved across the bay to Muttur by boat under Major Azed but were cut off on the shore and annihilated, with more than 40 commandos killed. It was the biggest loss suffered by the army since the conflict had begun, and the fact that it was inflicted on the Special Forces made the blow particularly galling.[92]

Notes

1 P.A. Ghosh, *Ethnic Conflict in Sri Lanka and Role of the Indian Peace Keeping Force*, p. 96, http://books.google.com.au/books?id=YZscr75ijq8 C&pg=PA131&lpg=PA131&dq=operation+checkmate+IPKF&source= bl&ots=0XZJyh-Run&sig=LSoPlhN80q_ayOqT_JmQF21FV nc&hl=en&sa=X&ei=Ds-pT4S4H8uuiQfcvuWtAw&ved=0CFUQ6AE wAw#v=one page&q=operation%20checkmate%20IPKF&f=false
2 Ibid., p. 104.
3 Depinder Singh, *The IPKF in Sri Lanka*, (Trishul: Delhi, 2002), pp. 81–3.
4 Narayan Swamy, *Tigers of Lanka*, p. 268.
5 O'Ballance, *Cyanide War*, p. 100.
6 Gunaratna, *Indian Intervention in Sri Lanka*, p. 245. The Indians had estimated that the operation would take four days. Major James D. Scudieri, *The Indian Peace Keeping Force in Sri Lanka 1987–90: a Case Study in Operations Other than War*, (School of Advanced Military Studies, United States Army Command and General Staff College, Fort Leavenworth: Kansas, 1994), http://www.dtic.mil/cgi-bin/ GetTRDoc?AD=ADA294004, p. 24.
7 By this time, the Thirty-Sixth Infantry division joined the Fifty-Fourth.
8 Gunaratna, *Indian Intervention*, p. 244.
9 Depinder Singh, *IPKF in Sri Lanka*, pp. 93–4, pp. 32–3.
10 Gunaratna, *Indian Intervention*, pp. 242–3.
11 'We Will Fight and Go Underground – Mahattaya', D.B.S. Jeyaraj's Interview with Tiger deputy leader Mahattaya, *The Island*, 25.10.87, p. 7.
12 Manoj Joshi, 'The Price of Peace', *Frontline*, 18–31.03.89, p. 19 (17–21).
13 Ghosh, *Ethnic Conflict in Sri Lanka*, p. 130.
14 Ibid., pp. 129–30.
15 Gunaratna, *Indian Intervention*, p. 258.
16 Joshi, 'The Price of Peace', *Frontline*, 18–31.3.89, pp. 17–21.
17 'Indian Major and 18 IPKF Men Killed', *The Island*, 14.5.89, p. 1.
18 Depinder Singh, *IPKF in Sri Lanka*, p. 112, pp. 147–148.

The IPKF interlude 81

19 Joshi, 'The Price of Peace', pp. 17–21.
20 *Landmine Monitor Report 2000*, Human Rights Watch, 2000, p. 534. Some reports credited Prabhakaran with designing the 'Jony' mine named after an LTTE cadre who was killed by the IPKF. 'Prabha's Jungle Life', *Weekend*, 18.2.90, p. 6.
21 'The Disturbing Demand', *Frontline*, 10–23.06.89, pp. 110–11.
22 'India Withdraws Last of Its Troops', *Sydney Morning Herald*, 26.3.90.
23 Scudieri, *The Indian Peace Keeping Force*, p. 45.
24 Gunaratna, *Indian Intervention*, pp. 272–5; D.B.S. Jeyaraj, 'Tigers Leap in Different Directions', *The Island*, 20.9.87, p. 7.
25 Gunaratna, *Indian Intervention*, p. 277.
26 Narayan Swamy, *Tigers of Lanka*, pp. 304–8, 'In Tiger Country', *Asiaweek*, 26.1.90, p. 40 (35–41).
27 Political Correspondent, 'The Tiger-EPRLF Power Play Over North East', *Weekend*, 8.10.89, p. 5.
28 Ghosh, *Ethnic conflict in Sri Lanka*, p. 134.
29 Gunaratna, *Indian Intervention*, 291–4. T.D.S.A. Dissanayake claims the following material was given: T56: 500, AK47: 500, Chinese grenades: 5000, live ammunition: 200,000 rounds, jeeps: 20, cement: 200 tonnes. Dissanayake, *War or Peace in Sri Lanka*, p. 77.
30 'Battle for Batticaloa', *Sri Lanka Monitor*, British Refugee Council, v. 2, no. 8, nov.1989, p. 3.
31 Narayan Swamy, *Tigers of Lanka: Boys into Guerrillas*, p. 309.
32 'North-East on a Knife-edge as Tamil Factions Clash', *Sri Lanka Monitor*, British Refugee Council, v. 2, no. 9, Dec. 1989, p. 1.
33 Ramesh Menon, 'Return of the Tigers', *India Today*, 15.4.90, pp. 123.
34 Rita Sebastian in Colombo and Lalit Pattajoshi, 'Pull-out Fall-out', *The Week*, 1.4.90, p. 28.
35 'In Tiger Country', *Asiaweek*, 26.1.90, p. 40 (35–41).
36 Ghosh, *Ethnic conflict in Sri Lanka*, p. 104.
37 Gunaratna, *War and Peace in Sri Lanka*, p. 72.
38 S. Venkat Narayan, 'A Visit to Jaffna', p. 6.
39 Rohan Gunaratna, 'Tiger Cubs in the Battlefield', *The Island*, 19.7.98, pp. 9–10.
40 Roy Denish, 'Tamil Rebels Preparing for a Bloody Vendetta', *Weekend*, 15.6.89, p. 1.
41 Iqbal Athas, 'The Mood in Jaffna', *Weekend*, 4.3.90, p. 25.
42 Munasinghe, *A Soldier's Version*, pp. 98–100.
43 Iqbal Athas, 'For the North, It's the Year of the Tiger', *Weekend*, 4.3.90, pp. 26–7.
44 'The Guerrilla Chief Emerges from His Jungle Hideout', *Sydney Morning Herald*, 3.4.90.
45 Ramesh Menon, 'Return of the Tigers', *India Today*, 15.4.90, pp. 123 (117–123).
46 Iqbal Athas, 'The North South Talks', *Weekend*, 3.6.90, pp. 6–7. The Sixth Amendment enacted in August 1983 made it unlawful for anyone in or outside Sri Lanka to 'support, espouse, promote, finance, encourage or advocate the establishment of a separate State within the territory of Sri Lanka'.

82 The IPKF interlude

47 Thomas Abraham, 'Fragile Peace', *Frontline*, 9–22.06.90, p. 18.
48 Keith Noyahr, 'The Siege of Kiran', *Sunday Times*, 24.6.90, p. 8; Mendis, *Assignment Peace*, pp. 132–3; Roy Denish, 'North East Flare up', *Weekend*, 17.6.90, pp. 6–7; *Sri Lanka Army*, pp. 445–448.
49 Mendis, *Assignment Peace*, p. 134, Wiiliam Clarance, *Ethnic Warfare in Sri Lanka and the UN Crisis*, (Vijitha Yapa: Colombo, 2007), p. 112.
50 Gamini Obeysekera, 'The Long March to Kiran Victory', *Weekend*, 24.6.90, pp. 4–5; 'Taking a Hammer at the LTTE', *The Island*, 24.6.90, p. 5.
51 Gamini Obeysekera, 'The Long March', pp. 4–5, Mendis, *Assignment Peace*, pp. 138–9; Rohan Gunasekera and Shamindra Ferdinando, 'Hooded Men Identify Tigers', *The Island*, 1.7.90, p. 1.
52 Taking a Hammer at the LTTE', *The Island*, 24.6.90, p. 5.
53 Mendis, *Assignment Peace*, p. 141.
54 Gunasekera and Ferdinando, 'Hooded Men Identify Tigers', p. 1.
55 John Lyons, 'Cold Blooded Butchery on Paradise Island', *Sydney Morning Herald*, 30.6.90.
56 Sena Warusahennedi, '200 Burnt Bodies Found', *The Island*, 22.7.90, p. 1.
57 Suresh Mohamed, 'Troops Poised to Take Jaffna Fort', *The Island*, 26.8.90, p. 1.
58 Rita Sebastian, 'Three Month Battle for Jaffna Fort', *Tamil Times*, 15.9.90, p. 4 and 16; Roy Denish, 'Fort Liberation', *Weekend*, 16.9.90, pp. 6–7.
59 Ibid., p. 4 and 16; Roy Denish, 'Fort Liberation', *Weekend*, 16.9.90, pp. 6–7.
60 Suresh Mohamed, 'Govt. Forces Pull Out of Jaffna Mandaitivu', *The Island* (International Edition), 3.10.90, p. 1.
61 One analyst opined that the evacuation may have been due to a need to forestall an Indian intervention and the fear of Tiger attacks in the South. However, the difficulty of preventing another siege from developing would have been a more likely cause. Taraki, 'Why Was the Jaffna Fort Evacuated?', *The Island*, 30.9.90, p. 10.
62 Norman Palihawadana, 'Tiger Bullets Greet Journalists', *The Island*, 28.10.90, p. 9; Shamindra Ferdinando, 'Sri Lanka Gets a Wartime Prize', *The Island*, 21.10.90, p. 12.
63 For the capture of Kokavil, see Roy Danish, 'The Kokavil Blackout', *Weekend*, 15.7.90, pp. 6–7; Hiranthi Fernando, 'Don't Worry Sir, I Will Fight Till I Die', *Sunday Times*, 1.10.00, http://sundaytimes.lk/001001/plus4.html (5.10.11); Shanika Sriyananda, 'Saved Through Blood, Sweat and Tears', *Sunday Observer*, 12.6.11, http://www.sundayobserver.lk/2011/06/12/fea02.asp, Adele Balasingham, *Women Fighters*, p. 69; Munasinghe, *A Soldier's Version*, p. 106; Dharmasiri Gamage and Tilak Senenayake, 'Next Ten Days Most Crucial', *Observer*, 22.7.90, pp. 1 and 17.
64 Mendis, *Assignment Peace*, pp. 154–5.
65 Roy Denish, 'The Taking of Mankulam', *Weekend*, 22.7.90, p. 6.

The IPKF interlude 83

66 For Mankulam see 'Political Correspondent', 'What Went Wrong at Mankulam?', *Sunday Times*, 2.12.90, p. 4; Roy Danish, 'Setback at Mankulam', *Weekend*, 2.12.90, pp. 6–7; Amantha Perera, 'Samthaanams Rain Down on Defence Lines', *Sunday Leader*, 11.5.08, http://www.thesundayleader.lk/archive/20080511/defence.htm; Roy Denish, 'Kumarappa', Tigers' New Grenade, *Weekend*, 9.12.90, p. 6; D.B.S. Jeyaraj, 'Balraj: Legendary Commander of the LTTE', http://dbsjeyaraj.com/dbsj/archives/2177 (5.10.11).

67 Rohan Gunaratna, 'Tiger Cubs and Childhood Fall as Casualties in Sri Lanka', http://fosus2.tripod.com/fs980720.htm

68 Taraki, 'Silvathurai – Why Did LTTE Do It?', *The Island*, 31.3.91, p. 9.

69 This was 'Operation Rana Derana'. Roy Denish, 'Operation Rana Derana', *Weekend*, 25.11.90, pp. 18–19, Roy Denish, 'Tigers Retreat from "Mined" Island', *Weekend*, 4.11.90, p. 3.

70 Taraki, 'Silvathurai – Why Did LTTE Do It?', *The Island*, 31.3.91, p. 9.

71 Mendis, *Assignment Peace*, p. 189, 'Tigers Stop Shelling Army Camps after Heavy Toll', *Sunday Observer*, 24.3.91, p. 1; Rohan Gunasekera, 'Army Halts Rebel Attacks on Camps', *The Island*, 24.3.91, p. 1; Shamindra Ferdinando, 'The Importance of Securing the Wanni', *The Island*, 24.3.91, p. 7; Adele Balasingham, '*Women Fighters*', p. 81; Shamindra Fernando, 'The Finest Hour of the Armed Forces', *The Island*, 31.3.91, p. 9; *The Sri Lanka Monitor*, British Refugee Council Newsletter, no. 38, March 1991, p. 1.

72 D.B.S.Jeyaraj, 'The Taking of Elephant Pass', *Frontline*, 13–26.05.00, http://frontlineonnet.com/fl1710/17100100.htm

73 K.T. Rajasingham, 'Sri Lanka the Untold Story', chapter 50 http://www.atimes.com/atimes/South_Asia/DG27Df02.html

74 Adele Ann Balasingham, *Women Fighters of Liberation Tigers*, pp. 85–6; Ranil Wijeyapala, 'Gallant Hero Defends Elephant Pass', *Sunday Observer* 11.1.10,http://www.sundayobserver.lk/2010/07/11/sec03.asp

75 Ranil Wijeyapala, 'Gallant Hero Defends Elephant Pass', Mendis, *Assignment Peace*, p. 219.

76 It had also been surmised that the Tigers' real aim all along was to compel the surrender of the camp and capture its weapons and equipment. UTHR (J) Report no. 8, Chapter 5, http://www.uthr.org/Reports/Report8/chapter5.htm#a

77 Dinesh Watawana, 'Troops Sound Victory Trumpet', *Sunday Times*, 4.8.91, p. 1.

78 Gamini Obeysekera, 'The Long March to Kiran Victory', *Weekend*, 24.6.90, pp. 4–5; Taking a Hammer at the LTTE', *The Island*, 24.6.90, p. 5; Keith Noyahr, 'The Siege of Kiran', *Sunday Times*, 24.6.90, p. 8; *Sri Lanka Army*, p. 448.The claim that the Tigers made use of chemicals was supported by diplomatic representatives in Colombo, according to one report. The chemicals were believed to be industrial chlorine and phosphine. According to the report, the chemicals were delivered in home-made grenades and the attack was made on the eighteenth. John Lyons, 'Rebels use Chemical Warfare on Army', *Sydney Morning Herald*, 29.6.90.

79 Roy Danish, 'Setback at Mankulam', *Weekend*, 2.12.90, pp. 6–7; Amantha Perera, 'Samathaanms Rain Down on Defence Lines', *Sunday*

84   The IPKF interlude

Leader, 11.5.08, http://www.thesundayleader.lk/archive/20080511/ defence.htm; Roy Denish, 'Kumarappa', Tigers' new grenade, *Weekend*, 9.12.90, p. 6.

80 According to one report, this attack took place later when many of the soldiers had vacated the camp. 'Ravana', 'The Black Tiger Phenomena, Its Origins and Their Targets', *The Island*, 14.11.93, p. 11.

81 Quoted in *The Sri Lanka Monitor*, British Refugee Council Newsletter, no.38, March 1991, p. 1. Later, Adele Balasingham placed the number of female cadres killed at 9. Balasingham, *Women Fighters*, p. 82. See also Rohan Gunaratna, 'Tiger Cubs and Childhood Fall as Casualties in Sri Lanka', http://fosus2.tripod.com/fs980720.htm (5.10.11)

82 Ben Bavinck, *Of Tamils and Tigers: a Journey through Sri Lanka's War Years*, (Vijitha Yapa: Colombo, 2011), p. 198, UTHR(J) Report no., Chapter 5, http://www.uthr.org/Reports/Report8/chapter5.htm#a

83 Chandima Wickremesinghe, 'Terrorists Suffer Heavy Casualties; Jaffna Fort Holds Out', *Sunday Times*, 24.6.90, p. 1.

84 Sri Lanka: Conflict of June 1990, UTHR(Jaffna), Jaffna Sri Lanka (Typescript), pp. 14–19.

85 T.B. Subramaniam, 'Adding to the Arsenal', *Frontline* 3.8–16.8.91, p. 39. Some Tiger sources disclosed to *Frontline* that the rebels possessed a couple of SAMs, although they were not in working order.

86 *Sri Lanka Army*, p. 465; Edward W. Desmond, 'A New Kind of Warfare', *Time*, 16.9.91, pp. 30–1 (30–31).

87 'Taraki', 'Grads of Tigers Defence College', *The Island*, 3.4.94, p. 7.

88 Political Correspondent, 'Straining at Ants and Swallowing Elephants', *Sunday Times*, 21.7.91, p. 4.

89 Jagath P. Senaratne, *Sri Lanka Air Force: A Historical Retrospect*, vol. II, 1985–1997, (Sri Lanka Air Force: Colombo, 1998), p. 132.

90 Adele Balasingham, *Women Fighters*, p. 81. Another report refers to him as 'Major' Dampo and gives his real name as Thayaparan Mulankavil. 'Ravana', 'The Black Tiger Phenomena, its origins and their targets', *The Island*, 14.11.93, p. 11; 'Taraki', 'Mainland Mannar under LTTE Control', *The Island*, 22.8.93, p. 7. Taraki believes that this was the crucial moment in the attack. Mendis says it was blown up by the fire from the camp. Mendis, *Assignment Peace*, p. 184.

91 Adele Balasingham, *Women Fighters*, Edward W. Desmond, based on reports by Anita Pratap in Jaffna, 'A New Kind of Warfare', *Time*, 16.9.91, p. 31 (30–31).

92 'Special Correspondent', 'Tigers on the Retreat', *Sunday Times*, 24.6.90, p. 4, Mendis; *Assignment Peace*, p. 1, Rohan Gunasekera and Shamindra Ferdinando, 'Govt. and LTTE agree on Ceasefire', *The Island*, 17.6.90, p. 1.

Chapter 5

The army on the offensive

From early to mid-1991 after overcoming the immediate threat to the camps in the peninsula and withstanding rebel attempts to eliminate the military camps in the periphery of the Wanni, the government went on the offensive to regain the strategic advantage. The search for a political solution to the ethnic issue was still on the cards. But with the rebels still controlling much of Jaffna and the Wanni sinking under Tiger control, the military imperative had now become stronger. Peace negotiations, without regaining the strategic initiative, would place the government at a weak position. Moreover, Indian intervention was no longer a threat after the IPKF's experience. The LTTE's fatal mistake of assassinating Rajiv Gandhi in May 1990 had also hardened India's attitude towards the Tigers, already soured by the post-accord experience. And even though the losses in the Wanni had dampened the initial enthusiasm for a quick victory, the Tigers' failure to capture Silvathurai and Elephant Pass boosted the morale of the Security Forces, convincing them that their superior resources could prevail over the enemy despite the Tigers' growing semi-conventional capability. The trick was to come up with an effective strategy.

The military's strategy from early 1991 followed two broad objectives: keeping the Tigers bottled up in the Jaffna Peninsula and disrupting their operations in the Wanni. The ultimate goal was the weakening of the rebels and the capture of Jaffna. This was not an easy task; on the one hand, it required an assault on territory where the rebels were well entrenched, while on the other hand the Security Forces were still small in number and their firepower only marginally superior to that of their opponents. The successful execution of the strategy required careful planning and the overhauling and revamping of the Security Forces.

86 The army on the offensive

Rearming the forces

The onslaught by the rejuvenated Tigers showed up the inadequacy of the armed forces available to combat the rebels. The 'armour' was still generally road bound, which made them more vulnerable to ambushes. Tracked vehicles would have enabled the forces to go to the rescue of the beleaguered garrisons such as Kokavil and Mankulam, moving cross-country without risking mine-infested roads. The need for tracked armour was also brought home in no uncertain terms when the army's 'armour' got bogged down in the sand during 'Operation Balavegaya'. Exhausted soldiers pushing Saladin armoured cars out of sand pits had been one of the most enduring images of the campaign. The armoured vehicles were also very vulnerable to RPG fire. To make matters worse, they also lacked ammunition; the 76mm shell used by the Saladins, the biggest armoured vehicle in the army, was becoming a rare commodity in international arms markets as few of these vehicles were being manufactured. The air force was in no better shape. The entire fleet of helicopters was battle damaged and did not have the armour protection to ward off the Tigers' .50 machine guns, especially at close range, which precluded them from approaching Tiger bunkers. The Siai Marchettis were too slow and their bombs too small, while the Y-8s were woefully inaccurate.[1] They also made a loud droning sound which alerted the enemy to their approach.[2]

There had been little improvement in the army's arsenal since 'Operation Liberation.' Attempts had been made to replenish the armoured corps from the late 1980s, but despite the allocation of more than Rs 200 million for the purchase of armour in 1987, no movement was made, reportedly due to the failure to agree on the best model to purchase, the focus being on European models.[3] The air force had too made no new acquisitions. The navy was the only arm that made substantial additions to its inventory; six more Dvoras were inducted into the fleet along with nine locally built inshore patrol boats and three Killer class South Korean patrol boats in 1988.[4]

The need for more soldiers was also apparent. At the outbreak of hostilities in June 1990, the army hovered around 50,000, organised in five regiments and three divisions.[5] But these numbers were clearly inadequate for the demands of the new war. For the first time, the Sri Lankan Security Forces had been called upon to fight a war simultaneously on several fronts, and this stretched their limited manpower resources. Recapturing the outposts, holding them, and patrolling the hostile hinterland all required increased commitments in manpower, especially when it became evident that the war was not going to end soon. As early as mid-July 1990, the army commander Major General Gerry de Silva had candidly conceded to the *Asian Defense Journal* that the army did not have enough troops to hold every area.[6] And as the hopes for a quick victory receded and the military suffered setbacks, it was clear that to be competitive against a revitalised enemy the Security Forces needed more men and better equipment. The initial reaction from the public quickly allayed any concerns of a lack of recruits. The response was overwhelming. Encouraged by the prospect of a fight to the finish, over 25,000 people flocked to the army headquarters, eager to join the good fight.[7] Contributions flowed into the Defence Fund – Rs 13.5 million by 6 p.m. on June 23 along with a further $3,000 in foreign exchange.[8]

By December 1990, however, the optimism had faded. The Tigers' pounce had been checked in the towns in the East and the military strongholds in the peninsula remained intact, but the Wanni had fallen to the rebels. The loss of lives too had been commensurate with the loss of territory, the military losing in six months more men than it lost in six years of conflict (1981–87). The shocking defeats in the Wanni and the attendant loss of life and limb dampened the zeal of the youth. Still, the numbers climbed steadily, if slowly. By 1991, there were 70,000 enlisted, and by 1994 this had increased to 105,000 including 42,000 active reservists.[9]

The government also scrambled to upgrade and update the equipment of the Security Forces. The defence budget was increased by a massive 50 per cent in 1990 in response to the outbreak of the war, from $257 million to $383 million. This was 15 per cent of the total budget (in comparison, 1987 defence spending was 17 per cent of the budget). $295 million were set aside for 1991 (8.5 per cent of the total budget), not including supplementary estimates.[10] The bulk of the expenditure was on military hardware – new armour, artillery and ammunition for the existing fleet being at the top of the list. However, it was not easy to obtain weapons and equipment. A deal for 76mm ammunition with Australia fell through when it became public and Australia withdrew from it. But new sources of weapons opened up with the breakdown of the Soviet Bloc. The Conventional Forces in Europe Treaty (CFE) led to a drastic reduction in the number of armoured vehicles, artillery pieces, attack helicopters and combat aircraft. This opened up a big weapons market for countries in the developing world, which were looking for cheaper weapons from less scrupulous sources.[11] By October 1991, 25 main battle tanks had arrived from Eastern European

88 The army on the offensive

sources. There was also China, a long-time arms supplier to Sri Lanka. In early 1991, the army purchased 12 Type 59–1 long-range field guns (130mm) from China North Industries Corporation (NORINCO) to provide support for isolated camps.[12] A Chinese delegation that visited the island in early 1991 also offered the answer to the army's quest for tracked armour. They brought with them a catalogue which listed a range of armoured vehicles, and the T-85 and T-86 IFVs caught the eye of the army top brass. Several vehicles were promptly ordered and they arrived in the island in late 1991.[13]

The air force also joined the race to modernise. In 1990, they had already purchased four Bell 212 helicopters, three Siai Marchetti SF 260s and three Y-12s. The following year, seven Chinese-built FT5/7 and F7 Jet Fighters (one FT-7 Jet Trainer, two FT-5 Jet Trainers and four F-7BS single seaters) were added to the fleet. The F7s were interceptors, but the air force technicians fitted the machines with locally manufactured bombs, turning them into ground-attack aircraft.[14]

In 1992, the SLAF boosted its ground-attack capability by purchasing two IA58 FMA Puccara ground-attack aircrafts, purpose-built for counter-insurgency warfare. In 1993, two more were purchased.[15] The Puccara was a dedicated counter-insurgency attack aircraft, not a jet trainer that could be converted to a ground-attack role like the Siai Marchetti or the Tucano. It had twin engines, which made it safer, and it could carry twice the war load of a Tucano including six guns in the nose. It could also take off and land on rough airstrips.[16] The advent of the F7s and the Puccaras gradually pushed the infamous 'barrel bombers' to the background and finally into obsolescence, the Y-12s now reverting to its former role of designated transports.[17]

But the transport challenges of the new Ealam War were too much for the Y-12s to handle. With the development of siege situations in the Wanni there was a growing need for aircraft that could deliver troops to the battlefield, quickly and safely, something for which the Y-12s were woefully inadequate. To address this need, three Mil7 transport helicopters were purchased in 1993. In the following year, three more were added to the fleet. Unlike the Bell 212/412, the Mil7 could carry 24 men, which was a big boost to the Security Forces' ability to replenish isolated garrisons. It could also carry a range of armaments including rockets and missiles.[18]

The navy also upgraded its fleet. In 1990, two 201 class patrol boats and one Israeli Shaldag fast patrol boat were purchased. The Shaldag had been rejected by the US navy and the Israeli navy. In 1991, the navy added two P151 patrol boats and three Haizui class and a Yuquin class landing craft capable of hauling 46 tons. In 1992, they also acquired four wooden 111 coastal patrol crafts to operate from command vessels.[19] The navy also purchased three new Chinese-built gunboats at Rs 150 million each. They were named Ranaviru, Ranasuru and Ranasiri. By late 1992, the navy had increased its fleet to 15 FACs, four landing crafts, three surveillance command ships and scores of locally and foreign-built patrol craft.[20]

However, acquiring new equipment solved only one part of the problem. The cash-strapped Sri Lankan government also found that obtaining second-hand weapons and equipment came with caveats. Some of the Chinese IFVs were found to be in bad condition. Recovery vehicles were not delivered, while spare parts were lacking. The machine guns were dysfunctional, the periscopes refused to work and, to make matters worse, the service manuals were in Chinese![21] Some of the MBTs also quickly developed engine problems and broke down, while defence experts expressed concerns about their weight that had the potential to cause difficulties in the sandy terrain in the North and during amphibious landings.[22] Obviously, beggars could not be choosers.

Hunting the Tiger in the Wanni

Although dominating the Wanni was important, venturing into this lair of the Tiger was a challenging task. Clad in thick jungle, much of the region was ideal guerrilla territory. The rebels were very familiar with the area, while the government forces knew little of the region. Furthermore, even if the troops captured this expanse of land, holding it – especially maintaining the long supply line to Jaffna – could become a nightmare for the army, which simply did not have enough men to dominate the Wanni while maintaining a presence in the East and the peninsula.

Therefore, the objective was not 'real estate' but to draw out and kill as many Tigers as possible – a 'seek and destroy mission', as one senior military officer explained.[23] Such operations, it was expected, would eventually weaken the Tigers to an extent that it would enable the Security Forces to move in and occupy the Wanni. In the Wanni, the army also had the advantage of the services of the PLOTE, now sworn enemies of the LTTE and possessing considerable local knowledge.[24]

The operations probed the Wanni from several directions. From March 1991 to May 1992, the army launched forays into the region from the direction of Mannar, Vavuniya, Janakapura and Mullaithivu. They were all incursions in strength into rebel territory with the troops

90 The army on the offensive

returning to base after the operations. In the operation from Mullaithivu launched in May 1992 (Operation Sathbala), a base was set up at Alampil on the Nayaru lagoon, but this was withdrawn later that year.

A year and a half of nibbling at the periphery of the Tiger's domain produced mixed results. The Security Forces captured some of the key bases of the Tigers, but whether this caused a serious setback to the enemy is arguable. The problem with such operations was that as long as the army showed no intention of holding onto territory the Tigers could avoid contact with them. The Wanni was a vast area and the army was only pushing and prodding at its periphery. The rebels had plenty of space to conduct tactical and strategic retreats. The army also gave the rebels sufficient warning by the ponderous nature of their operations. Reflecting the change from a guerrilla to a semi-conventional conflict in the North, the Security Forces deployed thousands of soldiers backed by armour and heavy artillery. For instance, Wanni Wickrema 1, launched on May 2 1991, involved two brigades, Kanthaka and Vikum, each made up of two infantry battalions, altogether over 3,000 soldiers. The troops were supported by long-range fire from the newly acquired 130mm artillery firing from Thalladi, Vavuniya and Gajabapura bases. A small group of commandos and 'armour' – Saladin armoured cars and Ferret Scout cars along with Saracen and Buffel APCs – also took part in the operation. In 'Operation Sixer' launched in mid-1991, the army was also employing the recently arrived T-86 wheeled and T-85 tracked IFVs.[25] Air support was provided by Siai Marchettis and helicopter gunships (Bell 212 and Bell 412). As the advance was through thick scrub that cut down visibility and made movement difficult, the army took a leaf out of the Tigers' combat manuals, using an armour-plated bulldozer to clear a path through the scrub.[26]

Not surprisingly, many of the camps were abandoned by the rebels at the approach of the army. Resistance was generally light in western Wanni. Further to the east, there was some resistance, the most serious fighting taking place around Puvarasakulam and Pandivirichchan during Wanni Wickrema II, where street fighting reportedly cost more than 30 army lives.[27] Losses for the rebels were also heavy; the army recovered the bodies of 40 Tigers after the battle.[28] Apart from this, resistance was negligible. Even in the East, despite heavy fighting in the operations around Mullaithivu only a handful of rebel corpses were recovered. No doubt, the Tigers removed some of their dead and wounded, but these numbers could not have been very great.

The capture and destruction of the bases undoubtedly caused serious disruption to the rebels' operations. Many of the camps were extensive, equipped with accommodation and training facilities for large numbers of cadres. But these could be re-occupied once the army had withdrawn. The large camp at Parappakadanthan in Mannar which was captured during 'Operation Tiger Hunt' in March–April 1991 had to be recaptured in 'Operation Seegrapahara' more than a year later. In Mullaithivu, the slow advance had also given the rebels ample time to relocate the all-important weapons making machinery.[29]

The operations also cost the Security Forces heavily, particularly in Mullaithivu. Troops faced a barrage of 'arul' grenades and well-laid fields of 'Jony' mines. The advance became so hard that the soldiers struggled to move more than a few metres a day. While the armour buoyed their confidence at times, the troops were also finding it to be a burden in the thick jungle where infantry had to be deployed ahead to protect the vehicles. Tigers took advantage of the close country to once again zero in on the IFVs, deploying RPG sections of seven men and two launchers to hunt them. An army officer recalled how these squads seemed to know exactly where to aim their rockets. Their fire damaged one T-86 and another T-85. And while the army claimed to have killed scores of rebels without many bodies to show for it, they returned laden with heavy casualties of their own. In 'Operation Lightning Strike' launched in August–September 1991 in the Weli-Oya Mullaithivu region, the troops suffered 74 killed and 278 wounded. Of the wounded, 83 lost a foot – the price exacted by the Jony mine.[30]

Strangling Jaffna

In Jaffna too, the army did not want to launch an all-out assault to capture the peninsula. The lessons of Operation Liberation and the IPKF's incursion into Jaffna taught that such an attack would inevitably lead to heavy civilian casualties. The campaign to clear the environs of the fort of rebel bunkers had also demonstrated how costly it would be to the troops if they were to take on well-entrenched rebel positions. Therefore, Jaffna was not to be taken in one fell swoop. First it was to be strangled, gradually.

In October 1991, the army wrested control of the string of islands off the western coast of the peninsula and sealed off the peninsula from the mainland across the lagoon. Phase One of the operation (October 18) captured Kayts and Mandaithivu and the other islands. Phase Two launched on October 22 made a seaborne landing on the mainland to capture the area between Kalmunai and Pooneryn.[31] The control of the islands restricted the Tigers' seaborne movement to and from the

92 The army on the offensive

peninsula from the western side, while the capture of Sanguppidy on the mainland cut off their remaining main supply route from the Wanni across the lagoon. With that, for the first time in five years, the military controlled both main supply routes into Jaffna Peninsula: the one via Sanguppidy and the one through Elephant Pass.[32] If these could be effectively controlled, the rebels could be prevented from obtaining succour from outside when the final assault was launched on Jaffna. It would also impede their relocation of vital resources and supplies to the mainland during such an operation.

In May 1992, while 'Operation Sathbala' was under way in Mullaithivu, the army launched several operations to tighten its grip on the ground in the peninsula. A combined air–land–sea attack was launched on Tiger camps on the coast between Thondamanar and Point Pedro while the army also broke out of Palali. 'Operation Sealion', the assault on the coastal belt, targeted rebel bases in Velvetithurai and Madagal by air, land and sea.[33] Backed by their new main battle tanks, the army also moved to Tellipilai to the west of Palali amid heavy resistance, capturing an area roughly 4 km by 2.5 km.[34] Thrusting westwards along the coast, they fought fiercely to capture Senthankulam on the coast. This was an important acquisition. A line of reefs obstructed the movement of ships off this stretch of the coast, but a break in the reefs at Senthankulam provided a safe passage which could be exploited for large-scale troop landing.[35]

The constriction of the peninsula was slowly being accomplished. But the battles were getting tougher. The struggle for Tellipilai was a case in point. The troops had to push their way through the minefields along a path cleared by an armour-plated bulldozer, while soldiers wearing 6-inch rubber-soled boots used rakes to remove the mines ploughed up by the tracks. Tanks followed the bulldozer, and in the wake of the tanks came the infantry. An armed helicopter hovered above, well out of reach of the .50 calibre machine guns, providing covering fire. The rebels who had had dug themselves in behind the railway bund resisted fiercely. It took some hard fighting and a pincer movement to remove them. The cost was heavy; the army lost 19 killed and 75 wounded. Despite all the precautions taken, some of the wounded lost their feet to mines. The army claimed to have killed more than 100 Tigers, but reportedly only nine bodies were recovered.[36]

But the noose continued to tighten around Jaffna. Since the relief of Elephant Pass in July–August 1991, the army had maintained a foothold at Vettilakerni, the place where the relieving troops had landed in July 1991, but this was not sufficient to close all movement. On July 2

The army on the offensive   93

1992, the armed forces launched Operation Balavegaya II to accomplish this. In a major operation that included several battalions of infantry supported by two squadrons of tanks and air cover, the beachhead was linked to the Elephant Pass camp and a swathe of territory linking the Kilali lagoon with the eastern coast was turned into a fortified zone. Blavegaya I demonstrated the need for tracked armour. Now the battle tanks were justifying their acquisition, negotiating the terrain well, taking on rebel defences sometimes independently of the infantry. Still, the Tigers fought hard, destroying one of the tanks with an RPG. In the air too, there were losses; one Y-8 on a bombing mission crashed and burned during the operation.[37]

But Jaffna was sealed. A major incursion into the peninsula was looking imminent now. The plan seemed to have been to advance through Jaffna through the largely open space between Araly and Pommaveli on the north-west coast of the peninsula.[38] This would avoid a campaign in the heavily populated area close to Jaffna city and make things easier for the troops and the civilians. Everything seemed to be falling into place for the Security Forces. The mood was buoyant. The Tigers were also said to be in desperate straits with their cash and arms reserves low and their cadres steadily disillusioned by their eroding strength.[39] The D-Day seemed only days away.

Then disaster struck. On August 8, Lieutenant General Kobbekaduwa, Major General Wijaya Wimalaratna and several other senior military men including Rear Admiral Jayamaha were killed when their land rover was blown up by a landmine on Kayts Island. They were on a reconnaissance mission in preparation for the upcoming assault on Jaffna.[40] After the death of the officers, the drive to take Jaffna began to lose its momentum. Now instead of the big push, several smaller operations were launched, mainly to consolidate the army's hold on the northern coast of the peninsula. On August 20 1992, Operation Earthquake extended their control over Madagal, where the Tigers had a radar station. In May during Operation Sea Lion, this area was bombed, but the station survived. 'Operation Earthquake' finally brought this area under the army's sway, extending the army's writ over the major part of Jaffna's northern coast to the west of Thondamanar.[41] On September 18, in another limited operation code named 'Chathuranga', the army also extended its control up to Pandatharippu about 2 km to the east and inland of Madagal.[42]

Despite the successes, these operations were little more than tinkering around the edges of the gains made earlier. Officially, the capture of Jaffna was still very much on the cards, but now there was no urgency,

94 The army on the offensive

no real drive. With the death of Kobbekaduwa and Wimalaratna, the heart had gone out of the campaign to take Jaffna. The Tigers – and the civilians – in Jaffna were safe, at least for the moment. So were the soldiers who were to conquer the Tiger stronghold.

Clearing the East

While the army engaged in a war of attrition in the Wanni and a slow but steady strangulation of the Jaffna Peninsula, the East remained restive. There the operations were of lower scale than in the North. No big battles took place here, no large-scale operations involving bulldozers crashing through the jungle. And it was in the East that the Security Forces also recorded their greatest success.

By now the East had become an important recruiting ground for the rebels. In the first two years of Ealam War II, the Tigers had lost a large number of cadres due to their tactic of trying to swamp army camps with massed attacks. Still, they were able to maintain high recruitment levels, mainly by drawing on young men and women from the East. About 900 of them are said to have been brought to the North in February and March 1993 in anticipation of an assault on Jaffna. According to one analyst, the fear of reprisals from the army after the Security Forces moved into the East was a major factor in driving young men and women – not to mention boys and girls – into the fold of the Tigers. The activities of Muslim home guards and other pro-government Tamil groups had also provided an added impetus. After June 1990, many young Tamils in the East were also frustrated by the lack of avenues for advancement; many were displaced and their education disrupted. For these young men and women in the East, joining the LTTE was an attractive proposition as the rebels looked after them. Many youths started working for them as labourers and in other capacities and later graduated to becoming full-fledged cadres. Tigers also used propaganda well to entice youngsters, highlighting the atrocities committed by the Security Forces and glorifying the deeds of the rebels.[43]

The control of the East then had a vital strategic advantage. Ealam War II had started with a struggle for the region, Tigers attempting to take over the province in what appeared to be a surgical strike on military and police posts. 'Operation Sledgehammer' and subsequent operations had pushed them back; the main towns were secured and several large rebel camps in the jungles were raided. By mid-February 1991, the army had even opened a route to Trincomalee from Batticaloa via Vakarai, enabling many refugees to resettle.[44]

However, although the army succeeded in re-taking the East, the rebels had simply melted into the jungle. In Batticaloa, the Security Forces had gained control of mainly the area between the lagoon and the ocean. The hinterland to the west across the lagoon remained Tiger country. So was the jungle-clad area south of Ampara town. Some of these hideouts were raided by the army and the STF, but still they achieved little in terms of killing or capturing rebels and their arms. The Tigers always managed to melt into the jungle without risking a major confrontation.

As the war in the North began to take the shape of a semi-conventional conflict demanding increasing troop commitments, the East began to pose a major strategic problem that was to remain with the Security Forces till the last phase of the war. As the army struggled to maintain pressure in the North, the Tigers began to gradually re-establish themselves in the East, taking advantage of the withdrawal of troops to beef up the forces in the North. The Tigers managed to slip through gaps in the army's defence lines between Gajabapura and Kokkuthuduwai to the north of Trincomalee now and then. They also used their fibre glass dinghies to induct men and material, moving close to the shore and beaching them and disappearing if the navy spotted them and gave chase.[45]

As the rebels began to reassert themselves, the Security Forces began to suffer. The fighting here took a different turn from the North. In the North, the rebels were defending territory, while in the East they were attempting to establish greater territorial control. Guerrilla tactics predominated with ambushes occurring with an increasing and alarming regularity, taking a steady toll of military patrols. By early 1992, these attacks had proved menacing enough for the Security Forces to confine their movements to the towns and the main roads. Batticaloa was a case in point. The Batticaloa town was a hub of activity with the Security Forces exercising considerable control over the town. Outside the town, the situation was not so settled. The Chenkaladi–Badulla highway was cut off. The Batticaloa–Habrana road was open, but travelling along it was hazardous as the Tigers were active in the jungles around it. Interestingly, the military told a visiting journalist that the soldiers controlled the main road only on Mondays, Wednesdays and Fridays, when they conducted patrols. On Tuesdays, Thursdays and Saturdays, they patrolled the railways line. On the days they did not patrol the road, no Sinhalese or Muslims were allowed to pass down the road as it was feared they would fall into the hands of Tigers. The trains operated only on the days the track was patrolled. Even Batticlaoa town was not free from LTTE pistol men.[46]

96 The army on the offensive

The army estimated there was a regular force of about 600 rebels in several camps in the eastern jungles. These bases were used to withdraw to after an attack. 'They operate in small groups of ten-fifteen or twenty people,' a military source explained. 'They can see when we move in large numbers, dodge our troops, hide their arms and mingle with the civilians.' Still, it was a far cry from the situation in the Wanni and parts of Jaffna where the Tigers enjoyed complete territorial control. In the East, the Security Forces had a degree of mobility which the army did not have in the Wanni and Jaffna. 'The big difference right now between the north and the east', the earlier source added, 'is that in the east we have to hunt the Tigers down; go searching for them. In the north the Tigers are just there.'[47]

And with the war in the North settling into a battle of attrition, hunting the Tigers was exactly what the army attempted to do, launching frequent drives to 'clear' the jungle bases of the rebels. These however had a sense of déjà vu to them. One example was 'Operation Eastern Cut-off', which took place in February 1992. Four infantry battalions and the Special Forces regiment backed by artillery and air cover tried to flush out the Tigers from the Thoppigala jungles deep in the hinterland of Batticaloa. Predictably, the rebels withdrew before the army reached the camps, leaving behind large stocks of food, grenades and mines. There were, however, no dead Tigers. The army gave a positive spin to the operation by saying it would be hard for the Tigers to rebuild their bases. But it was also clear that the rebels had also kept their forces intact.[48] And as 1992 drew to a close, the bloodletting showed little sign of abating, rebel ambushes taking a steady toll in life and limb. The result was a creeping death toll. August–September 1992 was a particularly bad period for the Security Forces in the East, more than 150 soldiers dying in rebel ambushes.[49] By the end of September 1992, the army had already lost the equivalent of a battalion to rebel ambushes in the East.[50]

The Security Forces' response to the rising death toll was predictable. They withdrew some of their smaller camps. Troop movements were only by large groups. But faced with the challenge of curtailing rebel activities with limited forces, they also resumed deep penetration operations using small groups of commandos and Special Forces, who were tasked with hunting the Tigers in their jungle hideouts. These small group operations eventually came to form the backbone of a successful campaign to clear much of the East of rebels. In 1993 with the North settled down to a stalemate and with no major operations to capture Jaffna in the offing, the army, under the leadership of Major General

The army on the offensive 97

Lucky Algama, focused on gaining control of the East. There were also strong political imperatives for this. The government wanted to hold provincial elections in the region, and for this they needed the Security Forces to be in control of the main population centres. Algama did not disappoint. He established a network of camps in strategic locations manned by volunteer force soldiers beefed up by mobile groups of commandos. These bases (called 'Forward operational Bases') were used as springboards for operations against the rebels in the area. These operations conducted by small groups of commandos and Special Forces placed the rebels under sufficient strain for them to gradually withdraw into safer areas near Verugal in the North and to a base near Thoppigala. While 'hearts and minds' operations were conducted in the cleared areas, the army surrounded the two main Tiger camps (the so-called 4–6 and 4–9 bases) and sent in the Special Forces to eliminate them. By January 1994, they had claimed to have killed more than 1,000 rebels in these small-scale operations. Harried, the eastern leader Karuna withdrew to the North with the survivors. The East was sufficiently normal for elections to be held in 1994.[51] By September 1993, the army even felt the south of Batticaloa secure enough for the STF to take over.[52]

The East was cleared. But the problem of the North still remained. In fact, the clearing of the East made any decisive moves in the North more difficult as the East required a large number of troops to keep it under control. Troops could be switched to the North only at the risk of denuding the East of much-needed manpower. This would be a problem that harried the Security Forces for many years to come.

Notes

1 Rohan Gunasekera, 'Military Modernization in Sri Lanka', *International Defense Review*, February 1991, pp. 107–8.
2 Rohan Gunasekera, 'Tiger Defences Overrun', *The Island,* 23.6.11, p. 7.
3 Defence Correspondent, 'Of Arms and Men and Machines of War', *Sunday Leader*, 7.5.95, p. 4.
4 Blodgett, *Sri Lanka's Military*, p. 103.
5 Ibid., pp. 114–5.
6 'General: Colombo Can't Defeat Tamils', *Asian Defence Journal*, September 1990, p. 110.
7 Wimalasena Fernando, 'To Serve in Defence of the Realm', *Weekend*, 1.7.90, pp. 7 and 49.
8 'Security Forces Advance on All Fronts in North and East', *Sunday Observer*, 24.6.90, p. 3.
9 Blodgett, *Sri Lanka's Military*, p. 117.
10 Rohan Gunasekera, 'Military Modernization in Sri Lanka', p. 107.

98 The army on the offensive

11 Rohan Gunasekera, 'Arms Trade in South Asia, *The Island*, 12.1.92, p. 6.
12 Blodgett, *Sri Lanka's Military*, p. 116.
13 Rohan Gunasekera, 'The Battle for Jaffna: primed for Action', *The Island*, 2.2.92, p. 5; *Sri Lanka Army*, p. 468.
14 Sunday Times Defence Correspondent, 'All about the Air Force', *Sunday Times*, 18.6.95, p. 10; Senaratne, *Sri Lanka Air Force*, pp. 119–20.
15 Senaratne, *Sri Lanka Air Force*, p. 140.
16 Rohan Gunasekera, 'Air Power in Ealam War', *The Island*, 21.2.93, p. 9.
17 Blodgett, *Sri Lanka's Military*, p. 370.
18 Senaratne, *Sri Lanka Air Force*, pp. 162–169; Blodgett, *Sri Lanka's Military*, pp. 124–5.
19 Blodgett, *Sri Lanka Military*, pp. 129–30.
20 'Navy Firepower Bolstered', *The Island*, 19.7.92, p. 1.
21 Rohan Gunasekera, 'The Battle for Jaffna: primed for Action', Defence Correspondent, 'Of Arms and Men and Machines of War', *Sunday Leader*, 7.5.95, p. 4.
22 'Army Stuck with Red Tanks', *Sunday Times*, 26.1.92, p. 1.
23 The officer was Colonel Shantha Kottegoda. Frederica Jansz, 'Victory at Vavuniya', *Sunday Times*, 12.5.91, p. 5.
24 Shamindra Ferdinando, 'The Army's Deadly Wanni Thrust', *The Island*, 17.2.91, p. 9.
25 Rohan Gunasekera, 'Army Captures Five Rebel Camps', *The Island*, 22.3.92, p. 9; Shamindra Ferdinando, 'Operation Sixer', *The Island*, 22.3.92, p. 9; Rohan Gunasekera, 'Tiger Set up Anti-tank Squads', *The Island*, 22.3.92, p. 1.
26 Rohan Gunasekera, 'The Army's Wanni Thrust, *The Island*, 19.5.91, p. 15; Mendis, *Assignment Peace*, pp. 204–6; Frederic Jansz, 'Victory at Vavuniya', *Sunday Times*, 12.5.91, p. 5; Rohan Gunasekera, 'A Signal Victory', *The Island*, 29. 9.91, p. 14; 'Operations Still on, Says Army', *Sunday Times*, 29.9.91, p. 3.
27 Rohan Gunasekera, 'Tiger Defences Overrun', *The Island*, 23.6.91, p. 9.
28 Rohan Gunasekera, 'Week-long Army Offensive Makes Tigers Withdraw', *The Island*, 23.6.91, pp. 1 and 3.
29 Rohan Gunasekera, 'A Signal Victory', *The Island*, 29. 9.91, p. 14; 'Operations Still on, Says Army', *Sunday Times*, 29.9.91, p. 3; 'A Body Blow', *The Sri Lanka Monitor*, British Refugee Council, no.44, Sept. '91, p. 2. Sarath Munasinghe gives a much higher casualty figure for both sides, 150 soldiers and 800 rebels killed, possibly an exaggeration. Munasinghe, *A Soldier's Version*, p. 120.
30 Rohan Gunasekera, 'Army Captures Five Rebel Camps', *The Island*, 22.03.92, p. 9; Shamindra Ferdinando, 'Operation Sixer', *The Island*, 22.3.92, p. 9; Rohan Gunasekera, 'Tiger Set Up Anti-tank Squads', *The Island*, 22.3.92, p. 1; Rohan Gunasekera, 'A Signal Victory', *The Island*, 29. 9.91, p. 14; 'Operations Still On, Says Army', *Sunday Times*, 29.9.91, p. 3, 'A Body Blow', *The Sri Lanka Monitor*, British Refugee Council, no.44, Sept. '91, p. 2; Munasinghe, *A Soldier's Version*, p. 120.
31 Dinesh Watawana, 'Jaffna Operations Achieve Objectives', *Sunday Times*, 27.10.91, p. 1.

The army on the offensive 99

32 Shmindra Ferdinando, 'Army Cuts off the Peninsula', *The Island*, 27.10.91, p. 7.
33 Mendis, *Assignment Peace*, pp. 268–9.
34 'Push to Jaffna', *Asiaweek*, 10.7.92, p. 46; 'Troops Meet Heavy Resistance as They Advance', *The Island*, 31.5. 92, p. 1.
35 'The Battle for Jaffna', *The Sri Lanka Monitor*, British Refugee Council, no.53, June 1992, p. 1.
36 John Colmey, 'In the Thick of a Jaffna Battle', *Asiaweek*, 14.8.92, pp. 66–70.
37 Rohan Gunasekera, 'Strangulation of the Jaffna Peninsula', *The Island*, 19/07.92, p. 9; Lt. Col. Ravi Pathiravithana, *Guerrilla Warfare – Discussing the use of Sri Lanka's Fleet of APVs and MBTs*, http://www.scribd.com/doc/52118278/GUERRILLA-WARFARE-DISCUSSING-THE-USE-OF-SRI-LANKA%E2%80%99S-FLEET-OF-APV%E2%80%99S-AND-MBT%E2%80%99S p. 15.
38 'Taraki', 'Recapturing Jaffna: Is It Feasible?', *The Island*, 29.8.12, p. 9.
39 Amaranath K. Menon, 'No Generals' War, but a Man-to-Man War, *The Island*, 16.8.92, p. 5 (From India Today)
40 Iqbal Athas, 'The Agony of Araly', *Sunday Times*, 16.8.92, p. 5.
41 Rohan Gunasekera, 'Key Sea Tiger Base Captured', *The Island*, 23.7.92, p. 11.
42 Mendis, *Assignment Peace*, pp. 284–5.
43 Taraki, 'Tiger Manpower: the Breeding Grounds', *The Island* 26.7.92, p. 11.
44 *Sri Lanka Army 50 Years On*, p. 362.
45 Rohan Gunasekera, 'The East Remains a Problem', *The Island*, 10.5.92, p. 9.
46 Dinesh Watawana, 'Batticaloa: one More Sunrise', *Sunday Times*, 16.2.92, p. 5.
47 Rohan Gunasekera, 'Operation Eastern Cut Off', *The Island*, 23.2.92, p. 11.
48 Ibid.
49 'Jaffna's Stalemate', *The Sri Lanka Monitor*, British Refugee Council, no. 56, September 1992, p. 1.
50 Rohan Gunasekera, 'Army's Dilemma in the East', The *Island*, 27.9.92, p. 13.
51 Defence Correspondent, 'Temporary Setback Turns Raw', *Sunday Leader*, 30.4.95, p. 7. In the first two months of 1994 alone, they claimed to have killed 100 rebels while losing only six of their men. 'Over 1000 Tigers Killed in First Two Months of '94', *Observer*, 6.3.94, p. 1.
52 Shamindra Ferdinando, 'STF Takes Over South of Batticaloa', *The Island*, 19.9.93, p. 1.

Chapter 6

The rise of the Sea Tigers and the battle for Kilali

While the Wanni quietened down and Jaffna remained besieged, the main action in the North shifted to the Kilali lagoon. It reflected the growing strategic importance of the sea to the Tigers and the Security Forces.

The Tigers at sea

The sea had always been important to the Tigers. The state of Ealam as envisaged by the Tamil separatists included a long shoreline, stretching from Halawatha on the west coast to the borders of the Hambantota District in the east. Even though this marked the furthest extents and most ambitious projections of the so-called Tamil homeland, even the coastline of the Northern and Eastern Provinces of Sri Lanka, the real bone of contention between the Sri Lankan government and the separatists, was very long. This was a boon to the rebels. It facilitated the growth of the armed movement by giving access to their 'rear base' in South India. The ocean was also vital for ensuring supplies through the LTTE's merchant fleet which anchored offshore until their deadly cargoes were emptied by lighter rebel craft. Last but not least, the rebels could also use the sea to shuttle men and material between their bases in the north-east.

The sea was also important to the Sri Lankan Security Forces. Since the late 1980s, the land route to Jaffna had been under increasing threat from the rebels in the Wanni, and as a result, the garrisons in the Jaffna Peninsula were coming to depend heavily on supply by the air force and the navy. This became even more pronounced after the fall of the Wanni heartland into rebel hands. Now the garrisons in Jaffna relied totally on air and sea-borne supplies.

This growing reliance on the air force and the navy made it important for the Tigers to find ways to threaten or cripple these vital links in order

The rise of the Sea Tigers 101

to increase the pressure on the troops in the peninsula. Undermining the air bridge was difficult without obtaining powerful anti-aircraft weapons, but harrying the navy was a real possibility given the Tigers' vast experience with naval operations. Therefore, it is not surprising that the Tigers developed a strong naval arm, aptly termed the Sea Tigers. As explained earlier, the formation of the Sea Tigers dates back to 1984, when the LTTE was beginning to explore opportunities for developing supply capabilities independent of Indian control. However, at this time their activities were limited to moving men and material from South India and ferrying supplies along the coast of Sri Lanka. The boats were fibre glass dinghies fitted with several outboard motors.[1] Later, when the LTTE developed their merchant navy, these dinghies also ferried their cargo to the coast from the ships anchored offshore. At this stage, despite the dangerous nature of their work, the boats were not armed; if confronted by the Sri Lankan navy, they relied on their speed to get away and as a last resort would open up with their small arms in defence.[2] The navy's big gunboats were too clumsy to tackle them, and when the navy inducted the faster Dvoras into service, the Sea Tigers tried using more outboard motors and keeping to shallow waters to avoid pursuit.[3] As explained elsewhere (Chapter 7), the Tigers had also begun to use limpet mines in an attempt to make the sea inhospitable for the navy, but these efforts were still in their infancy.

However, by the time of the outbreak of Ealam War II, the rebel navy had undergone a dramatic change. The dinghies now mounted weapons, usually a .50 machine gun. The standard dinghy was about 33 feet long with three or four outboard motors. Some were foreign built.[4] There were also the larger supply vessels fitted with either two 250 hp or five 85 hp outboard motors. In May 1991, the navy calculated that the Tigers had started with an original fleet of eight of these large boats.[5] They often sailed under the escort of one or two armed dinghies.[6] All Sea Tiger vessels generally had a low superstructure and angular construction, which enabled them to sail close to the waterline, avoiding detection.[7]

Their powerful outboard motors made it hard for the Dvoras to catch the Tiger dinghies, but the Sea Tigers were also developing bolder tactics to challenge the navy. A flotilla or 'swarm' of Sea Tiger boats would take on one or two naval craft, engaging them in a melee. This was often used to allow important elements of a convoy to get away. It also enabled the Sea Tigers to isolate navy crafts and sink or damage them severely, usually by firing at the outboard motors. At times, the Sea Tigers would also initiate attacks against navy vessels when circumstances were in their favour. However, whether on the defensive or offensive, like their land counterparts, the Sea Tigers also preferred to fight during the night or at dawn in order to avoid interception by air.[8]

Extensive naval operations were not possible without shore-based facilities. With the development of the rebel naval arm, Sea Tiger bases also cropped up all along the north-eastern coast, particularly on the northern coast of the peninsula and the eastern coast between Point Pedro and Mullaithivu. A radar station also was set up in Madagal on the northern coast of the Jaffna Peninsula, where the reef had a significant break. The rebel radar station functioned until the area reverted to army control in 'Operation Earthquake' in August 1992.[9] Undeterred, the Tigers shifted their base to Palaikkadu.[10] Despite increasing Indian surveillance, they also continued to operate from South India. In 1990, they had bases in South India in places such as Thanjavur and Coimbatore, which could not be completely shut down even with Indian naval patrolling.[11]

The Tigers were also improving their seamanship. In the 1980s, the Sea Tiger movements had been informed by traditional knowledge of the sea. Now, they began to make a detailed study of the ocean, mapping its perils and blessings. The Tigers were also stepping up their coastal defences in the Point Pedro–Mullaithivu coast and increasing their activities in the sea off Mannar.[12] The attempt to overrun Silvathurai had ended in failure but not the effort to dominate the region.

The emergence of the Sea Tigers as a separate and deadly arm of the rebels posed a serious challenge to the operations of the Sri Lankan navy. The arming of their craft enabled the Sea Tigers to carry out their activities in greater security. The armed dinghies could also threaten the navy's operations and make the ocean an inhospitable place for them. This had strategic significance as the Sea Tiger craft roaming the ocean could exert pressure on the naval supply lines with serious consequences. The damage or destruction caused to navy vessels would also add significantly to the government's mounting cost of waging war.

And the swarms of Sea Tigers were causing quite a lot of mayhem. Under the leadership of Thillaiambalam Sivanesan or Soosai, who became their commander in 1991, the Sea Tigers pressed their claim to the seas off the north-eastern coast of Sri Lanka. In one bold attack on August 29, 1992, they captured one of the navy's Inshore Patrol Crafts in Mandaithivu.[13] The following year, the navy suffered another serious setback when on August 29 a Dvora was sunk off Point Pedro, killing 11 on board. They also seized the boat's armaments – two 20 mm cannon, a .50 machine gun, personal weapons and a large quantity of ammunition.[14] The Tiger navy was also coming to play an active role in launching amphibious assaults. On October 1 1992, seaborne Tiger cadres launched a devastating attack on army-held positions at Kadaikadu south of Vettilakerni on the neck of the Jaffna Peninsula.[15]

Ominously for the Sri Lankan navy, the Tigers were also inducting their suicide cadres into their naval arm. The first 'Black Sea Tiger' suicide attack was carried out on July 10 1990 by 'Captain Collins' of Mannar, north of VVT coast.[16] In May the following year, another batch of Black Sea Tigers followed Collins's example, ramming SLNS *Abitha* about 6 miles north of Point Pedro, killing five and wounding about 20. Collins also gave his name to a sea mine the rebels were developing. The Jony mine's counterpart in the sea, the Collins mine, lay a few feet below the water level and exploded in the direction from which water pressure hit it from a speeding boat. In September 1991, one of them blew up an Inshore Patrol Craft between Karainangar and Nainathivu, killing seven including two officers.[17]

Much of the early Sea Tiger activity was concentrated on the Jaffna lagoon and the north-eastern shoreline. Gradually, to mount more pressure on their harried enemy, the Sea Tigers also began to make inroads into the western coast. In 1991, they had tried to dislodge the army from Silvathurai and bring that stretch of the coast under their control. But then the Sea Tigers were at their infancy. Now with their naval arm making great strides, the rebels tried again, setting up a Sea Tiger base in Mullikulam south of Silvathurai in early 1993 and developing it into a major centre of naval activity. With the rise of Mullikulam, Silvathurai became more vulnerable, and eventually the army decided to withdraw the garrison. In March 1991, the Tigers had sacrificed scores of young lives trying to overrun this camp. Now they forced it to shut down without firing a shot.[18]

But the navy also hit back, the Dvoras in particular, taking a heavy toll of Sea Tiger craft. By May 1991, the navy claimed it had destroyed six of the Sea Tigers' larger high-powered boats along with scores of smaller dinghies.[19] In January 1993, the Tiger merchant fleet also suffered a serious setback, this time in confrontation with the Indian navy. On January 13, the Indian navy intercepted the 280 ton cargo vessel MV *Ahat* in international waters 290 miles east of Hambantota and escorted it towards Tamil Nadu. The ship is said to have brought a cargo of AA missiles and anti-tank and anti-ship missiles. The ship's command refused to surrender for three days, and when finally the Indians closed in, they set fire to the ship. Among those perished was the former Jaffna LTTE leader Sathasivam Krishnakumar or 'Kittu' returning from

104 The rise of the Sea Tigers

England, where he had been based for some time. The Tigers are said to have been looking for heavy weapons to counter the SLAF and the army's tanks.[20]

The bloody waters of Kilali

It was the Kilali lagoon that was turning out to be the real battleground for the navy and the Sea Tigers. The lagoon, hemmed in by the peninsula to the north and the mainland to the south, was of great strategic significance, forming a link between Tiger-dominated peninsula and the Wanni. As Jaffna slowly strangled, this link became even more significant. In October 1991, the army and navy had established a beachhead at Comar south of army-controlled Mandaithivu Island and they went on to capture Sangupiddy ferry. About ten days previously, the army had also taken control of the islands to the west of Jaffna. These operations brought under military control one of the key entry points to the Jaffna Peninsula. In June 1991, the army had also taken over Kombadi and Ooriyan entry points near Elephant Pass. Finally, Operation Blavegaya II sealed off the neck of the Jaffna Peninsula completely from the mainland.

After the army repulsed rebel attacks on Elephant Pass, they banned all civilian traffic through Kombadi, Ooriyan and Sanguppidy and ordered the civilians to use the Elephant Pass causeway. The LTTE's response was to ban the use of Elephant Pass and order the civilians to use Ooriyan, Kombadi and Sanguppidy. The long-suffering civilians, more fearful of invoking the Tiger's wrath than earning the army's displeasure, began to use the entry and exit points designated by the Tigers. When the army took over these points too, the Tigers, rather than agreeing to let civilians pass through Elephant Pass, ordered them to use the Kilali lagoon.[21]

The Tigers had strong reasons for keeping Elephant Pass closed. According to analyst Taraki, this was due to their concern that the army would use it as an excuse to remove their camp at Vettilakerni and deploy the men elsewhere. The Tigers estimated that nearly 10,000 troops could be taken out of Pooneryn–Kalmunai point and Vettilakerni to be deployed elsewhere, especially in an assault on Jaffna. It was not something the rebels looked forward to with relish.[22]

The lagoon now became hotly contested territory. The rebels were frustrating the Security Forces' designs to control traffic to and from the peninsula, turning Kilali into an alternative route in and out of Jaffna, charging Rs 150 per head to ferry people across. Outmanoeuvred, the

The rise of the Sea Tigers   105

army declared the lagoon an exclusion zone in late 1992, forcing the much-harried civilians to go through army checkpoints at Elephant Pass. The Tigers placed their own barricades beyond this, obstructing traffic to force civilians to take the lagoon route.[23]

Evidently, the Tigers were not giving up the lagoon easily. It was not simply that the shallow expanse of water was a way to deny the army control over civilian movement – and make a tidy profit on the side. The rebels also used the Kilali route to reach India. They arrived on the mainland and then travelled through the Wanni jungles and reached the west coast between Puttalam and Mannar. From here they travelled to South India.[24]

For the Sri Lankan Security Forces, Kilali posed a challenge. It was hard for the navy to patrol the lagoon as the big Dvoras could not sail in the shallow waters. Only the Inshore Patrol Crafts were able to operate in the lagoon, and they were vulnerable to the armed Sea Tiger crafts.[25] On the other hand, the rebels could not be allowed to thumb their noses at the Security Forces with impunity. It was only a matter of time before something terrible occurred.

Several boats plying the lagoon were fired upon by the navy and a number of civilians were killed. On January 2 1993, in a widely publicised incident, the navy fired upon a flotilla of boats carrying civilians, killing about 35.[26] According to one source, in the first four months of 1993, a total of 328 civilians were killed in this fashion with thousands stranded on the lagoon's shores, waiting for a 'dash' across it.[27] On land in the peninsula, the blockade was beginning to bite. The smuggling of essential commodities to Jaffna was drastically curtailed, leading to severe hardships for the population. Fishing and agriculture were at a standstill with malnourishment increasing.

The Tigers' response to the clamping down on the Kilali lagoon came in devastating fashion. On November 16 1992, a suicide bomber drove an explosives-rigged motorcycle into the vehicle of the navy chief, Vice Admiral Clancy Fernando in Colombo, just outside the Galle Face Green. The vice admiral along with his flag lieutenant and driver were killed instantly.[28] On the night of August 26 1993, three days before they sank a Dvora off Point Pedro, the Sea Tigers struck in Kilali. They swarmed all over five patrol boats sent to intercept a convoy and sank two of them. Five bodies of navy men were recovered; four others were listed as missing in action.[29]

It was becoming clear that to enforce the blockade effectively the lagoon needed to be cleared of the Sea Tiger menace. But when the government's response came, it was on land, not in the sea.

Operation Yal Devi: September–October

In May 1993, Sri Lanka had a new president. Like many events in the island during the war, this too was the result of the rebels' handiwork. On May 1, the then president Ranasinghe Premadasa was blown up by a suicide bomber while he was taking part in his party's May Day procession. Only a week before, a suspected LTTE gunman had also assassinated Lalith Athulathmudali, the erstwhile Minister for National Security and sworn enemy of the Tigers and, in recent times, Premadasa. In the space of one week, the Tigers had removed two of the most charismatic and influential national leaders. Such was the power of the politics of murder.[30]

The new president, Dingiri Banda Wijetunge, took a hard-line stance on the ethnic issue. The security ruling out negotiations with the LTTE, he ordered the Security Forces to clear the North and the East for provincial elections as soon as possible.[31]

On September 28, the army launched Operation Yal Devi, the biggest military operation since the deaths of Lieutenant General Denzil Kobbekaduwa and Major General Wijaya Wimalaratna. Backed by tanks and other tracked armour, the army moved north-west of Elephant Pass, in three brigade groups of over 3,000 men, targeting Kilali town on the Thenmarachchi coast, now the only entry point to the besieged Jaffna Peninsula. The army planned to take Kilali and destroy the Sea Tiger facilities there. Kilali was also the key staging place for Sea Tiger operations in the lagoon and destroying it, it was hoped, would severely cripple their activities. The three brigades moved as part of one battle group without any attempt to secure the area they passed through and without any links stretching back to their base at Elephant Pass. It was a search and destroy mission in great strength, aimed at making a quick, aggressive dash to Kilali.

By the second day, they had reached the Pallai area on the Elephant Pass–Chavakachcheri road, driving the rebels and thousands of refugees before them towards Chavakachcheri.[32] Resistance was light; a skirmish left 37 soldiers slightly wounded. But on the second morning, the rebels sprang a deadly ambush, attacking the column from the right flank and trapping the soldiers in a narrow frontage. The battle raged until midafternoon as the long-range artillery from Elephant Pass joined air force ground-attack aircraft in punishing the rebels now swarming all over the battle group. By mid-afternoon, the rebels had been pushed back, but at a huge cost: the army lost at least 114 killed including six officers, while nearly 250 were wounded. The officers wounded included

The rise of the Sea Tigers 107

Brigade Commander Colonel Sarath Fonseka, who was struck by shrapnel towards the dying stages of the battle. Apart from the guns of the two tanks they destroyed, the rebels had also captured more than 80 rifles, two general-purpose machine guns and several light mortars and grenade launchers. The rebels admitted to losing 96, while the army claimed to have killed up to 300 Tigers. After Pulo Palai, rebel resistance died down. The army regrouped and continued its advance, reaching Kilali on October 2. There they found hundreds of boats and well-fortified camps. The boats, numbering more than 200, and the camps were destroyed while the pier was cratered. By October 5, the army was back in camp at Elephant Pass.[33]

The army claimed the operation was a success as it destroyed the fleet of boats the rebels used to ferry people across the lagoon and the harbour facilities at Kilali. The loss of Kilali, even though the army did not hold it, was a blow to the reputation of the LTTE, according to some analysts. It showed to the civilians that the Tigers could not prevent the army from capturing it and ensure security for the crossing.[34]

Within days, however, the rebels were back, their boats resuming the operations from where they had left, thousands of civilians again queuing up to make the precarious crossing.[35] Within weeks, they would also deliver the Security Forces a devastating blow, one that would dwarf the losses at Kokavil and Mankulam.

Operation Frog: November 11 1993

To the west, the Kilali lagoon is encompassed by a spit of land that looks like a spearhead on the map. Pooneryn camp and the Negathavanthurai naval base were set up on this narrow tongue of land, within 9 km of each other facing the Jaffna lagoon. The camp sat astride the Sanguppidy ferry and, together with the naval base, was well placed to watch the lagoon. Yet Pooneryn was also in a precarious position. Launching an attack across the shallow waters was not a huge problem for the rebels as they controlled much of the lagoon. For the military, reinforcing the camp in the case of such an attack was a serious challenge as heavy gunboats had to come all the way from the naval base at Trincomalee. Without them, only an amphibious operation using the covering fire of the lighter crafts was possible. An airborne landing always ran the risk of running into rebel heavy machine-gun fire.[36]

The Tigers struck on Thursday, November 11, launching 'Operation Frog'. At the time of the attack, the camp held about 1,300 soldiers belonging to the First Battalion Ceylon Light Infantry and the Third

108 The rise of the Sea Tigers

Battalion Gemunu Regiment. There were also about 300 sailors manning the naval radar station at Negathavanthurai.

On Thursday early morning amidst heavy rain, the LTTE cadres waded through the shallow waters off the coast of Negathavanthurai and attacked the naval detachment, killing the sailors manning the crafts and captured them. At the same time, other cadres infiltrated the Pooneryn camp from land and killed the crew manning the five 120mm mortars. They carried off two, while the others were left damaged. Soon the attack became general as the Tigers, including many female cadres, launched themselves at the defences in waves. The soldiers fought on, but the attackers were already inside the perimeter and the situation was rapidly deteriorating. Many soldiers panicked and were cut down by Tiger fire as they tried to find safety. Others tried to regroup and fight back, economising their ammunition.[37]

The air force dispatched reinforcements, but the Puccara and the Siai Marchettis that were sent from Palali were unable to attack the Tigers on the ground as they were too close to the defenders. However, they attacked rebel reinforcements coming across the lagoon, bringing some respite to the soldiers in the camp. Army commandos coming to the rescue aboard the landing craft 'Rana Gaja' from Kankesanthurai also ran into heavy fire from well-entrenched enemy positions on the shore, and the Dvoras which escorted the landing craft struggled to get close to the shore to provide fire support owing to the shallow water, further impeding the landing. Bowing to the inevitable, the navy finally ordered Negathavanturai to be abandoned. The desperate survivors – 48 sailors and 12 soldiers – waded through the lagoon to be picked up by dinghies from Elephant Pass.

Tigers continued to attack Pooneryn. More Tiger reinforcements were also pouring in, and another attempt to induct commandos – this time by air – was beaten off on Friday the twelfth. That night, the Tigers made a ferocious assault on the survivors at Pooneryn. Still, the base held, pockets of soldiers digging in to offer stubborn resistance. But the rebels had achieved their aim; having captured a large haul of weapons and ammunition and satisfied that they had given the enemy a terrible mauling, they began to withdraw. When the army reinforcements finally landed on Saturday morning, they met with very little resistance.

The rebels had dealt a shattering blow to the army and the navy. Between 400 and 600 soldiers and over 100 sailors were killed and about 600 soldiers and sailors were reported wounded. The navy lost five Inshore Patrol Crafts, while the army lost two 120mm mortars, two tanks, 12 five zero machine guns, 50 LMGs, 1 106mm RCL, 400 rifles

The rise of the Sea Tigers 109

and a huge stock of ammunition. One Puccara was damaged. One of the captured tanks was bombed and destroyed by the air force later when it was spotted being driven away, but the LTTE is said to have removed the gun from the tank.[38] The Tigers are supposed to have used more than 2,000 cadres in the assault, out of whom an estimated 700–800 were killed.[39]

The resistance to Yal Devi and the assault on Pooneryn underlined the rebels' growing credentials in semi-conventional warfare. In resisting Yale Devi, they had taken on a force with superior firepower supported by air cover and inflicted heavy casualties. At Pooneryn, they had swamped a large military complex, virtually wiping out the garrison. The actions, particularly the attack on Pooneryn, also demonstrated that the Tigers had learnt from their past mistakes in launching similar attacks, especially at Elephant Pass. At Pooneryn, they utilised their strengths while taking precautions to minimise the enemy's strengths. The attack, as usual, was meticulously planned. The rebels ensured that while they used massive force to overwhelm the camps they fortified the promontory overlooking the lagoon to prevent reinforcements from arriving. They used overwhelming force to crush resistance within a few days before reinforcements could arrive. The timing of the attack was also significant. The Tigers launched the attack during the monsoon when the weather afforded few clear skies for the air force.[40]

Coupled with the rise of the Sea Tigers, these demonstrations of defensive and offensive capability signified the evolution of the rebels into a serious force in the North. The Tigers were evolving, becoming more circumspect and finding ways to undermine the potential of the Security Forces and exploit their limitations. A new balance of power was emerging, the rebels making a strong contention for military parity.

Notes

1 *Sri Lanka Navy*, Sri Lanka Navy: Colombo 1998, pp. 89–90.
2 Martin Murphy, 'Maritime Threat: Tactics and Technology of the Sea Tigers', *Jane's Intelligence Review*, 1.6.06. Even the Indian navy found the Tiger boats too fast to catch. Sardeshspande, *Assignment Jaffna*, (Delhi: Lancer, 1992) p. 351. For an account of a battle between a naval craft of the Sri Lankan navy and a rebel dinghy with the Tigers using AK47s to fight off the pursuers, see Iqbal Athas, 'The Stinging Bee Experience', *Weekend*, 14.9.86, pp. 6 and 10.
3 *The Sri Lanka Navy: a Pictorial History*, p. 90.
4 Defence Correspondent, 'Terror at Sea', *Sunday Times*, 18.10.92, p. 5; Defence Correspondent, 'LTTE's Passage to India', *Sunday Times*, 18.10.92, p. 5; *The Sri Lanka Navy: a Pictorial History*, p. 106.

110 The rise of the Sea Tigers

5 Sugeeswara Senadhira, 'Navy Cripples LTTE Sea Power', *Sunday Observer*, 12.5.91, p. 1.
6 Defence Correspondent, 'Terror at Sea', Defence Correspondent, 'LTTE's passage to India'.
7 Paul A. Povlock, 'A Guerrilla War at Sea: The Sri Lankan Civil War', *Small Wars Journal*, P. 19, http://smallwarsjournal.com/sites/default/files/848-povlock.pdf
8 Martin Murphy, 'Maritime Threat: Tactics and Technology of the Sea Tigers', *Jane's Intelligence Review*, 1.6.06, *The Sri Lanka Navy: a Pictorial History*, p. 107.
9 Rohan Gunasekera, 'Key Sea Tiger Base Captured', *The Island*, 23.7.92, p. 11.
10 'Tigers Urged to Surrender', *Sunday Observer*, 11.4.93, p. 8.
11 Romesh Fernando, 'North East War Politico-military Dimension', *The Island*, 24.6.1990, p. 6.
12 Taraki, 'Tigers Roam the Seas', *The Island*, 28.6.92, p. 11.
13 Povlock, 'A Guerrilla War at Sea', p. 18, Shamindra Ferdinando, 'Eleventh Year of Ealam War', *The Island*, 27.12.92, p. 7.
14 'Prabha Steps on to the Frontline', *Sunday Times*, 19.9.93, p. 7.
15 Shamindra Ferdinando, 'Eleventh Year of Ealam War'.
16 Roy Denish, 'The Kokavil Blackout', *Weekend*, 15.7.90, pp. 6–7. The report mentions this incident having taken place off the east coast. One midshipman was killed and three sailors seriously wounded. Another report mentions a second LTTE cadre, 'Captain' Vinoth. According to this report, the navy vessel was sunk. 'Ravana', 'The Black Tiger Phenomena, Its Origins and Their Targets', *The Island*, 14.11.93, p. 11.
17 Shamindra Ferdinando, 'Crucial Battle for Control of Jaffna Lagoon', *The Island*, 21.2.93, p. 9.
18 'Taraki', 'Tigers' Interest in the Gulf of Mannar', *The Island*, 25.9.92, p. 9.
19 Sugeeswara Senadhira, 'Navy Cripples LTTE Sea Power', *Sunday Observer*, 12.5.91, p. 1.
20 'Piecing the Puzzle of the Kittu Drama', *Sunday Times*, 24.1.93, p. 5.
21 Shamindra Ferdinando, 'Crucial Battle for Control of Jaffna Lagoon'.
22 Taraki, 'Why Are the Tigers Not Opening Elephant Pass?', *The Island*, 14.2.93, p. 9.
23 'Who Is Gunning for Pottu Amman', *Sunday Times*, 17.1.93, p. 5. Under the ban, gazetted under section 5 (Chapter 40) of the Public Security Ordnance Emergency Regulations title 'Establishment of Prohibited Zone regulations no. 1 of 1992', only vessels belonging to the Sri Lankan navy or any vessel authorised in that behalf by the competent authority was allowed to use the lagoon. Political Correspondent, 'Bishop Moves onto the Chess Board', *Sunday Times*, 17.1.93, p. 4.
24 Defence Correspondent, 'LTTE's Passage to India', *Sunday Times*, 18.10.92, p. 5.
25 Ibid.
26 Shamindra Ferdinando, 'Crucial Battle for Control of Jaffna Lagoon'.
27 This was alleged by Rev. Selvadurai Jeyanesan of the Uniting Church, who was visiting Sydney in May 1993. Lousie Williams, 'Jaffna Children

The rise of the Sea Tigers   111

Brainwashed to Fight', *Sunday Times*, 30.5.93, p. 5, originally appeared in the *Sydney Morning Herald*.

28 'Navy Chief, Aides, Killed by Suicide Bomber', *Daily News*, 17.11.92, p. 1.

29 Niresh Eliathamby, 'Ferocious Naval Battle Rocks Jaffna Lagoon', *The Island*, 29.8.93, p. 9.

30 'Lalith Assassinated', *Sunday Times*, 25.4.93, p. 1, 'The President Is Dead', *Sunday Times*, 2.5.93, p. 1.

31 Political Correspondent, 'DB Sets Stage for Military Thrust', 12.9.93, p. 6.

32 Shamindra Ferdinando, 'The Battle for Kilali – the Army Fights Back', *The Island*, 3.10.93, p. 13.

33 For descriptions of this battle see, Defence Correspondent, 'Kilali: the Untold Story', *Sunday Times*, 24.10.93, p. 7; D.B.S. Jeyaraj, ' "Brigadier" Balraj; the Legendary Commander of the LTTE', *Transcurrents*, 27.5.11, http://dbsjeyaraj.com/dbsj/archives/2177 D.B.S.Jeyaraj, 'Theepan of the LTTE', *Transcurrents*, 4.4.12, http://dbsjeyaraj.com/dbsj/archives/5381; Munasinghe, *A Soldier's Version*, pp. 129–31; H.L.D.Mahindapala, 'The Day When the Tigers Fought and Ran', *Sunday Observer*, 10.10.93, p. 10, Shamindra Ferdinando, 'Kilali Offensive a Success Claims Army', *The Island*, 10.10.93, p. 13.

34 Taraki, 'Major Upset for LTTE', *The Island*, 3.10.93, p. 13.

35 The army admitted that the Tiger boas were back in business. 'LTTE Resumes Boat Service Across Lagoon', *The Island*, 10.10.93, p. 1.

36 'Pooneryn or Peace Road', *Sunday Times*, 11.12.94, p. 9.

37 Franklin S. Raviraj, 'We Were Taken by Surprise – Wounded Soldier', *The Island*, 21.11.93, p. 3.

38 Niresh Eliathamby, 'What Went Wrong?', *The Island*, 21.11.93, p. 9.

39 Ravana, 'The Assault on Pooneryn and LTTE's Eastern Strategy', *The Island*, 21.11.93, p. 9 and p. 12.

40 Taraki, 'Pooneryn: Prabha's Strategic Thinking', *The Island*, 14.11.93, p. 11.

Chapter 7

A new regime, a new war

By early 1994, the war had settled into a stalemate again. In the North, the Tigers still held on to the Wanni and much of the Jaffna Peninsula with the Security Forces unable to dominate the region. The rise of the Sea Tigers was making the naval lifeline to the North increasingly dangerous. On the other hand, the rebels were no closer to establishing complete control over the North and the East. Despite the emergence of the Tigers' naval arm, the Security Forces still held on to their camps in the peninsula. They also had cleared much of the Eastern Province of the rebel presence, forcing the bulk of the rebel forces in the province to retreat northwards.

It was in this context that on August 19 1994 Sri Lanka had a regime change. The electorate voted out the United National Party (UNP) government after 17 years, electing a government of the People's Alliance (PA). The wafer-thin parliamentary majority of the new government was turned into solid gain when Chandrika Kumaratunge, the leader of the PA, won the all-important presidential election in November. The PA's victory underlined the extent to which the war in the North and the East had become a factor in southern politics. The stalemate in the North and the continuing losses in the military had led to a war weariness which had resulted in the emergence of a strong peace lobby and a growing conviction among many people in the South that the war was unwinnable and that a negotiated settlement was necessary. Coupled with the tiredness with the UNP's 17-year rule, this translated into a victory for the PA which campaigned on a platform of bringing peace to the country.

The election of Kumaratunge was greeted with jubilation by the peace lobby. Finally, it was believed a genuine peace process could be started now that a government that had received a mandate for peace was in power. The government and the LTTE did not disappoint. The PA began to make peace overtures very early, partially lifting the economic embargo on the North on September 1 1994 and calling for peace talks.[1] The Tigers responded by releasing several policemen they had held for years. But perhaps to remind the government of the need to stay on the peace track, the rebels also blew up the navy vessel *Sagarawardena* anchored off Mannar on September 19. Events moved quickly now. First round of negotiations were held from October 13 to 14 1994. Over the next three months (from October 13 to 14 1994 till January 14 1995), three rounds of talks were held between the government and the LTTE. Things continued to look rosy. On January 5, the rebels and the government signed a ceasefire to come into effect from January 8 1995. But soon optimism began to turn into disappointment. Although initially some progress was made in the peace talks, they gradually got stuck on disagreements over priorities. The Tigers wanted the Pooneryn camp removed, a demand that the government was very reluctant to grant.

In a letter dated March 16 1995, the Tigers warned that they would be 'compelled to make a painful decision' if a favourable response was not received to their demands before March 28. While waiting for a response, the LTTE, for the first time, articulated their political demands. In their publication *Viduthalai Puligal* the Tigers called for federalism with self-rule, the recognition of the Tamils as a distinct nationality and the recognition of the Tamil People's right for self-determination.[2]

The government wished to have the next round of talks between May 5 and 10. But by April 18, they had received a letter from the rebels. As the government's responses and reactions fell short of their expectations, the Tigers decided to withdraw from negotiations, the letter informed. Return to war was swift and devastating. On the early morning of April 19, Black Sea Tigers blew up two navy gunboats berthed in the Trincomalee dockyard. Ealam War III was on.

The Eastern offensive

The ceasefire and peace process came as a much-needed respite for both parties. Even though neither party admitted it, after nearly three years of bloodletting in a war that had expanded in scale and intensity, both sides needed time to regroup. It is arguable that the new government, eager to deliver on the promise of peace, was genuinely hopeful of a settlement, but as their demands showed, the Tigers had little interest in a settlement. Their eyes were firmly on the final objective of Ealam, and to this end, they set about consolidating their position and undermining the government's authority.

The Eastern Province was their main target. In the East, the Security Forces had altered the strategic equation by clearing large areas and forcing the rebels to shift their operations to the North by early 1993.[3] But while the peace negotiations were in progress, the Tigers moved to reverse these gains of the Security Forces by infiltrating large numbers of cadres into the province. The rebels had begun entrenching themselves again in the province in 1994 and 1995. This was facilitated to some extent by the movement of a large number of troops from the region to carry out 'Operation Yal Devi' in the North in October 1993.[4] The relaxation of military operations after the advent of the PA government and the cessation of hostilities during the peace talks also enabled the Tigers to induct more cadres into the East. By early 1995, about 1,000 cadres had been reportedly re-inducted into the province in this fashion.[5]

Karuna, who had withdrawn with his men to the North in 1994, was also back, busily recruiting school-aged children in large numbers, showing them videos of their recent exploits, notably the devastating assault on Pooneryn.[6] The Tigers even tested their strength in the East by clashing with the army. As early as December 28, a group of rebels, said to number about 150, attacked the Thumpanaveli army camp in Batticaloa. The operation ended with heavy losses to the Tigers, but it showed that they were beginning to flex their muscles in the East.[7]

Alarmed by the deteriorating situation, the military repeatedly warned the government about the rebel build-up in the East.[8] The government, however, showed little inclination to upset the delicate peace process by raising the issue with the rebels. After years of bloodletting and campaigning on a peace platform, the PA had finally established some goodwill between the two warring parties. They were not prepared to jeopardise it just yet.

But on April 19 1995, all that ended. The sinking of the two gunboats sent shock waves through Colombo. There was a sense of déjà vu among the sceptics who were quick to draw parallels between the sinking of the gunboats and the Tigers' return to violence almost five years ago in June 1990. The rebels had taken the government for a ride yet again, and the government had allowed itself to be ridden by the Tiger. As world leaders hastened to condemn the attack, the Sri Lankan government rushed to assure a jittery public that it was only a temporary setback for the peace process. But to prepare for the worse, the economic embargo and the ban on fishing was quickly reinstated.[9] The Security Forces also got the green light to carry out limited offensive operations in the North and the East. But everybody hoped that it was only a minor flare up, not the beginning of another full-scale war.

A new regime, a new war   115

The Security Forces' response was measured. In the North, the navy launched a bombardment of suspected Sea Tiger bases in the Nagarkovil area on April 21.[10] There were no operations on the ground. For their part, the Tigers too claimed that the door to peace was still open. But demonstrating that the door to war was opened even wider, they continued with their offensive. In the North, they pounded the army camps with RPGs and mortars. The exchange of fire seemed to have caused no casualties, but it also did nothing to ease tensions.[11]

The violence escalated. The rebels now moved quickly to capitalise on the gains they had made in the East during the peace talks. In the early hours of April 21 1995, a force of Tigers estimated at about 700 attacked the army camp at Kattumurippukulam, one of the army's Forward Operational bases, 10 km west of Vakarai in the Batticaloa district. At least, 45 soldiers were killed while nearly 80 soldiers were listed as missing in action. The Tigers occupied the camp for several hours before withdrawing with captured weapons and ammunition.[12] The rebels followed up their exploit in Batticaloa with another deadly attack in Ampara. On May 8, they ambushed a party of STF commandos as they left their camp in Kanchikudichchi aru, killing 19 police commandos.[13] Now a string of attacks and ambushes assailed the Security Forces, taking a steady toll.[14] On May 23, in a particularly deadly attack, 27 soldiers were slaughtered in an ambush on a foot patrol between Panchinankerni and Kadjugama in the Vakarai area in Batticaloa.[15] The civilians were not spared either. The Sinhala border villages also came in for a new round of punishment. In an attack on the Sinhala fishing village at Kallarawa, south of Pulmoddai in the Trincomalee district, the rebels killed 42 civilians and wounded four soldiers from the nearby camp. Many of the soldiers from the camp took refuge in the jungle and returned later.[16]

Within a few weeks, LTTE operations in the Eastern Province had forced the army to withdraw many of its smaller detachments that were vulnerable to attacks.[17] Other border areas were also coming under pressure. The police post at Kelepuliyankulam on the Kebithigollewa–Vavuniya Road was stormed on May 10, killing ten policemen, five home guards and the wife of a home guard.[18] As reports of Tigers roaming ahead of the border areas trickled in, the whole frontline became jittery with the anticipation of more attacks.

The army responded to the rebels' belligerence by launching operations to clear the most vulnerable areas of the East, particularly areas around the border villages in the Trincomalee and Batticaloa districts. Going on the offensive in Batticaloa, troops moved up to Kathiraveli and Kamappanchenai and destroyed Tiger encampments. The rebels, however, vanished into the jungles. In the North, the army made a daring commando raid on the rebels' checkpoint north of Vavuniya at Vannadikulam near Omanthai. Heli-borne troops carried by MI17s and troops on trail bikes moving from Nochchimodai attacked the sentry point and destroyed it, losing three killed and claiming to have killed 18.[19]

The army was hitting back, but these actions were more like knee-jerk reactions than operations with a clear strategy. And by July 1995, despite limited successes, the pressure on the military was beginning to tell.

The North

While keeping the troops occupied in the East with frequent, deadly attacks, in the north the Tigers went for the jugular. The emergence of the Sea Tigers had made the naval lifeline to the north somewhat insecure. Now the Tigers moved to threaten the air bridge to Jaffna, perhaps as a preliminary to assaulting army positions in the peninsula. During the peace talks, they had acquired several anti-aircraft missiles, and now they tested them on the SLAF with deadly effect. On April 26, an AVRO on its way to Ratmalana from Palali became their first victim, when it was shot down with 48 people on board just outside Palali. A week later, another AVRO met the same fate while on its way to Palali from Ratmalana. An anti-aircraft missile hit it as it was coming to land in Palali. The aircraft broke into three pieces. All 52 on board perished.[20]

With the downing of the second AVRO, the air force immediately grounded its fleet, leading to the isolation of many camps in the North. Panic spread through the military as there were reports of rebel build-ups near major military camps, particularly Pooneryn. The Tigers were reported to be massing cadres; setting up defences, hospitals and other support services and converting dozens of confiscated tractors into improvised armoured vehicles mounted with .50 machine guns.[21] The spectre of another huge disaster began to haunt the military.

Fortunately for the government, no major attack materialised. The Tigers seemed to be content to keep the peninsula under siege while re-establishing themselves in the East. The air force remained out of the skies until May 7 when the F7s bore down on the suspected rebel concentrations around Paranthan and around Pooneryn.[22] With no more missile attacks, transport flights resumed several weeks later with the air force using smaller aircraft and the Y-12s as transports.[23] The air bridge was back in operation, but it would remain tenuous at best.

However, back in the sea and on land, things were taking a turn for the worse. A day after the downing of the second aircraft, the Tigers launched a fierce attack on an army outpost on Kayts Island, killing 18.[24] But this was nothing compared with the blow that fell two months later. On June 28, the Sea Tigers flexed their muscle again in the North, launching a devastating attack on the army camp on Mandaithivu Island, just west of the Jaffna Peninsula. Mandaithivu is the southernmost of the string of islands to the west of the Jaffna Peninsula. A force of Sea Tigers and seaborne Tigers, estimated at about 1,000, attacked the island in the early hours of the twenty-eighth and overran the defences. It involved extensive preparation – scores of boats, including 50 trawlers commandeered from Tamil Nadu fishermen and the water jets captured from Pooneryn in 1993, were used. The rebels also timed their attack well. At the time of the attack, the 700-man garrison at Mandaithivu was depleted as about half the soldiers were either on leave or waiting for transportation to Mandaithivu from Palali. The troops on the island also belonged to a newly raised battalion that had not seen major combat. The Tigers breached the defences without any great difficulty and went through the camp meticulously, killing and destroying. Summoned to the rescue, the air force struggled with its fleet of Bell 212s to induct troops into the disputed island; the newly acquired MI17s were not thrown into the fray as they were not being used in the North up till then. By the following morning, it was all over. The Tigers had cleaned up the camp and withdrawn with a large haul of weapons and ammunition, including two .50 machine guns, RPGs, heavy machineguns and 81mm mortars as well as over 150,000 rounds of ammunition. Over 100 soldiers lay dead, and many more wounded. The rebels placed their own losses at 11, although the army as usual claimed to have killed many more.[25]

Whether anybody liked it or not, Ealam War III was in full swing. And the pressure was mounting on the government to retaliate.

The taking of Jaffna

As the Tigers stepped up the offensive, the government pondered its options. The search for a political solution was not abandoned. The aim of the government's operations was the weakening of the enemy so that negotiations could be carried out from a position of strength. In essence, this was not different from the position of previous governments. However, the PA government showed a seriousness lacking in previous governments by offering a concrete set of proposals. These were vehemently opposed by the Sinhala nationalists and ridiculed by the LTTE and suffered an inevitable demise. But the government continued to explore other possibilities for a political resolution to the conflict while aiming for military dominance.

The rebel activities were at their most intense in the East, but it was the North that the government had in its sights. The reasoning was that if the Tigers were to be taught an unforgettable lesson it had to be taught not in the jungles of the East or the Wanni but in the Jaffna Peninsula where they ran their de facto state, with all the apparatus of an alternative administration. If Jaffna was taken, it would deal the rebels a shattering blow to their morale and military power, a blow from which they would find it hard to recover. The hopes of assaulting Jaffna had gradually receded after the deaths of Denzil Kobbekduwa and Wijaya Wimalaratna. It was now time to return to the charge with a vengeance.

With a major northern offensive in their minds, the army and the air force immediately went on missions to purchase new weapons and equipment to bolster their strike capability. Delegations were sent to China, the Czech Republic, Pakistan, Indonesia, Russia and the UK, while military teams from at least two countries were reportedly expected in the country to assess the threat from AA missiles.[26] Among the new weapons expected were dedicated helicopter gunships, something that the air force had badly wanted for a long time.[27] The army's firepower was also being boosted; new 122mm guns were being expected towards the end of the year.

After several probing attacks, which tested the rebel defences and extended the perimeters of the Palali camp, the main assault on Jaffna was launched on October 16. The previous offensive to capture territory in the Jaffna Peninsula, 'Operation Liberation', had involved 5,000–10,000 troops. It was the first ever brigade-size operation launched by the Sri Lankan army and was considered a landmark in the army's operational evolution. But it paled in comparison with what the army launched to capture Jaffna in October 1995. 'Operation Riviresa', which began on October 17 1995, unleashed nearly 30,000 troops on Jaffna. The troops belonged to three divisions: the Fifty-First, Fifty-Second and Fifty-Third, and were supported by battle tanks and APCs on the ground and the air force's ground-attack fleet in the sky. The navy patrolled the ocean, preventing rebels from fleeing the onslaught.

Unlike its predecessor 'Operation Liberation', which tackled Vadamarachchi, Operation Riviresa' went for Valikamam, the heart of the Tigers' de facto power in the peninsula. The aim was to deal the Tigers a crushing blow. Accordingly, the troops advanced in two columns from

Palali along a narrow corridor bordered on the east by the Jaffna–Point Pedro road and in the west by the Jaffna–Palali road (about 5 km apart). The strategy was to seal off the main population centres of Valikamam – which were to the west of the advancing columns – from the rest of the peninsula before taking the city.

The battle was tough, but after several weeks of slow, grinding advance, the army finally entered Jaffna in the first week of December. In the first half of 1996, two other operations, Riviresa II and III, brought the other two sectors of Jaffna, Thenmarachchi and Vadamarachchi, also under government control. After more than a decade, Jaffna was finally in government hands.

The capture of Jaffna showed that if they mustered large enough forces with sufficient firepower the government forces could prevail over the Tigers in open confrontation. As in 1987, the rebels' resistance to the advance consisted mainly of fighting from fortified positions and using booby traps. At some points, they also threw in their improvised 'armour'. But these were no match for the army's heavy artillery and tanks and APCs.[28] The built-up nature of the city and the low-level locations of rebel bunkers made it hard for the tanks to manoeuvre and engage the enemy, but this was overcome by flattening the buildings with their guns and tracks to clear pathways and fields of fire.[29] By the third week of December, at least two Mi24 helicopter gunships had also arrived, and these provided an added punch to the advance. The heaviest rebel resistance came at Neerveli on the Jaffna–Point Pedro Road. Here, the Tigers had one of their main bases complete with underground command structures and hospitals. The fortifications were impressive, said to resemble World War II German fortifications on the French coast. They fought fiercely for nearly two days (October 29 and 30) in defence of their base, but in the end the superior firepower of the army prevailed. Opportunely for the army, the 122mm artillery had just arrived, and now they were used to batter the rebel defences to submission. The Tigers lost heavily here; among their dead was Akila, the leader of the LTTE's women's wing, and many other female cadres. The army too suffered in the two-day battle, losing 73 killed. In the rebel base, the forces found a fully equipped, air-conditioned, three-storey underground hospital and an underground 'airbase' in which a partially assembled aircraft was found.[30]

However, even though the rebels had few answers to the army's advance, the battle for Jaffna also showed that capturing the city was only a small part of the battle. The assault had killed many rebel cadres, but it had failed to destroy the rebel army. Overall, despite some losses in men and material, the Tigers managed to evacuate the bulk of their forces and heavy equipment to the Wanni without exposing them to the full might of the military's onslaught. About 4,000 cadres had been removed to Mannar, Kilinochchi and Mullaithivu. The fierce resistance put up in places such as Neerveli was largely to delay the advance of the army and remove the arms and equipment.[31] It was a story repeated in the capture of the other parts of the peninsula, especially Vadamarachchi. The army found the Sea Tiger camps and bunkers along the coast of Velvetithurai and Point Pedro coast empty. It was learnt later that the Sea Tigers had relocated their assets to the Mullaithivu coast in anticipation of an army attack on the area soon after the fall of Valikamam.[32] There was minimal resistance to the army's advance into Vadamarachchi. The operation was completed in 36 hours with the loss of only two soldiers, both to sniper fire.[33]

If the assault on Jaffna had expected to deal the Tigers a crippling blow, it had fallen short of its mark. What was even more worrying was the civilian exodus. As it appeared that the army juggernaut could not be stopped, the Tigers had begun to evacuate Jaffna. The fall of Neerveli was the cue. While rearguard action continued, the bulk of the rebels and the civilian population were now moved across the Jaffna lagoon to Chavakaccheri. As the monsoon rains poured down, the Tigers exhorted the civilians to leave, evoking the spectre of a terrible fate if the army moved in. A refugee woman recalled how the rebels toured the town, announcing over loudspeakers how a 'demonic force' would attack them and that the rebels were going to resist them. 'Since we are going to resist every inch against a state drunk with racism, you people must evacuate this same night.'[34] With the guns booming in the near distance, few people dared to check the veracity of such claims by staying on.

Once out of Jaffna, thousands of refugees gathered in makeshift camps in Chavakachcheri and many converged in Kilali to escape from the peninsula altogether. Some travellers who managed to reach the South described Chavakachcheri as a 'vast gypsy camp site' with refugees sheltering under banyan trees.[35] As the army advanced, the Tigers transported many of these civilians across the lagoon, the passage now free of charge as the rebels were keen to encourage the exodus. When they arrived on the mainland, the civilians were transported in tractors to shelters prepared to house them.[36] The Wanni was steadily turning into a haven for desperate people from Jaffna, its camps filling with thousands of hapless souls.

The evacuation of the bulk of the Jaffna population was a significant political and military victory for the Tigers. It secured for the LTTE its revenue and recruitment base and denied the government the control of the Tamil population. The government was mainly in control of real estate. The civilians who were necessary to turn the military victory into a political triumph were gone.

An expanding war

Furthermore, the rebels' military response also showed that even though they had no answer to the government's onslaught they were still a potent force. The battle for Jaffna had not been as sanguinary as expected in some quarters, but it had still cost the lives of over 300 soldiers with nearly a 1,000 wounded.[37] Several armoured vehicles had also been damaged, while one of the Mi24s had received a mauling. However, these were minor concerns compared with the rebels' ability to bring the war to areas outside the North.

Their most ambitious effort, however, went awry. While the army launched its probing attacks in the peninsula, Prabhakaran unleashed his cadres on the string of army camps that defended the 'border villages' in the north-east. On July 28, a force of over 500 heavily armed LTTE cadres moved out of their bases in the jungles near Mullaithivu to attack the military camps in the Weli Oya area: the Kokkuthuduwai, Jayasinghepura, Janakapura and Kokilai army camps. This, however, proved to be a catastrophe for the Tigers. Tipped off by an informant, the army was waiting for them. The hunters were ambushed. With the element of surprise lost, the Tigers suffered horrendously, battered by artillery and mowed down by small arms. Shattered by the rude surprise, the rebels tried to flee through the jungle only to be harried by the air force. A large group of them that gathered on the beach was attacked and scattered by bombers, while naval gunfire pounded them from the sea. It was as a one-sided battle as one could hope for. The army recovered the bodies of 182 rebels, many of them mere children. The number that died in the jungle from air force attacks and wounds or the numbers that suffered injuries were not known, but it was estimated that up to 300 may have perished. The army suffered little: Only two soldiers were killed and 22 wounded.[38]

It was a morale-boosting victory for the army and a shattering defeat to the rebels, their biggest reverse since the failure to capture Elephant Pass in 1991. But the rebels had better luck with later attacks in the East. By the end of October, the Tigers had shot and hacked to death more than 120 civilians in the Ampara, Polonnaruwa and Moneragala Districts.[39] More alarmingly, they also brought the war to the capital, again.

122 A new regime, a new war

In August, not long after the Weli Oya debacle, a suicide bomber set off a powerful explosion outside the office of the chief minister for Western Province, killing 23 people and wounding nearly 50. Colombo was jolted again, the city bracing for more attacks.[40] Then in the early morning of October 20, a group of Tiger cadres in battle fatigues sneaked into the Kolonnawa refinery and blew up six oil tanks storing diesel, kerosene and aviation fuel. Another group fired mortars at the Orugodawatta crude oil storage facilities, destroying two more fuel tanks.[41] On December 11 1995, a female suicide bomber blew herself up outside the army headquarters, killing 11, while on January 31 1996 the Tigers struck again in Colombo, setting off a bomb at the base of the Central Bank building, killing 91 and injuring nearly 1,400.[42]

In Jaffna too, things were not going all that well for the army. The army had definitely scored a major victory by occupying the peninsula, but it was also being forced to spread itself thin on the ground. Civilians returning to the Wanni from Jaffna in early 1996 told of many localities in Valikamam without the presence of the army.[43] The rebels had also left a number of cadres in the peninsula to cause as much mayhem as they could. Soon, they also began to infiltrate the peninsula. Crossing the lagoon in small numbers from their safe haven in the Wanni, they joined the few cadres still operating in the peninsula and began operations. As early as March 18 1996, 18 new recruits from the Gajaba Regiment died when their tractor was attacked with an IED in Mallakam within the Valikamam area. Twenty-two others were wounded.[44] In May 1996, an air force vehicle was fired on by unknown gunmen in Jaffna.[45] Again, in May (twenty-seventh), rebels fired at a motorcycle carrying two army personnel around 5 p.m. south of Kuppilan, killing one and wounding the other.[46] In June 1996, senior military officials were speaking of a group of around 30 Tigers who were roaming around in Valikamam, targeting military personnel.[47] On July 4, the Tigers raised the stakes, targeting a government minister. Housing Minister Nimal Siripala de Silva narrowly escaped a female suicide bomber, who blew herself up at a function attended by the minister. The Jaffna commander Brigadier Hamangoda and 26 others were not so lucky.[48] A few days later on July 15, a gun battle broke out between a large group of rebel infiltrators and the army at Sarasalai South in Thenmarachchi, killing 13 soldiers. The situation was so critical that artillery and mortar fire had to be called from nearby military bases, forcing the rebels to withdraw with their casualties.[49] By September, sporadic clashes between the army and the rebels were very frequent, with skirmishes and mine attacks taking place almost on a daily basis. Both sides suffered only minor losses in these confrontations, but they were sufficient to keep the army occupied and a large number of soldiers tied down in the peninsula.[50]

The rebels also kept up the pressure on the air and naval lifelines to Jaffna. On January 22 1996, they shot down a Mi17 transport helicopter with 39 troops aboard including seven officers. The helicopter was ferrying troops from Palali to Vettilakerni when it was targeted by rebels from a dinghy east of Point Pedro.[51] The helicopter crashed into the sea, the bodies of 16 of the slain washing ashore east of Point Pedro a few days later.[52] The Tigers also struck at sea. On October 16,, on the eve of the launch of Operation Riviresa, the Sea Tigers attacked and sank a cargo ship taking food to the North at the Trincomalee harbour, killing nine navy personnel.[53] On March 30, Black Sea Tigers rammed a Dvora between Vettilakerni and Chalai, sinking the vessel and killing 14 sailors including one officer. The Dvora was travelling from Kankesanthurai in a convoy which was attacked by up to 12 Sea Tiger boats. The navy claimed to have sunk three of the attacking boats.[54] On June 12, rebel frogmen gathered more scalps for the Sea Tigers when they blew up two navy coastal patrol craft anchored at Karainagar. Three sailors were wounded while two were reported missing.[55]

These were rude reminders of the complexity of the rebel threat which the capture of Jaffna had done little to undermine. However, the biggest headache for the government was that the conquest of Jaffna had indeed exacerbated one of its biggest problems – the problem of supplying troops in the peninsula.

Notes

1 Colombo's Peace Gesture to Tamils', *The Age*, 1.9.94.
2 'Taraki', 'LTTE Outlines Its Demands', *The Island*, 9.4.85, p. 12.
3 'Prabha's Tactic; Wait and See', *Sunday Times*, 16.7.95, p. 6.
4 Taraki, 'Jaffna First Policy Dominates Tiger Thinking', *The Island*, 31.10.93, p. 7.
5 Sunday Times Military Analyst, ''LTTE Resorts to Cloak and Dagger Exercises', *Sunday Times*, 22.1.95, p. 9.
6 Defence Correspondent, 'Temporary Setback Turns Raw', *Sunday Leader*, 30.4.95, p. 7.
7 Sunday Times Defence Correspondent, 'Thumpaneveli Flares up in Midnight Drama', *Sunday Times*, 1.1.95, p. 8.
8 Rohan Gunasekera, 'Army Officers Worried', *The Island*, 29.1.95, p. 1.
9 'Tigers Explode Truce', *The Sri Lanka Monitor*, British refugee Council, no.87, April 1995, p. 1.
10 Panduka Senenayake, 'Navy Bombard Sea Tiger Base', *The Evening Observer* 21.4.95, Inform Clippings, April '95 p. 8. (Inform newspaper

124 A new regime, a new war

clippings were monthly digests of newspaper articles from major Sri Lankan newspapers produced by the NGO Inform Group based at 5 Jayaratne Mawatha, Colombo, Sri Lanka).

11 The army did claim they found the body of a guerrilla after the army retaliated to an attack on defence lines at Vettilakerni. 'LTTE Attacks in North Repulsed', *Daily News*, 21.4.95, Insight Clippings April '95, p. 7.

12 Gamini Wijayaratna, 'Tigers Overrun East Army Base', *The Island*, 23.4.95, p. 1. According to Iqbal Athas, the army lost 28 dead and 45 wounded. The Tigers used Pasilans, 60mm mortars and arul grenades along with small arms. Iqbal Athas, 'The Fight Back'. The Ministry of Defence gave the final death toll as 28 killed and 45 wounded, saying that all those feared missing in action had returned to the camp after taking cover in the surrounding jungle. Daryl de Silva, 'Defence Ministry Confirms Final Tally at 28 Killed, 45 Wounded', *Daily News*, 24.4.95, Insight Clippings, April '95, p. 10.

13 Premalal Wijeratne and Rajika Jayatilake, 'All Unquiet on the Eastern Front', *Sunday Leader*, 14.5.95, p. 4.

14 'Ealam War III Toll: April 19 – May 27', *Sunday Times*, 28.5.95, p. 8.

15 Shamindra Ferdinando, 'Tigers Kill 27 Soldiers in Second Attack in EAST', *The Island*, 24.5.95, Insight Clippings, May '95, p. 8.

16 Iqbal Athas, 'A Grim Story', *Sunday Times*, 28.6.95, p. 9.

17 Military Analyst, 'Prabha's Tactic; Wait and See'.

18 'Tiger Rampage at Kelepuliyankulam', *Sunday Times*, 14.5.95, p. 5.

19 Iqbal Athas, 'The Fight Back'.

20 Iqbal Athas, 'The Avro Disaster and Oliver's Twist', *Sunday Times*, 7.5.95, p. 9.

21 Iqbal Athas, 'Pooneryn; the Scenario for Big Showdown', *Sunday Times*, 14.5.95, p. 9.

22 Ibid.

23 Sunday Times Defence Correspondent, 'Scotch Rumours on LTTE', *Sunday Times*, 21.5.95, p. 7.

24 T.D.S.A. Dissanayake, *War or Peace in Sri Lanka*, p. 123.

25 Defence Correspondent, 'The Mandaithvu Debacle', *The Island*, 2.7.95, pp. 6 and 7, Taraki, 'LTTE Demonstrates Its Sea Power Again', *The Island*, 2.7.95, pp. 6 and 18, Iqbal Athas, 'Mandaithivu Was a Sitting Duck', *Sunday Times*, 2.7.95, p. 9, The Tigers are also said to have removed the cannon from one of the tanks stationed at Mandaithivu. Defence Correspondent, 'United We Stand, Divided We Fall', *Sunday Times*, 9.7.95, p. 6.

26 Iqbal Athas, 'Battle for the East Hots Up', *Sunday Times*, 21.5.95, p. 9.

27 Sunday Times Defence Correspondent, 'All about the Air Force', *Sunday Times*, 18.6.95, p. 10.

28 Shamindra Ferdinando and Norman Palihawadan, '47 Terrorists, 29 Soldiers Killed', *The Island*, 24.10.95, Inform Clippings, October '95, p. 5.

29 Ravi Pathiravithana, *Guerrilla Warfare: Discussing the Use of Sri Lanka's Fleet of APV's and MBT's*, p. 16.

30 Munasinghe, *A Soldier's Version*, p. 148; *Sri Lanka Army 50 Years On*, pp. 528–9; Premalal Wijeratne and Sasanka Samrakkoday, 'The Final Countdown', *Sunday Leader*, 5.11.95, p. 8.

A new regime, a new war 125

31 Nirupama Subramanyam, 'Wounded Yet Ferocious', *India Today*, 15.12.95, p. 48 (46–55); Taraki, 'Game Plan for a Grand Slam', *The Sunday Times*, 3.3.96, p. 7.
32 Iqbal Athas, 'Leave Issue Alerts Forces', *Sunday Times*, 3.3.96, p. 7, Iqbal Athas, 'The Navel Op That Beguiled the Tiger', *Sunday Times*, 9.6.96, p. 7.
33 Ibid.
34 Quoted in 'Terror Road', *The Sri Lanka Monitor*, no. 93, Oct. 1995, The British Refugee Council, London, p. 2.
35 Ananth Palakidnar, 'Tigers Dig-in for 'Last stand' in Jaffna', *Sunday Observer*, 5.11.95, p. 1.
36 Iqbal Athas, 'Daring Jaffna Thrust a very Costly Effort', *Sunday Times*, 26.11.95, p. 7.
37 'Army Issues Comeback Call to Deserters', *Sunday Times*, 26.11.95, p. 1. By late November, the army announced a death toll of 322 soldiers and 10 officers with 972 soldiers and 42 officers wounded. The Tigers casualties were put at 1,600 killed and 3,750 wounded.
38 'Forces Hit Back Kill 218 Tigers', *Daily News*, 29.7.95, Inform Clippings, July '95, p. 11; Geoff Wijesnghe, 'LTTE suffers worst defeat in conflict', *Daily News* 29.7.95, Inform Clippings July '95, pp. 11–12.
39 Nirupama Subramanyam, 'Fight to the Finish', India Today, 30.11.95, p. 68 (inset) (64–69)
40 Norman Palihawadana and Shamindra Ferdinando, 'Bomb Blast in Colombo Kills 23, Nearly 50 Wounded', *The Island*, 8.8.95, Inform Clippings August '95, p. 1.
41 Premalal Wijeratne, Asgar Hussein, Pearl Thevanayagam and Sasanka Samarakkody, ' Colombo Crippled by LTTE', *Sunday Leader*, 22.10,95, p. 1.
42 LTTE Bombing of Central Bank, 31 January 1996', 'http://www.lankalibrary.com/phpBB/viewtopic.php?t=1592
43 Taraki, 'Game Plan for a Grand Slam'.
44 Iqbal Athas, 'Hardly Three Weeks Away', *Sunday Times*, 24.3.96, p. 9.
45 Defence Correspondent, 'Jaffna: signs of Sunrise', *Sunday Times*, 26.5.96, p. 8.
46 'Tigers Strike in Waligamam', *The Island*, 27.5.96, Inform Clippings, May '96, p. 6.
47 Iqbal Athas, 'The Navel Op That Beguiled the Tiger', *Sunday Times*, 9.6.96, p. 7.
48 Iqbal Athas, 'Elite US Commandos in Lanka', *Sunday Times*, 7.7.96, p. 7.
49 Shamindra Ferdinando, 'Tigers Kill 13 Soldier', *The Island*, 15.7.96, reproduced in Inform Clippings, July, 1996, p. 2.
50 Defence Correspondent, 'Quiet on the N-E Front', *The Island*, 22.9.96, p. 12.
51 'SLAF Helicopter Carrying 39 Shot Down by Tigers', *The Island*, 23.1.96, Inform Clippings January '96, p. 11.
52 'Nineteen Bodies of Helicopter Crash Victims Washed Ashore', *The Island*, 31.1.96, Inform Clippings, January '96.

126 A new regime, a new war

53 'Operation Sunray', *Sunday Leader*, 22.10.95, p. 4.
54 Shamindra Ferdinando, 'Fourteen Sailors Killed', *The Island* 31.3.1996, Inform Clippings, March '96, p. 9.
55 'Shamindra Ferdinando, Two Naval Craft Blown Up', *The Island*, 12.6.96, Inform Clippings, June '96, p. 3.

Chapter 8

The problem of the Wanni

With the fall of Jaffna, the government's attention now focused on the Wanni. The Wanni had seen little action since mid-1992, when the army ended the last of its major operations to degrade rebel power in the region. Now it loomed as the major Tiger stronghold, a vast contiguous territory over which the rebels had near-complete control. By the time the armed forces launched its assault on Jaffna, this rebel bastion had undergone a remarkable transformation with serious implications for the Security Forces' occupation of the Jaffna Peninsula.

Fortress Wanni

As explained earlier, the military operations to disrupt rebel activities in the Wanni in the early 1990s did little to erode their power. But an unintended consequence of these operations was the turning of the interface between rebel- and army-controlled Wanni into a fortified frontier with serious implications for future operations. This was the Forward Defence Line, a veritable modern replication of World War I battlefield conditions in late twentieth-century Sri Lanka.

As the name implies, the Forward Defence Line, or the FDL as it came to be known, was a defensive construction. It had been taking shape since the beginning of Ealam War II, with the gradual erosion of the army's presence in the Wanni, eventually becoming a line of demarcation between the territories controlled by the army and the LTTE. By late 1993, it had stabilised across northern Sri Lanka, running to the north of Vavuniya, from Malwathu Oya in the west to Mahakachchakodiya in the east. Nochchimoday, north of Vavuniya, was the last government-held post on the Vavuniya–Jaffna Road. The vast area of the Wanni beyond that was Tiger country.[1]

128   The problem of the Wanni

An army officer, Lt Colonel Raj Vijayasiri explains the configuration of the FDL:

> In the FDL concept, a bunker line surrounds the whole area. The bunkers are located every thirty to forty meters depending of the terrain. The area forward of the bunker line was mined and concertina wire was employed. A two-meter high earth wall was built in the gaps between bunkers. The bunkers were manned day and night by two to four soldiers. The command and control, fire support and logistic elements were located inside the bunker line.[2]

In the Jaffna Peninsula, a similar line had been constructed across the neck of the peninsula. Bulldozers had piled sand into a 2-metre-high wall running all the way from Vettilakerni on the coast to the Elephant Pass base. Two fences were erected in front of the wall, and the ground beyond the fences was liberally strewn with anti-personnel mines. Sentry points stood along the earth bund at regular intervals. Another defence line circumvented the Palali base, protecting it from rebel attacks and keeping the Tiger mortars well away from the airstrip.[3] Tall watchtowers studded its perimeter, giving the base the appearance of a fortress.[4]

Indeed, the FDL turned the entire rebel-held Wanni into a veritable fortress, marking its land frontier with a trench and bunker line. When the army advanced, the FDL moved forward, the bulldozers that cut through the scrub also digging up the trenches and throwing up earthen embankments. When the advance stopped and an area was occupied, the trenches sprouted bunkers at intervals and the entire line stabilised to form fresh, static, fortified line of defence. Behind this line, the army had its main bases, complete with long-range artillery that could provide fire support for the troops in the bunkers. The large bases at Gajapbapura, Thalladi and Vavuniya performed this function.

This was, no doubt, a rather ponderous way to conduct war. But for the army, the FDL was a valuable strategic and tactical tool. It provided a secure forward position from which the troops could launch offensive operations against enemy positions. It also helped the army to interrupt communications between the East and the North. The defence line cut through the land routes which the rebels used to move between the Eastern and Northern Provinces and impeded their supply operations. The FDL was also a cordon around Sinhala villages in the East and the North Central Province, which were of great strategic value to the Security Forces' operations.

The problem of the Wanni   129

But the FDL posed its own problems. Manning the long bunker line spread the army thin as thousands of soldiers were required to hold the static defences. It also posed problems for the soldiers' morale. The troops manning the forward positions often lived under trying conditions, always on the alert and experiencing poor living conditions in their crude dugouts. They frequently lacked necessities of all kinds, including first aid supplies and ammunition. Another problem was boredom – soldiers spending months at the frontlines without leave, following a monotonous routine of guard duties and patrols.[5] Such problems played havoc with the motivation of the frontline troops, placing them in a less than optimum condition for carrying out their duties.

To make matters worse for the soldiers, the FDL was also vulnerable to frequent attacks. Unlike the rebels, the army did not have the luxury of happening upon the enemy with little notice. Their major attacks often gave the game away, and the Tigers simply melted into the vast Wanni jungles. The Special Forces did carry out small group operations, but these were not substitutes for the large, noisy jungle bashings. On the other hand, the FDL provided the rebels with plenty of targets to attack to deplete the army's strength as well as divert attention from major operations. Often enjoying the element of surprise, the rebels could pick vulnerable places in the bunker line or pounce on patrols to launch frequent pinprick attacks to keep the soldiers on their toes, bleeding them and drawing them into a war of attrition. Occasionally, these attacks were carried out on a larger scale as well-coordinated and organised operations aimed at causing maximum destruction. Such attacks often took place during major military operation elsewhere, to distract the army from their main focus.

The most vulnerable section of the FDL was in the East. There the FDL cut through the Tigers' passage between the North and the East, the heavily guarded Sinhala settlements adding to the impediments to the rebels' movements. It also gave the area greater strategic importance, inviting some of the deadliest rebel ambushes and assaults. One of the biggest attacks on this part of the 'frontier' came on July 25 1993, on the tenth anniversary of the 1983 riots. In a well-planned and coordinated attack, the Tigers overwhelmed the Janakapura army camp. The rebels penetrated the defence perimeter of the camp at a time when a considerable number of the soldiers were out on ambush duties and overran the camp in the space of three hours. Surprised, the soldiers offered little resistance, many being gunned down during a mad scramble to escape. The official death toll was 24 with 18 missing. Again, the Tigers kept the nearby Kokkuthuduwai and Kovil Point camps occupied by diversionary attacks.[6] Arms and equipment worth Rs 50 million were also captured by the rebels. The captured weapons and equipment included 44 T56 rifles, one machine gun, four RPG launchers, three mortars, two tractors, one motorcycle and a bulldozer.[7]

Wanni and the A9

Thus, by the time Jaffna was captured, the Wanni had turned in to a near-impregnable rebel stronghold separating Jaffna from the government-controlled south of the island. What the capture of Jaffna did was to worsen this physical isolation of the peninsula from the South caused by this consolidation of rebel control of the Wanni. On the one hand, the Tigers were now in greater strength than ever before in the Wanni astride the A9. On the other hand, the number of soldiers needed to be supplied in the North had increased markedly with the capture and occupation of Jaffna. By early March, there were nearly 70,000 troops stationed in the peninsula.[8] It placed an increasing burden on the already overworked air force and navy. In the five years leading up to 'Operation Riviresa', the average annual flying hours for the air force flights operating between Jaffna and the South had clocked 14,000 hours annually. After Riviresa, it jumped to 22,500 hours, a substantial increase.[9] The air force had even hired private AN 24s flown by Kazakh pilots to maintain the air bridge to Jaffna.[10] With the Tigers acquiring AA missiles and the Sea Tigers a constant menace, such supply runs were becoming increasingly risky. The crushing expense of keeping the lifeline open was also a drain on the government's already-lightened purse.

There were several options now for relieving this pressure. One was to open the Jaffna–Kandy Road, by pushing north from Vavuniya or south from Elephant Pass. Another option was to open an MSR along the Weli–Oya–Kokkuthuduwai–Alampil–Mullaithivu–Puthukkudiyuruppu–Pranthan–Elephant Pass axis in the east. The third alternative was to push along the Mannar–Pooneryn road in the west. The problem with all these options required large-scale operations that would tax the resources of the already-stretched Security Forces. Any of these options required a major military undertaking in the Wanni. But tackling the Wanni was a daunting prospect. The army had absolutely no presence in the Wanni except on the coast and along the FDL in the south. To the north, there was Elephant Pass and Pooneryn, while to the west was the camp at Thalladi (and the military presence on the island of Mannar). In the east, Mullaithivu stood as the only military base between the peninsula and Weli Oya. To the south, the army's Forward Defence Lines started from Paymaduwa to the south-west of Vavuniya and extended north-eastwards, in an axis that included Chettikulam and Puvarasakulam until it reached Nochchimodai to the north of Vavuniya on the Vavuniya–Elephant Pass road. Here it curved south-eastwards, encompassing Mamaduwa and Mahakachchikodiya and Kudakachchikodiya. This 80 km bunker line then ran into the line of fortified Sinhala villages that included Padaviya and the Weli Oya settlements.[11]

The army, however, had reasons to be optimistic about undertaking operations in the Wanni. The battle for Jaffna had shown that the LTTE was no match for the army in conventional fighting if the army brought massive force to bear on the rebels. A major offensive in the Wanni was likely to repeat this success. There was also the feeling that the rebels were scraping the barrel in terms of manpower. 'Many of their cadres are teenagers now,' a military official told *Jane's Intelligence Review*. 'They have lost many of their adult fighters, especially mid-level leaders.'[12] The army spokesman had even declared that the rebel supremo Prabhakaran was 'nervous', ordering his cadres to attack any target out of sheer desperation.[13]

There were also other reasons for the Security Forces to be confident. Since Riviresa, their conventional capabilities had increased. In late 1995, three Mi24s had been purchased along with three Antonov AN-32B transports. In 1996, six Kfir aircraft and four more Antonovs were purchased along with four more Mi24s.[14] The Kfirs were equipped with two 30mm cannons and air-to-ground weapons including bombs, rockets and even missiles. These added substantially to the offensive capability of the air force.

The main problem was manpower. Despite repeated attempts to raise the numbers of Security Forces, the army had not succeeded in persuading enough young men to fill the ranks. In November 1995, the need for recruits was so great that the army announced they were to recruit 10,000 fresh troops who were to be sent to replace the dead and wounded soldiers in the North after being given a crash course of eight weeks instead of the normal four months. An amnesty was also issued to deserters to enable them to rejoin the army.[15] But whether the numbers were there or not, the army had to make a move to reopen the road to the Wanni. It cost too much to keep it closed. The preference seemed to be for the approach up the eastern coast, where Mullaithivu formed a convenient halfway point. The camp could be used as an anchor for the advance to or from Elephant Pass.

But before the army could make a move, the rebels struck. The blow fell on Mullaithivu.

Mullaithivu, Sath Jaya and Edibala

After the fall of Jaffna, the Tigers had been looking for a way to redeem their lost prestige, especially in the eyes of the Tamil diaspora which had become a major source of financial and moral support, and dispel the growing belief that they were a spent force. True, they had managed to remove the bulk of their forces, their military hardware and, very importantly, a large portion of the population of the peninsula to the Wanni, but all that could not hide the fact that they had conceded Jaffna. It was imperative that they retook Jaffna if they were to achieve their goal of Ealam. But that was clearly in the distant future. Before that, they had to regain some respect. A big military victory could reverse their fortunes.

Mullaithivu was a perfect target. The Mullaithivu camp had begun as a small establishment in the late 1970s, but by mid-1990s it had expanded to become the base for a brigade, spreading over a large area encompassing the former Mullaithivu town which had been abandoned by now. The camp measured about 5 km north–south and 2.5 km across with a perimeter about 15 km long. To the east, the camp was bounded by the sea and to the west by an open lagoon area. To the north and the south spread a landscape of secondary scrub jungle and palm trees. In July 1996, the camp was home to two infantry battalions supported by a troop of artillery. The camp also had a few naval personnel who operated a ground-based radar that covered the seafront.

The base was important for the military. Since it was the only military base located on the eastern coast, it could monitor the Sea Tiger activities and give early warning to the naval convoys that went past this area on their way to and from Jaffna. The navy could use it in an emergency as a supporting base. It was also important to the military as a staging base if they were to launch operations inland.

On July 18, the Tigers launched a massive attack code named 'Unceasing Waves' on the camp and breached the defence lines. As the garrison struggled to hold on to parts of the camp, the government dispatched heli-borne commandos as reinforcements, landing them at Alampil about 4 km south of Mullaithivu. By the time the commandos reached the camp amidst heavy resistance on the twenty-fifth, the battle was over. The relief column found a scene of utter destruction and desolation. The camp was flattened and the smell of death hung everywhere. As they surveyed the scene in amazement, they were joined by a handful of survivors. Eleven soldiers had saved themselves by hiding in a well, while a few others had taken refuge in the jungle. These seemed to be the only soldiers to have come out of the maelstrom alive.[16]

The problem of the Wanni 133

The final death toll is obscure. The rebels claimed to have killed over 1,200 soldiers. The official death toll from the government stood at fewer than 500, while other sources put it at around 1,500, more than the losses for the whole of 1995.[17] This may be too high as according to the government there were only 1,407 personnel in the camp at the time of the attack.[18] Apart from the few soldiers who joined the relief column and a few dozen who made the long trek through the jungle to reach Weli Oya, there were no survivors.[19]

The government later gave the figures at over 700 killed. The deputy defence minister said that 415 soldiers whose bodies had been handed over to the G.A. Kilinochchi had been classified as 'missing in action'. The government also claimed to have killed 1,500 rebels. Forty-three survivors had also made their way to different camps. The Tigers gave their casualty figures at 275 'boys and girls'. They claimed to have captured two 122mm artillery pieces with a range of 30 km. Independent sources said up to 1,000 rebels were killed or wounded during the operation.[20] According to the army, the rebels also took about 1,000 shells for the 122mm artillery pieces along with three Buffel armoured vehicles.[21]

It was the biggest defeat for the army in the Ealam war. It showed that the Tiger was far from tamed and that the end of the war was a long way off.

The army's retaliation came the following day. It took the form of a massive assault southwards from Elephant Pass in the direction of Kilinochchi. Code named 'Sath Jaya', the operation was a retaliatory strike which also doubled as a potential drive to reopen the A9.

Paranthan fell on the twenty-eighth, but the going became tough after that. The rebels resisted fiercely and the troops were brought to a halt outside Kilinochchi on August 8. They resumed the advance again on September 22 in the face of ferocious counter-attacks and finally succeeded in capturing the town on the twenty-sixth by performing a pincer movement. By then, the rebels had vanished. The army entered Kilinochchi on the twenty-sixth to be greeted by a town deserted by all except a few stray dogs.[22]

But the Tigers were not giving up their Wanni capital easily. On January 9 1997, they launched a fierce counter-attack, unleashing about 2,000 cadres on the Elephant Pass and Paranthan Forward Defence Lines. The defences at Paranthan were breached, while a diversionary attack was made on Elephant Pass. The heavy artillery at Paranthan was particularly in danger of being captured by the rebels. The situation was so critical that the commandos of the air mobile brigade had to be airlifted from Batticaloa, where they were conducting operations, while thousands of troops were also rushed in from camps in Jaffna. The troops from Kilinochchi also joined the fray. The reinforcements enabled the embattled soldiers at Paranthan to finally beat off the attack. Again the toll was heavy. The army lost 223 killed and over 400 wounded, while the Tigers admitted to losing 170 killed. The army also lost a substantial part of their armoury at the Kilinochchi–Paranthan complex. The Tigers claimed to have captured three 120mm mortars, three .50 machine guns and hundreds of automatic rifles along with as much ammunition as they could carry while destroying two 130mm guns and nine 122mm guns. The army claimed they destroyed the guns themselves to prevent them from falling into enemy rebel hands.[23]

The army did not make further incursions into the Wanni until the following year. In February 1997, they went on the offensive again, launching 'Operation Edibala'. The operation linked Mannar with Vavuniya. The FDL that defended the predominantly Sinhala villages in the Anuradhapura and Vavuniya districts had left a big gap to the west, between the defence line and the army base at Thalladi. Much of this area was occupied by the Wilpattu National Sanctuary, but the reserve was also a safe haven for the rebels as well as a corridor for them to approach the Sinhala villages in north-eastern Anuradhapura. Operation Edibala closed this gap of about 60 km by capturing the remaining extent of the Vavuniya–Mannar road. About 20,000 troops broke out of their defence lines in Puvarasakulam under cover of heavy artillery fire and advanced towards Mannar. Compared with Sath Jaya, this was a cakewalk. The most serious response of the LTTE came when they shelled Vavuniya town for two consecutive days on February 9 and 10, using their newly acquired long-range artillery from Mullaithivu, killing two policemen. The attacks also forced the air force to move its base from Vavuniya to Anuradhapura.[24]

The capture of the highway ended 12 years of Tiger dominance in the region. It also meant that supplies could now be moved by land instead of sea, thus freeing the navy from having to escort cargo ships.[25] It also brought the army closer to establishing that elusive MSR along the Mannar–Pooneryn axis. Following Edibala, the coastal belt between Halawatha and Puttalam was declared a no-go zone. This strengthened the gains of Edibala by obstructing sea-borne rebel infiltration.[26]

Operation Jayasikurui

After the capture of Kilinochchi, speculation was rife about a big military push to link Vavuniya with Kilinochchi. Despite the loss of

Mullaithivu and the high price paid for Kilinochchi, there was still a surfeit of optimism in government circles. The armed forces now stood at around 95,000 including recalled reservists. The government had also spent heavily on weapons in 1996–97, purchasing an additional 15 main battle tanks from the Czech Republic and 14 patrol craft (nine Super Dvoras from Israel and five Trinity Class ships from the US) and another medium-size landing craft from China. More APCs (BTR80) and 152 mm guns were also expected shortly from China.[27] The Tigers, despite their recent performance in the Wanni, were not believed to number more than 6,000.[28] The lack of serious resistance to Operation Edibala was also seen in defence circles as an indication that the rebels were desperately weak.[29]

The big push finally came on May 17. Code named 'Operation Jayasikurui' or 'Victory Assured', it involved a northwards thrust along the A9 towards Kilinochchi by nearly 20,000 troops belonging to the Fifty-Fifth and Fifty-Third Divisions. The Fifty-Fifth had been raised specifically for this campaign. It included the Commando, Special Forces and Airmobile Brigades. The Twenty-Third was pulled out of Jaffna to be redeployed. The troops also included a contingent of naval troops trained in guerrilla warfare.[30]

Initially, the advance was along two axes: the Fifty-Fifth Division advanced northwards along the A9, while the Fifty-Third broke out of the defences in Janakapura in the Weli Oya area and moved in a north-westerly direction towards the Puliyankulam–Mullaithivu road.

The operation had all the hallmarks of previous incursions into the Wanni. It was another 'jungle bashing operation' but in far greater strength than ever before. Along with the advancing columns went a fleet of earth moving machines, many of which had been acquired for this operation. They cut through the scrub, clearing a path for the armour and the infantry to advance. The Fifty-Fifth Division moved in two columns, about half a kilometre on either side of the A9, avoiding the road for fear of landmines.[31] As the troops advanced, artillery began pounding enemy targets in the Wanni from the army's bases in Vavuniya, Weli Oya and Kilinochchi. In the sky, surveillance and ground-attack air-craft circled, watching for signs of enemy presence.

The operation began promisingly, the columns advancing briskly in the first few days. But soon resistance began to stiffen, the rebels counter-attacking fiercely, launching a series of counter-attacks code named 'do or die', using large numbers of troops. It was not until August 6 that the troops from Fifty-Third and Fifty-Fifth Divisions were able to finally link up about 2 km south of Puliyankulam.[32] By then, the Tigers' strategy

136 The problem of the Wanni

was becoming clear. They were not going to melt into the jungle as in the case of previous army incursions into the region. Instead, they were going to bleed the army dry, exacting a heavy toll in lives and hardware as they fell back gradually. They were also aiming to strengthen themselves by capturing as much booty as they could.

The soldiers inched ahead. Puliyankulam railway station, slightly to the west of the town, was captured on August 20 after fierce hand-to-hand fighting. The railway station was found to be completely stripped of anything useful, the Tigers removing all the rails and sleepers to build their defences.[33] It was not until November that the army was finally able to claim the town.

Rebel resistance now centred on Mankulam. And as the army struggled to manoeuvre around the town, the rebels now made a surprise move. Early morning on February 1, they attacked Kilinochchi. Led by at least one captured tank and armoured personnel carriers, along with suicide cadres, they stormed the defence lines from the east, west and the south. Despite heavy resistance from the army, they pushed the troops back from the defence lines, capturing the Kilinochchi town itself. The army admitted to pulling back 1.5 km, but in reality they gave more ground, ceding the entire town area to the rebels. They also claimed to have thwarted an attempt by the rebels to capture a 130mm artillery piece.[34] In an attempt to neutralise the army's firepower, the Tigers also launched a commando raid on the army artillery base at Iyakachchi in Jaffna. The army reported the attack as thwarted with all 12 infiltrators killed, but the infiltrators managed to damage the 200-foot communication tower.[35] The army was still fighting to regain the lost defences a week later, facing stiff resistance from the rebels who rained mortar and artillery fire on them. According to the army, a 4 km area between the two sides had become a no-man's-land.[36] The rebels remained in the captured southern defences of the complex, the captured defence lines giving them the advantage of keeping the area under army control under surveillance, which enabled them to direct intermittent artillery and mortar fire on the army defences.[37] They also used the captured defence lines as launching pads for artillery strikes on Paranthan and Elephant Pass. Ironically, the defence lines built with heavy concrete to withstand rebel artillery fire now thwarted the army and the air force from destroying them.[38]

To the south, Jayasikurui troops continued their attempt to encircle Mankulam, but as at Puliyankulam, they were prevented by heavy resistance from completing the pincer. It was not until September 30 that the army was finally able to claim the town. A two-pronged attack closed in on the town, soldiers from the eastern pincer wading through Kanakarayankulam River against stiff resistance.[39] Mankulam, the town that eluded the army for nearly a year, was finally in their hands.

The capture of Mankulam, however, came as a hollow victory. While the troops were still bogged down around the town, the Tigers claimed a bigger prize: Kilinochchi. On September 27, they launched Operation Unceasing Waves II, simultaneous attacks on Paranthan and Kilinochchi, penetrating the defences which included 30-foot earthen banks.[40] At the time of the attack, the defence perimeter stretched nearly 27 km north–south and 4–6 km east–west. The rebels picked their time well; the assault coincided with the withdrawal of the Special Forces Regiment, an infantry battalion and several main battle tanks and artillery pieces to Mankulam, weakening the defences at Kilinochchi.[41] And again, as usual, stealth preceded the storm; under cover of artillery and mortar fire, the rebels infiltrated teams of commandos who guided the attackers and helped direct artillery fire on gun positions and command posts. One or two captured tanks and an armoured vehicle filled with explosives were also used to blast holes through the defence.[42] Before long, the defence line between Paranthan and Kilinochchi was split and the strong points at Kilinochchi isolated and exposed to the enemy's fury.[43] By the morning of the twenty-eighth, the situation seemed hopeless. The troops, battered and demoralised, were ordered to withdraw to Paranthan. But the retreat soon turned into a rout. Reinforcements sent from Elephant Pass and Paranthan battled through heavy artillery fire, but to no avail. All hopes of holding on to Kilinochchi had evaporated by now. Tigers claimed to have destroyed two battle tanks, while another was destroyed by retreating troops.[44] Over 40 'soft skinned' vehicles also fell into the hands of the rebels along with some water bowsers. One resourceful artillery officer managed to save three 120mm mortars while blasting their ammunition. A few armoured cars were also saved.[45]

The government issued conflicting casualty figures.[46] But it was clear that the army had met with a crushing defeat, even more devastating than the defeat at Mullaithivu. An army survivor who escaped to Paranthan remembered how the road was so covered with dead bodies that it was hard for him to get through.[47] Again, the Tigers thought to have been on their last legs had stood up and delivered a shattering blow to the enemy.

Jayasikurui was finally terminated on December 2 1998. By then, with the Tigers back in Kilinochchi, the operation was all but dead. Now a new offensive called 'Rivibala' was launched towards Oddusudan, about

138 The problem of the Wanni

11 km from Mankulam on the Mankulam–Mullaithivu road. The objective was to create a buffer between the rebels and Mankulam and also to squeeze the Tigers further into the Mullaithivu jungles. By the end of the day, the town was in government hands; there was little resistance.[48] With 'Rivibala' major military operations ended in northern Wanni. The defence lines would remain more or less static for nearly a year. The attention now shifted to the western half of the Wanni, where more rude surprises awaited the army.

Ranaghosa

The western Wanni had been relatively calm since 'Operation Edibala' brought the Vavuniya–Mannar highway under government control. The FDL now extended all the way from just north of Vavuniya to Mannar with a break at Uyilankulam, where another entry point to rebel Wanni had been established.[49] Apart from occasional minor attacks on the FDL, there had been little fighting along this front. But with Jayasikurui petering out in northern Wanni, the army turned its attention to this sector, leading to another bloody yet ultimately futile Wanni venture.

The operations were code named 'Ranaghosa' and targeted both the seaboard and the interior. The attempt to open the A9 was now all but shelved; the focus was shifting to edging up along the western coast to open an alternative route through Pooneryn. The capture of the seaboard could also deny the Tigers a stretch of the coast vital for their supplies from the neighbouring subcontinent.[50] A thrust inland into western Wanni could also disrupt rebel operations in the areas of Tunukkai and Mallavi, which had become important centres of Tiger activity in the region.

'Operation Ranaghosa' was launched in several phases from March through September 1999. The army, in this instance, the Fifty-Third and Fifty-Fourth Divisions, brought a large area in western Wanni under government control. On the western coast, they moved up to Pallamadu on the A32, and from there the government's gains extended eastwards along a concave line running through Periyamadu to the west of Mankulam. The initial phases of the operation were relatively bloodless except for a sustained artillery barrage on the Thalladi camp during the second phase of the operation in mid-March. At the end of the artillery blitz, 11 soldiers lay dead while 15 others were wounded. A number of vehicles and a large quantity of supplies including fuel were destroyed.[51] As the troops progressed northwards, the resistance stiffened. The advance along the A9 was brought to a halt at Pallamadu.[52]

To the east of the A32, the army's attempts to move north of the Periyamadu tank in September were foiled by a fierce counter-attack. The Tigers showered them with heavy artillery and mortar fire. And as the artillery roared, rebel cadres engaged the enemy in close quarter fighting, forcing them to return to their original positions with heavy losses. More than 50 soldiers were reported killed; among them was a group of 15 soldiers who were encircled and wiped out. The rebels also captured more than 50 assault rifles, several RPG launchers and one PKMG along with thousands of rounds of ammunition. The bodies of the 15 men killed in the encirclement were later handed over to the ICRC.[53]

With the debacle at Periyamadu, the campaign to secure the western Wanni ended. The operations had captured large chunks of territory at relatively less cost than Jayasikurui, but they were still nowhere closer to achieving their main objective of opening a main supply route to Jaffna. Instead, they had occupied more territory that tied down large numbers of soldiers, police and airmen. The Wanni had become an expanse that swallowed men and equipment that the government could ill afford to lose.

The Wanni campaign – reflections

Why was it so difficult for the government forces to capture the Wanni?

The biggest challenge was the lack of control over the vast expanse of the Wanni itself. Since the intensification of the separatist struggle in the mid-1980s, there had been very little military presence in the Wanni heartland and since 1990 there had been absolutely no such presence. The only army bases were in the periphery and some, like Mullaithivu, were isolated. Lack of presence resulted in the lack of intelligence. The army knew little or nothing about what passed in the Wanni heartland. Even in the few peripheral bases, the troops had little dominance over the surrounding countryside. At Mullaithivu, their vision of the terrain had ended just beyond the barbed wire and they had paid dearly for this blindness. During Sath Jaya too, the army found it was groping in darkness. Demonstrating their lack of familiarity with the terrain, the advancing troops stuck to the axis of the main roads despite having tracked armour that allowed them to manoeuvre cross-country. During Jayasikurui, it resulted in the slow extension of a bulging salient along the axis of the A9, providing the rebels with long flanks that could be attacked. Almost all the rebel counter-attacks fell on these vulnerable flanks.

An officer, Lt Colonel Janaka Masakkara, was candid in his assessment. The Tiger, he said, knew the land very well, while the soldier had to advance with a map in one hand. He believed that about

70 per cent of the land must be known and familiar to the army before they can combat the enemy. 'But what happens is that before the soldiers can get a fair amount of knowledge of the ground, the enemy starts to attack.'[54]

The lack of intelligence of enemy positions meant that although they had superior numbers and firepower the Security Forces could not use them with optimum effect. To make matters worse, they also found that some of the new technology they had acquired was of little use. The army had acquired several mortar locating devices at the cost of US$11 million (Rs 660 million), but these were found to be of little use.[55] The army was also struggling with huge logistical problems. Holding the ever-lengthening FDL required large reserves of manpower. The army started with two divisions numbering nearly 20,000 men, but as the advance continued, these numbers began to be thinly spread. The tendency was to use less trained troops to hold the FDL on the flanks, while the hardened soldiers slogged it out at the spearhead of the advance. This was fraught with huge risks as the army found out very early in the campaign. On June 10 1997, the first rebel counter-attack on Thandikulam cut through the FDL manned by police and the navy, leading to massive losses in men and material. The problem became more and more acute the further the army advanced. In November 1997, it was reported that a large number of troops were being pulled out of the Valikamam sector in Jaffna to take part in the Jayasikurui campaign.[56] Predictably, rebel attack spiked in the peninsula following this.[57] During the Ranaghosa operations, many troops manning the defences on the Mannar–Chettikulam road were deployed in the western Wanni, replacing them with police.[58]

A more serious development was the increasing use of commandos and Special Forces to do the work of regular army troops. They were being deployed in large numbers very much like regular troops and to perform duties that were usually the work of regular troops. Inevitably, their quality declined. The result was heavy casualties to these troops.[59]

The problem of dealing with the extending FDL was also complicated by the mounting casualties, which chipped away at the army's numbers. The battles for Puliyankulam and Mankulam and the savage counter-attacks by the rebels exacted a high price. By mid-August 1997, about 600 soldiers including 14 officers had been killed while 3,200 were wounded.[60] By the end of the year, over 1,000 soldiers had been killed with more than 5,000 wounded with about half the A9 yet to be captured.[61] The toll increased as the battle for Mankulam progressed. The loss of Kilinochchi added to the toll.

The problem of the Wanni 141

The increasing casualties and the aimless slogging up the A9 also intensified desertion. By mid-1997, their numbers exceeded 10,000, including 200 officers.[62] These numbers increased in the next year. On October 15 1998, the army spokesman Sunil Tennekoon revealed at a cabinet press briefing that about 5,000 soldiers had deserted during the last three months alone. According to him, the overall number of deserters stood at 25,000 in May that year.[63]

The continued bloodletting at the front was also making it hard to recruit new soldiers. The army was holding military 'tattoos' in villages and country towns, but the response was dismal.[64] The army was planning to visit schools in a bid to entice school leavers to join the army with a plan to raise 15,000 troops to make up the shortfall.[65] Another recruitment drive in August 1999 fell far short of its mark. The army began interviews on August 16, hoping to recruit 10,000 soldiers, but after a couple of weeks only 1,500 had enlisted. The target was then reduced to 2,500. In frustration, the army blamed government politicians and foreign-funded NGOs for hampering recruitment drives by their emphasis on peace.[66] Hard pressed for troops, the government also issued amnesties to army deserters. By mid-1998 about 14,500 of these had surrendered.[67] Some deserters who volunteered to return, it was reported, had reportedly been sent to the third perimeter defence lines. Here they were detailed for cooking and other similar duties. It was even claimed that some who didn't like this treatment had chosen to cross over to the rebels![68]

While the army struggled with numbers and intelligence, the rebels enjoyed several advantages. They were at home in the terrain. They knew the land well and they also knew where the enemy was; compared with the army, the Tigers had few long-range guns, but they knew where to train them as the locations of the FDLs and the bases were no secret. They also made certain they gathered intelligence about army positions. Civilians entering LTTE-held areas were grilled for information, while infiltrated agents among civilians passed information about the army's defences. The army's Forward Defence Lines were constantly monitored for signs of troop movements.[69] In a sense, this was a replication of what the Tamil militants had done in the 1980s when they held the army under siege. Now similar tactics were being employed on a much larger scale for a similar outcome.

Thus, while the army stumbled blindly into the Wanni, the Tigers were able to assemble large forces close to the FDL to launch attacks. The information about the layout of camps and bases was also used to infiltrate commando groups to carry out surgical strikes behind enemy

142 The problem of the Wanni

lines during major attacks. This had happened at Pooneryn and Mullaithivu as well as during the numerous counter-attacks during Jayasikurui. Such tactics enabled the Tigers to make optimum use of their main ground attacks, using human wave assaults and their other great asset in the Wanni – their long- and medium-range artillery. These included the 122mm guns captured from Mullaithivu as well as the 120mm mortars taken from Pooneryn along with new weapons acquired from foreign sources through their overseas procurement network. This last was said to include two MBRLs and several 122mm and 130mm artillery guns.[70] The MBRLs had been used with some effect against troops in western Wanni, especially in the bombardment of the Tahalladi camp.[71] Many of the heavier guns were said to have been concealed in pillboxes to secure them against air attacks.[72] These 'stand-off' weapons increased the Tigers' ability to take on the army from a distance; they could also provide a much more devastating prelude to their mass attacks than their earlier arsenal of assorted mortars. However, it was still the mortar that caused the biggest concern for the army. They pummelled the advancing troops during both Jayasikurui and Rana Ghosa, inflicting the majority of the casualties.[73] The heavy dependence on mortars also underlined the availability of ample reserves of ammunition for these weapons. These stocks were boosted by the hijacking of a Sri Lanka-bound freighter carrying a load of mortars for the Sri Lankan army in May 1997.[74] Equipped with these, they could go on fighting for a long time, inflicting heavy losses on the enemy from a distance. Moreover, their commando attacks on army artillery positions also reduced their vulnerability to artillery fire. And despite the heavy losses suffered in battle, they still had plenty of cadres to sacrifice.

These factors combined to make the armour and the air power of the Security Forces of limited value. Crashing along blindly in close country, tanks and APCs were vulnerable to artillery and RPG fire of the rebels who knew where the enemy was. The Tigers were able to offset the advantage of air power by 'hugging' the enemy – maintaining close proximity to the enemy. This made it difficult for the small fleet of Kfirs to attack them for fear of hitting their own troops. It was a tactic they had practised since the battle for Elephant Pass in 1991, and it paid dividends again during the assault on Kilinochchi.[75] In addition, the Kfirs lacked the manoeuvrability required to engage ground targets closely. Helicopter gunships were able to do this, but the rebels countered them by deploying anti-aircraft guns that kept them at bay. By February 1998, the air force had lost two out of the original fleet of five Mi24s to ground fire and the air force was clamouring for at least

The problem of the Wanni 143

three more Mi24s.[76] In June 1998, one more Mi24 was lost, placing the remaining machines under severe strain.[77] In 1996 and 1999, the air force's wish was granted and two additional Mi24s and five Mi35s – export version of Mi24 – were purchased, but the threat to them still remained.[78]

All this placed the government's Wanni adventure on a precarious footing. A severe loss of men and material and an overextended FDL held by despondent troops was the inevitable outcome. It was only a matter of time before the whole enterprise unravelled, with shocking results.

Notes

1 Shamindra Ferdinando, 'Vavuniya Is Calm but. . . .', *The Island*, 26.9.93, p. 9.
2 Lt Col. Raj Vijayasiri, A Critical Analysis of the Sri Lankan Government's Counter insurgency campaign, Master's Thesis, US Army Command and General Staff College, Fort Leavenworth, Kansas 1999, p. 44.
3 Adele Balasingham, *Women Fighters*, pp. 115–16.
4 Franklin Raviraj, 'Inside Jaffna', *The Island*, 27.1.91, p. 9.
5 Rohan Gunasekera, 'Army's Dilemma in the East', *The Island*, 27.9.92, p. 13; 'Scribe', 'Carnival and War – For How Long?', *Sunday Times*, 20.6.93, p. 6; *Sri Lanka Army*, pp. 524–5.
6 The Sunday Times Military Affairs Correspondent, 'Janakapura's Day of the Jackal: Army Suffers Its Worst Defeat in Ealam War as Camp Run Over', *Sunday Times*, 1.8.93, p. 7.
7 'Weli Oya Death Toll Rising – 54 Now', *Daily News*, 27.7.93, pp. 1 and 16.
8 Paul Harris, 'Sri Lankan Forces Pushed to the Limit', *Jane's International Review*, 1.4.96.
9 Harry Gonetilleke, 'Operation Edi Bala – a Military or Political Imperative', *Weekend Express*, 9.3.97, p. 4. Goonetilleke attributes the figures to the air force commander.
10 Rohan Gunasekera, 'Tigers Lick Their Wounds but Prepare to Hit and Run', *Jane's Intelligence Review*, 1.2.96, v. 3, no. 2.
11 'Sumedha', 'Road to Mannar and the Key to Peace', *Sunday Times*, 2.3.97, p. 10.
12 Gunasekera, 'Tigers Lick Their Wounds but Prepare to Hit and Run'.
13 Daryl de Silva and Pearl Thevanayagam, 'Commandos Battle on to Mullaithivu', *Weekend Express*, 20–21.7.96, p. 1.
14 Blodgett, *Sri Lanka's Military*, p. 125, Senaratne, *Sri Lanka Air Force*, p. 191.
15 'Army Issues Comeback Call to Deserters', *Sunday Times*, 26.11.95, p. 1.
16 Paul Harris, 'Asia, Bitter Lessons for the SLA', *Jane's Intelligence Review*, 10.01.96.
17 Ibid.

144 The problem of the Wanni

18 Premalal Wijeratne and Winston de Valliere, 'Killing Fields of Kilinochchi', *Sunday Leader*, 11.8.96, p. 4.
19 Paul Harris, 'Asia, Bitter Lessons for the SLA', *Jane's Intelligence Review*, 10.01.96.
20 Amit Baruah, 'The Kilinochchi Stand-off', *Frontline*, 6.9.96, p. 131 (130–1). Sarath Munasinghe says 2 officers and 66 men reached Weli Oya through the jungle. Munasinghe, *A Soldier's Version*, pp. 156–7.
21 Amit Baruah, 'Operation Sath Jaya III', *Frontline*, 1.11.96, p. 61. (59–62). Other sources reported the army as disclosing the number of shells lost at 6,000. Premalal Wijeratne and Sasanka Samarakkody, 'Edibala Overshadowed', *Sunday Leader*, 23.2.97, p. 5.
22 Defence Correspondent, 'Black Tigers at Service Funerals', *The Island*, 8.10.96, p. 8.
23 Defence Correspondent, 'Paranthan Death Toll: 171 Soldiers and at least 171 Tigers', *The Island*, 12.1.97, p. 10 and 12; Shamindra Ferdinando, 'Army Admits Destruction of Long-range Guns', *The Island*, 12.1.97, p. 1; Iqbal Athas, 'The Paranthan Comeback', *Sunday Times*, 12.1.97, p. 7; Iqbal Athas, 'Not Losing Is also Winning: the Paranthan Poser', *Sunday Times*, 19.1.97, p. 7; Mendis, *Assignment Peace*, pp. 427.
24 Mendis, *Assignment Peace*, p. 429; Premalal Wijeratne and Sasanka Samarakkody, 'Edibala Overshadowed', *Sunday Leader*, 23.2.97, p. 5; 'Operation Edibala Enters Its Fourth Day', *Weekend Express*, 8–9.2.97, p. 1.
25 Premalal Wijeratne and Sasanka Samarakkody, 'Edibala: Mission Accomplished', *Sunday Leader*, 2.3.97, p. 4.
26 Premalal Wijeratne and Sasanka Samarakkody, 'Sea Tigers Put Forces between the Devil and the Deep Blue Sea', *Sunday Leader*, 20.4.97, p. 4.
27 *Sri Lanka Army 50 Years On*, p. 554.
28 The figures are given by the International Institute of Strategic Studies, quoted in Roy Denish, 'Death at Dark Midnight', *Sunday Leader*, 30.11.97, p. 8.
29 'LTTE Had Been Weakened Says Amy Chief', Sunday Times Interview with Army Commander Rohan Daluwatte, *Sunday Times*, 2.3.97, p. 7.
30 Mendis, *Assignment Peace*, p. 443.
31 Defence Correspondent, 'Driving a Stake into the Tiger's Heart', *The Island*, 18.5.97, p. 10.
32 Defence Correspondent, 'Jubiliation as Two Army Divisions Link up at Puliyankulam', *The Island*, 10.8.97, p. 10.
33 Shamindra Ferdinando, 'Heavy Tiger Losses in Wanni Offensive', *The Island*, 25.8.97, Inform Clippings, August '97, pp. 4–5; Roy Denish, 'Push and Pull for Puliynkulam', *Sunday Leader*, 31.8.97, p. 9, Defence Correspondent, 'Tigers in Do-or-die Stand at Puliyankulam', *The Island*, 4.8.97, p. 10.
34 'Taraki', 'Operation Checkmate in Killinochchi – LTTE Style', *Sunday Times*, 15.2.98, http://sundaytimes.lk/980215/taraki.html; 'Taraki', 'Changing Strategies and Kilinochchi Gamble', *Sunday Times*, 22.2.98, http://sundaytimes.lk/980222/taraki.html; Iqbal Athas, 'Credibility Crisis Hits Forces Gains', *Sunday Times*, 8.2.98, p. 9.

The problem of the Wanni 145

35 Shamindra Ferdinando, 'Over 200 Tigers, 20 Soldiers Die in Kilino-chchi Battle', *The Island*, 2.2.98, reproduced in Inform Clippings, Feb.1998, p. 1; P.S. Suryanarayana, 'The Battle for Kilinochchi', *Frontline*, 20.3.98, p. 60 (59–61). Another report says that it was artillery fire that damaged the tower. P. Karunakaran, 'LTTE Opens All Fronts', *Weekend Express*, 7–8.2.98, p. 7.

36 Shamindra Ferdinando, 'Stiff Resistance Despite Heavy Artillery Bombardment', *The Island*, 7.2.98, reproduced in Inform Clippings Feb, 1998, p. 2.

37 P.S.Suryanarayana, 'The Battle for Kilinochchi', *Frontline*, 20.3.98, p. 60 (59–61)

38 Roy Denish, 'Mirusuvil Massacre', *Sunday Leader*, 22.2.98, p. 7.

39 Roy Denish, 'Blackout in the Aftermath of a Fiasco', *Sunday Leader*, 18.10.98, p. 10.

40 Roy Denish, 'Ceaseless Waves' Swamp 'Assured Victory'', *Sunday Leader*, 11.10.1998, p. 8.

41 Munasinghe, *A Soldier's Version*, p. 171.

42 Vijayasiri, *A Critical Analysis*, p. 50.

43 'Kilinochchi Calamity: the Worst Debacle in 17 Years', *Sunday Times*, 4.10.98, http://sundaytimes.lk/981004/sitrep.html

44 'Kilinochchi Base Captured – LTTE', *Tamilnet*, 28.9.98, http://www.tamilnet.com/art.html?catid=13&artid=2112

45 Munasinghe, *A Soldier's Version*, p. 170.

46 The Ministry of Defence: KIA – 4 officers and 182 other ranks, MIA – 18 officers and 771 other ranks, WIA – 21 officers and 401 other ranks. 'MoD Issues Casualty Figures', Tamilnet, 8.10.98, http://www.tamilnet.com/art.html?catid=13&artid=2153. Before that, another military spokesman had given the figures of 632 killed and 432 wounded. The ICRC claimed they had handed over 600 bodies to the army. Iqbal Athas, 'Censorship Resurrecting the dead', *Sunday Times*, 11.10.98, http://sundaytimes.lk/981011/sitrep.html

47 Marwaan Marcan-Markar, 'Sleepwalkers and Slaughtered Sheep', *Sunday Leader*, 11.10.98, p. 8.

48 'Op Jayasikurui the Longest Ever Military Campaign Called Off', *Sunday Times*, 6.12.98, http://sundaytimes.lk/981206/sitrep.html

49 Marawaan Marcan-Markar, 'Crossing the Border', *Sunday Leader*, 7.3.99, p. 11.

50 Defence Correspondent, 'On the Road Again, This Time It's the Right One', *The Island*, 4.7.99, p. 8.

51 Iqbal Athas, 'Now, an Artillery War', *Sunday Times*, 21.3.99, http://sundaytimes.lk/990321/sitrep.html, Roy Denish, 'Tigers Pound Thallady Camp, *Sunday Leader*, 21.3.99, p. 13, D.B.S. Jeyaraj, 'Strategic Changes in Wanni', *Frontline*, 23.2.99, p. 59 (57–60)

52 Roy Denish, ' "Ready disorder" by Tigers Limits Army Advance', *Sunday Leader*, 4.7.99, p. 7.

53 Iqbal Athas, 'Rana Ghosa V Disaster Bares Tiger Build – up', *Sunday Times*, 19.9.99, http://sundaytimes.lk/990919/sitrep.html; Roy Denish, 'Army, LTTE Suffer Heavy Toll at Periyamadhu', *Sunday Leader*, 19.9.99, p. 11 (Athas says more than 50 killed and over 400 wounded.

146 The problem of the Wanni

Denish says over 100 killed and at least 700 wounded. He also says state radio had announced 660 wounded, Tiger casualties considered heavy but not known for certain.) Tigers claimed to have collected 20 SLA bodies and claimed only 19 of their cadres died. Tamilnet, 'SLA advance Thwarted – Vot', 12.9.99, http://tamilnet.com/art. html?catid=13&artid=3916; Defence Correspondent, 'Debacle at Periyamadu', *The Island*, 19.9.99, p. 9.

54 Wilson Gnanadass, 'The Northern Wasteland', *Sunday Leader*, 27.10.96, p. 4.

55 Roy Denish, 'Political Overtones in Military Appointments', *Sunday Leader*, 13.8.00, p. 4; Taraki, 'The Deepening Theatre of Operation', *Sunday Times*, 8.2.98, p. 10.

56 P. Karunakaran, 'Mullaithivu Debacle, Monsoon to Decide Jayasikurui', *Weekend Express*, 8–9.11.97, p. 1.

57 P. Karunakaran, 'Jayasikurui and Heroes Week', *Weekend Express*, 22–23.11.97, p. 1.

58 Taraki, 'Ealam War Growing More Complex', *Sunday Times*, 21.3.99, http://sundaytimes.lk/990321/taraki.html

59 Vijayasiri, *A Critical Examination*, p. 52. In one major debacle, the Tigers ambushed Special Forces troops used in this fashion on December 5 1997 beyond Puliyankulam. Over 150 troops, mostly commandos, were killed. See Iqbal Athas, 'Worst ever Commando Debacle', *Sunday Times*, 7.5.96, p. 9, Roy Denish, 'Troops Walk into Tiger Trap', *Sunday Leader*, 14.12.97, p. 5.

60 Shamindra Ferdinando, 'Tigers Targeting Tanks in Fierce Battle', *The Island* 21.8.97, Inform Clippings August '97, p. 3.

61 Roy Denish, 'Bloodiest Year at the Battlefront', *Sunday Leader*, 28.12.97, p. 9.

62 Premalal Wijeratne and Sasanka Samarakkody, 'Saga of Capturing Vessels Continues', *Sunday Leader*, 13.7.97, p. 4.

63 Zacki Jabbar, 'Army Deserters Stand at 5,000', *The Island*, 16.10.98, Inform Clippings, October '98, p. 14.

64 Marwaan Marcan Markar, 'Troopers Who Refuse to Charge', *Sunday Leader*, 10.5.98, p. 11.

65 'Army Turns to Schools for 15,000 Troops', *Sunday Times*, 3.5.98, Inform Clippings, May '98, p. 4; Chris Kamalendran, 'Commander: Army Will Go to Schools', *Sunday Times*, 10.5.98, Inform Clippings, May '98, p. 8.

66 Shamindra Ferdinando, 'Forces Recruit More Men, Criticise Politicians for Hampering the War Effort', *The Island*, 5.9.99, p. 1.

67 Jabbar, 'Army Deserters Stand at 5,000'.

68 Roy Denish, 'Desertion and Defection', *Sunday Leader*, 25.10.98, p. 13.

69 Rohan Gunaratna, 'Tamil Tigers Burning Bright', *Himal*, April 1999, p. 37 (34–9), Vijayasiri, *A Critical Analysis*, p. 50.

70 Rohan Gunaratna, 'LTTE Adopts Heavy Artillery', *Jane's Intelligence Review*, 1.6.01.

71 Iqbal Athas, 'Now, an Artillery War', *Sunday Times*, 21.3.99, http://sundaytimes.lk/990321/sitrep.html

72 Taraki, 'The Deepening Theatre of Operation', *Sunday Times*, 8.2.98, p. 10.
73 In early 1998, the army commander Sri Lal Weerasooriya revealed to visiting journalists that the Tigers were depending heavily on their mortars. P. Karunakaran, 'Claymore Claims Army and PLOTE Members', *Weekend Express*, 16–17.5.98, p. 6.
74 Gunaratna, 'Tamil Tigers Burning Bright', p. 34.
75 Roy Denish, 'Savage Onslaught on Key Camps', *Sunday Leader*, 8.2.98, p. 4.
76 Shamindra Ferdinando, 'Air Force Seeks More Copter Gunships', *The Island*, 15.2.98, p. 1.
77 P. Karunakaran, 'Mi-24 Crashes Killing Crew', *Weekend, Express*, 28.6.98, Inform Clippings, June '98, p. 5.
78 Blodgett, *Sri Lanka Military*, p. 125.

Chapter 9

The East in ferment

The East had always been a sideshow to the campaigns and battles in the North, but it was a sideshow with serious strategic significance. A considerable number of troops were required to hold it, and keeping the region under control while launching major campaigns in the North was a daunting task. As the battle for the Wanni raged, there was every sign that the government was losing the struggle for the dominance of the East.

If the government had lost much of its hard-won advantage in the province during late 1994 and early 1995, in the lead-up to and during the assault on Jaffna, the East had slipped further from their grasp, creating a strategic problem as serious as the need to open the MSR. During probing operations leading up to Operation Riviresa, the army had withdrawn large numbers of troops from the province, vacating a number of camps. These included several army detachments in the Thoppigala jungles used by elite forces as launching pads to intercept and destroy small rebel hit teams. Riviresa swallowed more troops. Before the operation, a recruitment drive had been launched, but the army had managed to secure only about 7,000 youths, still about 10,000 shorter than the number they needed.[1] As a result, more troops had to be called from the East. Accordingly, the army withdrew from the Kathiraveli, Mankerni, Patchenai, Vakarai, Pannichchakerni, Karadiyanaru and Kaddamuruvikulam in the middle of 1995.[2]

While the army marched into Jaffna, the East, now denuded of troops, beckoned the rebels. The Tigers now roamed freely in the hinterlands of the Batticaloa and Trincomalee Districts. This included the strategically important Vakarai to the north of Batticaloa, with its coastline that enabled the Tigers to move cadres and material in and out of the district. The Tigers now established themselves here in strength, turning it into one of their strongholds in the Batticaloa District. The military withdrawal continued in the following year as Operation Sath Jaya began to take its toll. As many as 44 STF and army camps were reportedly withdrawn from the north and west of Batticaloa to feed the operation.[3]

Impotent incursions

The Security Forces tried to stem the tide by making forays into rebel-dominated territory in the East. Between April 1995 and the end of 1996, they launched more than a dozen operations in the province, often using air support, the majority of them in Batticaloa and Ampara.[4] On January 17 1996, the commando and Special Forces regiments penetrated deep into enemy-held territory in the Thoppigala jungles in Batticaloa. This was the beginning of a series of such operations in the district. But, despite claims of rebel camps destroyed and large areas cleared, there were few real gains. For instance, the bases claimed to have been captured in Special Forces raid deep into the Thoppigala jungles in Batticaloa in January 1996 included the 'Karuna' camp with 20 huts and buildings and a 500-bed rebel hospital, but the casualty figures and captured items told the story. Only one soldier was killed with 33 wounded. Twenty-five Tigers were claimed to have been killed, but few arms or bodies were found. What was captured was mainly provisions, uniforms and vehicles.[5] A large number of trucks, vans and tractors were also destroyed in the operation.[6]

In late February 1996, the army claimed to have destroyed a rebel base at Mulaivadduvan, 28 km west of Batticaloa, killing at least 30 rebels, even though the rebels admitted to losing only 9. Again no bodies were found.[7] On March 3, the troops attacked the camp at Tharavikulam and found it vacated by the rebels, capturing only provisions, a generator, a TV set, two video decks, a roneo machine, two typewriters, a table fan, four lorry batteries and propaganda material.[8] The frustrating game of hide and seek continued. In July 1996, the Security Forces went on the offensive again in Batticaloa, launching 'Operation Sedapahara' to clear Vakarai. Heli-borne troops linked with two battalions landed by sea. They destroyed a number of rebel camps, but again the bulk of the rebel forces had withdrawn deep into the jungles.[9] The army was also given a stark reminder of the difficulty of clearing the East while the Wanni remained on the boil; the operation came to a premature end as many of the commandos involved in the operation had to be hastily airlifted to take part in the operation to rescue Mullaithivu.

It was clear that repeated attempts by Security Forces had failed to dislodge the rebels from the hinterland of the East, especially in the

150 The East in ferment

Batticaloa District. In Batticaloa, by March 1996, the army was in control only of the Batticaloa town with only one road link to the rest of the island – the MSR to Welikanda. Needless to say, this was becoming a favourite target of the Tigers.[10] The Maha Oya–Chenkaladi Road, opened during the 1992–94 period, was now again cut off while the Tigers roamed freely on either side of it. By early 1997, it was calculated that despite numerous raids by the Security Forces the rebels still maintained more than ten major camps in the Batticaloa District alone.[11] The Security Forces, plagued as they were by the lack of manpower, could only hope to harass them with frequent operations that had little scope for dominating the lost territory for any length of time. One military source was quoted as saying that hunting the Tigers in the East was like punching holes in a paper bag. 'We clear the rebels from one place and they just pop up somewhere else,' he explained.[12]

A deadly guerrilla war

Although the rebels avoided confrontation when the Security Forces were on the attack, in true guerrilla fashion they continued to engage the enemy at times and places of their choosing. The cost was high for the Security Forces. On March 11 at Wellaweli, a village about 25 km south of Batticaloa, the Tigers ambushed and killed 23 STF men including three officers.[13] On March 23, an army patrol was ambushed at Vantharamoolai, a village 14 km from Batticaloa town, killing 40 soldiers and injuring 15. The army patrol was 100 men strong and was from the Sittandi camp on its way to investigate a rebel build-up in Vanthalamolai on the MSR from Welikande to Batticaloa.[14] Two days later, the Tigers struck in Trincomalee, killing 15 volunteer troops on a patrol on the Pulmoddai–Kebithigollewa road. Three men were wounded while one was missing. In just two weeks in March 1996, 133 security men had been killed.[15]

Rebels continued to step up their attacks in the province, especially in the Batticaloa District. It was reported that they had sent three specialised attack groups to the province to engage in hit-and-run attacks.[16] On May 6, they ambushed an army patrol at Mylathenna in Punani in the Batticaloa District, killing 12 soldiers.[17] Six days later, the rebels killed 14 soldiers and wounded 13 more at Shanthiveli in Batticaloa District. On May 27, eight soldiers including an officer in a volunteer unit were killed when Tigers attacked an army detachment at Meegasgodella about 6 km west of Kallar.[18] Another 14 soldiers were killed and four wounded in an ambush at Jayanthiyaya, Welikanda, in the Polonnaruwa District on June 9.[19]

The East in ferment 151

As they tightened their grip on the province, the rebels also became bolder, attacking isolated camps in force as they had done in the Wanni in 1990. On December 11 1996, a large group of rebels estimated at around 500, including many female cadres, assailed the STF base at Pulukunawa about 19 km from Ampara town off the Ampara–Maha Oya Road. The base was garrisoned by about 140 men and also functioned as an artillery support base for operations in the surrounding area. The majority of the men were from the STF with a small contingent from the artillery regiment to work the piece of 85mm artillery that was in the camp. The Tigers overran the camp, killing 42 and wounding many more. The rebels claimed they had control of the camp for two and a half hours during which they completely destroyed the base. Among the booty they claimed were the 85mm artillery gun, a mortar, 70,000 rounds of small arms ammunition in addition to 165 shells for the artillery piece. They admitted to losing 26 of their cadres.[20]

The guerrilla attacks continued. About 1,500 rebel guerrillas were keeping nearly 30,000 Sri Lankan troops and police tied down.[21] And soon, the rebels upped the ante. On March 6 1997, a force of several 100 rebels attacked the army camp in Vavunathivu, on Buffalo Island in the Batticaloa lagoon. The camp was manned by about 250 soldiers of the Sixth Gajaba Regiment and the National Auxiliary Guard.[22] There were no heavy weapons except .50 machine guns and the camp possessed no tanks or APCs. The rebels blew up the bridge at Valairavu, the only link between the island and the mainland, to prevent reinforcement from arriving and made a sustained effort to overrun the camp till past midday. According to some officers, the assault, made in waves, was preceded by a heavy bombardment and an attack by suicide cadres on the defence lines. The bombardment was carried out with mortars as well as the 85mm cannon captured from Pulukunawa.[23]

The intensity of the rebel attack pushed the army from the first line of defence. With the fate of the camp hanging in the balance and a major debacle unfolding at the doorstep of Batticaloa town, the army was rallied by Captain Sudath Dabare. The officer, wounded in both eyes, went on fighting gallantly, and under his leadership the men held on till morning, even launching a counter-attack and capturing the first line.[24] Finally, the attack was repulsed but only when army reinforcements arrived in boats along with air force gunships and ground-attack aircraft. But the Tigers had exacted a heavy toll. When they finally withdrew, they left 63 soldiers and two junior officers dead and 105 wounded. Rebels admitted to losing 83 killed.[25] The army denied the rebels captured any weapons, claiming that after the battle they recovered two

RPG launchers, two 40mm grenade launchers, 15 T56 assault rifles, four T-81 rifles, ammunition, a canter truck and two tractors.[26]

The attack on Vavunathivu was accompanied by an audacious attack on the Three Brigade Headquarters in the centre of Batticaloa town. A barrage of mortar and artillery fire fell on the brigade headquarters, killing two female police officers and a policeman and wounding six other policemen.[27] Further north in Trincomalee too, the Tigers pounced on the same day. Early morning on the sixth, while their colleagues stormed Vavunathivu, a group of Black Tiger commandos infiltrated the perimeter fences of the China Bay air force base and approached the hangars where the aircrafts were parked. They opened fire with small arms and RPGs, setting alight a Y-12 and destroying it. Another group of Tigers began lobbing mortars from near a railway track outside the base. When army-sent reinforcements arrived, the Tigers had melted into the jungle, leaving four of their dead with suicide jackets still intact.[28]

The Security Forces reacted violently to these triple attacks. The military launched an air, sea and ground assault on Sea Tiger bases in Alampil and Chalai. The navy blasted them from the sea, the air force's Puccaras and Kfirs bombed them, while the army shelled them from camps in the Weli Oya area. Casualties among the rebels were not known.[29]

A 'liberated zone'

In the wake of Jayasikurui, the East sank further under rebel control. The STF pulled out of several camps in the interior. The Wellaweli camp was withdrawn to the Black Bridge in Chenkaladi. Many of the outposts were now manned by police. These men were 'combat trained', but they were no substitute for the STF or regular army. The government held on to the Habarana–Vaalachchenai road, but much of the Batticaloa District to the west and north of the lagoon and to the south up to the border of Ampara district was now more or less Tiger country, a 'Liberated zone'. The A5 from the Black Bridge in Chenkaladi up to Maha Oya was now a main supply route for the LTTE. This was quite similar to the situation in the Wanni, where the Tigers controlled a large swathe of territory, but unlike in the Wanni where the rebel-held territory was clearly demarcated by the FDL and the coast, the Tiger-controlled territory in the East was loosely defined by the jungle, partially government-controlled highways and the coast. This made it possible for the Tigers to infiltrate government-controlled territory which was also facilitated by the presence of a largely Tamil-speaking population in the more densely populated urban areas of government-held Batticaloa. This made even the Batticaloa

The East in ferment   153

town area vulnerable to area rebel attacks. In June 1997, the Tigers even dared to lob a few mortars in the direction of the ASP's office. The bombs only succeeded in killing an unfortunate farmer, but the attack underlined the rebels' ability to strike in the heart of government-controlled territory.[30] A few weeks later on August 24 1997, they struck again, firing three mortars at the army detachment in the municipal building in Batticaloa town itself, killing two soldiers and wounding 15.[31]

In the large expanse of territory under their control, the rebels had established a parallel government as they did in the Wanni and in Jaffna before its capture. They maintained tax collecting centres and police stations, raising revenue and administering law and order; the rebels were taxing the farmers, Rs 500 per acre in addition to a part of the harvest. A local journalist who visited Kokkadicholai found the rebels also actively engaged in civic work, building wells, ensuring school function and carrying out welfare programs. Tiger police stations and Kangaroo courts dispensed justice. Tigers' shrines to the dead were also proliferating. Still, the region functioned under a system of dual control, under the rebels and the government. In the schools was taught the Sri Lankan state's version of history as well as the Tigers' version.[32] The 'liberated' East was also proving to be a more fertile recruiting ground for the rebels. The displacement and destitution caused by the military operations was pushing more and more young people into the fold of the Tigers, who had now effectively become the government in the area.[33] While the Tiger cemeteries proliferated, so did the young men and women who would end up entombed in them.

In this 'liberated zone', Vakarai was an area that the Security Forces were desperate to clear. The Tigers were using Vakarai to send reinforcements and supplies to the North, and as Operation Jayasikurui continued to struggle against stiffening rebel resistance, stemming this flow became important. On June 22 1999, 'Operation Indra Sera', a joint army, navy and air force operation, was launched to capture the region. Finally, the Security Forces announced the capture of the strategic town, destroying the port maintained by the rebels at Vakarai along with a hospital and several other minor camps. The Tigers offered initial resistance but withdrew into the jungle after blowing up the Vakarai hospital and removing whatever they could.[34] The Security Forces claimed to have killed 33 rebels. This time the government forces were there to stay; the government announced plans to open services in the area in a bid to restore formal government control.[35]

The army remained in Vakarai, setting up camps and distributing relief to the civilians. On September 1 1999, they extended their control

154 The East in ferment

to Kathiraveli to the north. This time the Tigers withdrew without a fight. But they remained a potent threat. On August 9 1999, a Black Tiger cadre entered the Vakarai camp, posing as a civilian seeking relief supplies, and blew himself up, killing Major G. B. J. Karunanayake and wounding three others.[36]

As the new millennium approached, there was little appreciable change in the situation in the East. The vast hinterland to the west of Batticaloa and the south of Ampara still remained Tiger country, only occasionally penetrated by Security Forces' operations. These operations did little to break their hold on the area as the Security Forces always withdrew back to their bases. The loss of Vakarai was a significant blow to the Tigers, but the army's hold on the town was still not firm. The rebel attacks also continued throughout the province, taking a steadily increasing toll. On occasion, their attacks could still extend to the border villages. On September 18 1999, following an air force bombing raid of Pudukuduirippu, an estimated 75 rebels hacked and stabbed to death 54 Sinhalese villagers in Gonagala settlement of 31 Colony in the Ampara District. The Tigers came to the village early in the morning and went from house to house hacking and stabbing people.[37] The attack highlighted another more brutal dimension to the precarious security situation in the region.

Notes

1 Sunday Times Defence Correspondent, 'Pressure on the LTTE Chief', *Sunday Times*, 27.8.95, p. 9.
2 Shamindra Ferdinando, 'Tigers Vacate Taravikulam Camp', *The Island*, 22.1.96, Inform Clippings, January '96, p. 10.
3 'Taraki', 'Government Clings on Despite Stiff Opposition', *Sunday Times*, 8.9.96, p. 7.
4 Seanaratne, Sri Lanka Air Force, vol. 1, pp. 182–200 lists 14 operations in the East, the majority of them in Batticaloa and Ampara. These were only the operations in which the air force took part.
5 Mendis, *Assignment Peace*, pp. 376–8. Another report says the hospital had 200 beds. No bodies seemed to have been found. Srian Bulathsinhala, 'Troops Smash Tiger Bases in Thoppigala', *The Island*, 21.1.96, Inform Clippings January '96, p. 9.
6 Norman Palihawadana, 'LTTE Cadres Flee Thoppigala Camps', *The Island*, 22.1.96, Inform Clippings January '96.
7 'Over 50 Tigers Killed in N-E Clashes', *Daily News*, 4.3.96, Inform Clippings, March '96, p. 2.
8 Trincomalee group correspondent, 'Troops Destroy Camp, Capture Large Haul of Equipment', *Daily News*, 5.3.96, Inform Clippings, March '96, p. 2.

The East in ferment 155

9 'Troops Overrun Five LTTE Camps', *The Island*, 12.7.96, Shamindra Ferdinando and Norman Palihawadana, 'Nine More Terrorists Killed, Vakarai Town Captured', *The Island*, 13.7.96, both reproduced in Inform Clippings, July 1996, p. 1.

10 Iqbal Athas, 'Leave Issue Alerts Forces', *Sunday Times*, 3.3.96, p. 7.

11 Premalal Wijeratne and Sasanka Samarakkody, 'Tigers Brace for Big Forces Op', *Sunday Leader*, 27.4.97, p. 7.

12 Paul Harris, 'Sri Lankan Forces Pushed to the Limit', *Jane's International Review*, 1.4.96.

13 Shamindra Ferdinando, 'Twenty Three STF Men Killed in Terrorist Attack in East', *The Island*, 12.3.96, Inform Clippings March '96, p. 4.

14 Sunday Times Military Correspondent, '40 Troops Killed by LTTE in Batti', *Sunday Times*, 24.3.96, Inform Clippings March '96, p. 7.

15 Norman Palihawadan and Shamindra Ferdinando, 'Fifteen Soldiers Killed in East', *The Island*, 26.3.96, Inform Clippings, March '96, p. 8.

16 'Taraki', 'Government Clings on Despite Stiff Opposition', *Sunday Times*, 8.9.96, p. 7.

17 '18 Tigers, 12 Soldiers Killed', *Daily News*, 7.5.96, Inform Clippings, May '96, p. 2.

18 Shamindra Ferdinando and Norman Palihawadana, 'Eight Army Men Killed', *The Island*, 28.5.96, Inform Clippings, May ' 96, p. 6.

19 Norman Palihawadana, 'Fourteen Soldiers Killed', *The lsland*, 10.6.96, Inform Clippings, June '96, p. 2.

20 Premalal Wijeratne and Sasanka Samarakkody, 'STF Suffers a Severe Setback', *Sunday Leader*, 15.12.96, p. 4, G. Nadesan 'LTTE "urmal" publishes Pulukunawa captured arms list', *Weekend Express*, 21–22.12.96, p. 4.

21 Rohan Gunaratna, 'Tamil Tigers Burning Bright', *Himal*, April 1999, p. 36.

22 Defence Correspondent, 'Tigers Counterstrike to Their Edi-Bala Shame Goes Wrong', *The Island*, 9.3.97, p. 10. According to another report, only 150 soldiers from the two aforementioned units were present. Shamindra Ferdinando, 'Two of LTTE's Frontline Leaders Killed', *The Island*, 10.3.97, Insight clippings, March '97, p. 7.

23 Defence Correspondent, 'Tigers Counterstrike to Their Edi-Bala Shame Goes Wrong', *The Island*, 9.3.97, p. 10; Iqbal Athas, 'Tiger Triple Jump in the Eastern Theatre', *Sunday Times*, 9.3.97, p. 5; Shamindra Ferdinando and Norman Palihawadana, 'Nearly 275 Tigers and Soldiers Killed in Vavunathivu', *The Island*, 8.3.97, Inform Clippings, March '97, p. 6.

24 Sumadhu Weerawarne, 'An Unlikely Hero', *The Island*, 30.3.97, p. 6.

25 Iqbal Athas, 'Tiger Triple Jump in the Eastern Theatre' *Sunday Times*, 9.3.97, p. 5; Defence Correspondent, 'Tigers Counterstrike to Their Edi-Bala Shame Goes Wrong', *The Island*, 9.3.97, p. 10.

26 Shamindra Ferdinando, 'Two of LTTE's Frontline Leaders Killed', *The Island*, 10.3.97, Inform Clippings, March '97, p. 7.

27 Iqbal Athas, 'Tiger Triple Jump in the Eastern Theatre', *Sunday Times*, 9.3.97, p. 5.

28 Defence Correspondent, 'Tigers Counter Strike to Their Edi-Bala Shame Goes Wrong', *The Island*, 9.3.97, p. 10; Iqbal Athas, 'Tiger Triple Jump in the Eastern Theatre' *Sunday Times*, 9.3.97, p. 5.

156 The East in ferment

29 Defence correspondent, 'Three Pronged Surprise Assault Smashes Tiger Bases', *The Island*, 16,3.97, p. 8.
30 Roy Denish, 'The East: Thorn in the Side of Assured Victory', *Sunday Leader*, 29.6.97, p. 4.
31 Roy Denish, 'Push and Pull for Puliyankulam', *Sunday Leader*, 31.8.97, p. 9.
32 Mawaan Macan Macar, 'South West of Batti: State in the Making', *Sunday Leader*, 8.6.97, p. 4, Marwaan Marcan Markar, 'Criminals in the East', *Sunday Leader*, 5.4.98, p. 8.
33 'Taraki', 'Government Clings on Despite Stiff Opposition', *Sunday Times*, 8.9.96, p. 7.
34 'Troops Capture Vakarai', *Daily News*, 23.6.98, Inform Clippings, June '98, p. 4.
35 'Army Captures Vakarai', *Sri Lanka Monitor*, no. 125, June 1998, http://brcslproject.gn.apc.org/slmonitor/june98/cont.html
36 P. Karunakaran, 'LTTE Intensifies Attacks to Coincide with PA's Fifth Year', *Weekend Express*, 14–15.8.99, p. 7, 'Vaharai Black Tiger Attack', *Sri Lanka Monitor*, no. 139, August 1999, http://brcslproject.gn.apc.org/slmonitor/August99/vaha.html
37 Chris Kamalendran, 'Pre Dawn Horror in Ampara: 54 Killed as LTTE Unleashed Terror on Villagers', *Sunday Times*, 19.9.99, Insight Clippings September '99, p. 1.

Chapter 10

The rise and fall of the Unceasing Waves

As the millennium drew to a close, the LTTE considered itself ready to make a decisive shift in the military balance. The army's offensive had ground to a halt, costing them much blood and treasure. There was again great war weariness in the South with no end in sight to the long-drawn out war. On the other hand, although they had lost much territory, the Tigers had also been able to deliver some morale-denting blows to the army. They had also acquired much booty, a huge arsenal that could keep them fighting for a long time to come. And although they had lost many good fighters, the survivors had been steeled by the experience. It was now time to unleash these seasoned veterans and devastating firepower in a wave of fire and steel that would turn the tide of war decisively in their favour.

Back to square one in the Wanni

On the night of Sunday, November 1 1999, a group of around 150 Tiger commandos infiltrated the defences around Oddusudan. The defence lines south of Oddusudan were manned by the Second Battalion of the Gajaba Regiment (2GR), while to the west it was occupied by sailors from the navy's north-east command. Cutting through the barbed wire and sneaking behind the defence lines, the rebel commandos attacked the enemy from the rear, spreading confusion. Soon larger groups of rebels assailed the defence lines in that sector from the east and the north. As their gunners rained mortars, artillery and multi-barrel rocket fire on the enemy, they punched a hole through the Gajaba Regiment's defences in a short time, cutting off the Oddusudan area.

As communications between Oddusudan and the other bases broke down, panic began to spread along the defence lines. Reinforcements sent from the southern and western sectors of the army-occupied territory had to withdraw under heavy fire while the rebels pushed themselves through the army's defences between Oddusudan and Nedunkerni. Soldiers from the broken 2GR fell back on Nedunkerni to the south, while the sailors tried to make a stand further east towards Olumadu, abandoning Oddusudan altogether.[1]

Soon shells began falling in the vicinity of the army positions in Kanakarayankulam further to the south, causing casualties and setting alight an ammunition dump that blew up, destroying several buildings.[2] It was now apparent that the attack was not just another counter-attack that aimed at capturing weapons and inflicting maximum casualties. The Tigers seemed to be aiming at a bigger prize. By Thursday, Nedunkerni too had been abandoned, the troops in the eastern flank of the A9 in full retreat towards Gajabapura to the south, leaving behind truckloads of weapons and equipment. Further north, Mankulam held out, but only briefly. With the Tigers swarming all over the defences on the eastern flank, the town now faced the terrifying prospect of being cut off. As Ampakamam and Olumadu to the east of the town fell, Mankulam, now increasingly isolated, finally yielded, and the soldiers from the garrison joined the panic-stricken exodus south. Everywhere to the north of Kanakarayankulam, the defences were crumbling now, soldiers throwing down their weapons and streaming southwards. Behind them, the rampant Tigers surged, now moving along the A9 in vehicles. Kanakaranyankulam fell next as the army fell back on Puliyankulam.[3]

Further east, shells were falling around Padaviya, sending shock waves through the border villages. To the south, Vavuniya became a ghost town, abandoned by its residents who feared the rebels were unstoppable. An estimated 100,000 people began to fill refugee camps to the south.[4] The army was at their heels. By November 7, Puliyankulam too was abandoned as the army fell back on Omanthai, the last major town before Vavuniya. Here they dug in, boosted by fresh troops and artillery fire from Vavuniya.[5] Deterred by the stiffening resistance, the Tigers' southward advance finally came to a halt on the outskirts of Omanthai, and the army consolidated its positions, preventing further loss of territory. Omanthai would remain the northernmost point of government control till the very end of the Ealam Wars.

But to the west of the A9, the rebels rolled on. As the army rallied at Omanthai, the Tigers shelled and stormed the defence lines in western Wanni, the lines that marked the conquests of the 'Rana Ghosa' operations. Periyamdau fell, and pummelled by barrages of heavy artillery, Palampiddy and Pallamoddai also soon succumbed. Madhu now lay exposed, and by November 18, the shrine and all the outlying areas

The rise and fall of the Unceasing Waves   159

were in rebel hands. Within a week, the Tigers had pushed the army back to the Vavuniya–Mannar Road, and the army base at Thallady itself was coming under heavy artillery fire.[6]

Within a week, the Tigers had taken back the territory the army had spent nearly two and a half years capturing at the cost of thousands of lives. The precise numbers in killed and wounded were never officially disclosed. However, it is safe to estimate that it was well above 1,000. The rebels also captured a large quantity of arms and ammunition, including armoured cars and artillery.

It was a debacle which had panic written all over it. Very early during the offensive, the Tigers had damaged two Mi24 gunships, the aircraft on which air support for the ground operation had depended so much, forcing the air force to take their machines out of the skies. Then, to make matters worse, a Buffel APC loaded with valuable communication equipment on its way to Kanakarayankulam from the forward areas got stuck in soggy ground and fell into the hands of the rebels, forcing the military to maintain radio silence. Without any communication with their superiors and devoid of any direction, the troops did the only natural thing under the circumstances: they took to their heels.[7]

For the government and the Security Forces, it was a shattering blow to their morale. Months of 'conquests' in the Wanni had been lost – in a matter of days. Hundreds of soldiers had perished and an invaluable arsenal had fallen into enemy hands. Moreover, the sudden loss of vast swathes of territory in the Wanni had also left the military bases in the periphery of this area vulnerable to the brunt of the Tigers' fury. Suddenly, the war they had hoped to take to the enemy had returned to their doorstep.

Return to Elephant Pass

Early in December 1999, soldiers on guard at Iyakachchi detected several LTTE cadres infiltrating the defences. The army shot the intruders dead.[8] Although the daylight infiltration came as a surprise, the fact that the rebels were carrying out surveillance of the vast military complex was not new. The military had suspected, for months, that the Tigers were preparing another assault on Elephant Pass. After the devastating rolling back of the Jayasikurui gains, this became even more probable.

Elephant Pass in 1999 was a world removed from the base it was in 1991, when the Tigers had launched their 'mother of all battles' to swamp it. The base was now a sprawling complex, extending from the mainland to the south of the lagoon all the way to the eastern seaboard

160   The rise and fall of the Unceasing Waves

of the peninsula, covering an area about 23 km long and 8–10 km wide.[9] The front of the complex facing the Wanni was protected by the Paranthan camp, while the rear projected into the peninsula and was well guarded by a number of smaller fortified bases at Iyakachchi, Kadaikkadu and Vettilakerni, giving the base protection in depth. The camp at Iyakachchi also protected a freshwater well vital for the survival of the troops. The base was garrisoned by the Fifty-Fourth Division and was also supported by long-range artillery from the Pallai base further to the north. The A9 functioned as a main supply route from the army's bases in Jaffna while the Kadaikkadu–Vettilakerni base provided a beachhead for seaborne supplies. The whole base had been laid out according to Western defensive principles and was considered impregnable by an enemy without air support.[10]

On December 11, just days after the army intercepted the rebel infiltrators at Iyakachchi, the Tigers' Unceasing Waves reached this formidable fortress. Wary of repeating the mistakes of 1991, the Tigers sought to strangle the sprawling base rather than attacking it head-on. Seaborne Tigers arrived on the shores of Vadamarachchi in three waves and, after fierce fighting that left scores of rebels and soldiers dead, gained control of a strip of coast about 3 km in length between Vettilakerni and Kadaikadu.[11] The army was facing a serious problem. Tiger beachheads on the Vadamarachchi coast cut off Elephant Pass from their sea–land supply route, making the army depend on the main supply route with Jaffna for supplies. However, attempts to move further inland from the beachheads failed as the rebels faced stout resistance. But to the south, the Tigers succeeded in pushing the army out of Paranthan. Now the Tigers' heavy artillery was also coming into action, the 122mm guns opening up from Pooneryn and pounding the area north of Elephant Pass in the Thenmarachchi sector. Shells were also beginning to land around the defences at Iyakachchi.[12] It was an unsettling reminder of the insecurity of the peninsula against the Tigers' long-range weapons. Meanwhile, fearing a rebel drive to completely cut off Elephant Pass, the army moved the crack Fifty-Third Division, which consisted of an air mobile unit, a Special Forces unit and a mechanised infantry unit, to Elephant Pass.[13]

For the next three months, the rebels occupied themselves with exchanging artillery fire with the army at Elephant Pass.[14] But ominously, they were also beginning to make inroads into the peninsula across the lagoon. By late January 2000, there were indications that the rebels had gained a foothold not only in Thenmarachchi but also in Valikamam.[15]

Back in Elephant Pass, the rebels picked up from where they had left. On March 26, seaborne rebel commandos landed near Nagarkovil further to the north. Joining the men who were already manning the beachhead around Vettilakerni, they extended the beachhead, taking control of the eastern coast of Vadamarachchi all the way south from Nagarkovil. Realising that the thin strip of coast was becoming increasingly untenable, the army withdrew across the lagoon to Thenmarachchi. With the coast under their control, the rebels thrust inland. While one group moved north-westwards, another attacked southwards, moving on the main army defences. From the south, more rebels joined the fight, about 400 seasoned cadres under the veteran leader Theepan wading through the Chundikulam lagoon to attack the army lines to the west of Vettilakerni and east of Elephant Pass. At the same time, a unit of the rebel commandos raided the army positions at Pallai, a major road junction to the north of Iyakachchi. They put out of action 11 artillery pieces crippling the army's firepower. Then, to make matters worse, led by the veteran commander Balraj, the Tigers cut across the narrow lagoon and seized a 4 km strip of the MSR north of Iyakachchi, clashing with army commandos in the process. The situation was getting desperate now. The army sent its men to the rescue from the north, but at least two determined attacks by army commandos with armoured support failed to dislodge the Tigers from the A9. Elephant Pass was now virtually cut off.

Faced with the prospect of being choked in their base, the army cleared an alternative route to the west of the A9 to rejoin the MSR via a circuitous route. But this road too was coming under pressure from rebel attacks. On April 18, they also thrust southwards towards Iyakachchi. As rebel cadres assailed the Iyakachchi defences, their comrades on the mainland moved on the south-eastern defences of the Elephant Pass main camp, the 'armoured' units of the rebels made up of captured and improvised armour spearheading the assault. The end was close now. Iyakachchi finally succumbed on April 21, and with their freshwater source gone and the rampant Tigers swarming towards the main base from the north and the south, the army began to vacate Elephant Pass. Taking circuitous routes to avoid rebel artillery, the soldiers withdrew to Kilali, abandoning heavy weapons and equipment. In the process, many succumbed to dehydration and heat. The Tigers moved into the Elephant Pass camp in the afternoon of the twenty-second, and the following morning the LTTE flag flew over Elephant Pass for the first time since the separatist conflict began. The army had destroyed much equipment, but still the rebels captured a massive arsenal including several heavy artillery pieces, tanks and armoured vehicles. As many as 800

162   The rise and fall of the Unceasing Waves

soldiers are said to have perished in the disastrous trek from the doomed camp. These included Special Forces Expert and Deputy Commander of Fifty-Fifth Division Brigadier Percy Fernando who died in battle and Colonels Neil Akmeemana, Bhatiya Jayatileka and Hari Hewarachchi who died of dehydration. It was the biggest defeat suffered by the Sri Lankan armed forces in the history of the separatist war.[16]

Using a euphemism that had by now become a hallmark of the Security Forces' admissions of defeat, the army announced that it had 'readjusted' its Forward Defence Lines.[17] The Security Forces also tried to downplay the loss of weapons, admitting to losing only one 152mm gun to the rebels, but the Tigers later issued photographs of three 152mm cannon, which were published in the pro-rebel *Tamil Guardian*.[18] The army commander Sri Lal Weerasooriya later gave a more candid explanation for the withdrawal, saying that it was better to save the troops and use them later.[19] For their part, the rebels were clear about their achievements and goals; they proclaimed the victory as 'facilitating the LTTE to gain its strategic goal of liberating Jaffna'.[20]

The capture of Elephant Pass was a remarkable military feat, a masterpiece of manoeuvre warfare. The sprawling complex had been considered impregnable by any enemy without any air support. But the Tigers had taken it by outmanoeuvring the army. Rather than going for a frontal attack to swamp the defences as they had tried in 1991, the rebels had cut off the supply lines to the army – first the seaborne supply route and then the MSR with Jaffna. When the freshwater supply at Iyakachchi was lost, holding on to the base became suicidal. Retreat was the only sane option left for the army.

Rampant Tigers

After the loss of Elephant Pass base, the army had pulled back to Pallai further north on the A9. On April 30, under intense artillery and mortar attack, the army 'readjusted' its lines again, vacating Pallai and retreating in the direction of Eluthumaduval on the A9.[21] The defence lines were now stabilised, anchored on Kilali in the west and Nagarkovil in the east. But the Tigers were not letting up. After a brief lull, they pounced again. While a diversionary attack was launched against the army's positions in the Nagarkovil–Kilali axis, the rebels moved in on Thenmarachchi. The Tigers already had established positions in the Thenmarachchi sector at Ariyalai and Thanankilappu, and now with the aid of more cadres ferried across the lagoon from the mainland, they extended their hold. Heavy fighting raged in the Ariyalai and Thanankilappu areas as

The rise and fall of the Unceasing Waves   163

the rebels made repeated attempts to storm the Navatkuli bridge that linked Thenmarachchi with Valikamam.[22] In desperation, the air force bombed the Sanguppiddy causeway that linked the mainland with the peninsula and claimed to have destroyed the Tigers' communication tower at Pooneryn.[23] But all that was to no avail. Navatkuli fell after a ferocious onslaught, and after another fierce battle, the Tigers captured the large army base at Kaithady, advancing up the Kaithady–Kopay road northwards. Meanwhile, another group of rebels landed at Colombuthurai and moved up the coast, reaching the outskirts of Jaffna town. In a tacit admission of the steady rebel encroachment, the government announced that the army had, again, 're-adjusted' their defences 'temporarily towards Colombuthurai east'.[24] By May 20, Tiger heavy artillery shells began falling on the outskirts of the Palali airbase.[25]

In Thenmarachchi, the army faced an increasingly desperate situation: the town of Chavakachcheri, the largest urban centre in Thenmarachchi, was becoming steadily isolated. The rebels had quickly fanned out and captured the key Sarasalai junction of the Chavakachcheri–Point Pedro Road, making the army's positions in Chavakachcheri increasingly untenable. By May 20, the Tigers were claiming the capture of the town.[26] That left the army with only one major camp in Thenmarachchi – in Kodikamam. On May 29, they struck back from there and succeeded in pushing into Sarasalai, but a determined rebel counter thrust pushed them back to base.[27]

By this time, however, the rebel offensive was beginning to show signs of petering out. The rebels had withdrawn from some areas close to the Jaffna city and seemed unable to proceed beyond Nagarkovil–Kilali axis and Meesalai. An attempt to push northwards in Thenmarachchi and threaten Vadamarachchi west was thwarted at Varani even though the air force lost another Mi24 helicopter during the battle.[28] But another attempt by the army to advance in the direction of Sarasalai also ended in failure as the troops were forced to return to their original positions amidst heavy artillery and mortar fire.[29] But there were no further advances from the Tigers either. The amazingly rapid advance had finally slowed and then stalled, the juggernaut grinding to a halt within sight of victory.

After months of crushing everything in their path, the waves had finally foamed out. The tide was about to turn in the North.

Arms to the rescue

On August 10 and 11, the Sri Lankan air force launched bombing raids on enemy lines in the Nagarkovil area. On August 16, they also bombed

164 The rise and fall of the Unceasing Waves

the Columbuthurai and Sangupiddy jetties.[30] The raids were carried out by MiG-27s, a new addition to the air force's inventory. In early August, Sri Lanka took delivery of four of these aircraft from the Ukraine. The single seater supersonic jets were piloted by foreigners from undisclosed countries and carried 23mm guns and a sophisticated missile delivery system. They could also reach Jaffna Peninsula within 7 minutes of take-off.[31] Several Kfirs had also arrived from Israel, further boosting the air force's ground-attack capability.[32]

The aircraft were part of a scramble for weaponry by the beleaguered Sri Lankan government. With the Tigers clawing at Jaffna's gates, the government went into panic mode, shopping for arms and equipment to stem the rebel tide, facilitated by a massive 800-million-dollar defence budget. They re-established diplomatic relations with Israel, discontinued in the early 1990s, to facilitate the acquisition of the Kfirs. More than 40 T-55 battle tanks were also expected from the Czech Republic.[33] Iran is said to have provided mortars, while Britain also rushed in helmets, body armour and two Hercules C-130 transport planes.[34] The Mi24s and the old Bell helicopters were fitted with the latest anti-missile systems obtained from Israel.[35] At least, 36 new Infantry Fighting Vehicles were also expected from Russia.[36] Three plane loads of ammunition also arrived from Pakistan which also chipped in with a donation of 10 MBRLs. More were expected from China and the Czech Republic.[37] Half the MBRLs from Pakistan were immediately put into action against the enemy in Jaffna. Later, 16 more MBRLs arrived from the Czech Republic along with 10,000 122mm rockets for them.[38]

These acquisitions boosted the firepower, defence and morale of the Sri Lankan Security Forces and helped the government to stem the rebel tide. The enhanced air power was instrumental in constraining the movement of rebel artillery.[39] The MBRLs in particular proved to be a great boon to the struggling Sri Lankan army. These weapons could unleash volleys of up to 40 rockets at a time, and their devastating fire was more than anything the rebels had been forced to face until then. The slowing of the Tigers' march owed much to this new phenomenon on the battlefield.[40]

The tide turns

With new weapons of unprecedented potential, the army switched on to attack mode. It began offensive operations just as the rebel offensive was starting to lose its steam. On September 3, after several days of heavy bombardment with MBRLs and other heavy artillery, troops of

The rise and fall of the Unceasing Waves   165

the Fifty-First and Fifty-Third Divisions launched a major offensive to capture lost territory in the Thenmaracchi and Valikamam sectors. Code named 'Rivi Kirana', the operation was launched south-eastwards from Sarasalai and eastwards from Colombuthurai. This, however, achieved little. The first thrust moved some distance before being beaten back by exceptionally intense mortar and artillery fire, which resulted in heavy casualties. The thrust from Colombuthurai, which was the main attack, advanced about 500 metres but no further due to heavy fire. The rebel artillery from Pooneryn zeroed in on the advancing soldiers, while the mortars from rebel positions in the peninsula rained down on them, causing heavy losses. More than 125 were killed and over 800 wounded.[41]

Undeterred, the army continued to probe rebel defences. From September 10 onwards, a series of operations gradually pushed the Tigers further away from the Jaffna town, recapturing the Navatkuli bridge.[42] On September 17, the army made a major breakthrough in Thenmarachchi. Six battalions from the Fifty-Third Division and two battalions from the Fifty-Second Division moved in a pincer, encircling the Chavakachcheri town. As the air force along with MBRLs and artillery fire pummelled rebel defences, the two arms of the pincer closed southwest of the town. The rebels had vacated the town by then, but Chavakachcheri was finally back in government control. The army met some fierce resistance but most of it from the rebels' civilian 'border force' and new female recruits.[43]

The troops took possession of a devastated town. The use of heavy firepower, especially the MBLRs, had pulverised Chavakaccheri, Jaffna's second-largest town which had boasted nearly 100,000 inhabitants in its heyday. Buildings were flattened, coconut trees ripped apart. According to the army, the town was hit by nearly 3,000 shells fired by both sides.[44] Fortunately, no civilians were around at the time of the battle. If there were any, none would have survived, a visiting Indian journalist quipped wryly.[45]

The army's gains enabled them to interdict the Tigers' supply lines to Jaffna from the mainland. Over the next few months, the army gradually extended its control over the areas lost to the rebels in May 2000. In a series of operations code named Kinihira 1–8, they expanded its control around Chavakachcheri to free the main supply lines to the town from rebel control, pushing the enemy south of the A9. By the end of 2000, the entire A9 barring 2 km east of Jaffna town was in army hands. The gains, however, were not made without loss. The army faced stubborn resistance from the rebels, particularly from their mortars, losing more than 100 killed and 200 wounded while claiming to have killed over 300 rebels.[46] By the beginning of 2001, at the end of Kinihira 8, the troops had recaptured almost all the lost territory in Thenmaracchi and Valkiamam. Kinihira 8 captured the remaining stretch of the A9 and also gained control of Ariyalai and Thanankilappu. By now, rebel resistance had completely petered out. Only two soldiers suffered minor injuries from an IED.[47]

Within six months, the Tigers had lost much of the territory they had gained in Thenmarachchi and Valikamam. Their conquests in the neck of the Peninsula were all that was left to them.

On December 21 2000, the Tigers finally declared a unilateral ceasefire. The government rejected it. The army was by now eyeing the rebel-controlled area beyond the Muhamalai–Nagarkovil defence lines, the last remaining Tiger territory in the Jaffna Peninsula. To wrest control of this territory, they launched 'Kinihira 9' in January 2001. In two phases, the army captured an extent of 17 square kilometres on Thenmarachchi, extending the defence lines up to Ponnar and Muhamalai, but the cost was heavy: over 100 soldiers and officers were killed and more than 550 wounded by Tiger artillery and mortar fire.[48] Then three months later, the Security Forces launched another ambitious drive to extend its gains. Code named 'Agni Khila' or Rod of Iron, its objective was to capture Pallai. On April 24 2001, the army broke out of its defence lines at Muhamalai, moving on either flank of the A9; the Fifty-Fifth Division moved on the eastern flank and the elite Fifty-Third Division on the western flank. They did not advance very far. Running into a minefield, they were showered with heavy artillery and mortar fire, forcing them to return to their original positions. The loss was staggering; over 200 killed and nearly 2,000 wounded.[49]

With Agni Khila ended the major fighting in Ealam War III. But the Kinihira operations ended its decisive – perhaps the most decisive – phase of the entire Ealam War. With the Unceasing Waves crashing against the gates of Jaffna, the Tigers had reached the high watermark of their military prowess. But the waves had failed to break through. The prize – Jaffna – had been tantalisingly within their grasp, but the rejuvenated Sri Lankan military had raised the stakes. Then, within six months, they had also lost much of the territory they had gained in Thenmarachchi and Valikamam. The war had reached a stalemate again with positions roughly back to where they were after the fall of Mullaithivu.

The failure of the rebels owed much to a combination of their depleted resources and the rejuvenation of the Sri Lankan Security Forces. The reality was that the dogged resistance to the Jayasikurui campaign, while bleeding the army dry, had also cost the rebels heavily. In March 1998, the rebel commander Karuna admitted on rebel radio that they had lost 1,165 cadres killed in resisting Jayasikurui from May to December 1997. According to the army, rebel losses were higher. In May, the army claimed that monitored broadcasts of a speech by Prabhakaran admitted to losing 1,300 cadres in opposing Jayasikurui.[50] The capture of Kilinochchi alone is said to have cost the rebels a massive 717 killed. According to the analyst Sivaram, the Tigers had lost around 3,000 killed and wounded in opposing Jayasikurui. These included some of their toughest and most experienced cadres.[51]

When they launched their assault on Jaffna, the rebels were already constrained by the loss of many of these veteran fighters in stalling Jayasikurui. The assault on Jaffna depended heavily on long-range firepower with only a small hard core of around 1,500 drawn mainly from the commando, armoured, Sea Tiger and women's units engaged in direct confrontation with the enemy.[52] The superior firepower of the Security Forces, particularly the galling fire of the MBRLs, fell heavily on these cadres, decimating them. According to Army Commander Lionel Balagalle, the Tigers had admitted to losing 2,019 cadres during the first ten months of 2000, a huge loss to an organisation already plagued by a heavy attrition rate.[53] By the time they lost Chavakachcheri, the rebels had already pulled out many of their experienced cadres from the line of fire, preserving them for future offensives and manning the frontline mainly with the civilians trained in combat and new female recruits.[54] The army too lost heavily, 266 killed and over 2,000 wounded in September and October alone, according to Balagalle, but the rebels found it harder to absorb their losses.[55]

The rebels had learnt a painful lesson common to all predominantly guerrilla armies that pursued conventional campaigns with limited resources: unless you gained a decisive advantage quickly your moment would be lost, perhaps forever. But the army too had learnt a lesson, that while their firepower could dent the attack of the enemy it was not sufficient to drive them away completely, especially from well-entrenched positions. The rebel lines at Muhamalai had proven resilient against the armour and infantry attacks of the Security Forces, protected as they were by mines and long-range artillery. The scenario would be repeated many more times before the end of the war.

Penetrating the Tigers' den

While the Tigers were struggling to hold on to their gains in Jaffna, the Security Forces launched a series of deadly covert operations to strike

168 The rise and fall of the Unceasing Waves

at the rebels behind their lines. This was not a new phenomenon in the Ealam Wars. In the late 1980s, the Special Forces had experimented with their 'tracker teams' that spent days behind enemy lines, hunting the rebels. During Operation Jayasikurui, small groups of soldiers had operated ahead of the FDL, engaging enemy troops in their own territory, killing them and making them feel generally insecure.[56] These were not exactly deep penetration operations, but still they were proactive ways of engaging the rebels. But the attacks that materialised in 2001 were of a far deadly kind. Here were groups of assassins, highly trained and motivated, striking deep within rebel territory with deadly effect. Until then, it was only the army that felt insecure in their rear. The country beyond the FDL was secure rebel territory. Now, for the first time in the war, that rear was being invaded by a silent, deadly enemy.

The attackers, as it was later revealed, belonged to a special group within the Sri Lankan Special Forces. Said to be the brainchild of the former Army Commander Lionel Balagalle, the members of these teams came from all three ethnic groups in Sri Lanka. There were ex-rebels, members of anti-Tiger Tamil groups, Muslim militants and carefully selected Sinhala personnel. They were given highly specialised 'commando'-type training at home and abroad.[57]

The Deep Penetration Units endeavoured to deny the enemy the initiative by operating in their domain, providing valuable intelligence of the enemy territory, a crucial element lacking in the army's military planning. They also carried out some spectacular attacks on high-profile enemy targets. On May 15 2001, a vehicle carrying the LTTE political chief Thamilselvam and five cadres on their way to a meeting with a Norwegian peace facilitator was struck by a landmine in the Mallawi–Kokavil area. Thamilselvam escaped unhurt, but one of the cadres was killed.[58] In June, the head of Batticaloa district intelligence 'Lt Col.' Nizam died in a similar mysterious claymore attack in Vavunathivu.[59] On September 26, another senior leader 'Colonel' Shankar met his death in similar circumstances, this time in Oddusudan, heart of the Tiger rear.[60] Several others narrowly escaped death. These included Deputy Military Chief 'Col.' Balraj, the eastern commander 'Col.' Karuna and eastern political chief Karikalan.[61]

The Tigers were naturally concerned. The attacks were occurring in areas deep behind their lines. Indeed, no Sri Lankan soldiers had come that far for nearly ten years. The army however promptly denied any involvement.[62] But it was now clear to everybody that a covert war was being fought behind enemy lines. It was also clear that this war was deadly enough for the rebels to be seriously concerned.

The rise and fall of the Unceasing Waves 169

Whether the Deep Penetration operations could have made a crucial difference to the outcome of the conflict is arguable. They had the potential to place the rebels under severe pressure when combined with more conventional operations. But by the time Colonel Shankar was killed, it did not really matter. By then, two far more spectacular attacks that shook Sri Lanka and the world had begun to alter the course of the conflict.

Notes

1 Iqbal Athas, 'Years of Gains Lost in Days', *Sunday Times*, 7.11.99, http://sundaytimes.lk/991107/sitrep.html, P. Karunakaran, 'Debacle at Oddusudan: was It the Failure of Intelligence?', *Weekend Express*, 6–7.11.99, p. 6.
2 P. Karunakaran, 'Debacle at Oddusudan'.
3 Athas, 'Years of Gains Lost in Days'.
4 V. Suryanarayan, 'Land of the Displaced', Frontline 22.6.01, p. 62 (61–3).
5 Roy Denish, 'Army in Disarray', *Sunday Leader*, 7.11.99, p. 6; D.B.S Jeyaraj, 'LTTE Offensive', *Frontline*, Nov. 27 – Dec 10, 1999, http://www.frontline.in/fl1625/16250040.htm; Roy Denish and Asgar Hussein, 'Vavuniya Turns into Ghost Town', *Sunday Leader*, 14.11.99, p. 1; Leon Berenger and Kris Kamalendran, 'Mass Exodus from Wanni', *Sunday Times*, 14.11.99, http://sundaytimes.lk/991114/frontm.html#1LABEL1; Defence Correspondent, 'Military in Worst Debacle in Nine Years', *The Island*, 7.11.99, p. 9.
6 D.B.S Jeyaraj, 'LTTE Offensive', *Frontline*, Nov. 27 – Dec 10, 1999, http://www.frontline.in/fl1625/16250040.htm, 'Tigers Say Thallady Forward Defence Overrun', *Tamilnet*, 24.11.99, http://tamilnet.com/art.html?catid=13&artid=4243), P. Karunakaran, 'Madhu, Periyamadu Fall to the LTTE', *Weekend Express*, 20–21.11.99, p. 1.
7 Jeyaraj, 'LTTE Offensive', Athas, 'Years of Gains Lost in Days'. Athas says the two helicopters were only damaged, but Jeyaraj says they were shot down.
8 Iqbal Athas, Tiger Waves Smashed at Elephant Pass, *Sunday Times*, 12.12.99, http://sundaytimes.lk/991212/sitrep.html
9 D.B.S. Jeyaraj, 'The Taking of Elephant Pass', *Frontline,* 13–26.5.00, http://www.frontlineonnet.com/fl1710/17100100.htm
10 'EPS Fall: Reassessing LTTE's Manoeuvre Warfare Prowess', http://www.tamilnet.com/art.html?catid=79&artid=8839 (The article does not have a byline, but the style suggests that it is by 'Taraki'.)
11 Athas, Tiger Waves Smashed at Elephant Pass, Roy Denish, 'Setback for Tigers at Elephant Pass', *Sunday Leader*, 19.12.99, p. 7.
12 Sunil Jayasiri and N. Parameshwaran, 'Tiger Shells Shock Jaffna', *Daily Mirror*, 13.12.99, Insight Clippings, December '99, p. 24.
13 D.B.S. Jeyaraj, 'Another LTTE Offensive', *Frontline,* v. 17, no. 8, Apr. 15–28, 2000, http://www.flonnet.com/fl1708/17080520.htm, 'Creeping

Advantage in Jaffna', *Tamilnet*, 10.2.00, http://www.tamilnet.com/art. html?catid=79&artid=7408

14 Roy Denish, 'Soldiers in Need of "relief"', *Sunday Leader*, 23.1.00, p. 10.

15 Roy Denish, 'Red Herring for Independence', *Sunday Leader*, 6.2.00, p. 10; 'Creeping Advantage in Jaffna'.

16 For descriptions of this battle, see Jeyaraj, 'Another LTTE Offensive', 'Elephant Pass Troops stand Firm', *Sunday Times*, 19.12.99, http:// sundaytimes.lk/991219/sitrep.html; Jeyaraj, 'The Taking of Elephant Pass'; Paul Harris, 'LTTE Turns up Heat in Sri Lankan Power Struggle', *Jane's Intelligence Review*, 21.8.00; Iqbal Athas, 'The Great Escape from Elephant Pass', *Sunday Times*, 18.2.01, http://sundaytimes. lk/010218/sitrep.html

17 P. Karunakaran, 'Ealam War III Enters Sixth Year', *Weekend Express*, 23.4.00, p. 5.

18 Iqbal Athas, 'How Operation Kinihira Won Chavakachcheri', *Sunday Times*, 24.9,00, http://sundaytimes.lk/000924/sitrep.html (The pictures were published in September 2000.)

19 V.S.Sambandan, 'The Fall of Elephant Pass', *Frontline*, 12.5.00, p. 124.

20 Ibid. (124 and 126)

21 Iqbal Athas, 'News Blackouts: Rumours Rule the Day', *Sunday Times*, 7.5.00, http://www.sundaytimes.lk/000507/sitrep.html

22 *The Island* reported that two officers and 31 soldiers were killed in fighting in the Ariyalai and Thanankilappu areas on May 10 and 11. 'Fighting Continues in the North', *The Island*, 12.05.00, http://www.island. lk/2000/05/12/islnews.html#

23 T.N. Gopalan, 'Deadlock at Jaffna Doorstep' http://www.telegraphindia. com/1000513/front_pa.htm

24 Gopalan, 'Deadlock at Jaffna Doorstep'.

25 D.B.S. Jeyaraj, 'The Battle for Jaffna', *Frontline*, May 27–June 9, 2000, http://www.frontlineonnet.com/fl1711/17110120.htm

26 'Tigers Take Key Jaffna Town', *BBC News Online*, 21.5.00, http:// news.bbc.co.uk/2/hi/south_asia/757484.stm

27 Iqbal Athas, 'An Uneasy Lull', *Sunday Times*, 4.6.00, http://sunday times.lk/000604/sitrep.html, D.B.S.Jeyaraj, 'A Deceptive Calm', *Frontline*, v. 17, no. 13, 24.6–7.7.00, http://www.frontlineonnet. com/fl1713/17130310.htm

28 Iqbal Athas, 'Troops Brace to Face Stepped Up Attacks', *Sunday Times*, 28.5.00, Athas, 'An Uneasy Lull', Jeyaraj, 'A Deceptive Calm', *Frontline*.

29 Iqbal Athas, 'Attacks Disrupt KKS Port and Palali Airfield', *Sunday Times*, 11.7.00, http://sundaytimes.lk/000611/sitrep.html

30 Mendis, *Assignment Peace*, p. 532.

31 Roy Denish, 'Under Surveillance', *Sunday Leader*, 6.8.00, p. 13.

32 Raj Chengappa and Roy Denish, 'Return of the Tiger', *India Today*, 22.5.2000, p. 32 (28–32).

33 Iqbal Athas, 'Sri Lankan Army Inspects Czech Main Battle Tanks', *Jane's Defence Weekly*, 19.7.2000.

34 Paul Harris, 'LTTE Turns up Heat in Sri Lankan Power Struggle', *Jane's Intelligence Review*, 21.8.00.

The rise and fall of the Unceasing Waves 171

35 Janaka de Silva, 'Prabhakaran in a Winning Position', *Sunday Leader* 24.12.00, p. 7.
36 Military Balance, 2001, p. 159, BMP-2
37 Robert Karniol, 'Rocket Boost for Sri Lanka', *Jane's Defence Weekly*, 27.6.00.
38 The Czech Republic also provided eight MF-55A bridge layers, 16VT-53 armoured recovery vehicles, three mobile workshop vehicles and 12 TATRA T815 tank transporters. Iqbal Athas, 'Sri Lanka Army Inspects Czech Main Battle Tanks'.
39 S. Chandrasekaran, 'India in the "active" mode', South Asia Analysis Group, Notes and Updates, Sri Lanka: update no. 20, 12.7.00, http://www.southasiaanalysis.org/%5Cnotes2%5Cnote110.html (21.2.00).
40 Paul Harris, 'LTTE Turns up Heat in Sri Lankan Power Struggle', *Jane's Intelligence Review*, 21.8.00, D.B.S.Jeyaraj, 'A Deceptive Calm', *Frontline*, vol. 17, Issue, 13, 24.6–7.7.00, http://www.frontlineonnet.com/fl1713/17130310.htm
41 Iqbal Athas, 'The Millennium Thrust That Failed', *Sunday Times,* 10.9.2000, http://sundaytimes.lk/000910/sitrep.html; Roy Denish, 'Motives behind the Push', *Sunday Leader*, 17.9.00, p. 13, Shamindra Ferdinando, 'Chava Now a Devastated Town', *The Island*, 22.9.00, http://www.island.lk/2000/09/22/news09.html
42 Iqbal Athas, 'How Operation Kinihira Won Chavakachcheri', *Sunday Times*, 24.9,00, http://sundaytimes.lk/000924/sitrep.html; Janaka se Silva, 'September's Campaign without Equal', *Sunday Leader*, 1.10.00, p. 10.
43 Iqbal Athas, 'How Operation Kinihira Won Chavakachcheri', Janaka De Silva, 'September's Campaign without Equal'
44 Janaka De Silva, 'September's Campaign without Equal'.
45 Nirupama, Subramaniam, 'Army Takes Back Ghost Town', *The Hindu,* 21.9.00, http://hindu.com/2000/09/21/stories/03210007.htm
46 Janaka De Silva, 'Uncertain Waves and Political Manoeuvres', *Sunday Leader*, 31.12.00, p. 10.
47 Iqbal Athas, 'After the Truce, War Drums from the LTTE', *Sunday Times,* 21.1.00, http://sundaytimes.lk/010121/sitrep.html
48 Iqbal Athas, 'Troops on the Road to Elephant Pass', *Sunday Times,* 28.1.01, http://sundaytimes.lk/010128/sitrep.html (Another report says 54 men and officers were killed while over 230 were injured.) P. Karunakaran, 'Unexpected LTTE Resistance Stalls Knihira IX', *Weekend Express*, 21.1.01, p. 5.
49 Iqbal Athas, 'How "Operation Rod of Iron" Misfired', *Sunday Times,* 29.4.01, http://sundaytimes.lk/010429/sitrep.html (acc. 24.2.12); Nirupama Subramaian, 'Starting All Over Again', *Frontline*, 25.5.01, p. 57 (57–8)
50 Shamindra Ferdinando, 'Jayasikurui Operation Kill 1.300 Tigers Admits Prabhakaran', *The Island*, 14.5.98, Insight Clippings, May '98, p. 2.
51 'EPS Falls: Reassessing LTTE's Manoeuvre Warfare Prowess' http://www.tamilnet.com/art.html?catid=79&artid=8839
52 D.B.S. Jeyaraj, 'Another LTTE Offensive', *Frontline*, 28.4.00, p. 53. (52–5)

172 The rise and fall of the Unceasing Waves

53 Lieut. Gen. Lionel Piyananda Balagalle's Interview with *Jane's Defence Weekly*, 19.1.01.
54 Iqbal Athas, 'How Operation Kinihira Won Chavakachcheri'.
55 Lt. Gen. Lionel Piayananda Balagalle's interview with *Jane's Defence Weekly*, 19.1.01.
56 Munasinghe, *A Soldier's Version*, p. 206.
57 D.B.S. Jeyaraj, 'LRRP Infiltration Demolishes Impregnable Tiger Terrain Myth', http://transcurrents.com/tamiliana/archives/575
58 N.Subramanyam, 'LTTE Come under Bomb Attacks', *The Hindu*, 16.8.01, http://www.hindu.com/thehindu/2001/08/16/stories/03160005.htm; Rohan Gunaratna, 'LTTE Adopts Heavy Artillery', *Janes Intelligence Review*, 1.6.01.
59 N. Subramanyam, 'LTTE Come under Bomb Attacks', *The Hindu*, 16.8.01, http://www.hindu.com/thehindu/2001/08/16/stories/03160005.htm
60 'LTTE Condemns Assassination of Senior Leader', http://www.tamilnet.com/art.html?catid=13&artid=6340; D.B.S.Jeyaraj, 'Death of a Tiger', *Frontline*, 13–26.10.01, (v.18, no. 21), http://www.frontlineonnet.com/fl1821/18210570.htm
61 D.B.S. Jeyaraj, 'LRRP Infiltration Demolishes Impregnable Tiger Terrain Myth', http://transcurrents.com/tamiliana/archives/575
62 'Army Denies LTTE Accusation of Killing Shankar', http://www.island.lk/2001/09/28/news01.html

Chapter 11

The peace that failed and the reconquest of the East

In the early hours of July 24 2001, a small group of Tamil Tigers armed to the teeth with mortars, RPGs and assault rifles sneaked through the security ring at the Katunayake air base. Methodically, they began to attack the fleet of ground attack and transport aircraft belonging to the Sri Lankan air force, reducing them to flames and heaps of twisted metal. Then they took their mayhem to the neighbouring Katunayake airport, where the same treatment was meted out to the commercial planes belonging to Sri Lankan Airlines. By morning, crack army commandos had arrived and many of the attackers were dead. But the damage had been done. Two Kfirs, two Mi17s, one MiG-27 and three Chinese K-8 trainer aircraft were completely destroyed. In the Katunayake airport, three aircraft belonging to the Sri Lankan Airlines also lay in ashes. The damage was estimated at approximately $450 million. The cost to the economy and the morale of the nation: priceless.[1]

Six weeks later on September 11, two hijacked aircraft flew into the World Trade Centre in New York, killing more than 3,000 people and prompting the outraged Western countries to launch a 'War against Terrorism'. By the end of the year, the US and its allies had invaded Afghanistan, and any country or organisation connected with what was deemed terrorism was coming under increasing pressure. Along with the Katunayake attack, this new international mood paved the way for the reactivation of the long-dormant peace process in Sri Lanka.

The elusive peace

Towards the end of the campaign for the dominance of Jaffna in 2000, with neither side able to gain a commanding position over each other, the rebels and the government had again begun moving towards

174 The peace that failed and the reconquest

negotiations. As explained elsewhere, both sides had never eschewed peace talks in principle. Indeed, both parties averred that they were for a negotiated settlement and that the military operations were to achieve a position of strength from which to negotiate. It is arguable that the government under Chandrika Kumaratunge still had a genuine commitment to a political solution and wished to present it from a position of strength, while the LTTE wished to achieve a strategic equilibrium that would move them as close as possible to their ultimate goal of Ealam. Negotiations for the Tigers were a means of achieving or sealing this final goal. Each party achieving a position of dominance was a prerequisite for talking to the other.

While struggling for the strategic advantage, the Sri Lankan government had been working on its blueprint for the settlement of the ethnic issue. This was a new constitution developed in consultation with the main opposition party, the UNP. But when the proposals were finally brought in, in 2000, the UNP opposed it, citing the provision for the continuation of the president's term until the next elections as objectionable. The Sinhala nationalists joined the fray and the proposals were doomed to end the same way as many others before them. For their part, the Tigers showed little interest in the proposals calling for negotiations but with third-party facilitation.

However, at the end of 2000 with both parties totally exhausted without either obtaining a significant strategic advantage, a return to peace negotiations seemed inevitable. There was also a growing public opinion against the continued bloodletting that seemed to go nowhere. Norway had been chosen as a facilitator acceptable to both parties. The 'peace process', however, moved sluggishly with the government insisting on a time frame for peace talks and the need to discuss substantive issues earlier on and the Tigers not responding positively. Too much time was being spent on debates and disputes without any real urgency.

The Tigers' assault on Katunayake was a means of manipulating the pace and direction of the peace process. The need became even more urgent with the United States' declaration of the 'War against Terrorism'. With world opinion turning rapidly against terrorism, the rebels felt increasingly constrained to make peace. For the Sri Lankan government, the airport attack was a wake-up call, showing that it could not expect to gain decisive military leverage over the enemy. The backlash against terrorism after the terrorist attacks on the US could not change the ground situation in Sri Lanka where the need for talks rather than more fighting was becoming increasingly apparent. Peacemaking was also helped by a change of government in Sri Lanka. Fresh elections were called in December 2001 and the People's Alliance government was roundly defeated by an electorate that was growing weary of the prolonged war. The new prime minister, Ranil Wickremesinghe, began to move the peace process ahead, and in February 2002 the LTTE and the government, under Norwegian auspices, signed a ceasefire.[2] For the first time since the war began, a Sri Lankan government had signed a deal with the LTTE. Peace seemed closer than ever before.

According to the ceasefire agreement, the government and the LTTE were to have control over the areas already under their dominance. Unarmed rebel cadres were allowed to enter government-controlled areas for political work and neither party was to move munitions, explosives or military equipment into the area controlled by the other. The embargo on the flow of goods and travel between the North and the South was to be lifted. The government was to disband paramilitary groups but 'continue to perform their legitimate task of safeguarding the sovereignty and territorial integrity of Sri Lanka without engaging in offensive operations against the LTTE'. A Ceasefire Monitoring Committee made up of members from Nordic countries was to monitor the progress of the agreement.[3]

Hopes rose when the Tigers held six rounds of talks with the Sri Lankan government from September 2002 to March 2003. The first few rounds were quite promising. A number of key issues such as resettlement, reconstruction and rehabilitation were discussed. For the first time, the Tigers also demonstrated a willingness to accept something less than a separate state. The promise of peace, however, was a mirage. Talks soon got tense over the issue of dismantling high-security zones in the North. The Sri Lankan military was not prepared to remove the high-security zones unless the rebels made a commensurate reduction in their armed strength. Just before the fifth round of talks on February 7 2003, a naval confrontation between the Sri Lankan navy and the LTTE also added to the tensions. The Tigers unilaterally withdrew from negotiations on April 24 2003, citing the slow implementation of the agreements reached during the last six months.[4]

The LTTE now submitted a set of proposals for Interim Self-Government Administration (ISGA). It proposed an Interim Self-governing Authority for the Northern and Eastern Provinces for a period of five years. While accommodating Sinhala and Muslim communities, which inhabit the two provinces, the authority was to be under the control of the LTTE. The authority was to have very wide-ranging powers, including borrowing externally and external trade. It also proposed the recognition of the Sea Tigers as a legitimate naval unit and called for the demarcation of areas for LTTE's naval training.[5]

The proposals caused an uproar in the South as Sinhala hardliners saw it as further proof of the LTTE's unwillingness to give up a separate state. Adding to the tensions was the report that the rebel merchant navy was continuing to replenish the Tigers' arsenal, running the gauntlet of navy ships. Several shipments were intercepted and at least two sunk by the navy.[6] But the weapons and munitions kept coming in much to the alarm of the Sri Lankan government. Perhaps the most ominous development for the government was the rebel build-up in Trincomalee. In August 2003, the media published a map of Trincomalee, which showed a number of new LTTE camps to the north and south of the Kottiyar Bay.[7] The ceasefire had recognised the LTTE's control over the territory it held on December 24. This territory was clearly demarcated in the North, but the boundaries were hazy in the East, especially in Trincomalee. Now the Tigers seemed to be exploiting this lack of clarity to encroach on the area to the south of the Trincomalee harbour, particularly in the Sampoor area. If the Tigers could set up artillery in these bases, the harbour and port could become seriously vulnerable.[8]

While the debate on the ISGA proposals heated up, the president intervened. On November 11 2003, Chandrika Kumaratunge took over the ministries of defence, interior and mass communications.[9] The resultant stand-off led to fresh elections being held on April 8 2004. The elections brought the United People's Freedom Alliance (UPFA) into power with Mahinda Rajapaksa, who had the firm backing of the Sinhala hardliners, as prime minister.

Presidential elections were also looming, and when the Supreme Court ruled that Chandrika Kumaratunge could not contest for the presidency a third time, the choice fell on the charismatic and populist Prime Minister Mahinda Rajapaksa. The LTTE called for a boycott of the elections. In the closest presidential poll in Sri Lanka's history – and perhaps the most decisive – Rajapaksa emerged the winner. After his election, Rajapaksa appointed his brother Gotabhaya as the secretary to the Ministry of Defence in November 2005. In December, the government appointed Lieutenant General Sarath Fonseka as the commander of the army. All three were men who saw little merit in pursuing peace with the LTTE.

Sri Lanka now had a political and military leadership that matched the growing hawkishness of the Tigers. The government still made the customary pronouncements in support of peace talks, but the military option was now being considered seriously for the first time in the history of the conflict. And unlike previous governments, who, even if they had so wished, did not possess the wherewithal to pursue a 'military solution', the new regime also had an unprecedented military superiority over the rebels.

The balance shifts

The military balance had begun to change even before the ceasefire. As noted earlier, with the Tigers clawing at the gates of Jaffna, the government went on an arms buying spree, which increased the firepower of its forces by leaps and bounds. The disastrous Agni Kaila offensive in April 2001 showed the army the need for even greater firepower to dislodge the Tigers from their entrenchments. With the ceasefire coming into effect, the government moved to redress this situation. By 2002, the army had nearly doubled its artillery, from 97 in 2001 to 187 in 2002, while the number of APCs rose from 158 to 204, largely due to the acquisition of the BMP-2s from the Russian Federation. Between 2001 and 2002, the air force had also purchased two MiG-27s, one MiG-23, at least ten Mi35 attack helicopters and ten transport planes. The last included three AN32s.[10] To boost their surveillance capability, a more sophisticated model of Unmanned Aerial aircraft (UAV) was added to the air force's inventory.[11]

The navy also made great strides. In 2005, in order to meet the challenge of the enemy's naval threat, the Sri Lankan navy set up the Small Boat Squadron (SBS) and the Rapid Action Boat Squadron (RABS), which were equipped with small, heavily armed Inshore Patrol Crafts (IPC). These boats, the smallest of which were the 23-foot Arrow Boat, were developed by the Sri Lankan navy and were equipped with a heavy machine gun and several light machine guns. They were trained to attack rebel boats using an arrowhead formation that would swamp the enemy crafts with numbers and firepower.[12] The SBS was also being trained to carry out surveillance inside the Tigers' naval territory and also to function as the navy's equivalent of the long-range reconnaissance unit, carrying out surveillance and strikes deep within enemy territory.[13]

On the other hand, there were serious setbacks for the rebels. The tsunami of 2004 that devastated the coastal areas of Sri Lanka fell heavily on the Tigers, especially their naval wing. Among the thousands that died in the north-east of the island were an estimated 2,800 LTTE cadres, the vast majority of the Sea Tigers. 'In seven to 10 minutes, it was all over – radar and communications facilities, munitions dumps and dry docks were all basically devastated,' an intelligence source was quoted as saying.[14] The rebels' naval arm had been thoroughly degraded and it would never regain its former prowess.

To make matters worse, the rebels also faced a serious rift within their ranks. In March 2004, Karuna, the rebel commandant in the East, raised the standard of revolt, complaining of the discriminatory treatment of the eastern cadres and declaring his intentions of functioning

178 The peace that failed and the reconquest

independently. He requested a separate ceasefire with the Sri Lankan government, which was rejected by the latter. Faced by the biggest ever split in their ranks, the Tiger leadership acted ruthlessly. While infiltrators terrorised Karuna supporters in the East, the regular troops of the rebels – which included hundreds of eastern cadres stationed in the North – attacked the renegade's eastern stronghold. While one group landed on the east coast and outflanked Karuna, another group crossed the Verugal, using a ruse to make Karuna's men drop their guard. Outflanked and outmanoeuvred, Karuna's force, said to number 3,000–4,000 cadres, disintegrated, many of his cadres surrendering to the LTTE and Karuna himself escaping to the capital with a few trusted associates, while some of his loyal cadres reportedly took refuge in Sri Lankan army camps on the Batticaloa–Polonnaruwa Border.[15]

Thus ended the most serious rift within the rebel ranks. The ease with which the renegade faction was cowed belied the gravity of the split for the LTTE. They had lost one of their most experienced commanders, one who knew the LTTE intimately, and they had not lost him to death but to defection. It seriously weakened the rebels' hold on the East and strengthened the government's hand by gifting them a rebel leader with invaluable insight into the LTTE's military organisation.

The rebel offensive

With the election of Mahinda Rajapaksa, the stage was set for the escalation of tensions between the government and the rebels. Rajapaksa had campaigned on a platform for renegotiating the ceasefire and had had the backing of southern hardliners including the JVP. In no mood to conciliate, the Tigers exploited the situation to push and prod the government. Even while the peace talks continued, the LTTE had carried out a systematic campaign of assassinations to consolidate their position. Their victims included their rivals and government intelligence personnel. One of the most prominent to be murdered was Major T. Nazim Muthaliph of the Sri Lanka Military Intelligence. On May 31 2005, he was gunned down as he waited in traffic.[16] By mid-2005, more than 400 people had been killed in a brutal campaign of assassinations. These included 147 civilians, 36 political activists and 37 Security Forces personnel.[17] Now with a new hard-line government in power, the Tigers shifted gear. From December 2005, the rebels began to mount pressure on the government through a series of attacks on the Security Forces. Claymore attacks in the North and the East claimed more than 150 lives of government troops. Civilians also came in for punishment. In one devastating attack on a passenger bus, more than 60 people were killed in Kebithigollewa in the Anuradhapura District.[18] Counter-violence by Security Forces aggravated the situation. Soon after the attack on the bus, air force jets bombed suspected rebel targets around Mullaithivu.[19] The ceasefire was looking increasingly fragile.

In the East, the Tigers battled Karuna's cadres. Despite failing to mount a serious challenge to the LTTE immediately, Karuna's hard core were able to continue operating in Batticaloa, particularly in the coastal belt much to the chagrin of the Tigers. The LTTE succeeded in killing some of Karuna's men, but it also lost some of its own. A notable loss to the Tigers was E. Kausalyan, the head of its political wing. He was killed in an ambush along with five others in February 2005, as they travelled back to Batticaloa after overseeing reconstruction efforts in a region hard hit by the December 26 tsunami.[20] In May 2006, they were also implicated in the death of Colonel Ramanan, the chief LTTE intelligence operative in the East.[21]

Despite continued efforts of international backers of the peace process, the violence continued. Events took a turn for the worse when peace talks were finally scheduled for April 24–25 2006 in Geneva. The Tigers cancelled the talks, citing transport restrictions. They strongly objected to the Sri Lankan navy's supervision of their eastern leaders travelling to the North to attend a meeting.[22] On April 23,, six rice farmers were found killed in Gomarankadawala in the East. Two days later, the Tigers struck in Colombo by deploying a suicide bomber to assassinate the army commander Lieutenant General Sarath Fonseka.[23] The attack failed and Fonseka survived. In retaliation, the Sri Lankan air force carried out bombing missions, two Kfir and two F-7 aircraft targeting Tiger positions around Trincomalee, particularly around Sampoor, Koonitheevu, Iraalkuli, Ilakkanthai and Uppaaru. Dvora FACs shelled the coastal areas, while long-range artillery and MBRLs from the Monkey Bridge camp in Trincomalee joined the attack.[24]

The doors to peace were closing fast. The last one would close with a little known anicut in Trincomalee.

The last battle for the East

The Mahaveli River that flows into the Indian Ocean at Trincomalee bifurcates at a place a few miles north of the border between the Trincomalee and Polonnaruwa districts. One of the branches continues on as the Mahaveli River, while the other now becomes the Mavil Aru. The Mavil Aru anicut had been constructed across a canal carrying water

180 The peace that failed and the reconquest

from this stream. The sluice gates in the anicut controlled the water to about 30,000 acres of land, giving sustenance to several thousand peasant families from Sinhala, Muslim and Tamil communities.[25]

On July 20 2006, with the peace process in steady decline, the rebels decided to up the ante. They closed the Mavil Aru sluice. They had closed the sluice in June 2005 too but had reopened it soon afterwards, following intervention by the Ceasefire Monitoring Committee. This time, however, the Tigers stood their ground, despite repeated pleas by the Monitoring Committee. Predictably, the move aroused the indignation of the southern public, already chafing at the Tigers' assassination and claymore attack spree. It was seen as part of the same strategy of provocation and confrontation, the closing of the sluice calculated to drive the people from their land in order to establish rebel control over a contiguous area from the south of Trincomalee to Batticaloa.[26] The Tigers, however, presented their aims in humanitarian terms. They claimed that the sluice was closed by the local community in protest against the government's failure to implement an irrigation scheme in the area.[27] If the sluice was to be opened, they said, the government had to resume work on the Eachchalanpattu irrigation scheme and provide speedy relief to the people in the area who were displaced by the tsunami. They also had to stop the aerial bombing of targets in the North and the East.

The deadlock continued, and thousands of acres of paddy land began to dry up without water, driving thousands of peasant families to despair. In the South, as Sinhala nationalist elements capitalised on the incident, pressure for stronger action by the government began to mount. As the tension escalated, the air force carried out several air raids on rebel positions south of Trincomalee.[28] The raids continued in the next few days, the air force targeting rebels' positions further south in Batticaloa, including the LTTE's conference centre at Karadiyanaru, 24 km west of Batticaloa town.[29]

On July 28, the army finally began operations to reopen the sluice. A force of about 2,000 soldiers from the Sri Lanka Light Infantry and the Gemunu Watch led by a contingent of commandos marched on the sluice as part of a move dubbed a 'Humanitarian operation' to open the sluice gates and bring relief to the peasants. Tiger resistance was light at the start. But soon heavy artillery and mortar fire began to zero in on the soldiers, and the advance began to get bogged down amidst mounting casualties. But the troops inched their way amidst the rain of mortars.[30] Realising that the army could not be halted, the Tigers declared on August 8 that they had opened the sluice as a humanitarian

The peace that failed and the reconquest   181

gesture. The government strongly denied it, claiming the troops had captured the sluice and reopened it themselves. What exactly happened is not clear, but what is certain is that it was a victory for the government – and the hardliners.

But by this time what had started as a minor flare-up was threatening to become a conflagration. On Tuesday, August 1, while the battle for Mavil Aru was still raging, the Sea Tigers went on the attack. From their base in Sudaikuda near Sampoor, they swarmed out to attack the *Jetliner*, a passenger ferry bringing over 800 troops from Kankesanthurai to Trincomalee. As the navy's Small Boat Squadron and Fast Attack Crafts went into action, the 122mm artillery and 81mm mortars of the rebels opened up from Sampoor, targeting the Trincomalee naval base. The navy, however, succeeded in forcing the Sea Tigers to withdraw, saving the ferry from certain disaster and claiming to have destroyed three Sea Tiger boats in the process.[31]

Clearly, the rebels were working according to a bigger plan, trying to cripple the naval movement between Trincomalee and Jaffna. Another siege of Jaffna appeared to be imminent. But then, at dawn the following day – August 2 – the Tigers flexed their muscles in the East again. As artillery and mortar fire rained on the Muttur jetty, rebel cadres infiltrated the town from the west, pushing out the army and police checkpoints and overrunning much of the town. Only the police station bolstered by a navy detachment held out. A quick-witted naval officer utilised an MBRL parked in the naval dockyards to keep the enemy away from the jetty while the Security Forces gathered reinforcements. Over the next two days, hundreds of naval ratings poured into the Muttur jetty. As the troops moved in to clear the town, heavy fighting broke out, with both sides resorting to artillery. Again the Security Forces prevailed. By the end of the week, the Tigers had been ejected, even though the rebels claimed they withdrew. The navy admitted to losing 14 men, while the rebels claimed they had the bodies of 40 slain soldiers.[32]

The rebels may have been foiled at Muttur, but their rampage was not limited to the town. While Muttur burned, the Tigers laid siege to several army camps to the south of Trincomalee. In a move reminiscent of their sweeping assault in June 1990, the Tigers attacked the Kattaparichchan, Selvangar and Pahala Thoppur camps, placing the small garrisons under strain. But here too, the soldiers held out, now boosted by support from helicopter gunships and artillery fire. From the naval dockyards, the MBRL again belched its fire, keeping the assailants at bay.[33]

Then, just as the dust from the battle was settling down in Muttur and Mavil Aru, the Tigers made their expected pounce on Jaffna.

From August 11, they launched a multi-front assault on Security Forces' defences in the North. Supported by their long-range artillery that opened up from Pooneryn, rebel cadres attempted to overwhelm the defences at Muhamalai by land, while Sea Tiger boats approached Kilali, hoping to storm the defences on the coast. The land attack met with some success, the Tiger assault troops pushing back the army from several bunkers in the Muhamalai FDL. But a counter-attack soon drove them back.[34] However, the naval assault turned out to be a costly failure. The Tigers had miscalculated their timing; as the flotilla approached the shore at low tide, the battle tanks and MBRLs on the shore easily picked them off, blowing the boats to bits, killing dozens of cadres.[35] The Tigers also attempted to land on the islands of Mandaithivu and Kayts, but here too their success was short-lived. Parts of the islands were occupied by the rebels on the eleventh before they were ejected by the Security Forces the following day.

But the rebel attack was by no means over. While the struggle for the FDL and the islands went on, the rebel artillery went into action. Shells from their long-range guns in Pooneryn began to descend on Palali, causing damage to the runway. On August 12, the rebel guns in the East also joined in, opening up on the naval dockyards in Trincomalee.[36]

For the next few days, the Tigers continued their fruitless assault on the defences in the North to no avail. But fighting was gradually fizzling out now, both sides considerably exhausted by attack and defence. By August 25, the army managed to finally eject the weary rebels out of the bunkers they had captured on the eleventh.[37] After two weeks of fighting, the frontlines remained more or less the same as they were before the rebel assault. But hundreds had died in the bloody struggle. The army admitted to losing 131 offices and soldiers killed and over 170 wounded while claiming that they had killed and wounded hundreds of rebel cadres. This may have been an overestimate, but the fact that the Security Forces buried over 100 bodies of fallen rebels suggests that the Tigers too had suffered severely in their aborted attacks.[38]

From Sampoor to Thoppigala

After their failed offensive in Muttur and Jaffna, the Tigers seemed content to go on the defensive. It was now the government that took the initiative. With the situation in the North stabilised, the Security Forces moved on to the attack, focusing on the Eastern Province. The government was still paying lip service to negotiations, but all indications were that it was now determined to pursue the military option till its logical conclusion – the destruction of the LTTE. Despite misgivings in some quarters, especially the peace lobby and some of the government's international backers, this approach was receiving considerable support from a southern public now frustrated with the peace process and what was seen as the LTTE's provocation of military confrontation. The Sinhala hardliners backed the government all the way. For many years, they had argued that this was the only option and that the war was 'unwinnable' because this option had not been tried seriously. Now that they had a political and military leadership that seemed to believe in this option, they rallied around it.

The Security Forces lost little time in pursuing the Tigers. The immediate objective was Sampoor where the Tigers had located their artillery, threatening Trincomalee harbour. But the ultimate goals of the Security Forces were far more ambitious than that: the recovery of the entire province. And unlike the previous operations in the region, this was to be one which would clear the province completely and hold it, rather than simply push the rebels out of the main population centres and into the jungles.

The rebel territory south of Trincomalee included much of the coastline between Trincomalee and Batticaloa, extending along the coast just below the Kottiyar Bay all the way down to Kadjuwatte to the north of Batticaloa. To the south of this, the government held on to the coastal belt to the east of the lagoon, while the rebel territory skirted around this stretch of land to swallow the vast hinterland to the west and to extend south across the A5 highway. To the north of Batticaloa, Vakarai functioned as their major stronghold, while to the south Kokkadicholai had emerged as the centre of rebel authority. To the west, the deep jungles around the Thoppigala rock provided sanctuary for numerous bases and training facilities.

The army started methodically, beginning with the rebel bases closest to the Trincomalee harbour and the biggest threat to the naval facilities there. On August 28, troops broke out of the Thoppur, Kattaparichchan and Mahindapura camps and advanced towards Sampoor. They captured Kattaparicchan on August 31, crossing the Kattaparichchan bridge and capturing Tiger camps on the far side. By the end of the first week, they had also captured the villages of Senaiyoor, Ganeshapuram and Ambalnagar.[39] Despite vowing to defend Sampoor tooth and nail, the Tigers withdrew across the Verugal River into the Batticaloa District with their heavy artillery. On the night of September 3, the rebels vacated Sampoor town completely and the army moved in and took full control the following day.[40]

The campaign to recapture the area south of the Verugal River began in late October 2006. The army advanced on Vakarai from three directions – Mahindapura in the north, Trikonamadu nature reserve in the west and Kadjuwatte – the last military camp on the A15 before rebel held territory – in the south. While the ground troops plodded on, navy vessels patrolled the ocean, on the lookout for any rebels fleeing from the region or for reinforcements coming in. The troops moved steadily despite heavy resistance. The Tigers had blown up the Panchenikerni bridge across the Upparu lagoon, but on January 19, Special Forces commandos dived into the lagoon and crossed the lagoon underwater, surprising the enemy. This was the cue for the rebels to withdraw. As the LTTE fled northwards, the troops moved in to take charge of Vakarai. The Tigers tried to make a stand just to the south of the town, but their defence lines were breached again at Panchinankerni on January 16. The army surged north.[41]

The Tigers had already begun withdrawing their heavy weapons in December when it appeared that they could not prevent the army from advancing. Now they retreated into the jungles, regrouping in the thickly forested hinterland to the west.[42] As they withdrew, the army continued its northward advance, clearing the area of any lingering rebels, finally bringing the entire area under army control. By January 20, the government forces were in complete control of Vakarai. For the first time since 1996, the A15, the main road from Batticaloa to Trincomalee, came under government control.

As it became clear that the Tigers were not likely to hold out, the civilians, fearing an all-out assault by the Security Forces, began to stream out of Vakarai. Using whatever routes they could find, they trekked through the jungles to find places of safety. By late December, nearly 30,000 had moved out of the region, filling refugee camps in government-controlled areas.[43] As the army moved in to take Vakarai in January, the remaining thousands of civilians poured out of the area.[44]

The battle for Vakarai cost the army 45 killed and 108 wounded while the rebels' deaths were estimated at 71.[45] Evidently, the rebels had managed to extricate themselves with light losses. But the battle cost them heavily in terms of war material. After the capture of Vakarai and the clearing of the surrounding areas, the army recovered a massive haul of weapons. Despite attempts to move out their heavy weapons, the Tigers had not been able to remove their heavy artillery. The army recovered two partially destroyed 152mm guns and two 122mm guns, along with over 750 T56 rifles and nearly 70,000 T56 rounds. The four heavy guns had been interred in trenches about 15 feet deep. The army also found

The peace that failed and the reconquest 185

a large number of vehicles including tractors, double cabs and buses, many of them destroyed beyond use.[46]

The biggest blow for the rebels, however, was the loss of control over the Vakarai coast. Along with the loss of the coast around the Trincomalee harbour, this closed off all access to the sea in the East, south of Trincomalee, thereby blocking their seaborne supply routes. The control of the A15 also eased the Security Forces' logistical problems.

Meanwhile, further south in Ampara too, the Security Forces were making headway. While the army was advancing on Vakarai, the STF launched an operation, code named 'Niyathai Jaya', to clear the Kanchikudichchi aru jungles in Ampara. On January 4 2007, as the STF advanced the Tigers retreated, offering only token resistance. By the beginning of February, the area was declared cleared of major rebel concentrations, the STF having captured nearly 20 rebel camps of various sizes along with many vehicles, generators and other equipment that pointed to a well-entrenched base complex. Only four members of the STF were reported wounded due to mines and no LTTE casualties were reported, a sign that the rebels had chosen to abandon the camps rather than stand and fight.[47] But the Tigers had been made to withdraw from one more area in the East, another nail in the coffin of their eastern domain.

The attention of the Security Forces now shifted to the Thoppigala region and the area south of the A5 in Batticaloa, the last rebel stronghold in the East. Like many other places in the province, the Thoppigala area had fallen back under the rebels' control after troops were summoned for operations in the North in the mid-1990s. Since then, the Tigers had held on to the vast jungle fastness despite several operations aimed at shaking their grip on it. The jungles around the rock concealed numerous rebel bases, especially in the Narakamulla area. The rock and the jungles surrounding it also formed part of the vast hinterland of Tiger country to the west of Batticaloa, straddling the Maha Oya–Chenkaladi highway (A5) and extending all the way south to the border with Ampara. This was where the Tigers withdrew after the loss of Vakarai. It was estimated that around 300–400 rebels had retreated there with some of their remaining heavy weapons.[48] It was their last stronghold in the East, their last refuge.

The army gave them little respite. By early March 2007, operations to clear the area were well under way. By the third week of March, the Unnichchai tank, where the rebels had entrenched themselves, had fallen but only after fierce resistance.[49] With Unnichchai in the bag, the army now extended their control gradually up to Vavunathivu to the east, establishing a line of control across the rebel territory, splitting it into two. The area south of this line was now gradually reduced, eliminating the last pockets of rebel control in the region. One of the rebel strongholds to fall under the Security Forces' control was Kokkadicholai, which had functioned as a key LTTE administrative centre. It boasted numerous new buildings including a modern conference facility. Now, as the army closed in, the rebels abandoned all that, preferring to withdraw north of the A5 rather than defend the town. The army entered the town on March 28.

Now the attention focused on the A5. Troops moved north-west from Vavunathivu and took Karadiyanaru on the highway.[50] Despite some resistance, the rebels gradually withdrew deeper into the jungles. By late April, they had relinquished the highway completely, moving further into the terrain covered with scrub jungle to its north. The army now pushed on across a landscape that had few roads and settlements, an area that had been Tiger country for more than a decade.[51] By the end of June, they had finally reached the general area of Narakamulla on the fringes of Thoppigala, capturing the Tigers' main bunker line. The rebels retreated, leaving behind a haul of small arms and a large fleet of vehicles including double cabs, trailers and canter trucks.[52]

With Narakamulla gone, the rebels continued to resist, but this was now more like a delaying tactic to enable their cadres to slip through the army cordon. By now the rebels were beginning to retreat from the East itself. As many as 200 are said to have filtered through the army cordon by this time, led by the eastern rebel commander Ramesh.[53] When the army finally reached the coveted Thoppigala rock in the second week of July, the remaining Tigers had long melted into the jungle to begin the long trek north. Among the booty recovered by the army were two badly damaged 120mm mortar pieces along with a large cache of small arms and ammunition. An MBRL and a SAM were also recovered. The MBRL which had four barrels had been dismantled and smeared with grease before being buried.[54] The rebels had also torched a large number of vehicles. The army found some of the bases at Thoppigala and Narakamulla extremely well situated, some impervious to artillery fire. As testimony to a more peaceful past, the dome of a temple stood on top of the rock with paintings of deities. An LTTE cadre had left his slippers there.[55]

Within a year of provoking a confrontation at Mavil Aru, the rebels had lost the East completely. To be sure, there was still an LTTE presence in the province. According to some analysts, the rebels still hovered in the coastal area and in the jungles in small groups but only as intelligence and assassination squads.[56] In July 2007, it was reported that a group of 50 rebels had infiltrated the East. Suspected Tiger guerrillas shot dead the chief secretary of the Eastern Provincial Council, Herath Abeyweera. The next day, they shot dead an army captain and wounded two soldiers at Sittaru near Kantalai in the Trincomalee district.[57] Suspected LTTE cadres ambushed a patrol of Sri Lankan soldiers in the Inguruhinna area of the Thoppigala region in Sri Lanka's Eastern Province as late as November 27 2008, killing one soldier.[58] But these were the groans of a mortally wounded Tiger. As a fighting force, the LTTE was finished in the East.

A new battlefield equation

The rebels' unsuccessful attempt on Jaffna and the failure to defend the East showed how far the military balance had shifted. The Jaffna offensive was a far cry from the devastating rebel onslaughts in Ealam War III. Not only did they fail to capture any significant amounts of weaponry and equipment but the Security Forces also regained the lost ground without delay. The bunkers lost at Muhamalai were captured within 72 hours, and the ejection of the Tigers from the islands was even quicker.[59] There were several reasons for this. The grinding resistance to Jayasikurui and the battering received at the hands of rejuvenated and refurbished Sri Lankan forces in their repulse from Jaffna in 2000 had drained the rebels of experienced cadres, and clearly, they had not recovered from that yet. And they were now hurling themselves against a military that had acquired far heavier firepower than it possessed in 2000. They had managed to preserve much of their artillery in Pooneryn, but exposing their cadres on the ground to the fury of the MBRLs and the air force's MiGs was a different proposition altogether. It was as if the Tigers had tried to roar but had produced only a whimper. It would set the tone for their operations for the next three years.

In the East too, the rebels faltered, this time in defence. This owed in a large measure to the approach of the Security Forces – strategically and tactically. Led by the tenacious Fonseka and Rajapaksa, in their drive for the East the Security Forces had demonstrated a clarity of purpose and a determination rarely shown in previous campaigns. This was not a campaign to push the rebels back from the main population centres or to clear the main supply routes. This was an operation that clearly aimed at removing the LTTE from the East for good. The methodical reduction of rebel territory demonstrated this, ending with the capture of Thoppigala.

188 The peace that failed and the reconquest

The military tactics also showed how far the Security Forces had travelled since they last ventured into rebel territory in the region. On the one hand, they deployed a firepower that was never previously seen in the East. Days of heavy bombardment carried out by the MiGs and Kfirs from the air and artillery, including the devastating MBRLs from the ground, battered rebel defences and morale alike. The armoured vehicles provided mobility as well as fire support for the advancing troops, moving through the dense brush and pounding suspected rebel positions ahead.[60] For the first time in the East, main battle tanks were firing their guns on enemy positions in the Thoppigala jungles, augmenting the barrage of MBRL, artillery and aerial bombing.

In the ground operations, regular army movements were combined with Special Forces and small group operations. The latter were carried out by the Special Forces attached to the brigade groups as well as ordinary soldiers trained as Special Infantry Operations Teams (SIOT). The concept of using small groups of highly trained soldiers to assail enemy frontlines was introduced in 2002 on a limited scale. It was expanded during Ealam War IV to include many of the soldiers engaged in the frontlines. The aim of the program was to train units of eight men with special skills who could act independently of their main unit for a limited period of time, usually for 48 hours. Their training involved survival techniques, communication, night fighting, marksmanship, handling explosives, medical skills and using signals communications to coordinate artillery and airstrikes. These men would move 1 or 2 km from the baseline and carry out surveillance and elimination of enemy outposts. Each group was tasked with killing at least one rebel a day. Once the groups had established dominance over the area ahead of the defence line, the baseline would move ahead to occupy the dominated area.[61]

Such tactics had been part of the Security Forces' operations since the late 1980s. But until the post-2006 phase of the war or Ealam War IV, they were overshadowed by the large troop movements, and sometimes, as we have seen elsewhere, the commandos even became part of these movements. But now small group operations came to play a prominent tactical role on their own. In Sampoor, the attacks were spearheaded by small groups of Special Forces troops, who moved in advance of the main bodies of troops to dominate the area ahead. They carried out sabotage work, disrupting communications and making the enemy feel insecure in his territory. The main formations of infantry followed in their wake to consolidate the area.[62] The tactics were repeated in Vakarai. Led by Colonel Prasanna Silva, the troops lived in the jungle for weeks, sustained by their ration packets. Their operations made the jungles around

Vakarai increasingly inhospitable for the rebels who now found themselves reduced to the same predicament they had hitherto subjected the government troops. They were being confined to the towns and villages while the jungle came to be dominated by small, highly mobile groups of Special Forces. The vehicular movement along the roads became risky as they were vulnerable to ambushes.[63]

At Thoppigala too, small groups of commandos from the Second and Third Commando Regiments fanned out, probing Tiger defences. Several eight-man teams of the Long Range Patrol (successor to the Long Range Reconnaissance Patrol) ventured into enemy territory, scouting and disrupting communications. The regular ground troops from the Seventh Sri Lankan Light Infantry and Sixth, Seventh, and Eighth Battalions of the Gemunu Watch followed.[64]

This combination of heavy pummelling and stealth succeeded in achieving what the Security Forces had not been able achieve for nearly 15 years – the complete clearing of the East. But perhaps the biggest blow to the rebels was struck outside the island, in the US and the ocean. They demonstrated the extent to which the international climate had changed to the detriment of the Tigers' cause.

The choking supply lines

In the battles for Jaffna and Muttur, the Tigers had offered little resistance to the air force, raising speculation among Sri Lankan defence circles about the state of their arsenal of anti-aircraft missiles. The answer to this was revealed in the most unfortunate way for the Tigers. In August 2006, the US thwarted an attempt by LTTE operatives in the US to obtain a cache of weapons worth $1 million including 20 SA-18 heat-seeking, surface-to-air, anti-aircraft missiles; 10 missile launchers and 500 AK-47s. The two men accused of the act were arrested in Canada and were expected to be extradited to the US to stand trial.[65] The incident showed that the rebels were struggling to make the missiles they already possessed operable and came as a serious setback to their efforts to redress it.[66] This enabled the air force's jets and helicopters to prowl the skies without molestation during the recapture of the East.

The defensive strategy of the rebels in the East was dictated partly by their circumstances in the province. They had a semi-conventional arsenal but a small force. The artillery was not placed in expectation of a conventional battle but to threaten the harbour. The few heavy guns they had were no match for what the army could bring to bear on them. Among the booty recovered by the army at Thoppigala were

190 The peace that failed and the reconquest

an MBRL and a SAM. The MBRL which had four barrels had been dismantled and smeared with grease before being buried.[67] But there was another side to this lack of firepower. Throughout the campaign, the MBRL and the heavy artillery had been used sparingly, hinting at a lack of ammunition. The dwindling stock of shells underlined a crisis in supply. The Tigers' seaborne supply lines were also being gradually choked. This was a direct result of the growing confidence of the Sri Lankan navy at sea, backed by the resources of Indian intelligence. On September 17 2006, a combined air and naval attack sank one of the Tigers' merchant ships, bringing a supply of arms and munitions for the rebels. The shipment was supposed to have included mortars, artillery, anti-aircraft missiles and other munitions.[68] With Sampoor lost and the army poised to move on Vakarai, these would have provided a welcome succour to the retreating Tigers. But this was only the beginning. During the next year, the Sri Lankan navy went on the offensive, sinking as many as six more of the rebels' 'floating warehouses'. The last four were sunk deep in international waters, close to Australia's maritime border.[69]

The loss of the ships on top of the failure in obtaining the SAMs dealt a severe blow to the rebels' chances of retaliating against the army. For years, they had depended on these vessels to replenish their arsenal and fight the Sri Lankan forces to a standstill. Now, having committed themselves to a conventional war against an enemy using unprecedented firepower, they needed an ever-increasing supply of weapons, especially ammunition, to fight back. But little was getting through and the rebels' heavy weapons, particularly the MBRL, though they remained a menace in the East, spewed their venom sparingly.

The sinking of the rebel merchant fleet deep in international waters also demonstrated a remarkable confidence on the part of the Sri Lankan navy. It also owed a lot to the intelligence provided by India.[70] Every six months, the officers of the Indian navy and coast guard met their Sri Lankan counterparts to discuss strategies and other related matters.[71] They could place in the hands of the Sri Lankan navy vital information only their sophisticated surveillance equipment could gather. Not only India but also the US provided the Sri Lankan navy with intelligence gathered by the US Pacific command through signals and imagery intelligence.[72] In short, the rebel merchant navy was not only fighting the Sri Lankan navy but also the vast resources of the Indian and US naval establishments.

Faced by a vastly superior enemy and limited means of engaging him, the Tigers opted to go on the defensive. Their strategy was to hold out as long as possible and preserve their weaponry and cadres as much as possible. The rebels' deadliest retaliations came in the form of unconventional attacks. On October 16, a suicide bomber driving an explosives-laden Isuzu half lorry exploded his deadly load in Boraluwala, Digampathaha, near Habarana where a large number of sailors had gathered while going on and returning from leave. The blast killed at least 116 and wounded more than 130.[73] Two days later, on October 18, the rebels launched a daring attack on the navy detachment in Galle. Entering the harbour while posing as fishing boats, five Sea Tiger boats attempted to attack the navy crafts and buildings in the harbour. The attack caused more panic than damage; 13 sailors and 8 civilians were injured, a sailor and a civilian succumbing to their injuries later. An Inshore Patrol Craft (IPC), a coastal patrol boat, a Dvora Fast Attack Craft (FAC) and the non-operational sub chaser SLNS Parakrama were damaged along with two oil tanks and two buildings. All five rebel crafts were destroyed by the navy, who also claimed they had killed 15 of the attackers. The bodies of three of them later washed ashore near the naval establishment.[74] Then, on December 1 2006, the Tigers went for the jugular. A suicide bomber tried to ram Gotabhaya Rajapaksa's motorcade with his explosive-rigged three-wheeler. The attack failed. Gotabhaya survived to live with renewed zeal to see the back of the Tigers.

In hindsight, the loss of the East seems to suggest that the rebels had made a blunder in provoking another war. But the Tigers' decision to opt for another round of military confrontation should be seen in the context of their overall strategy and the situation they found themselves in after the ceasefire agreement. Complete independence had always been the LTTE's final goal and peace talks had been a way of moving closer to that. The peace process after the Ceasefire Agreement was not going the way they wanted, and they were being increasingly constrained by the involvement of international players. While a political settlement was always possible, it was never likely to be what they desired: total independence. Trapped within their own goals and the constraints of the ceasefire, war was looking increasingly like an attractive, and to them perhaps the only, option. The Tigers had made all their gains mainly through military prowess and they had come tantalisingly close to sealing their claims to the North in 2000. One more push, using the strength they had acquired during the ceasefire, would get them just over the line. And even if they failed, another protracted war, against a government seen as a hard-line Sinhala regime, could give them the leverage they needed to bring the peace process back on to a more favourable track. In the circumstances, it would prove to be not only suicidal but also an understandable response from an organisation whose singleness of purpose flew in the face of reality.

Notes

1 Nirupama Subramanian, 'Terror at Katunayake', *Frontline*, 17.8.01, pp. 51–3; Rohan Gunaratna, 'A Wake up Call', *Frontline*, 31.8.01, pp. 52–4.
2 'Sri Lanka Seals Truce Deal', http://news.bbc.co.uk/2/hi/south_asia/1835737.stm
3 For the full Ceasefire Agreement see http://www.norway.lk/Embassy/Peace-Process/Role-of-Norway/
4 V.S.Sambandan, 'Peace Process in Trouble', *Frontline*, 23.5.03, pp. 128–30.
5 M. Balasuriya, *Rise and Fall of the LTTE*, (Colombo: 2011), pp. 151–4.
6 Iqbal Athas, 'Attack on Tiger Ship – a Job Well Done', *Sunday Times*, 13.3.03, http://www.sundaytimes.lk/030316/index.html; Iqbal Athas, 'Navy between Bravery and Brickbats', *Sunday Times*, 22.6.03, http://www.sundaytimes.lk/030622/index.html
7 Iqbal Athas, 'Tiger Trap for Trinco Siege', *Sunday Times*, 3.8.03, http://www.sundaytimes.lk/030803/index.html
8 Chandraprema, *Gota's War*, pp. 263–4; D.B.S. Jeyaraj, 'Wretched of the North East Lanka Earth', http://transcurrents.com/tamiliana/page/20?s=jeyaraj
9 V.Suryanarayan, 'Stepping Stone to a Separate State', *Frontline*, 21.11.03, pp. 15–16.
10 Blodgett, Sri Lanka's Military, pp. 138–41. The artillery pieces were mainly 122mm, 152mm and 130mm pieces. *Military Balance*, 2002, Central and South Asia, p. 135.
11 Moorcraft, *The Total Destruction*, p. 66.
12 Tim Fish, Sri Lanka Learns to Counter Sea Tigers' Swarm Tactics', *Jane's Navy International*, March 2009, pp. 21–3.
13 Paul A. Povlock, 'A Guerrilla War at Sea: The Sri Lankan Civil War', *Small Wars Journal*, 9.9.11, pp. 31–2, http://smallwarsjournal.com/sites/default/files/848-povlock.pdf
14 Anthony Davis, 'Tamil Tigers Seek to Rebuild Naval Force', *Jane's Intelligence Review*, 1.3.05.
15 D.B.S.Jeyaraj, 'The Fall of Karuna', *Frontline*, 7.5.04, pp. 122–4; V.S.Sambandan, 'A Rebellion in the East', *Frontline*, 26.3.04, pp. 114–16; Iqbal Athas, 'LTTE in Move to Destabilise East', *Sunday Times*, 30.7.06, http://sundaytimes.lk/060730/index.html
16 Col. A. Hariharan, 'LTTE and Ceasefire Violations', http://www.southasiaanalysis.org/%5Cpapers15%5Cpaper1406.html (4.9.12)
17 V. Sambandan, 'War by Other Means', *Frontline*, 18.6–1.7.05 (v. 22, no. 13) http://www.frontlineonnet.com/fl2213/stories/20050701002304200.htm
18 Kesara Abeywardana, 'Last Post for Victims of Brutal Terror', *The Nation*, 18.6.06, http://www.nation.lk/2006/06/18/newsfe1.htm
19 Sri Lankan Kfir Jets Bomb Mullaithivu; Sampoor Under Artillery Attack, Tamilnet, 15.6.06, http://www.tamilnet.com/art.html?catid=13&artid=18513

The peace that failed and the reconquest   193

20 'Hundreds Gather for the Funeral of the Slain Tamil Tiger', *Gulf News*, 11.2.05, http://gulfnews.com/news/world/other-world/hundreds-gather-for-funeral-of-slain-tamil-tiger-1.276968 (4.9.12)

21 'Tigers Flash War Alert after Leader Death', *The Telegraph*, Calcutta, 23.5.06, http://www.telegraphindia.com/1060523/asp/foreign/story_625 8616.asp; 'Eastern Promise: Sri Lankan Troops Turn Tigers Back into Guerrillas', *Jane's Intelligence Review*, 20.9.07.

22 'Until the hurdles in front of us to attend Geneva talks are removed and a more conducive environment created, our team is unable to come to the talks,' the Tigers said in a letter to the Norwegian facilitators. 'Tamil Tigers Harden Talks Stance', *BBC News*, http://news.bbc.co.uk/2/hi/south_asia/4911554.stm

23 Alex Perry, 'If This Is Called Peace. . . .', *Time Magazine World*, 30.4.06, http://www.time.com/time/magazine/article/0,9171,501060508–1189385,00.html

24 'Mini War in Sampoor', *Daily Mirror*, 26.4.06, http://archives.daily mirror.lk/2006/04/28/opinion/04.asp

25 Iqbal Athas, 'Ealam War IV Rages on Several Fronts', *Sunday Times*, 13.8.06, http://www.sundaytimes.lk/060813/columns/sitrep.html

26 Iqbal Athas, 'LTTE in Move to Destabilise East', *Sunday Times*, 30.7.06, http://sundaytimes.lk/060730/index.html

27 B. Muralidhar Reddy, 'Water War', *Frontline*, 15–25.8.06, v. 23, no. 16, http://www.frontlineonnet.com/fl2316/stories/2006082500 1405400.htm

28 Iqbal Athas, 'LTTE in Move to Destabilise East'.

29 'Air Strikes Target LTTE Camps in Batticaloa', *The Island*, 30.7.06, http://www.island.lk/2006/07/30/news2.html

30 Iqbal Athas, 'The Ealam War IV: Trinco in danger', *Sunday Times*, 6.8.06, http://sundaytimes.lk/060806/index.html

31 Norman Palihawadana, 'Tiger Attack on Troop Carrier Repulsed, Trinco under LTTE Fire', *The Island*, 2.8.06, http://www.island. lk/2006/08/02/news1.html Athas, 'The Ealam War IV: Trinco in Danger'.

32 Chandraprema, *Gota's War*, p. 324, Iqbal Athas, 'The Ealam War IV: Trinco in Danger', 'Heavy Fighting in Muttur as Death Toll Rises', *Sunday Leader*, 6.8.06, http://www.thesundayleader.lk/archive/20060806/news.htm

33 Chandraprema, *Gota's War*, pp. 326–7.

34 Ranga Jayasooriya, 'Tiger Offensive Repulsed in Kilali', *Observer*, 20.8.06, http://www.sundayobserver.lk/2006/08/20/fea17.asp; Iqbal Athas, 'LTTE Planning Big Hits', *Sunday Times*, 1.10.06, http://sundaytimes. lk/061001/Columns/sitreport.html

35 Iqbal Athas, 'LTTE Planning Big Hits', Ranga Jayasooriya, 'Tiger Offensive Repulsed in Kilali'.

36 Iqbal Athas, 'Heavy Battles in North and East', *Sunday Times*, 13.8.06, http://sundaytimes.lk/060813/index.html

37 Iqbal Athas, 'LTTE Takes Beating; but a Long Way to Go', *Sunday Times*, 27.8.06, http://sundaytimes.lk/060827/index.html

194 The peace that failed and the reconquest

38 Ranga Jayasooriya, 'Tigers Planning Major Attack During Monsoon Season', *Observer.*
39 D.B.S. Jeyaraj, 'Army Seizes Four Villages around Sampur', *Sunday Leader*, 3.9.06, http://www.thesundayleader.lk/archive/20060903/news.htm#Army
40 D.B.S.Jeyaraj, 'Simmering East Set to Explode', *Sunday Leader*, 10.9.06, http://www.thesundayleader.lk/archive/20060910/issues.htm
41 Iqbal Athas, 'Vakarai: the Reality Behind the Euphoria', *Sunday Times*, 21.1.07, http://sundaytimes.lk/070121/Columns/sitreport.html; Amantha Perera, 'Beyond Vakarai', *Sunday Leader*, 28.1.07, http://www.thesundayleader.lk/archive/20070128/defence.htm
42 Amantha Perera, 'LTTE Regrouping in Jungles', *Sunday Leader*, 28.1.07, http://www.thesundayleader.lk/archive/20070128/news.htm#After
43 D.B.S. Jeyaraj, 'Civilians Suffer in Battle over Vaharai', *Sunday Leader*, http://www.thesundayleader.lk/archive/20061224/issues.htm
44 Amantha Perera, 'Beyond Vakarai'.
45 Sri Lal Seneviratne, *Negenahira Mudageneema*, Self-published, Honganji Graphics, Naranhenpita Sri Lanka 2008, pp. 36–7.
46 Ibid., p. 36.
47 Mendis, *Assignment Peace*, pp. 653–6.
48 Amantha Perera, 'War Comes Full Circle', *Sunday Leader*, 15.7.07, http://www.thesundayleader.lk/archive/20070715/defence.htm
49 'Corporal Nuwan Tharanga: Fallen Hero at Thoppigala', http://www.sundayobserver.lk/2008/03/16/mag04.asp
50 'Special Forces Poised to Capture Thoppigala Jungle', http://www.sundayobserver.lk/2007/06/24/fea02.asp
51 'Battle for Thoppigala Erupts Again', *Sunday Times*, 10.6.07, http://www.sundaytimes.lk/070610/News/news4.html
52 Ranil Wijayapala, 'Liberation Thoppigala', *Sunday Observer*, 11.10.09, http://www.sundayobserver.lk/2009/10/11/sec03.asp
53 Amantha Perera, 'War Comes Full Circle', Iqbal Athas, 'Heavy Casualties as War Intensifies', *Sunday Times*, 24.6.07 http://www.sundaytimes.lk/070624/Columns/sitreport.html
54 'Troops Recover LTTE Multi Barrelled Rocket Launcher', http://www.lankalibrary.com/phpBB/viewtopic.php?f=2&t=3650&start=0
Sri Lal Seneviratne, *Negenahira Mudageneema*, pp. 48–9.
55 Santush Fernando, 'How Thoppigala Fell Like Nine Pins', http://www.nation.lk/2007/07/22/militarym.htm
56 D.B.SJeyaraj, 'Eastern Cauldron', *Frontline*, 24.8.07, p. 47 (45–8)
57 Iqbal Athas, 'East: the Aftermath', 22.7.07, http://www.sundaytimes.lk/070722/Columns/sitreport.html
58 'LTTE Militants Kill Sri Lankan Soldier in Thoppigala', *Jane's Intelligence Review*, 1.12.08.
59 Tom Farrel, 'Northern Exposure: the Next Stage in Sri Lanka's War', *Jane's Intelligence Review*, 15.11.07.
60 Ravi Pathiravithana, 'Guerrilla Warfare: Discussing the Use of Sri Lanka's Fleet of APVs and MBTs', p. 17.
61 Chandraprema, *Gota's War*, 395–6, Sergei De Silva, *Janes Intelligence Review*, 13.11.09.

The peace that failed and the reconquest 195

62 Ranga Jayasooriya, 'Fall of Sampur', *Sunday Observer,* 10.9.06, http://www.sundayobserver.lk/2006/09/10/fea05.asp Chandraprema, *Gota's War*, p. 332.

63 Ranil Wijayapala, 'Liberating Vakarai', *Sunday Observer,* 20.9.09, http://www.sundayobserver.lk/2009/09/20/sec03.asp Chandraprema, *Gota's War*, 347–8.

64 Santush Fernando, 'How Thoppigala Fell like Nine Pins'; Iqbal Athas, 'Army Holds Jaya Pirith; Tigers warn of Bloodbath', *Sunday Times,* 7.3.07, http://sundaytimes.lk/070311/Columns/sitreport.html

65 The men were finally extradited in December 2012 after their lengthy appeal in the Canadian Supreme Court failed. http://www.priu.gov.lk/news_update/Current_Affairs/ca201212/20121229extradited_tamil_tigers_arraigned_in_us_federal.htm, 'Extradited Tamil Tigers Arraigned in US Federal Court to Face Terrorism Charges', 'Two Men Who Tried to acquire Cache of Weapons for Terror Group Extradited', http://www.gsnmagazine.com/node/28137

66 See also Tom Farrel, 'Eastern Promise – Sri Lankan Troops Turn Tigers Back into Guerrillas', *Jane's Intelligence Review*, 20.9.07.

67 'Troops Recover LTTE Multi Barrelled Rocket Launcher', http://www.lankalibrary.com/phpBB/viewtopic.php?f=2&t=3650&start=0; Sri Lal Seneviratne, *Negenahira Mudageneema*, pp. 48–9.

68 Mendis, *Assignment Peace*, pp. 623–8.

69 Paul A. Povlock, 'A Guerrilla War a Sea', *Small Wars Journal,* 9.9.11,pp. 36–7,. http://smallwarsjournal.com/sites/default/files/848-povlock.pdf

70 There were also suggestions that American satellite intelligence may have had a hand in locating the floating warehouses. Povlock, 'A Guerrilla War a Sea', p. 36.

71 John Cherian, 'New Delhi's Dual Approach', 21.11.08, v. 25, no. 23, *Frontline,* http://www.frontlineonnet.com/fl2523/stories/20081121 252312800.htm

72 Hashim, *When Counterinsurgency Wins*, p. 175.

73 Iqbal Athas, 'Real Heroes and Mock Heroics', *Sunday Times,* 22.10.06, http://sundaytimes.lk/061022/Columns/sitreport.html

74 Iqbal Athas, 'Real Heroes and Mock Heroics', *Sunday Times,* 22.10.06, http://sundaytimes.lk/061022/Columns/sitreport.html; Harishchandra Gunaratna, 'Tiger Bid to Blast Galle Naval Base Foiled', *The Island,* 19.10.06, http://www.island.lk/2006/10/19/news1.html

Chapter 12

The rolling up of the Wanni

With the East slipping from the rebels' grasp, the Wanni was shaping as the decisive – and final – battleground. The Tigers had been attacked in this stronghold many times in the past, and each time they had succeeded in bouncing back. But as they braced for the final assault of the Sri Lankan Security Forces, a repeat performance was appearing to be a daunting prospect.

Return to the Wanni: prospects and challenges

The loss of the East, and the failure to obtain vital supplies from abroad, placed considerable strain on a rebel war machine already beginning to stutter and creak. To be sure, in the Wanni the rebels possessed several advantages. They had been in control of this area for a long time and were familiar with the terrain. They also had had a long time to prepare defences. Being a contiguous area, the Wanni also had internal lines of communication that were largely secure. And being a large region with areas of thick forest cover, there was wide room for manoeuvre and retreat in comparative security. The East, in comparison, had been complex. The Tiger territories were ill defined and somewhat scattered rather than contiguous; Tiger-dominated settlements lived cheek by jowl with areas dominated by the Security Forces. The only contiguous areas where the population was under the control of the LTTE was the coastal strip from Vakarai to Sampoor and the area west of Batticaloa, which included the Thoppigala rock. These, however, were much smaller areas with little room for manoeuvre. The STF and the army were never far away.

But in the Wanni, the LTTE also faced some serious problems. Being a large area, it required a large army to defend it, especially if it was to be defended on multiple fronts. The LTTE of 2007 simply lacked

The rolling up of the Wanni   197

this. It was estimated that the Tigers had about 7,000–7,500 troops under their command. Many of their more experienced cadres and some of their leaders were dead. Many – about 1,200 cadres according to government estimates – were also tied up at Muhamalai, facing the Fifty-Fifth and Fifty-Third Divisions that were threatening to push southwards. So far, they had presented a wall of steel to the government troops, but in order to continue their resistance they had to maintain a strong presence across the neck of the peninsula. Southern Wanni and Mullaithivu had about 3,000 cadres each with several hundred guarding the rebel supremo Velupillai Prabhakaran.[1] Chances of increasing these numbers were limited considering that their eastern recruiting grounds were now lost.

All this left only a limited number of battle-hardened troops to defend the southern, eastern and western borders of the Wanni. The Tigers possessed a powerful arsenal of heavy and long-range artillery that could engage the enemy from a distance, but whether this was an adequate compensation for the lack of many foot soldiers was left to be seen. The Tigers' spectacular assaults in the past had been a combination of long- and medium-range artillery fire and massed attacks. They still possessed the firepower, which included several long- and medium-range guns acquired since 2000, but this meant little without the troops to take advantage of it on the ground. Another drawback was that, being a contiguous area, the Wanni could also be systematically rolled up, reduced gradually. The long coastline could also be blocked while internal lines could be made insecure by aerial bombardment and operations by Deep Penetration Units.

When the campaign in the Wanni opened in 2007, the Sri Lankan military was well placed to exploit these drawbacks. The army now had a strength of around 100,000.[2] This was only marginally bigger than the army that fought the disastrous campaign in the Wanni in 1997–99, but in the context of the depletion in the enemy ranks, these numbers were formidable. Moreover, these numbers were now backed by unprecedented firepower. The Sri Lankan military forces went into Ealam War IV with a massive superiority over the Tigers in firepower. As explained earlier, the rebel onslaught on Jaffna in 2000 had seen the government scramble to beef up its military hardware. During the period of relative calm and peace following the ceasefire, this arsenal had been further boosted. When the army began prodding rebel defences in the Wanni in 2007, it possessed over 60 main battle tanks, 217 APCs (35 tracked) and a massive artillery train including 40 each of 130mm and 152 artillery and 22 multi-barrelled rocket launchers. The air force too had been boosted; it now had 17 Fighter ground-attack aircraft (MiG 27 and Kfir) and 14 attack helicopters (Mi24 and Mi35).[3] Boosting this arsenal were artillery locating radars received from China. These replaced the outdated and malfunctioning radars received in the late 1990s from the US and promised to be a huge asset in tackling the rebels' mortars.[4] Locating enemy targets was further facilitated by the introduction of a new version of UAV to the air force.[5] Combined with the aforementioned introduction of arrow boats into the navy, the Security Forces were well equipped to take on the rebels in their Wanni stronghold from land, air and sea.

There was also the Karuna factor. Even though the Sri Lankan military establishment never admitted it, it stands to reason that the defection of a man of such vast experience and knowledge could have only enhanced the Security Forces' knowledge about the enemy's capabilities and mindset. No one on the government's side knew the enemy better than he did. It was an advantage that the Security Forces could ill afford to neglect.

Thus, on paper at least, the Sri Lankan forces had an edge over the rebels in the Wanni. But except for potential insights from Karuna, this was nothing new. The army had enjoyed superiority over the enemy in numbers and firepower throughout the conflict, but the Tiger had always found a way to overcome it. If the Tiger was to be hunted successfully in the Wanni, it would have to be a question not only of firepower and numbers but also their deployment.

Into the Wanni

By the end of 2007, fighting had become general along the Wanni with the army beginning to probe rebel defences. As in the East, the army's objectives in the Wanni were in marked contrast to the previous attempts to penetrate the region. Unlike in the 1990s, the Security Forces had as their objective not the opening of a road or merely destroying rebel camps but of eliminating the enemy. Military movements were aimed at exerting maximum pressure on the enemy and steadily eroding their power until it was permanently erased. It was to be the most determined and single-minded operation in the entire Ealam War.

To achieve this objective, the Security Forces opened multiple fronts in the Wanni. There was already one active front at Muhamalai. The western Wanni was to be the second front. Here, two divisions engaged the Tigers, the Fifty-Seventh to the east of the Giant's Tank and the Fifty-Eighth operating to the west of the reservoir. The Fifty-Eighth

Division began operating in two brigade groups, the 581st and 582nd, but later in the year a third group, the 583rd Brigade, was added. In December, another front was opened up in eastern Wanni with the newly raised Fifty-Ninth Division taking on the Tiger defences ahead of Weli Oya.

Of all these theatres, western Wanni was clearly shaping up as the main theatre of fighting. The army's objective was to take over the so-called rice bowl of Mannar and then move northwards, rolling up the rebel-held western coast. This was important for several reasons. The control of the west coast would deny the Tigers access to the Tamil Nadu coast from which military and medical supplies were smuggled in. Viduthalathivu on the coast was a major Sea Tiger base and functioned as the main link between South India and the west coast and also as the point of origin for many Sea Tiger operations off that coast. Capturing that would make the Tigers seriously consider relocating their assets to the east coast. Along the western coast also lay the A32, a potential MSR to Jaffna. Opening this route, rather than the A9, was fraught with fewer problems when it came to defending the gains, as it lay along the coast and was never too far from supply from the sea. The navy could also defend one flank from possible rebel attacks. The terrain north of the rice bowl was also more open and conducive to the deployment of armour which could facilitate rapid movement as well as the offensive capabilities of the ground troops. The open terrain could also negate rebel attempts to outflank them from the east to some extent. Besides, in the east and close to the A9, the rebels were in greater strength as their nerve centre Mullaithivu lay on the east coast with easy access to the A9 axis. These factors made advancing up the west coast a far more attractive proposition than moving up the east coast or the A9.[6] The army had attempted to accomplish this during the Rana Ghosa operations, but it had ended in a costly failure. Now it was time to try it again, under a new vision, with new hardware against a weakened enemy.

Of the two divisions engaged in western Wanni, the Fifty-Eighth was to move closer to the coast while the Fifty-Seventh was to advance on its flank, neutralising enemy threats in the interior, both divisions rolling up the western Wanni together. The Fifty-Ninth Division in the east was to roll up the eastern coast, edging up to the rebel stronghold on Mullaithivu, and hold that front while the west was won. The eastern front would be the hinge on which the campaign in the west would swing.

In the Mannar rice bowl, fighting focused on the town of Adampan. Here two roads running north–south and east–west through western Wanni met, turning it into a strategic road junction. Capture of

200 The rolling up of the Wanni

Adampan could place the military one step closer to the Tiger stronghold of Viduthalathivu and eventually to its objective of closing the western seaboard. It would also disrupt the rebels' supply lines to their troops in the eastern part of Mannar.[7]

After a painfully slow campaign, Adampan was captured on May 9 2008. In the meantime, the Fifty-Seventh Division continued its manoeuvres to the west of Vavuniya. By the end of 2007, they had pushed the Tigers back from several villages to the north-west of Vavuniya including Periyathampanai.[8] Thampanai was taken on December 25.[9] The army was inching its way towards the prize catch of the Madhu shrine, which was eventually brought under control on April 24. Fighting now centred on Palampiddy, a major Tiger base in the area, located about 8 km north of Madhu. This is an important junction that links Viduthalathivu in the north-west, Madhu in the south, Mullikulam in the south-east and Nedunkanda in north-east. The government announced its capture on May 17.[10]

By now the eastern Wanni had also come alive with fighting. On December 11 2007, fighting broke out in the Kokkuthuduwai area.[11] The Fifty-Ninth struck beyond Kokkuthuduwai, negotiating fields of pressure mines, keeping the rebels on their toes.[12] By the end of June 2008, the army was about 25 km from the rebels' main Mullaithivu base, within reach of artillery fire.[13]

Slowly but surely, the Wanni was being rolled up. On June 30, the Fifty-Seventh and Fifty-Eighth Divisions linked up south of Periyamadu.[14] By July 16, Viduthalathivu had fallen.[15] Illuppaikadawal to the north of Viduthalathivu succumbed on July 20, and on August 2, Velankulam, the last town in Mannar, was in army hands.[16] In the meantime, the Fifty-Seventh Division moved further inland, on the eastern flank of the Fifty-Eighth, to tackle the Mallavi–Tunukkai stronghold of the rebels. This was a vital road link between the A9 and western Wanni with roads fanning out to Velankulam and Illuppakadawai in the west and Kokavil and Mankulam in the East. Capturing the town would choke rebel supplies to their embattled cadres in the west as well as along and beyond the A9. Mallavi was also a largish town with several government buildings and dozens of shops. It was the third-largest town after Kilinochchi and Mullaithivu in LTTE-held areas. Tunukkai fell to the Fifty-Seventh Division on August 22 followed by Mallavi on September 1.[17]

To the west, the Fifty-Eighth Division powered ahead of Velankulam, on the road to Pooneryn. This was where the rebels had sited some of their heavy artillery that could reach Palali and Muhamalai. If Pooneryn could be taken, it would eliminate this danger. It would also complete the control of the western coast. By early September, the army was prodding Tiger resistance to the north-east of Naachchikuda, another Sea Tiger base. The troops bypassed the Sea Tiger stronghold and cut off the Mannar–Pooneryn Road (A32) from the north. Its supply routes cut off, and the town fell to the army on October 29.[18] The Fifty-Eighth Division now raced towards Pooneryn, while the Fifty-Seventh edged towards Kilinochchi from the south and the south-west. As civilians evacuated Kilinochchi en masse, the army announced that it would fire the first artillery rounds into Kilinochchi in the first week of October.[19] On October 1, as expected, the Fifty-Seventh Division opened up on Kilinochchi with its heavy guns, plastering the town and environs with long-range artillery fire for three days, while the air force unloaded its deadly cargoes on the rebel capital.[20]

For a moment, the rebels appeared determined to make a stand before their capital. In an email interview with the Indian magazine *Nakeeran*, Prabhakaran was full of bravado. Capturing Kilinochchi was nothing more than a daydream of the Rajapaksas, he asserted.[21] But in the trenches where the rebels faced the military juggernaut, the retreat continued. To add to the rebels' woes, the army was opening more fronts in the Wanni. In the first week of November, they introduced a new task force, TF III, which was inducted between Fifty-Seventh Division and TF II, and it was heading towards Mankulam, forcing the rebels to divert more cadres to watch its movements.[22] On the western coast, the Fifty-Eighth Division raced northwards. By the second week of November, they were in control of Devil's Point on the coast and were poised to cut off Pooneryn.[23] The Tigers were now faced with the problem of standing and fighting for Pooneryn and risking the loss of their heavy guns or withdrawing. They made a determined stand at Nallur but failed to prevent it from falling on November 15. The rebels now scrambled to save their precious hardware. When Fifty-Eighth Division reached Pooneryn, the Tigers had vanished, towing their artillery along.[24]

With Pooneryn in the bag, the Fifty-Eighth Division started moving south-east along the B69 highway heading towards Paranthan. After fierce battles, the division breached rebel defences to the north of Paranthan, while to the south, the Fifty-Seventh also broke through, fighting knee deep in the monsoon mud in the Adampan area.[25] On December 31, despite heavy resistance, Task Force 1 of Fifty-Eighth Division took the heavily fortified Paranthan town, under the cover of artillery fire and ground-attack aircraft as well as armour support. By the evening of January 1 2009, they had reached the Karadipokku junction just north of Kilinochchi town. The other military formations began converging on Kilinochchi from the east, west and south. By January 2, the troops were in control of the Kilinochchi railway station.[26]

The rebels now staged yet another retreat. Their capital was finally in government hands. The daydream had come true.

With the fall of Kilinochchi, the rebels on the Muhamalai line faced an increasingly untenable position. To be sure, they were still offering stiff resistance. Faced with the threat of being sandwiched between Task Force 1 advancing north from Paranthan and the Fifty-Third and Fifty-Fifth Divisions marching down from the north, the rebel cadres at Muhamalai finally began to fall back. Even as the withdrawal began, the army began its move from the north on January 6. The rebels fought a delaying action, trying to inflict maximum casualties while their heavy weapons and the bulk of their forces were evacuated. The Fifty-Third Division and the Fifty-Eighth Division eventually linked up at Elephant Pass on January 9.[27]

By the third week of January, Task Force 1 was well on its way towards Mullaithivu along the A35 that linked Paranthan with Mullaithivu. The Tigers now held on to only two major urban centres in the interior, Visvamadu and Puthukkudiyuruppu. The former was considered to be where many of the rebels' artillery pieces were based. On the coast, they still held on to Mullaithivu and Chalai. Now the army converged on these last remaining rebel bastions from the north, south and west. Off the east coast, the navy kept up a tight surveillance, deploying their vessels in three rings to prevent rebels from escaping and supplies from trickling in.

By the end of the month, Visvamadu too had fallen.[28] This was followed by Chalai, the last Sea Tiger bastion. The Fifty-Fifth Division moving south from Elephant Pass fought for five days to capture the base, overcoming fierce resistance. Chalai fell by February 5. Among those believed killed were the deputy Sea Tiger leader Vinayagam and several other senior Sea Tiger leaders.[29]

The advance continued. The Fifty-Seventh Division had halted operations to function as a reserve division holding Visvamadu, while the Fifty-Eighth Division now continued the offensive, moving towards Puthukudiyiruppu from the north and the west. To the south of the A35, the Fifty-Ninth Division was closing in.[30] On March 3, the army captured the Puthukkudiyuruppu junction. The rebels had dug themselves in, taking refuge in concrete bunkers, turning this last semi-urban area they had under control into a veritable fortress. They fought hard, exacting a heavy price for the ground they yielded, claiming the lives of

The rolling up of the Wanni   203

80 soldiers from the Fifty-Eighth Division before they abandoned the town.[31] The fortunes of the war were heading in only one direction now.

In the south, Mullaithivu fell on January 25. The Fifty-Ninth Division advancing from the south found four earth bunds blocking its way, but artillery, rocket and air strikes made short work of these. Under cover of night, Special Forces troops crossed the Nanthikadal lagoon and fixed a cable across the water to enable other troops to cross over and take the rebels on their flank. By nine in the morning, the town was in the hands of the Security Forces.[32]

The rebels were now trapped within an area roughly 200 square kilometres in extent. Their numbers too had dwindled. According to military intelligence, they had only about 2,000 cadres left in January.[33] The surviving hard-core Tigers probably did not number more than a few hundred. It was the lowest point the Tigers had ever reached in their long and bloody campaign.

A new kind of war

The campaign that began the rolling up of the Wanni was very different from the previous campaigns in the region. Unlike Jayasikurui and Rana Ghosa, which relied on heavy movement of troops and machines crashing through the jungle, aiming at overrunning vast swathes of territory, this campaign laid emphasis on quick, deadly jabs at the enemy, using small groups of infantrymen. Initial advances by the Fifty-Seventh Division had tried to follow the previous patterns of ponderous movements, inviting costly retaliation.[34] But after their failure, the army opted for the same tactic that had paid dividends in the recent campaign in the East: less conspicuous but deadly assaults by SIOT teams.

The SIOT operations aimed at steadily bleeding the enemy and gaining ground without exposing the troops to too much danger. Large troop movements brought down artillery fire on the soldiers, causing heavy casualties. This was particularly suicidal in the area west of the Giant's Tank, where the advance lay mainly over open ground. Using the small groups to infiltrate and kill the enemy was a far less costly option than moving troops over open ground. They also made use of the commandos and Special Forces to their full potential. Unlike previous campaigns where commandos had been used in large numbers much in the fashion of regular troops, now they were being deployed in a capacity where their special skills could be properly harnessed.

The experience of Corporal Nuwan Tharanga of the Alpha Group of the Second Commando Regiment underlines the nature of these operations. Tharanga's team was chosen to reconnoitre an enemy position near the Giant's Tank in April 2008. Early morning (around 4 a.m.) on April 24 2007, they crawled and crept towards the rebel camp. The bund was heavily mined and booby-trapped while a drain defended it from the front. Tharanga and his men tried to remove some of the booby traps but then decided to wade across the drain waist deep in muddy water. As they emerged on the enemy's side, they were detected and a fire fight ensued, the commandos capturing the bunker with the loss of several men. But now they were assailed from another underground bunker and the men withdrew to regroup. After about 15 minutes, they assaulted the bunker from two directions and finally captured it.[35]

Such operations dominated the army's campaign in the Wanni in the Fourth Ealam War. The general advances were usually made at break of dawn once the enemy frontlines had been badly mauled. Then the operations resumed until the time came for another general advance. This was how the army had inched their way up to and around Adampan. It was largely an infantryman's war, fought in the shadows in the night and the early dawn. It was not until March 2008 that Mi24 gunships had joined the fight for the first time. Hitherto, only fixed-wing, high-altitude aircrafts had been used to target Tiger assets deep in the Wanni.[36]

But the SIOT teams would not have been able to carry out their deadly missions without the support of artillery. The massive firepower of the refurbished Sri Lankan army was often utilised in support of the men on the ground, the army utilising their massive artillery train to provide a high gun density over any given area.[37] They shattered enemy defences and bolstered their morale. The barrages by the multi-barrelled rocket launchers in particular were an awesome experience of sight and sound, as one journalist discovered:

> . . . . at 1:40 a.m. we were witness to a spectacle we would never forget. A salvo of about 20 shells were fired from a multi barrel launcher into enemy territory lighting up the sky with streaks of light for a few seconds as we clearly saw through the lattice work above our door. Though we were a few hundred metres from the firing site, the ground shaking noise was enough to send a chill down our spine. No living creature would want to be at the receiving end of such awesome fire. It immediately gave us a firsthand hint as to what the Americans meant when they crowed about giving the Iraqi army 'shock and awe' with their fire power as they invaded that country.[38]

The rolling up of the Wanni   205

One can simply imagine the impact of these weapons on the receiving end.

In tackling rebel strongholds using these tactics, the army also took a leaf out of the Tigers' book. At the height of their triumphant Unceasing Waves operations in 1999–2000, the Tigers had cut off supply routes to main army bases, forcing the army to give them up. Now the army also applied similar pressure, manoeuvring around the centres of resistance and threatening to constrict them. Almost all the rebel bastions were captured in this fashion.

And while the SIOT teams nibbled at the enemy frontlines, the Security Forces also continued to make the rebels feel insecure behind their lines. Deep Penetration Units were now back in action. In August 2007, a high-ranking rebel medical cadre was killed by a DPU attack on the A9 road near Mankulam. Three months earlier, another attack had taken place about 8 km south of Kilinochchi.[39] On January 5 2008, the unit bagged one of their biggest prizes. They shot and killed Shanmuganathan Ravi Shankar alias 'Colonel' Charles, who was the head of the LTTE military intelligence. Charles was the mastermind behind numerous terror attacks, including the assassination of Ranjan Wijeratna and the Central Bank bombing. He was killed while he was in western Wanni, assisting in the fortification of Viduthalathivu.[40]

Beyond Admapan the country opened up the soggy, marshy ground, giving way to more open land with many abandoned paddy fields that enabled armour also to play a more active role in the advance.[41] Against Naachchikuda, low-flying aircraft also joined the fray, carrying out bombing raids against enemy positions for the first time.[42] But the operations by small groups still played a major role. At Velankulam, while the air force, armour and regular troops launched a frontal assault on the defences, commandos slipped through the rebel net to assail the defences from the East. On August 2, the town was in army hands.[43] At Tunukkai too, small groups of soldiers moved through scrub jungle to outflank rebel defences around the Vavunikulam tank.[44] This was a world removed from the blind jungle bashing during Jayaskikurui.

But all these successes were not obtained cheaply. As the experience of corporal Tharanga illustrates, the Tigers fought tooth and nail for their Wanni stronghold, striving to inflict maximum casualties on the invaders. Corporal Tharanga had found the bund of the Giant's Tank so liberally laced with booby traps and mines that he had to cross the ditch in waist-deep water. Many soldiers got caught in such traps and suffered as a result. The cost was high. According to figures disclosed in parliament, in February 2008, 104 military personnel were killed while 822 were wounded (the number of missing in action was not disclosed).[45] In the following month, there were 93 deaths while 686 were wounded.[46] By the time Adampan fell, the army had lost 248 killed and 1,308 injured.[47] But the army was now big enough to absorb these losses. With the gains in the Wanni, recruitment was picking up. In the first half of 2008, there was still a reluctance to join up, but with the increasing gains made in the Wanni there was a significant boom in the figures in the latter half of the year. Between January and November 2008, nearly 38,000 heeded the military's call to join.[48] During the same period, about 11,000 had also deserted, but the net gain was significant. The aggregate of Security Forces was now reported at roughly 300,000.[49]

In the peninsula too, the army adopted an approach similar to its tactics in the Wanni. The Muhamalai defences were proving impregnable to frontal attacks. Several factors contributed to this. The narrowness of the neck of the peninsula made it easy to defend. The terrain is largely open with grasslands, sand dunes, scrub jungle, marshy land and coconut and palmyra groves, presenting obstacles to advancing troops as well as little cover to them. The narrowness of the area and the natural obstacles to an advancing army also enabled defending troops to concentrate fire on the attackers, anticipating their approach along predictable lines. There was little room to manoeuvre and outflank each other. A well-entrenched army supported by heavy artillery could cause havoc among advancing troops. The army and the LTTE had bolstered their defences with such weapons. The fact that both sides had also placed some of their crack units added to the challenge. The rebels had placed up to 1,000 of their battle-hardened cadres here, while the army had placed their two experienced divisions, the Fifty-Fifth and the Fifty-Third, facing the rebels. The defence lines were also heavily fortified and laid in several tiers. In some places, they were said to be spread no more than 30 yards apart. To complete the picture of impregnability, the no-man's-land was liberally strewn with mines.[50]

After several frontal attacks ended in heavy casualties, the army began employing Deep Penetration Units to probe rebel lines, carrying out their deadly work behind enemy defences. In an attack on June 26 2007, one such group ambushed a rebel vehicle with a claymore. No casualties were reported, but the attack showed that the army was switching to a different mode of operations in the theatre.[51] The army also raised the Mechanised Infantry Brigade attached to the Third Division to the status of a new division. The division consisted of an eclectic collection of the army's infantry fighting vehicles: BTR-80A, BMP-2, Type 63 and WZ551. The military personnel deployed in this unit came from the Third Light Infantry Battalion, Tenth Sinha Regiment, Fourth Gajaba Battalion, and Fifth and Sixth Reconnaissance regiments of the Sri Lanka Armoured Corps.[52]

The army employed the new mechanised unit in making short sharp incursions into Tiger territory. These were costly, but the army high command felt that the price was not too high considering the advantage it obtained. After one particularly bloody incursion in April 2008, the army commander Sarath Fonseka conceded heavy losses but explained it as the cost of a successful strategy to bleed the enemy who was losing their veteran fighter without any significant gains. 'A few more such attempts will bring the LTTE to its breaking point from which it would soon meet its fate,' he explained.[53] As in the Wanni, the army was willing to bleed in order to drain the enemy of blood they could ill afford to lose.[54]

Notes

1 Tom Farrel, 'Northern Exposure: the Next Stage in Sri Lanka's War', *Jane's Intelligence Review*, 15.11.07.

2 Iqbal Athas, 'Heavy Casualties as War Intensifies', *Sunday Times*, 24.6.07, http://www.sundaytimes.lk/070624/Columns/sitreport.html

3 *Military Balance*, 2007, p. 324–5.

4 Chandraprema, *Gota's War*, p. 422.

5 Moorcraft, *The Total Destruction*, p. 66.

6 An excellent analysis of these factors appears in Lt Col. Susantha Seneviratne and Ruwan Harischandra, *Negenahira Mudhagath Meheyuma*, Pahana Publishers, Colombo, 2003, pp. 89–100. Also Iqbal Athas, 'Three Different Thrusts into Rebel Strongholds', *Sunday Times*, 20.2.07, http://www.sundaytimes.lk/080120/Columns/sitreport.html

7 D.B.S. Jeyaraj, 'So Near and Yet So Far in the Mannar War Theatre So Far', http://transcurrents.com/tamiliana/archives/555 (17.10.11).

8 Iqbal Athas, '2008 Year of War, Ban on LTTE Likely', *Sunday Times*, 30.12.07, http://www.sundaytimes.lk/071230/Columns/sitreport.html

9 http://www.satp.org/satporgtp/detailed_news.asp?date1=12/26/2007&id=1#1

10 'Troops Regain Palampiddy', *Daily News*, 19.5.08, http://www.daily news.lk/2008/05/19/sec01.asp

11 Amantha Perera, 'Wanni FDLs Heat up', *Sunday Leader*, 16.12.07, http://www.thesundayleader.lk/archive/20071216/defence-.htm

12 Iqbal Athas, 'Three Different Thrusts into Rebel Strongholds', *Sunday Times*, 20.2.07, http://www.sundaytimes.lk/080120/Columns/sitreport.html

13 Amantha Perera, 'Military Engages Tigers on Six Fronts', *Sunday Leader*, 29.6.08, http://www.thesundayleader.lk/archive/20080629/defence.htm

14 Amantha Perera, 'Troops Gain Strategic Bay', *Sunday Leader*, 20.7.08, http://www.thesundayleader.lk/archive/20080720/defence.htm

208   The rolling up of the Wanni

15 Chandraprema, *Gota's War,* p. 422, Col. Hariharan, 'War after the Fall of Vidatalativu', *The Island,* 23.7.08, http://www.island.lk/2008/07/23/features1.html

16 D.B.S. Jeyaraj, 'Frontline Positions Shift Rapidly in Northern Theatre of War', http://transcurrents.com/tc/2008/08/post_18.html 'Troops Capture LTTE's Last Stronghold in Mannar District', http://www.defence.lk/new.asp?fname=20080802_06

17 D.B.S. Jeyaraj, 'Frontline Positions Shift Rapidly in Northern Theatre of War', Amantha Perera, 'Wanni Fighting Takes Heavy Toll on Both Sides', *Sunday Leader,* 7.9.08, http://www.thesundayleader.lk/archive/20080907/defence.htm

18 Ranil Waijayapala, 'Crossing of Strategic Earth Bund', *Sunday Observer,* 6.12.09, http://www.sundayobserver.lk/2009/12/06/sec03.asp, Shamindra Ferdinando, 'Mission Accomplished on Western Flank', 25.11.12, *The Island,* http://www.island.lk/index.php?page_cat=article-details& page=article-details&code_title=66895

19 Amantha Perera, 'The Battle for Kilinochchi', *Sunday Leader,* 28.9.08, http://www.thesundayleader.lk/archive/20080928/defence.htm

20 Amantha Perera, 'Tiger Administrative Structure Hit', *Sunday Leader,* 12.10.08, http://www.thesundayleader.lk/archive/20081012/defence.htm

21 'Capturing Kilinochchi Is a Daydream of the Rajapakses', *Sunday Leader,* 26.10.08, http://www.thesundayleader.lk/archive/20081026/interviews-1.htm

22 'Pooneryn as Good as Fallen', *The Nation,* http://www.nation.lk/2008/11/09/militarym.htm Amantha Perera, 'Army Eyes New Northern Supply Route', *Sunday Leader,* 9.11.08, http://www.thesundayleader.lk/archive/20081109/defence.htm

23 Amantha Perera, 'Army Moves to Cut Off Pooneryn', *Sunday Leader,* 16.11.08, http://www.thesundayleader.lk/archive/20081116/defence.htm

24 Iqbal Athas, 'Fall of Pooneryn: Crushing Blow to Tigers', *Sunday Times,* 16.11.08, http://www.sundaytimes.lk/081116/Columns/sitreport.html Amantha Perera, 'Mode Shift on the Northern Frontline', *Sunday Leader,* 23.11.08, http://www.thesundayleader.lk/archive/20081123/defence.htm

25 Iqbal Athas, 'Mortar Monsoon, Fierce Battles Knee Deep in Mud', *Sunday Times,* 21.12.08, http://www.sundaytimes.lk/081221/Columns/sitreport.html

26 'Lankan Forces Capture Two Key LTTE Bastions; 50 Tigers Killed', *India Today,* 1.1.09, http://indiatoday.intoday.in/story/Lankan+forces+capture+2+key+LTTE+bastions;+50+Tigers+killed/1/24142.html Amantha, Perera, 'Troops Enter Killi with Multi Pronged Attack', *Sunday Leader,* 1.4.09, http://www.thesundayleader.lk/archive/20090104/defence.htm

27 Ranil Wijayapala, 'Muhamalai, Sornapattu and Strategic Elephant Pass Fall in a Row', *Sunday Observer,* 27.12.2009, http://www.sundayobserver.lk/2009/12/27/sec03.asp

28 'Sri Lanka Army Gains Control over Visvamadu Town', *India Today,* 29.1.09, http://indiatoday.intoday.in/story/Sri+Lankan+army+gains+control+over+Visuamadu+town/1/26672.html

The rolling up of the Wanni 209

29 'Tamil Tigers' Biggest Sea Base Chalai Captured', http://www.lanka library.com/phpBB/viewtopic.php?f=2&t=4678; Asif Fuard, 'The Fall of Chalai and the Death Knell of Sea Tigers', *Sunday Times*, 8.2.12; http://www.sundaytimes.lk/090208/News/sundaytimesnews_16.html (9.9.12)

30 Ranil Wijayapala, 'Desperate LTTE Attempts to Reverse Security Forces' Victories', http://www.sundayobserver.lk/2009/02/15/sec03.asp

31 Ranil Wijayapala, 'Troops Marching on LTTE's Last Terrain', *Sunday Observer*, 8.3.09, http://www.sundayobserver.lk/2009/03/08/sec03.asp; Chandraprema, *Gota's War*, p. 458, 'House to house Fighting Delays final Victory', *The Nation*, 8.3.09, http://www.nation.lk/2009/03/08/militarym.htm

32 Ruwan Weerakoon, 'LTTE Cornered and Cut Off', http://www.thebottomline.lk/2009/01/28/defence_col.htm

33 Muralidhar Reddy, 'Cornered Tigers'.

34 C. A. Chandraprema, *Gota's War*, p. 393–4.

35 'Nuwan Tharanga: Fallen Hero at Thoppigala', *Sunday Observer*, 16.3.08, http://www.sundayobserver.lk/2008/03/16/mag04.asp

36 Amantha Perera, 'Teddy Bears and Flying Gunships Make the Script', *Sunday Leader*, 9.3.08, http://www.thesundayleader.lk/archive/2008 0309/defence.htm

37 Moorcraft, *The Total Destruction*, p. 52.

38 Rohan Abeywardena, 'Where Men Fight and Guns Boom', *Sunday Times*, 27.1.08, http://www.sundaytimes.lk/080127/News/news0011.html

39 Amantha Perera, 'Govt. Troops Advance Beyond Silvathurai', 9.9.07, http://www.thesundayleader.lk/archive/20070909/defence.htm

40 Iqbal Athas, 'Charles: LTTE's Prince of Faceless Terror', *Sunday Times*, 8.1.07, http://www.sundaytimes.lk/080113/Columns/sitreport.html; D.B.S.Jeyaraj, 'Col' Charles: the Tiger Mastermind behind LTTE attacks outside North-East', http://dbsjeyaraj.com/dbsj/archives/14588

41 Pathiravithana, *The Use of Main Battle Tanks*, p. 18.

42 Ranil Waijayapala, 'Crossing of Strategic Earth Bund', *Sunday Observer*, 6.12.09, http://www.sundayobserver.lk/2009/12/06/sec03.asp, Shamindra Ferdinando, 'Mission Accomplished on Western Flank', 25.11.12, *The Island*, http://www.island.lk/index.php?page_cat=article-details& page=article-details&code_title=66895

43 D.B.S.Jeyaraj, 'Frontline Positions Shift Rapidly in Northern Theatre of War', http://transcurrents.com/tc/2008/08/post_18.html; 'Troops Capture LTTE's Last Stronghold in Mannar District', http://www.defence.lk/new.asp?fname=20080802_06

44 Ranil Wijayapala, 'Troops Zoom in on Kilinochchi', *Sunday Observer*, 24.8.08, http://www.sundayobserver.lk/2008/08/24/sec03.asp; Shamindra Ferdinando, 'Army Takes Commanding Position West of A9 . . . Bags Tunukkai, Eyes Mallavi, Mankulam under Threat' *The Island*, 23.8.08, http://www.island.lk/2008/08/23/news2.html; D.B.S.Jeyaraj, 'Frontline Positions Shift Rapidly in Northern Theatre of War'.

45 Iqbal Athas, 'Troops Make Progress but Major Battles Ahead', *Sunday Times*, 9.3.08, http://www.sundaytimes.lk/080309/Columns/sitreport.html

46 Iqbal Athas, 'Jeyaraj; Probe on Who Failed and What Next', *Sunday Times*, 13.4.08, http://www.sundaytimes.lk/080413/Columns/sitreport.html

210 The rolling up of the Wanni

47 Chandraprema, *Gota's War*, p. 422. The bulk of the casualties was caused by booby traps, landmines, artillery and mortar fire rather than close confrontation. Iqbal Athas, 'Continued LTTE Resistance Prolongs Sri Lankan Conflict', *Janes Defence Weekly*, posted on 28.2.08.

48 Iqbal Athas, 'Mortar Monsoon, Fiercest Battles Knee Deep in Mud', *Sunday Times*, 21.12.08, http://www.sundaytimes.lk/081221/Columns/sitreport.html

49 Iqbal Athas, 'Ealam War IV: Which way the last phase next year/' Sunday Times, 28.12.08, http://www.sundaytimes.lk/081228/Columns/sitreport.html

50 Amantha Perera, 'Wanni Battle Takes Its Toll', *Sunday Leader*, 21.12.08, http://www.thesundayleader.lk/archive/20081221/defence.htm

51 Amantha Perera, 'War Comes Full Circle', *Sunday Leader*, 15.7.07, http://www.thesundayleader.lk/archive/20070715/defence.htm

52 D.B.S.Jeyaraj, 'Tigers Get Ready to Face the Mechanised Infantry of the Army in the North', *Transcurrents*, 25.3.08, http://transcurrents.com/tamiliana/archives/category/transcurrents-newsfeatures/page/3

53 'Muhamalai Attack: LTTE's Defeated Aim'.

54 In the operation launched on April 23 2008, the army claimed they had repulsed a rebel attack and advanced 600 metres into enemy territory killing or critically wounded at least 160 rebels. If it was true, they also paid a high price for their daring. The official toll was 43 soldiers killed, 33 missing and 126 wounded. Unofficial figures spoke of a death toll well over a hundred. Iqbal Athas, 'The Aftermath of Muhamalai Confrontation', *Sunday Times*, 27.4.08, http://www.sundaytimes.lk/080427/Columns/sitreport.html, 'Muhamalai Attack: LTTE's Defeated Aim', http://www.defence.lk/new.asp?fname=20080426_06

Chapter 13

The last retreat of the Tamil Tigers

For the Tigers, the government's Wanni campaign posed serious challenges. They were being assailed from several fronts – the eastern and western Wanni. Their options were limited by their circumstances as well as the strategy of the Security Forces. In the 1990s, their response to Security Forces' incursions into the Wanni was a combination of guerrilla and conventional tactics. Against operations Wanni Wickrema, Lightning Strike and Sixer, they withdrew deeper into the Wanni while sometimes inflicting heavy casualties on the advancing enemy. Their response to Sath Jaya was more conventional with the use of artillery and mass attacks. Against Jayasikurui, they combined dogged frontal resistance with devastating flank attacks. Such tactics were now difficult to employ. The army was advancing on a wide front, not just prodding the Wanni in one corner or trying to cut through it, and it was bent on capturing and occupying all of the Wanni permanently. Strategic retreat could mean the permanent loss of territory with no other place to retreat. Withdrawal was also made difficult by the army's use of small groups to nibble at the defences rather than massive troop movements which were easy to detect and avoid. There was the possibility of the enemy overextending his lines of advance, especially as the army was advancing across the Wanni, but assailing this line was fraught with risks. On the one hand, the army was now in far greater strength than during any previous incursion into the Wanni in terms of numbers as well as firepower. On the other hand, the Tigers had very limited manpower to launch such offensives with. As explained earlier, the devastating mass attacks during Jayasikurui, while dealing staggering blows to the enemy, had also taken a crippling toll of the rebels' manpower. Some of their best troops were also stationed in Muhamalai. Given the superiority of the enemy's firepower, exposing them in frequent offensive operations was not prudent. The steady choking of their overseas supply routes also placed constraints on their heavy and long-range artillery. They needed to husband their men and material carefully and use them at the most opportune moment. Reverting to a purely guerrilla-type campaign was also not practicable in the Wanni. That would mean relinquishing the territorial gains made with huge sacrifices and also jettisoning the arsenal of heavy weapons and other conventional military resources built up painstakingly over many years. Opening a new front in the East was always appealing but not very viable anymore. With the help of Karuna, the army was well in control of the region, and with their diminished numbers it was too much of a risk to divert scarce resources away from the Wanni, the heartland and the last stronghold of their power. This was not a time for adventure but tact and resourcefulness.

Their attempts to redress the situation betrayed their desperation. With the outbreak of hostilities, the rebels had started raising a civil defence force, which included old men in their 60s and 70s. They also began forcibly recruiting children turning 17. 'The young are conscripted in the manner that cattle come of age are taken to the slaughter house,' despaired the University Teachers for Human Rights in one of their reports.[1] Such attempts were as desperate as they were futile; old men and young teens were no substitutes for seasoned fighters. The Tigers' strategy in battle betrayed the realisation of this reality. Early in the Wanni campaign, the leader of the Tigers' political wing Suppiah Thamil Selvam spelled out the rebel strategy in defensive terms. 'The LTTE is maintaining patience and still restricting itself to a defensive war,' he said, speaking to Tamilnet on August 19 2007. 'By doing so, it wishes the international community to realise the futility of achieving peace by dealing with such a government.'[2] The Tigers were also expecting the army's occupation of the East to complicate their drive for the North. While admitting that the loss of the East was a setback, the rebel spokesman Rasiah Ilantharian also reminded reporters that the army was not in an advantageous situation due to the capture of the East. 'If you want to control one region, you may have to lose control over another region,' he insisted.[3] Obviously, the rebel spokesman was thinking of the army relinquishing the East in the mid-1990s in order to support the invasion of Jaffna and the Wanni. Perhaps, the Tigers seemed to be thinking the army would find itself in a similar predicament.

Such reasoning is borne out by the rebels' response to the army's advance in the Wanni. While the resistance was stiff, the emphasis was on preserving the experienced cadres as much as possible and inflicting maximum casualties on the enemy. Sri Lankan soldiers storming rebel positions often found them held mainly by inexperienced cadres,

The last retreat of the Tamil Tigers 213

sometimes even by the recently raised Civil Defence Force. Although their main task seemed to have been to prevent the bunkers from falling to the army, too often they fell back in the face of attacks, leaving the army to occupy their positions. This, however, was not the end of the struggle for the army as the rebels had heavily booby-trapped the bunkers and mined the approaches to them.[4] On March 11 2008 alone, the engineering troops removed 53 anti-personnel mines from the general area of Kollomodai.[5] From further north in their Wanni heartland, the rebel artillery boomed while their snipers picked off soldiers groping their way through the mines and traps.[6] Such tactics contributed heavily to the casualties suffered by the eight-man teams and were an effective way of bleeding the enemy cheaply.

And while the army struggled, the rebels hinted at bigger things to come. 'The Military has now realised [the LTTE] are stronger than they thought. We are only defending ourselves now. They will know more when we are forced to change that role,' an unnamed rebel source confided to *Jane's Defence Weekly*.[7] But when that change would come was still a question.

Gradually, the Tigers began inducting their seasoned cadres into the frontline, launching counter-attacks on the advancing enemy. Taking a leaf out of the Security Forces' fighting manuals and underlining their own shortage of troops, these attacks were carried out by small groups. Some of their veteran leaders were also playing an active role in the defence now; Bhanu, Jeyam, Sornam, Ramesh, Amiuhab, Vidusha, Letchumanan and Velavan were reported to be in the thick of the campaign.[8] Under their auspices, the Tigers launched a major attack at dawn on February 20 on troops ahead of Uyilankulam. The troops were consolidating the positions they had occupied just two days before, and the Tigers were evidently looking to push them back before they had dug themselves in. The rebels moved in several small groups and attempted to storm the newly established fortifications, evidently striving to husband their experienced cadres by launching them in small units. The battle went on for several hours, the Tigers being backed by their 122mm artillery and 81mm mortars. The attack was repulsed with the Security Forces claiming the biggest rebel death toll – since the end of the ceasefire. They admitted to losing three killed and 20 wounded.[9]

As the army inched their way northwards, the Tigers also sought to divert their attention away from the Wanni. On January 28, their long-range guns at Pooneryn opened up on Palaly, firing 12 130mm shells at the base. Many VIPs who were flying to Jaffna to attend a medal ceremony were turned back.[10] The rebels also resorted to more traditional

214 The last retreat of the Tamil Tigers

guerrilla and terrorist attacks to keep the enemy off balance, showing that they were still capable of launching carefully planned and coordinated guerrilla action. On October 22 2007, with the campaign in the Wanni gathering pace, they launched a stunning attack on the Sri Lankan air force base at Anuradhapura. During the early hours of the morning, a group of 20–25 LTTE 'Black Tiger' commandos entered the base by cutting their way through the perimeter fence. Once inside, they neutralised the sentry points and the artillery and anti-aircraft guns and began pounding the aircraft on the runway as well as inside the hangars. When the attack ended late in the morning, at least seven aircraft including two unmanned aerial vehicles, an Mi17 and an Mi24, were completely destroyed and one Mi24 and three Mi17s damaged. A Bell 212 that got airborne during the attack also crashed, killing all four airmen on board, adding to the carnage and destruction. Among the aircraft destroyed was also a Beechcraft surveillance plane worth 14 million pounds. Twenty-one of the attackers lay dead along with 14 Security Forces personnel.[11]

Clearly, the aim of the attack was to destroy the fleet of aircraft at the base and cripple the air force's ability to take part in the operations that were beginning in the Wanni. If they could not get the missiles to blow the enemy planes out of the sky, the Tigers showed that they were prepared to take on the enemy's fleet on the ground. The attack had all the hallmarks of previous Black Tiger assaults – intelligence gathering, careful planning, rehearsing and training. The commandos knew their tasks and carried them out efficiently and ruthlessly. They were in control of the base from approximately 3 to 9 in the morning, carrying out their work of methodical destruction. According to analyst B. Raman, no other terrorist organisation in the world would have been capable of organising such a raid.[12]

Further south, the rebels employed their signature tactic outside the North and the East – terrorism. In 2007 and 2008, several parcel bombs ripped through buses packed with passengers, killing dozens of men, women and children. In the worst attack in April 2008, on a bus at the Piliyandala bus station, 23 people died while more than 50 were wounded.[13]

Such attacks caused considerable havoc to the morale of the southern public and the Security Forces. The loss of aircraft in particular was a severe blow as air power played a crucial role in the advance into the Wanni. The terrorist attacks again proved that the Tigers, though severely wounded, were still capable of biting anywhere in the island. But any optimism the Tigers may have felt was dashed by continuing

The last retreat of the Tamil Tigers 215

setbacks. On November 2 2007, only days after the attack on Vavuniya, an air strike deep in rebel territory killed Thamilselvan.[14] He was the public face of the LTTE and one of the highest-ranking rebels to be killed. It was also significant that he was killed by an airstrike, delivered by the air force the rebels had sought to cripple with their attack on the Anuradhapura base. In many parts of the south, people lit firecrackers and danced on the streets. The losses in Anuradhapura were forgotten.

The balance was steadily shifting in favour of the government forces. But the retreat continued. In desperation, the Tigers now threw up what came to be the hallmark of their defence in the Wanni. To the south of Viduthalathivu, the advancing troops came across what was to turn out to be a new defensive tactic. This was an earthen barrier built across the army's line of advance about 2 km south of the town. Tigers had resorted to earth bunds previously; during Operation Sath Jaya in 1996, the army came across a similar barrier built across the A9 north of Kilinochchi. But this was the first time the army had come across such a barrier in this war. The 'defensive mound' was interspersed with bunkers constructed with heavy logs every 100 metres or so. It was laid across the A32 as well. The Tigers appeared to have used heavy land moving machinery to construct the defence line, but had abandoned it as troops moved in.[15]

Hereafter, the earthen barrier became the rebels' main answer to the army's advance. Around the Mallavi–Tunukai complex, they erected another mound, manned by an estimated 150–200 cadres.[16] But the biggest and most impressive bund was raised further north to stall the northward drive of the army. It was a stupendous piece of work that was a reflection of the desperation as well as the fierce commitment of the cornered Tigers. The bund extended between Nachchikuda and Akkaraynakulam tanks – a distance of almost 30 km – with a trench in front facing an open area liberally strewn with mines. The bund was built in L-shaped sections that enabled the rebels to direct flanking fire on enemy troops breaking through it. A force of rebels estimated to be around 1,000 held the barrier. It was clear they were prepared to fight hard to prevent the army from rolling up the rest of the coastline and approaching Pooneryn and Kilinochchi.[17] Fight hard they did, but it was too little too late. The earthen bank was sufficient to delay the advance but not completely halt it. They were no match for the firepower at the Security Forces' disposal and the tactic of using small groups of specially trained troops. For instance, in mid-September against the barrier at Nachchikuda, a massive bombardment was launched using eight ground-attack aircrafts, Mi24s, artillery and MBRLs.[18] After this, the infantry broke through in several places and gradually extended their hold. By the end of October, the Fifty-Seventh and part of the Fifty-Eighth Division had taken much of the earth bund at Akkarayankulam and held it, despite fierce counter-attacks.[19] The price was high; the Fifty-Eighth Division alone had lost 153 soldiers, killed in breaching the rebel earthwork.[20] But the bund was taken. Undeterred, the Tigers shifted the bund to encircle Kilinochchi, realigning it to deal with the developing threat from the west and the north-west. The bund now ran like an 'L' from south of Nallur–Periyaparanthan area on the Paranthan–Pooneryn road, through Adampan to the north-west of Kilinochchi and then slanting east towards the Iranamadu Junction on the A9. As the army advanced on the bund, the rebels went on the attack, led by their veteran leaders Theepan, Swarnam and Lawerence. On December 20, as the Fifty-Seventh Division attempted to advance into enemy territory across the bund, the Tigers rained mortar and artillery fire on them, forcing them to retreat. The rebels were also said to be using one of their captured tanks and several boats deployed in the Iranamadu reservoir to provide fire support.[21] But again, this was too little too late. At Chalai too they rallied, erecting four consecutive earth bunds to thwart the approach of the army. But by now the battle had become a mismatch. Multi-barrel rocket launchers and heavy artillery pounded the bunds defended by heavy machine guns and mortars. The earthworks were captured one after the other and the troops surged forward.[22]

Ananthapuram

By late March, a steadily dwindling rebel army was being gradually pushed into an ever-shrinking area by a Sri Lankan army now numbering nearly 50,000. The Tigers were fast running out of space to retreat to and something needed to be done quickly. The much-anticipated decisive offensive needed to be launched – immediately. One advantage the Tigers now had was that with the abandonment of Muhamalai some of their toughest troops were now available for offensive action. This was the time to use them in a devastating counterstrike.

Since the loss of Kilinochchi, the Tigers had been trying to roll back the army lines, but without much success. In one such counter-offensive on February 5 2009, with the fate of Chalai hanging in the balance, they pounced on the army's defences to the west of the Nanthikadal lagoon. Led by their veteran leaders Lawrence and Swarnam and supported by heavy artillery fire, they infiltrated about 200 picked cadres through army defences and ambushed Sri Lankan military forces. The

The last retreat of the Tamil Tigers 217

attack delivered a jolt to the army; dozens were believed killed and wounded while several military vehicles were destroyed or damaged. But it was a futile, though gallant, gamble. Running against a cordon of nearly 50,000 troops was bound to end in failure. The army soon rallied, and after pounding a patch of jungle where the rebels had taken refuge, they unleashed the Special Forces on them. As Swarnam and Lawrence limped back to safety across the lagoon with the survivors, the soldiers piled up the trophies: 146 bodies, 268 assault rifles and 18 RPG launchers.[23]

Frustrated but not totally demoralised, the Tigers now decided on an even bigger offensive. In late March, they gathered at Ananthapuram a few kilometres to the north-east of Puthikuduiyirippu to plan the assault. Almost all the remaining Tiger leaders except Prabhakaran were there. Men and women of years, sometimes decades, of experience as fighters, men and women who had seen many defeats and triumphs, were now coming together to plot yet another, perhaps the most decisive, campaign in their careers. Along with them were some of their most hardened and devoted cadres and a potent arsenal that included several 130 mm artillery pieces.

The offensive never got off the ground. On April 3, the army succeeded in encircling the rebel force at Ananthapuram. After a fierce battle, two army pincers linked up at the Pachchapulmudai junction to the north-east of Pudukuduirippu town. The Tiger army was trapped.[24]

Despite repeated demands in Tamil over a loud hailer to surrender, the rebels stood their ground. A little over 100 surrendered. For the rest, a hail of fire awaited. From midnight on April 3, the pocket was subjected to a merciless air and land bombardment, the army and the air force pounding the patch of jungle where the rebels were holed up with a massive volume of bombs and shells. It is said that over 30,000 shells were fired on April 4 alone. Doomed, the Tigers fought back desperately and bravely, the artillery firing point-blank and at times horizontally at the enemy encircling them, while bands of rebels made ferocious attempts to break through the cordon. But it was a lopsided battle. By April 6, resistance had ceased. A few hundred rebels including 'Colonel' Bhanu had managed to escape, but the vast majority had perished under the devastating onslaught. By April 7, the army recovered 625 badly battered bodies.[25] Among them were the corpses of 'Colonel' Theepan; Vidusha, the leader of the women's wing; her deputy, Mohanaa; two leaders of the elite Jeyanthan Brigade, Keerthi and Nagesh, and senior leaders Gaddaffi, Ruban, Panjan, Nehru, Anton, Maankuyil, Amudha, Iniyawan, Aadithyan and Chitrangan. A senior Sea

Tiger Mahindan was also killed. The army also recovered a large haul of weapons including three 130mm guns, several heavy machineguns, one 30mm multi-barrelled anti-aircraft gun and dozens of assault rifles. Also recovered was the 85mm cannon lost to the Tigers at Pulukunawa in December 1996.[26]

The army did not come out of the battle unscathed, losing at least 135 killed, the majority of them from the Gajaba Regiment that bore the brunt of the rebels' resistance.[27] But the loss fell more heavily on the LTTE. They had lost their last remaining fighting force. There were no more leaders capable of organising an effective resistance and no army to organise it with. As a military force, the LTTE was now broken.

The last of the Sea Tigers

Chalai, which fell in February 2009, was the last Sea Tiger stronghold to succumb. But by then, the rebels' naval arm was only a shadow of its former self. As explained earlier, the Sri Lankan navy had wiped out the Tigers' merchant fleet in the high seas in 2006–7. Closer to the shore too, the rebel navy was struggling. In August 2006, they had invaded Kayts in force and had been repulsed without great difficulty. Another raid on the naval subunit on the Delft Island in May 2008 was more successful as the Tigers withdrew with two .50 guns two machineguns, one RPG launcher and two assault rifles.[28] As the army continued its advance in the western Wanni, a more audacious attack brought greater success. In June 2008, they launched a pre-dawn attack on the navy detachment at Erukkalamppiddi on the north-eastern shores of the Mannar Island. The rebels claimed they overran the detachment and were in control of the locality till 3.45 a.m. before withdrawing with arms and ammunition after destroying the electricity generator. They also claimed to have killed nine soldiers while losing five cadres. The navy said it repulsed the attack and lost only four killed and three wounded.[29]

As audacious as they were, raiding deep behind enemy lines, these attacks were whimpers compared with the daring and devastating attacks made by the naval arm of the Tigers in the previous phases of the war. A few bold ventures could not hide the fact that the Sea Tigers' power was on the wane, a reality underlined by their decreasing activity. While the Sri Lankan navy had 21 engagements with the Sea Tigers in 2006, with up to 30 craft on each side exchanging fire for over 14 hours on occasion, this number decreased to 11 in 2007 and then only four in 2008.[30] As if to taunt the once-vaunted rebel navy, the Sri Lankan navy's Special Boat Squadron had also raided the Iranathivu Island off the western coast in August 2008, venturing deep into rebel territory and returning without loss. Their booty consisted only of a couple of dinghies and a few medical and supply items, but it showed their ability to launch daring raids behind enemy lines.[31]

There were several reasons for this deterioration of the Sea Tigers. The rejuvenated navy with their fast-moving arrow boats was proving more than a match for them. Using swarm tactics that mirrored the once-feared manoeuvres of their enemy, the arrow boats took the battle to the rebels, confounding them and giving them little chance to rally. One of the few engagements between the Sri Lankan navy and the Sea Tigers in 2008 highlighted the changed balance of power in the sea. On the morning of September 18, not long after the hundredth arrow boat had been unveiled, boats from the SBS and RABS confronted a flotilla of Sea Tiger boats off the western coast and sank ten of them.[32]

Still recovering from the tsunami's depredations, the Sea Tigers were also reeling from a land, sea and air onslaught on their assets. As the campaign in the Wanni unfolded, the Sri Lankan air force began to step up strategic bombing runs over rebel territory, targeting among other things Sea Tiger bases. The loss of the coast below Trincomalee was another blow. Without access to the harbours on this strip of the coast, Sea Tigers lost much of their ability to launch surprise attacks on the navy in the East. As the army rolled up the western Wanni, they also lost all their bases on the western coast, including the important Viduthalathivu. When Chalai fell in February 2009, even the last base on the eastern coast was denied to them. Thereafter, the Sea Tiger activity was reduced to attempts to break the blockade and flee. Here too their weakness was manifest. Not long after the fall of Chalai, the Sea Tigers launched suicidal attacks on the troops holding the captured ground. The arrow boats were not even required now. The army alone managed to repulse them.[33]

The birth and death of a rebel air force

While the battle in the Wanni loomed, the Tigers also experimented with a new way of seizing the fast losing initiative. At midnight on March 25 2007, two little aircraft, no bigger than crop dusters, appeared over the Katunayake airbase and dropped four bombs on the hangars. Three of the bombs exploded, killing three airmen and wounding 14. Some of the helicopters in the hangars were also damaged. As the anti-aircraft guns in the airbase sprayed the sky with their bullets, the two little intruders flew away, unscathed.

220 The last retreat of the Tamil Tigers

Just over a month later, they were back. On April 29, while Sri Lankans were engrossed in the fate of their cricket team in the cricket world cup final, the aircraft returned, this time to bomb the oil refinery at Kolonnawa and the Shell gas complex at Kerawalapitiya. Both facilities suffered minor damage but, once again, the aircraft escaped.[34]

For the first time since World War II, Colombo had been bombed from the air, this time not by a foreign enemy but by a home-grown rebel air force.

The Tigers' fascination with air power has a long history. As early as the 1980s, they had been experimenting with air power. These attempts, however, were of the crudest kind. In early 1987, a visiting Indian journalist was shown a two-seater aircraft that was in the process of being assembled in a rundown 'arms factory." The visitor described with undisguised contempt the aluminium sheeting, the wooden propeller and the Volkswagen engine that was expected to power the machine to the sky. 'If you can make revolutions in such outfits,' the journalist wrote sarcastically, 'I shudder to think what would happen to this world.'[35]

What happened to these early efforts is not clear. But no LTTE aircraft took off to take on the Sri Lankan or Indian troops in the coming years. Then, in 1995 soon after the outbreak of Ealam War II, it was again reported that the Tigers had assembled a light aircraft, its parts smuggled into the northern coast. This was supposed to be a single seater and was expected to be used in a suicide attack.[36] The Tigers were supposed to have built a runway in Iranamadu in the Kilinochchi District. Speaking at a pro-Tiger demonstration in Paris in June 1995, Lawrence Thilagar boasted that the rebels would soon have their own air force.[37] This was probably a claim made to boost the confidence of the diaspora and encourage continuing support, but alarm bells began ringing when in October 1995 the army discovered a partially assembled aircraft in an underground 'airbase' in Neerveli.

As Ealam War III progressed, the 'Tiger air force' continued to make the news. In 1997, rumours were afloat as to what the rebel air arm was going to be like. The Tigers, it was reported citing 'informed sources', were going to clothe their airmen just like the Sri Lankan air force personnel. They were also going to have both male and female cadres. The Tigers, it was said, were planning to buy helicopter gunships from an unnamed Western source, and they were eying gunships that were more sophisticated than what the SLAF possessed![38]

In October 1998, the Sri Lankan air force confirmed, based on the information it had received, that the rebels were in now possession of an aircraft. It was believed to be a light helicopter, a R-44 two seater. It was

The last retreat of the Tamil Tigers 221

believed that the helicopter was used to strew flowers from the sky after Prabhakaran's Heroes Day speech in 1998. The air force was also distributing posters to airmen with pictures of the 'possible types of enemy aircraft'. The pictures showed light planes and helicopters.[39]

In January 2005, an unmanned aerial vehicle of the Sri Lankan air force relayed images of an air strip south-east of the Iranamadu tank, about 3,600 feet in length and capable of accommodating a range of aircraft. The UAV also identified two aircraft on the runway, one confirmed as a Czech-built Zlin Z-143 and the other possibly a light trainer. It was believed at this time that the LTTE had trained several of its cadres as pilots in France and the UK.[40]

Then after the bombing raid on Katunayake in March 2007, the Tigers finally unveiled their mystery air force. The pro-rebel Tamilnet website published photographs of the planes and the pilots – with their faces blurred – sitting with the rebel supremo Velupillai Prabhakaran. The pictures of the aircraft showed only the undersides of the machines, which showed bomb racks carrying four crude bombs in each plane. The only picture of the cockpit showed a two-member crew giving V signs as they prepared to leave for their mission. It was a proud moment for the rebels who had finally achieved their dream of having their air force, albeit a crude one.[41]

The antics of the rebel 'air force' showed the vulnerability of Sri Lankan air space to unconventional intrusions. Two little aircrafts had made a mockery of all the sophisticated weaponry that surrounded the city, and the air force's attack aircraft had been too 'modern' to hunt the crop dusters. The rebel aircraft, however, had little strategic or tactical value. The two Zlin- Z 143s did not have the capacity to inflict serious damage due to their inability to carry heavy ordnance and due to the inaccuracy of the delivery of their bombs. The attacks that followed the April 29 bombing demonstrated this well. The next air attack occurred in October during the rebel raid on the Anuradhapura airbase. Four bombs were dropped, taking advantage of the neutralising of anti-aircraft weapons by the rebel raiders on the ground. But the bombs did little damage, falling in and around the camp without causing too much harm apart from one which landed in a field, killing a dozen buffaloes.[42] This was followed on April 27 2008 by an attack on the FDL creeping up on rebel territory at Weli Oya. At approximately 1.45 a.m., at least two air Tiger aircraft dropped three but caused no damage.

On August 26 2008, a solitary rebel aircraft flew over the Trincomalee harbour and dropped at least two bombs. Several sailors were injured and some killed according to some reports. It was later revealed that the

222 The last retreat of the Tamil Tigers

target of the attack was the passenger ferry *Jetliner* which transported troops to and from Jaffna. The ship was unscathed.[43] On September 9 2008, the Tiger aircraft took on the Wanni Security Forces Headquarters in Vavuniya. The attack came in support of a group of Tiger commandos who had infiltrated the base. Thirteen soldiers and a policeman were killed. Two Indian radar technicians were wounded. Eleven of the 14 attackers were killed while the radar was damaged.[44] On October 28 2008, the rebel planes struck again, one aircraft dropping three bombs on the area headquarters at Tahalladi while the other continuing south to drop three bombs on the Kelanitissa power station. In the first attack, an airman and two soldiers were wounded. The power station sustained considerable damage estimated at over Rs 100 million.[45]

But such audacious 'raids' were not sufficient to turn the tide on the ground. The army continued to push the Tigers further and further into the Wanni. And as the Tiger territory shrank, the end began to loom for the plucky little air force. As the army advanced, one by one, rebel airstrips fell into their hands. One of these captured by the Fifty-Eighth Division north of Paranthan bore the sign of rebel ingenuity – it was little more than a stretch of the B69 highway marked off as an emergency runway.[46]

Finally, with the Wanni campaign all but lost, the Tigers launched their 'air force' in one last suicidal attack. On February 20 2008, the two aircraft swooped down on the Sri Lankan air force headquarters and the Katunayake airport. Both were shot down. The one that attacked the air force headquarters crashed into the nearby Inland Revenue Department building, causing a fire. The other crashed close to the airport. Both pilots were killed.[47]

With that ended the short but colourful campaign of the Tiger air force. They caused little damage and proved to be of little value in affecting the direction of the war. But the courageous forays of the rebel airmen caused considerable panic in the South and among the Sri Lankan security establishment and boosted the sagging morale of their ground troops facing annihilation on the shores of the Nanthikadal lagoon.

Nanthikadal

In early May 2009, the Sri Lankan army escorted a group of foreign journalists on a tour of the Wanni battlefront. As their convoy sped through the Wanni, the Australian journalist Matt Wade noticed how the villages they drove past were all deserted and wondered where all the

The last retreat of the Tamil Tigers 223

people were. He had seen many civilians in refugee camps in Vavuniya, but surely many more people had once populated this now desolate land?[48]

What Wade did not realise was that, at this time, the refugees in Vavuniya were the lucky ones. By now, the vast majority of the people in the Wanni were being crowded into a narrow spit of land surrounded by the Pudumatalan and Nanthikadal lagoons and the sea in Mullaithivu. Hemmed in by the advancing army and herded by the Tigers, they waited for an uncertain fate.

The exodus

Hundreds of thousands of hapless men, women and children, mainly Tamils from the North and the East, had become refugees in their own country during the different phases of the Ealam War. In previous bouts of the war too, the people in the Wanni had fled deeper into rebel-held territory, looking for safety and succour. But on those occasions, the civilians had not had to be part of the end of the war. The fate of the civilians in the last phase of the war was unique. This time they were being forced to play a crucial role in the brutal endgame.

The civilian exodus from Kilinochchi was a repetition of what had been happening in the Wanni since the beginning of the army's drive to capture the rebels' last stronghold. At the beginning of the offensive, according to the University Teachers for Human Rights, it was estimated that about 200, 000 civilians lived in LTTE-controlled Wanni. As the army pushed on and the rebels fell back, the civilians too withdrew deep into LTTE-held territory to escape the bombardment that accompanied the offensive. Rather than allowing them to move towards the Madhu Shrine, the Tigers shepherded them in the direction of Iluppaikkadavai and Mulankavil further north.[49] The exodus continued as the army advanced. Soon, Kilinochchi, the rebel capital, was fast filling with hapless refugees. By the end of September, their numbers had swelled to 140,000 according to the UN.[50] This was a figure disputed by the Nation Building Ministry, which claimed that only 89,000 people were living in the uncleared areas.[51] As the army intensified its campaign around Kilinochchi, many of them fled towards Mullaithivu, the last stronghold of the Tigers. Few heeded the government's call to leave the rebel-controlled territory. A number of factors contributed to this reluctance. No doubt the presence of the pro-government paramilitaries in Vavuniya, where the government had set up refugee camps, was a major deterrent as many refugees who had members in the LTTE would have feared persecution at their hands. Fleeing to India was also not an option anymore with the closest route blocked by the army's capture of the western coast.[52] The Tigers also prevented people from fleeing, especially young people who could be recruited for their war effort.[53]

Inevitably the refugees suffered – horrendously. Without basic necessities and their nerves strained by the brutal fighting that raged around them, the hapless men, women and children clung to the last vestiges of hope and dignity they had, expecting a miracle. The government dispatched weekly food convoys accompanied by UN international staff, but these did not always get through in time. Whether adequate supplies were being sent by a government that denied the existence of more than 100,000 mouths to feed is also a question. To add to their woes, the LTTE scoured the throngs of hapless humanity for new recruits to bolster their waning strength. Children under the age of 18 were increasingly being recruited, and each family in LTTE-controlled territory was being asked to contribute at least one family member. Every male between the ages of 18 and 45 was being required to undergo military training for two weeks.[54] According to the University Teachers for Human Rights, the rebels had recruited nearly 9,000 'very young' persons.[55] To make matters worse, in September 2008, the government ordered all United Nations and humanitarian agencies to withdraw their staff and operations from the Wanni, allowing only the International Committee of the Red Cross and the locally staffed Caritas to continue operations. Then in November, cyclone Nisha piled more misery on the long-suffering humanity, uprooting their miserable shelters and flooding their camps with torrential rain.[56] For the civilians of the Wanni, the nightmare seemed endless.

As the rebel-controlled territory shrank, the government searched for ways to separate the Tiger cadres from the civilians. A trickle of civilians had made the arduous journey across rebel lines into government-held territory, where they were detained in refugee camps under conditions marginally better than those faced by the masses in the Wanni.[57] But the vast majority of the civilians remained under rebel control, and they had to be weaned from the Tigers. This was imperative if the rebels were to be crushed with as little 'collateral damage' as possible. It is arguable whether the army would have cared much about the safety of the civilians if they had a free hand. It would not be surprising if many soldiers and their officers simply wanted to finish the war by annihilating the LTTE, even if it meant causing massive civilian casualties. Having fought tooth and nail to bring the Tigers to their knees and having suffered terribly in the process, it would have been natural to want to blast their way through the civilian shield, especially when the civilians' retreat with the Tigers could be interpreted as an extension of support for the rebels. But no doubt there was also a desire – at least in some quarters of the establishment – to finish the war with as little harm to the civilians as possible if that could be managed. This desire would have been strengthened by the military imperatives of the situation. Civilians mingling with the rebels made it practically difficult to identify and crush the rebel hard core whether one cared for civilian safety or not.

But as the endgame of the war approached, the need to ensure civilian safety was also being dictated by the growing international concern. In declaring a defensive war at the start of the war in the Wanni, Thamil Chelvam had expressed the hope that the international opinion would shift against the Sri Lankan government. This proved to be a miscalculation at this stage of the war. International opinion, led by India and Western nations, expressed disconcert at the renewal of the fighting but went no further than expressing concern and the hope that negotiations will recommence. There seemed no great urgency to save the LTTE from the Sri Lankan Security Forces. But now, as the LTTE continued to retreat and the civilians moved with them, international concern became more acute, the voices of caution louder and shriller. On February 3, Canada called for a ceasefire, and two days later on February 5, India expressed its 'deep concern' over the situation in Sri Lanka and went so far as to call on both the Sri Lankan government and the LTTE to end fighting.[58] A few days later, the UK too lent its voice to the growing calls for a ceasefire.[59] The international community may have had little sympathy for the Tigers, but it also had little stomach for seeing thousands of civilians perish with the rebels.

Calls for ceasefires had little impact on the warring parties. Sri Lanka rejected it out of hand, while the call did not even elicit a response from the Tigers. But with international opinion against the war gathering momentum, the Sri Lankan government implemented measures to ensure the safety of the civilians, declaring a no fire zone on January 21, designating a 32-square kilometre area 5 km north-west of Puthukuduyirupu between A35 highway and the Chalai lagoon as a conflict-free zone. The army promised not to fire into the safe haven and dropped leaflets, asking civilians to go there.[60]

But as the LTTE retreated further, the civilians too went with them. A few managed to filter through the rebel cordons, braving the shells and bullets. Such daring, though welcome from the government's perspective, also posed its own challenges to the army. On February 9, a suicide cadre posing as a fleeing civilian detonated a bomb at the Visvamadu transit welfare centre, killing 10 and wounding 64.[61] It was a calculated attempt to make the army wary of fleeing civilians, making it harder for the soldiers as well as the civilians.

The government declared another no fire zone on February 12, a 12 km long and 1–2 km wide strip of land along the coast of Mullaithivu. The safe haven extended from Vadduvakal in the south to Palamattalan in the north and was bordered by the Pudumatalan lagoon to the west. It encompassed several villages including Vellamullavaikkal, Karayamullivaikkal, Velayanmadam, Ampelavanpokkanai and Putumattalan. Over 200, 000 terrified and traumatised men, women and children now crowded into this thin stretch of land, awaiting their fate.[62]

This was where the civilians Matt Wade was looking for had gone.

The end

With the defeat of the last remaining military force of the LTTE at Ananthapuram, the attention now turned to the no fire zone. Predictably, the remaining LTTE cadres had taken refuge here among the civilians. Now several divisions of the army zeroed in on this strip of land with its seething mass of wretched humanity. As the army bore down, the Tigers threw up one last earth bund, a desperate measure to stave off imminent defeat. But this too was breached on April 20, exposing the rebel enclave to the army's assault.

As the army broke through the bund, thousands of civilians began to stream out of the area. Sri Lankan government put the number of these desperate souls at 49,000.[63] Then, as the Tigers retreated further into the no fire zone with tens of thousands of civilians still unable to leave, the army advanced from the north and the south along the coast and along the bank of the lagoon, crossing a landscape littered with the debris of a shattered rebel army and a brutalised people, and struck the final nail in their enemy's coffin by joining their forces advancing along the coast, sealing all hopes of escape for the Tigers. Out in the sea, the Sri Lankan navy circled, watching out for last-minute attempts by rebel leaders to break out.

The war was approaching its endgame. But the dying Tiger was putting up a ferocious fight. The capture of the bund at Pudumatalan had cost the army 224 dead and clearing the spit of land a further 225.[64] The army too held little back. A journalist who visited the area of the no fire zone recovered by the army saw signs of heavy shelling inside the zone. A middle-ranking army officer conceded that they had to use heavy weapons to neutralise rebel guns that had been placed inside the zone. 'The LTTE, which had positioned all the weapons in its possession inside the NSZ, was firing indiscriminately at the positions taken by the troops. We had no option but to neutralise them,' he explained. 'How else could we pave the way for the escape of the civilians and ensure minimum casualties of our men in the battlefield?' he asked rhetorically.[65]

With all hopes of holding out rapidly evaporating, the Tigers were now showing little interest in holding the civilians. On May 12 and 13, with rebel sentries withdrawn, the remaining civilians poured out of the safe zone.[66] By May 15, it seemed that after a long wait the army had finally cornered the remaining rebel leaders without their civilian shield. The Tiger was finally cornered. All that was needed was to move in for the kill.

What happened thereafter is likely to be debated for a long time. But suffice to say that surrounded by thousands of soldiers on a strip of sand about 1.5 km in extent the last of the rebels ended their lives the way they had lived: violently. Led by the last of their leaders, Soosai, Bhanu, Pottu Amman, and Prabhakaran himself, they reportedly made ferocious – and hopeless – attempts to break out across the lagoon but were met by an army determined to stop them and end the war that seemed all but over. Many broke through the defence lines, but none it seemed survived. Among those who perished were the remaining leaders of the Liberation Tigers of Tamil Ealam: the Sea Tiger leader Soosai, former Eastern Commander Swarnam, the heavy weapons expert Bhanu and the man who had eluded the Sri Lankan Security Forces for so long, Velupillai Prabhakaran himself. Also dead were scores of rebel cadres who had remained loyal to their leaders and their cause till the bitter end.[67] Also killed in the final hours were the head of the LTTE Peace Secretariat Seevarathnam Pulithevan and the Tigers' police chief Balasingham Nadesan. These latter two, it was later alleged, had been executed when they attempted to surrender along with their families and several civilians and rebel cadres negotiating with the government through the United Nations and the ICRC.[68] Pottu Amman's body was never found.

As victories go, it was a complete one. The Liberation Tigers of Tamil Ealam had been wiped out. Almost all its leaders and cadres were either killed or were in captivity. They had rarely given quarter to their enemy. Now they received none.

But the victory had come at a cost. According to official figures, more than 6,200 soldiers, airmen and sailors had died in Ealam War IV with 29,551 wounded. The Fifty-Eighth Division alone had lost 1,397 dead. The vast majority of these fatalities had occurred during the final stage

228 The last retreat of the Tamil Tigers

of the war after the fall of Kilinochchi. When one considers that at its peak the number of soldiers engaged with the enemy during the offensive in the Wanni was somewhere in the vicinity of 70,000, this was a horrific casualty rate, especially considering that the majority of the wounded would be disabled for life. The entire war had cost the Sri Lankan Security Forces 23,790 deaths since 1981. The number of rebel casualties was similar. In November 2008, they had admitted to losing 22,000 cadres since 1982.[69] Tens of thousands of civilians had also perished, sometimes brutally murdered, often callously ignored.

Notes

1 Amantha Perera, 'Behind the Frontlines', *Sunday Leader*, 13.7.08, http://www.thesundayleader.lk/archive/20080713/defence.htm
2 Amantha Perera, 'Defensive Tigers Warn of Lethal Days', *Sunday Leader*, 23.9.07, http://www.thesundayleader.lk/archive/20070923/defence.htm
3 'Sri Lanka's War Seen Far From Over', *The Washington Times*, http://www.washingtontimes.com/news/2007/jul/14/sri-lankas-war-seen-far-from-over/?page=2#ixzz2KmptE0gH
4 Amantha Perera, 'Lull in Battlefield as Focus Shifts to East', *Sunday Leader*, 16.3.08, http://www.thesundayleader.lk/archive/20080316/defence.htm
5 'Military Ups the Tempo', *The Nation*, 16.3.08, http://www.nation.lk/2008/03/16/militarym.htm
6 D.B.S. Jeyaraj, 'So Near and Yet So Far in Mannar Theatre so Far', http://transcurrents.com/tamiliana/page/3?s=jeyaraj
7 Iqbal Athas, 'Continued LTTE Resistance Prolongs Sri Lankan Conflict', *Jane's Defence Weekly*, 28.2.08.
8 D.B.S.Jeyaraj, 'So Near and Yet So Far in Mannar Thetatre So Far'.
9 Amantha Perera, 'The Battle for Admapan', *Sunday Leader*, 24.2.08, http://www.thesundayleader.lk/archive/20080224/defence.htm; 'Sri Lankan Troops kill 92 Tigers in Fresh Offensive', http://archives.dawn.com/2008/02/22/intl.htm ((13.2.13)
10 Rafik Jalaldeen, 'Forces Beat Back LTTE Artillery Attack', *Daily News*, 29.1.08, http://www.dailynews.lk/2008/01/29/sec01.asp (13.2.13)
11 Peter Foster, 'Tamil Tiger Suicide Squad in Audacious Attack', *The Telegraph*, 22.10.07, http://www.telegraph.co.uk/news/worldnews/1567103/Tamil-Tiger-suicide-squad-in-audacious-strike.html; B. Raman, 'No Crouching Tigers These', *Outlook India*, 23.10.07, http://www.outlookindia.com/article.aspx?235846; D.B.S. Jeyaraj, 'Anatomy of Tiger Assault on Anuradhapura Airbase', *Transcurrents*, 27.10.07, http://transcurrents.com/tamiliana/archives/400
12 B.Raman, 'No Crouching Tigers These'.
13 'Bus Bombing Kills 20 in Sri Lanka', http://www.theage.com.au/news/world/bus-bombing-kills-20-in-sri-lanka/2008/02/03/1201973719546.html, 'Bus Bomb Kills 23 Passengers Near Sri Lanka's

The last retreat of the Tamil Tigers 229

Capital', http://www.theage.com.au/news/world/bus-bomb-kills-23-passengers-near-sri-lankas-capital/2008/04/26/1208743266629.html, Sarath Kumara, 'Two Bus Bombs Kill More than 20 in Sri Lanka', http://www.wsws.org/articles/2007/jan2007/sril-j10.shtml

14 'Tamil Tiger Political Chief Killed in Sri Lanka Air Strike', http://afp.google.com/article/ALeqM5j-TOLA51vP-BoTQDVn2g7JLCjGww

15 Amantha Perera, 'Troops gain Strategic Bay', *Sunday Leader*, 20.7.08, http://www.thesundayleader.lk/archive/20080720/defence.htm. Other reports speak of heavy fighting to capture the earth bund. Ranil Wijatapala, 'Fall of Strategic LTTE Territory', *Sunday Observer*, 15.11.09, http://www.sundayobserver.lk/2009/11/15/sec03.asp

16 Chandraprema, *Gota's War*, p. 424.

17 Ibid., p. 425; Sergei De Silva Ranasinghe, "Good Education: Sri Lankan Military Learns Insurgency Lessons', *Jane's Intelligence Review*, 13.11.2009.

18 Tissa Ravindra Perera, *Wanni Awasan Maha Satana*, (Colombo: Pahan Publishers, 2009) p. 35.

19 Perera, Wanni Awasan maha satana, pp. 59–120 (passim).

20 Chandraprema, *Gota's War*, p. 425.

21 Iqbal Athas, 'Mortar Monsoon, Fierce Battles Knee Deep in Mud', 'How the Army Was Able to Capture Paranthan by the New Year', *Transcurrents*, http://transcurrents.com/tc/2009/01/post_219.html; 'Tigers Constructing Strong Defences Around 300 sq, KM in Eastern Wanni', http://transcurrents.com/tc/2008/12/post_203.html

22 'Tamil Tigers' Biggest Sea Base Chalai Captured', http://www.lankalibrary.com/phpBB/viewtopic.php?f=2&t=4678; Asif Fuard, 'The Fall of Chalai and the Death Knell of Sea Tigers', *Sunday Times*, 8.2.12, http://www.sundaytimes.lk/090208/News/sundaytimesnews_16.html

23 Asif Fuard, 'The Fall of Chalai and the Death Knell of Sea Tigers'; Tissa Ravindra Perera, 'LTTE Grand Assault Routed', *The Nation*, 15.3.09, http://www.nation.lk/2009/03/15/militarym.htm

24 Asif Fuard, 'Final Battle in the Midst of Civilians', *Sunday Times*, 12.4.09, http://www.sundaytimes.lk/090412/News/sundaytimesnews_14.html (9.9.12).

25 D.B.S. Jeyaraj, 'Anatomy of the LTTE Military Debacle at Ananthapuram', *Transcurrents*, 5.4.12, http://dbsjeyaraj.com/dbsj/archives/5404

26 For accounts of this battle see D.B.S. Jeyaraj, 'Anatomy of the LTTE Military Debacle at Ananthapuram'; Tissa Ravindra Perera, 'The Final Battle That Decimated the Tigers'; Shanika Sriyananda, LTTE's Waterloo', *Sunday Observer*, 12.4.09, http://www.sundayobserver.lk/2009/04/12/sec04.asp, Hashim, *When Counterinsurgency Wins*, p. 161.

27 Chandraprema, *Gota's War*, p. 458.

28 IIqbal Athas, 'Tale of Two Wars: Ground Battle and Media Battle', *Sunday Times*, 27.5.07, http://www.sundaytimes.lk/070527/Columns/sitreport.html

230 The last retreat of the Tamil Tigers

29 Amantha Perera, 'Sea Tigers Strike Again and Again', *Sunday Leader*, 15.6.08,http://www.thesundayleader.lk/archive/20080615/defence. htm
30 Paul A. Povlock, 'A Guerrilla War a Sea', *Small Wars Journal*, 9.9.11, p. 38, http://smallwarsjournal.com/sites/default/files/848-povlock.pdf
31 Amantha Perera, 'Heavy Fighting Ahead of Newly Gained Ground', *Sunday Leader*, 10.8.08, http://www.thesundayleader.lk/archive/ 20080810/defence.htm
32 R. Edirisinghe, 'Sri Lanka Navy Crush Sea Tiger Flotilla: 10 Sea Tiger Boats Sunk, 30 Cadres Killed', *Asian Tribune*, 18.09.08, http://www. asiantribune.com/?q=node/13302
33 Shanika Sriyananda, 'The Crawl to Terminate Sea Tigers', *Sunday Observer*, 15.3.09, http://www.sundayobserver.lk/2009/03/15/sec10.asp
34 Amantha Perera, 'Tigers Turn Party Poopers', *Sunday Leader*, 6.5.07, http://www.thesundayleader.lk/archive/20070506/defence.htm
35 S. Venkat Narayan, 'A Visit to Jaffna', *The Island*, 15.2.87, p. 6.
36 Premalal Wijeratne and Rajika Jayatilake, 'Al unquiet on the Eastern Front', *Sunday Leader*, 14.5.95, p. 4.
37 Sunday Times Defence Correspondent, 'All About the Air Force', *Sunday Times*, 18.6.95, p. 10.
38 Roy Denish, 'Flying Tigers to Prowl the Skies', *Sunday Leader*, 6.4.97, p. 8.
39 Roy Denish, 'LTTE Airstrike Power – the Truth Is Out', *Sunday Leader*, 6.12.98, p. 9.
40 N. Manoharan, 'Tigers with Wings – Air Power of the LTTE', paper no. 1720, Institute of Peace and Conflict Studies, http://www.ipcs. org/article/sri-lanka/tigers-with-wings-air-power-of-the-ltte-1720. html
41 'LTTE Releases Photographs of Air Mission', *Tamilnet*, 26.3.07, http://www.tamilnet.com/art.html?catid=13&artid=21668
42 D.B.S. Jeyaraj, 'Anatomy of Tiger Assault on Anuradhapura Airforce Base', *Transcurrents*, 27.10.07, http://transcurrents.com/tamiliana/ archives/400
43 'Air Attack Takes Attention Off Ground Battles', *Sunday Leader*, 31.8.08, http://www.thesundayleader.lk/archive/20080831/defence. htm
44 Iqbal Athas, 'Vavuniya Attack – How It Happened and Why', *Sunday Times*, 14.9.08, http://sundaytimes.lk/080914/Columns/sitreport.html
45 Iqbal Athas, 'They Came, They Bombed They Went Away', *Sunday Times*, 2.11.08, http://www.sundaytimes.lk/081102/Columns/sitre port.html; Amantha Perera, 'Tiger Air Show as Troops Move Forward', *Sunday Leader*, 2.11.08, http://www.thesundayleader.lk/archive/2008 1102/defence.htm
46 Amantha Perera, 'Mode Shift on the Northern Frontline', *Sunday Leader*, 23.11.08, http://www.thesundayleader.lk/archive/20081123/defence. htm
47 http://www.sundaytimes.lk/cms/article10.php?id=2380
48 Matt Wade, 'Inside Sri Lanka's Devastated Battleground', *Sydney Morning Herald*, 4.5.09, http://www.smh.com.au/news/world/inside-sri-lankas-devastated-battleground/2009/05/03/1241289038787.html

The last retreat of the Tamil Tigers 231

49 D.B.S. Jeyaraj, 'So Near and Yet So Far in Mannar Thetatre so Far', http://transcurrents.com/tamiliana/page/3?s=jeyaraj

50 Amantha Perera and Arthur Wamanan, 'Second Food Convoy Delayed', *Sunday Leader*, 12.10.08, http://www.thesundayleader.lk/archive/20081012/defence.htm

51 Ranil Wijayapala, 'Pudukuduyiruppu Awaits Final Battle', *Sunday Observer*, 8.2.09, http://www.sundayobserver.lk/2009/02/08/sec03.asp

52 'World Focus on Wanni Civilians', *SundayTimes*, 21.9.08, http://www.sundaytimes.lk/080921/Columns/political.html

53 'Trapped and Mistreated', *Human Rights Watch Report*, 15.12.08, http://www.hrw.org/node/77143/section/4 (UTHR claims that when more than 2,500 civilians expressed their willingness to move to government-controlled territory when the army was approaching Killinochchi in October 2008 the Tigers asked them to pay a large sum of money if they were to be released.) University Teachers for Human Rights (Jaffna) Special Report no. 31, http://www.uthr.org/SpecialReports/spreport31.htm#_Toc212879820 (20.2.13)

54 'Trapped and Mistreated'.

55 University Teachers for Human Rights (Jaffna) Special Report no. 31 http://www.uthr.org/SpecialReports/spreport31.htm#_Toc212879820

56 'Wanni Civilians Denied Relief and Freedom of Movement – Human Rights Watch', http://transcurrents.com/tc/2008/12/post_179.html

57 University Teachers for Human Rights (Jaffna) Special Report no. 31.

58 'Canada Joins all for Ceasefire in Sri Lanka', http://www.nationalpost.com/rss/story.html?id=1252491, 'India Asks Sri Lanka, LTTE to Stop Fighting' *Hindustan Times*, 5.2.09, http://www.hindustantimes.com/India-news/NewDelhi/India-asks-Sri-Lanka-LTTE-to-stop-fighting/Article1-375110.aspx

59 'Martin Calls for Ceasefire in Sri Lanka', http://www.belfasttelegraph.co.uk/breakingnews/breakingnews_ukandireland/martin-calls-for-ceasefire-in-sri-lanka-28465734.html

60 'Safe Zone in Sri Lanka Conflict', http://news.bbc.co.uk/2/hi/south_asia/7842612.stm

61 Ranil Wajayapala, 'Desperate LTTE Attempts to Reverse Security Forces' Victories', *Sunday Observer*, http://www.sundayobserver.lk/2009/02/15/sec03.asp

62 'No Fire Zone Declared Further Facilitating Civilian Safety', http://www.defence.lk/new.asp?fname=20090212_09

63 'Civilians Turn Pawns', *Headlines Today*, 21.4.09, http://indiatoday.intoday.in/story/Civilians+turn+pawns/1/38052.html

64 Chandraprema, *Gota's War*, p. 480.

65 B. Muralidhar Reddy, 'Final Assault', *Frontline*, 5.6.09, v. 26, no. 11, http://www.frontlineonnet.com/fl2611/stories/20090605261102400.htm

66 B. Muralidhar Reddy, 'Final Hours', *Frontline*, 19.5.09, v. 16, no. 12, http://www.frontlineonnet.com/fl2612/stories/20090619261200900.htm

67 D.B.S. Jeyaraj, 'The Last Days of Hiruvenkadam Velupilai Prabhakaran', http://dbsjeyaraj.com/dbsj/archives/615 (According to Gordon Weiss,

army officers had confided in him that Prabhakaran was killed in a mangrove swamp, cut down by RPG and heavy machine gun fire.) Gordon Weiss, *The Cage: The Fight For Sri Lanka and the Last Days of the Tamil Tigers*, Sydney, Macmillan, 2011, p. 224.

68 Gordon Weiss claims that the massacre is substantiated by the accounts of senior and lower ranking officers and enlisted men alike. Weiss, *The Cage*, p. 225.

69 'Victory's Price: 6200 Sri Lankan Troops', http://news.smh.com. au/breaking-news-world/victorys-price-6200-sri-lankan-troops-20090522-bi4f.html

Conclusion

The separatist War in Sri Lanka evolved from a very low-intensity conflict in the Jaffna Peninsula into a major conflagration that engulfed the entire country and devastated much of the North and the East of the island. Starting with the killing of a mayor, it ended with the deaths of over 100,000 people.

The long military contest between the Tigers and the government can be reduced to one of simple objectives. The Tigers wanted to dominate and rule the north and the east, and the government wanted to prevent that. The military operations were a means of achieving these objectives. What the Tigers captured, the government wished to recapture and vice versa. The brief suspensions in this tussle came once in the form of the Indian intervention and then twice as a result of the stalemates reached in 1994 and 2000.

The war followed a tortuous course, gradually escalating in intensity, scale and complexity. From a very low-intensity terrorist campaign, it evolved into a guerrilla war and then into a semi-conventional war. By the end of 1990, the Tigers had gained control over much of the territory it wished to rule, dominating much of the Jaffna Peninsula and the vast Wanni region, the latter gradually developing into their main military stronghold. The loss of the Wanni to the rebels in particular marked a turning point in the course of the war. On the one hand, it provided the rebels with a safe haven to retreat to and reorganise in. It was also an excellent way of placing the remaining army bases in the peninsula under pressure and finally removing their presence altogether in the drive to 'liberate' the entire North. For the Security Forces, the loss of the Wanni complicated things immensely. Now they had not only Jaffna to recapture and the East to pacify, but the vast stretch of the Wanni also required re-conquest.

The escalating war posed the Sri Lankan Security Forces a serious challenge. They were hardly professional forces, having been created only after independence in 1948 and having seen very little action. Their early responses betrayed this lack of experience as well as resources. Civilians came in for severe punishment due to the lack of professionalism as well as the backwardness of resources. When the war turned into a struggle for territory, the Security Forces were stretched further. Forced to fight on several fronts with limited resources, they chose to bleed the Tigers dry by continuous jabs in the Wanni while preparing for the recapture of Jaffna. At the same time, efforts continued to pacify the East. Of these operations, only those in the East produced positive results. The region was cleared of rebels ahead of provincial elections. But in the Wanni, the operations achieved little as the rebels retreated deep into the jungles. In the meantime, the death of Lieutenant General Koebbedauwa and several other senior officers ended the plan to recapture Jaffna. The peninsula was finally recaptured in 1995, but the strain on the already stretched Security Forces exacerbated after the event. The East was lost as troops were withdrawn and the influx of thousands more soldiers into Jaffna made the reopening of the MSR of paramount importance. This led to the disastrous campaign Jayasikurui, which overstretched the army and allowed the rebels to mount a devastating counter-offensive.

With the struggle for territory, the nature of the conflict also changed. While the struggle in the East remained very much a counter-insurgency war, the war in the North gradually assumed a conventional character with thousands of soldiers and rebel cadres involved in operations of manoeuvre and assault and defence of fixed positions. And as the military conflict evolved, so did the armies of the two protagonists. One of the fascinating aspects of the war is that the instruments with which the war was fought, namely the armed forces of the two protagonists, were created during the course of the war. Each major escalation of the fighting was usually preceded and followed by the acquisition of more deadly weapons and the expansion of forces, leading to an impressive evolution. The Tamil rebels started with a few dozen committed but ill-armed and trained militants fighting a Sri Lankan army which was small in numbers and, for a professional army, primitive in terms of training and equipment. During the course of the war, the Tamil Tigers built up armed forces that included heavy artillery and thousands of uniformed, highly trained and well-armed personnel and even created a small but lethal navy and a rudimentary air force. The Sri Lankan Security Forces expanded into tens of thousands of soldiers backed up by a growing fleet of tanks and APCs, a potent arsenal of heavy artillery and an increasingly sophisticated air force and navy. The war ended when one of these armed forces literally annihilated the other.

Despite the offensives, counter offensives and losses and gains in territory, the war can be seen as a long stalemate with both sides unable to achieve a decisive strategic advantage. There were several reasons for this. The Tigers were often able to offset the advantage the Security Forces had in terms of numbers and firepower. Frequently, the army's tactics also played into the Tigers' hands. The Tigers, on the other hand, did not possess the means to deal a death blow to the enemy. They besieged Jaffna but could not completely cut it off. Within this long stalemate, there were several major shifts in the balance of power. In May 1987, the Sri Lankan Security Forces appeared to be on their way to banish the Tigers into the jungles of the Wanni. In 1987–89, the IPKF had actually achieved it. In 1992, the Sri Lankan Security Forces seemed again poised to deal a decisive blow to the rebels in Jaffna. In 1995, the Tigers were hounded from Jaffna, and in 1997–99 despite stiff resistance, they seemed unable to halt the progress of the army into the Wanni. The tables were turned in 1999–2000. Following the rolling back of Jayasikurui gains and the capture of Elephant Pass, the Tigers seemed well placed to retake Jaffna but were stopped in their tracks by the refurbished Security Forces.

Of all these critical moments, the LTTE's failure to press home its advantage in 1999–2000 was perhaps the most decisive. The Tigers had reached their high watermark as a military force but could not simply deal the final blow. The long gruelling struggle to counter the Jayasikurui advance drained them of many experience cadres, while the devastating power of new weapons prevented them from making a quick dash for victory on the back of the triumph at Elephant Pass. The advantage that accrued to the Sri Lankan Security Forces as a result of the dramatic increase in firepower made another bout of semi-conventional war suicidal for the LTTE.

The problem was compounded by developments post-2000. After September 11, there was a massive backlash against terrorism, and the Tigers suffered heavily in the field of public relations due to this. Many countries came down heavily on them and actively collaborated with the Sri Lankan government in blocking avenues for the Tigers to raise funds and obtain weapons. The noose had been tightening on the Tigers for a while due to their intransigence and the blatant use of terror tactics without concern for civilian lives. But after the September 11 attacks, it became a stranglehold. One of the biggest blows to the Tigers was the loss of India's support. After the murder of Rajiv Gandhi in 1991, the Indian state turned against Prabhakaran, declaring him a wanted criminal. Not only did India remain aloof from the conflict but it also supplied

236 Conclusion

vital technology to combat them. At the same time, China emerged as a major backer of the Sri Lankan state, providing huge quantities of weapons and other equipment.

The split in the LTTE in 2004 was also helpful to the military. With the defection of Karuna, not only did the Tigers lose one of their most capable commanders, the government also gained the support and insight of a hardened Tiger leader with intimate knowledge of the LTTE. The result was a heavy boost to the military's intelligence network.

Furthermore in 2005, Sri Lankans also elected a government that was committed to a 'fight to the finish'. Unlike many previous governments, the Rajapaksa government also had the wherewithal to fight the war to a finish. Large amounts of military hardware had bolstered the military's strike capability, particularly its air arm. Combined with this firepower was the development of more sophisticated ways of dealing with the rebel forces. The Sri Lankan Security Forces had learned much from their failures in the 1990s. Blind jungle bashing with large forces was replaced by small group operations, while in the sea the swarms of arrow boats bested the Sea Tigers at their own game. The numbers of soldiers, airmen and sailors had also increased. The army in particular had expanded massively. This enabled the military to deploy a firepower that was of unprecedented ferocity and to sustain heavy casualties without losing the battle-worthiness of many units. Into this one must also factor in the willingness to accept heavy casualties, perhaps for the first time in the war, made possible by the availability of large numbers of troops.

In short, when Ealam War IV started in 2006, the Tigers had their backs to the wall. They still possessed a large army of well-armed, committed troops and a huge stockpile of weapons including heavy artillery, but in a long conventional war of attrition, they were no match to the Sri Lankan forces with their larger army and comparatively massive fire power. They could not count on any international sympathy. Prabhakaran had used up all his reserves of goodwill. India's desire to see the back of the Tigers also stifled the rebels' attempts to replenish their arsenal. Boosted by the support of Indian intelligence agencies, the Sri Lankan navy annihilated the rebels' merchant navy, dealing a death blow to their chances of fighting the enemy to a standstill.

When the campaign in the Wanni unfolded in 2007, the Tigers were trapped into fighting a conventional war of attrition with a dwindled pool of cadres and an arsenal that had little chance of being replenished. The Wanni which had been a safe haven for them when the Sri Lankan

Security Forces were small, ill equipped and inexperienced now became a death trap with the Security Forces having an unprecedented capacity to assail the enemy from land, air and sea. By employing a combination of heavy firepower and small group operations, the Sri Lankan forces gradually bled the enemy. The Security Forces also bled profusely, but unlike the rebels they were in a position to absorb their losses. Naively and foolishly, the Tigers looked to the world to save them, but no help arrived.

The ultimate military defeat of the Tamil Tigers was part of a long process that gradually weakened the rebels militarily as well as diplomatically and strengthened the Sri Lankan Security Forces and government. The tenacity and ferocity of their defence could only postpone the defeat, not avoid it.

Bibliography

Books

Alles, A. C., *The J.V.P. 1969–1989*, (Lake House: Colombo, 1990).

Balasingham, Adele, *Women Fighters of Liberation Tigers*, (Thasan Printers: Jaffna, 1993).

Balasingham, Anton, *War and Peace: Armed Struggle and Peace Efforts of Liberation Tigers*, (Fairmax Publishing: Mitcham, 2004).

Balasuriya, M., *Rise and Fall of the LTTE*, (Asian Network on Conflict Research: Colombo, 2011), pp. 151–4.

Bavinck, Ben, *Of Tamils and Tigers: a Journey through Sri Lanka's War Years*, (Vijitha Yapa: Colombo, 2011).

Blodgett, Brian, *Sri Lanka's Military, in Search of a Mission 1949–2004*, (Aventine Press: San Diego, CA, 2004).

Chandraprema, C. A., *Gota's War: the Crushing of Tamil Tiger Terrorism in Sri Lanka*, (Ranjan Wijeratne Foundation: Colombo, 2012).

Clarance, William, *Ethnic Warfare in Sri Lanka and the UN Crisis*, (Vijitha Yapa: Colombo, 2007).

De Silva, Gen. Gerry, *A Most Noble Profession: Memories That Linger*, (International Book House: Colombo, 2011).

Dewarajah, Lorna Srimathie, *The Kandyan Kingdom*, (Lake House: Colombo, 1972), pp. 35, 41 and 79.

Dissanayake, T.D.S.A., *War or Peace in Sri Lanka*, (popular Prakashan: Colombo, 1995).

Ghosh, P.A., *Ethnic Conflict in Sri Lanka and Role of the Indian Peace Keeping Force*, p. 96, http://books.google.com.au/books?id=YZscr75ijq8C&pg=PA131&lpg=PA131&dq=operation+checkmate+IPKF&source=bl&ots=0XZJyh-Run&sig=LSoPlhN80q_ayOqT_JmQF2lFVnc&hl=en&sa=X&ei=Ds-pT4S4H8uuiQfcvuWtAw&ved=0CFUQ6AEwAw#v=onepage&q=op eration%20checkmate%20IPKF&f=false.

Gunaratna, Malinga H., *For a Sovereign State*, (Sarvodaya Book Publishing Services: Ratmalana, 1988).

Bibliography   239

Gunaratna, Rohan, *Indian Intervention in Sri Lanka: the Role of India's Intelligence Agencies*, (South Asian Network on Conflict Research: Colombo, 1993).

Gunaratne, Rohan, *War and Peace in Sri Lanka*, (Institute of Fundamental Studies: Colombo, 1987).

Hashim, Ahmed S., *When Counterinsurgency Wins: Sri Lanka's Defeat of the Tamil Tigers*, (University of Pennsylvania Press: Philadelphia, 2013).

Hoole, Rajan *et al.*, *Broken Palmyra Broken Palmyrah: The Tamil Crisis in Sri Lanka, an Inside Account*, (Sri Lanka Studies Institute: Ratmalana, Colombo, 1992).

Donald L. Horowits, *Coup Theories and Officers' Motives: Sri Lanka in Comparative Perspective*, (Princeton University Press: Princeton, NJ, 1980).

Little, David, *The Invention of Enmity*, (U.S.Institue of Peace: Washington, DC, 1994).

Mendis, L.M.H., *Assignment Peace, in the Name of the Motherland*, (Author publication: Nugegoda, Sri Lanka, 2009).

Moorcraft, P., *Total Destruction of the Tamil Tigers: The Rare Victory of Sri Lanka's Long War*, (Pen and Sword Military: Barnsley, England, 2012).

Munasinghe, Sarath, *A Soldier's Version*, (Author publication: Colombo, 2000).

Muthukumaru, Anton, *The Military History of Ceylon – an Outline*, (Navrang: Delhi, 1987).

Narayan Swamy, M.R., *Inside and Elusive Mind*, (Konark Publishers: Delhi 2003).

Narayan Swamy, M.R., *Tigers of Lanka: from Boys to Guerrilas*, (Konark Publishers: Delhi, 1994).

O'Ballance, Edgar, *Cyanide War: the Tamil Insurrection in Sri Lanka 1973–88*, (Brassey's: London, 1989).

Perera, Tissa Ravindra, *Wanni Awasan maha satana*, (Pahan Publishers: Colombo, 2009).

Ponniah, S., *Satyagraha: The Freedom Movement of the Tamils in Ceylon*, (A. Kandiah: Jaffna, 1963P).

Ranatunge, Cyril, *Adventurous Journey, from Peace to War, Insurgency to Terrorism*, (Vijitha Yapa: Colombo, 2009).

Sardeshspande, Lt. Gen. S.C., *Assignment Jaffna*, (Lancer: Delhi, 1992).

Scudieri, D., *The Indian Peace Keeping Force in Sri Lanka 1987–90: a Case Study in Operations Other Than War*, (School of Advanced Military Studies, United States Army Command and General Staff College, Fort Leavenworth, Kansas, 1994), http://www.dtic.mil/cgi-bin/GetTRDoc?AD=ADA294004.

Senananayake, Capt. Tilak, *Vadamarachchi Vimukthi Meheyuma saha Uthure Satan* (Godage: Colombo, 2004).

Senaratne, Jagath P., *Sri Lanka Air Force: a Historical Retrospect*, vol II, 1985–1997, (Sri Lanka Air Force: Colombo, 1998).

240 Bibliography

Seneviratne, Col Susantha and Harischandra, Ruwan, *Negenahira Mudhagath Meheyuma*, (Pahana Publishers: Colombo, 2003).

Seneviratne, Sri Lal, *Negenahira Mudageneema*, (Self-pubished, Honganji Graphics, Naranhenpita, Sri Lanka, 2008).

'71 Aprel Mathakayan, 71 Sahodrathwa Sansadaya, Rajagiriya, 2006.

Singh, Depinder, *The IPKF in Sri Lanka*, (Trishul Publications: Delhi, 2002).

Sivanayagam, S., *Sri Lanka: Witness to History, a Journalis's Memoirs 1930–2004*, (Sivayogam: London, 2005).

Smith, Tim, *Reluctant Mercenary: the Recollections of a British Ex-army Pilot in the Anti-Terrorist War in Sri Lanka*, (The Book Guild: Sussex, UK, 2002).

Sri Lanka Army, '50 Years on'- 1949–1999, (Sri Lanka Army: Colombo, Sri Lanka, 1999).

The Sri Lanka Navy: a Pictorial History of the Navy in Sri Lanka [1937–1998], (Sri Lanka Navy: Colombo, Sri Lanka, 1998).

Weiss, Gordon, *The Cage: the Fight for Sri Lanka and the Last Days of the Tamil Tigers*, (Macmillan: Sydney, 2011).

Articles, pamphlets and theses (print and online)

Abeypala, H. W., 'Black Saturday's Slaughter House', *Weekend*, 15.02.87, pp. 6 and 11.

Abeywardana, Kesara, 'Last Post for Victims of Brutal Terror', *The Nation*, 18.6.06, http://www.nation.lk/2006/06/18/newsfe1.htm (10.02.12).

Abeywardena, Rohan, 'Where Men Fight and Guns Boom', *Sunday Times*, 27.1.08, http://www.sundaytimes.lk/080127/News/news0011.html (11.05.11).

Abraham, Thomas, 'Fragile Peace', *Frontline*, 9–22.6.90, pp. 18–19.

——— 'Pounding Jaffna', *Frontline*, 2–15.3.91, p. 56.

'Air Attack Takes Attention Off Ground Battles', *Sunday Leader*, 31.8.08, http://www.thesundayleader.lk/archive/20080831/defence.htm (15.06.12).

'Air Strikes Target LTTE Camps in Batticlaoa', *The Island*, 30.7.06, http://www.island.lk/2006/07/30/news2.html (06.06.13).

Alwis, William and Abeywardene, Srimal, 'Eleven Killed by Bomb in CTO', *Ceylon Daily News*, http://www.dailynews.lk/2009/06/08/fea10.asp (21.12.13).

'A New Spiral of Violence', *Asiaweek*, 24.5.85.

'Army Captures Vakarai', *Sri Lanka Monitor*, no. 125, June 1998, http://brcslproject.gn.apc.org/slmonitor/june98/cont.html (03.07.13).

'Army Eyes New Northern Supply Route', *Sunday Leader*, 9.11.08, http://www.thesundayleader.lk/archive/20081109/defence.htm (05.08.12).

'Army Issues Comeback Call to Deserters', *Sunday Times*, 26.11.95, p. 1.

'Army Officer for Jaffna', *Malaysian Straits Times*, 29.2.84.

'Army Stuck with Red Tanks', *Sunday Times*, 26.1.92, p. 1.

Bibliography   241

'The Army Will Stay On', (Athulathmudali's interview with *India Today*'s Dilip Bob and S.V. Venkatramani, *Lanka Guardian*, 1.7.87, p. 9 (9–10)).

Athas, Iqbal, 'Sri Lanka Strengthens Defence Forces', *Jane's Defence Weekly*, 3, no. 2, (12.1.85), p. 45.

—— 'The Fear of Living Dangerously', *Weekend*, 3.8.1986, pp. 11, 23.

—— 'The Grand Design', *Weekend*, 21.09.86, p. 8.

—— 'Rendezvous in Madras to Receive Seized Arms', *Weekend*, 08.03.87, pp. 7, 21.

—— 'Peace through the Ballot?', *Weekend*, 15.03.87, p. 7.

—— 'Bid to Internationalise Hostage Crisis by Tigers', *Weekend*, 29.3.87, pp. 7, 23.

—— 'The Vadamarachchi Landing', *Weekend*, 31.05.87, p. 6.

—— 'How Operation Jellyfish Stung India's Flotilla at the Kutch', *Weekend*, 7.6.87, p. 23 (6, 23).

—— 'The Post Vadamarachchi Crisis', *Weekend*, 14.6.87.

—— 'The Plot That Failed at the Airbase', *Weekend*, 21.6.87.

—— 'Tigers Explode Peace a Nelliady', *Weekend*, 12.7.87, pp. 6 (6 and11).

—— 'The 'Day after' Mood Plagues Jaffna', *Weekend*, 19.7.87, pp. 6 (6 and 19).

—— 'Island Pride and Prejudice', *Weekend*, 24.7.87, p. 6.

—— 'The Mood in Jaffna', *Weekend*, 4.3.90, p. 25.

—— 'For the North, It's the Year of the Tiger', *Weekend*, 4.3.90, pp. 26–7.

—— 'The North South Talks, *Weekend*, 3.6.90, pp. 6–7.

—— Iqbal Athas, 'The Agony of Araly', *Sunday Times,* 16.8.92, p. 5.

—— 'The Fight Back', *Sunday Times*, 30.4.95, p. 9.

—— 'The Avro Disaster and Oliver's Twist', *Sunday Times*, 7.5.95, p. 9.

—— 'Pooneryn; the Scenario for Big Showdown', *Sunday Times*, 14.5.95, p. 9.

—— 'Battle for the East Hots Up', *Sunday Times*, 21.5.95, p. 9.

—— 'Mandaithivu Was a Sitting Duck', *Sunday Times*, 2.7.95, p. 9.

—— 'Daring Jaffna Thrust a Very Costly Effort', *Sunday Times*, 26.11.95, p. 7.

—— 'A Grim Story', *Sunday Times*, 28.6.95, p. 9.

—— 'Leave Issue Alerts Forces', *Sunday Times,* 3.3.96, p. 7.

—— 'Hardly Three Weeks Away', *Sunday Times*, 24.3.96, p. 9.

—— 'Worst Ever Commando Debacle', *Sunday Times*, 7.5.96, p. 9.

—— 'The Navel Op That Beguiled the Tiger', *Sunday Times*, 9.6.96, p. 7.

—— 'Elite US Commandos in Lanka', *Sunday Times*, 7.7.96, p. 7.

—— 'The Paranthan Comeback', *Sunday Times*, 12.1.97, p. 7.

—— 'Not Losing Is Also Winning: the Paranthan Poser', *Sunday Times*, 19.1.97, p. 7.

—— 'Tiger Triple Jump in the Eastern Theatre', *Sunday Times*, 9.3.97, p. 5.

—— 'Censorship Resurrecting the Dead', *Sunday Times*, 11.10.98, http://sundaytimes.lk/981011/sitrep.html (09.07.13).

242 Bibliography

———— 'Now, an Artillery War', *Sunday Times*, 21.3.99, http://sunday times.lk/990321/sitrep.html (05.07.13).

———— 'Rana Ghosa V Disaster Bares Tiger Build – up', *Sunday Times*, 19.9.99, http://sundaytimes.lk/990919/sitrep.html (04.03.12).

———— 'Years of Gains Lost in Days', *Sunday Times*, 7.11.99, http://sundaytimes.lk/991107/sitrep.html (05.08.12).

———— 'Tiger Waves Smashed at Elephant Pass', *Sunday Times*, 12.12.99, http://sundaytimes.lk/991212/sitrep.html (07.10.13).

———— 'After the Truce, War Drums from the LTTE', *Sunday Times*, 21.1.2000, http://sundaytimes.lk/010121/sitrep.html (24.2.12).

———— 'News Blackouts: Rumours Rule the Day', *Sunday Times*, 7.5.2000, http://www.sundaytimes.lk/000507/sitrep.html (25.04.12).

———— 'Troops Brace to Face Stepped Up Attacks', *Sunday Times*, 28.5.2000.

———— 'An Uneasy Lull', *Sunday Times*, 4.6.00, http://www.sundaytimes.lk/000604/sitrep.html (21.12.13).

———— 'Attacks Disrupt KKS Port and Palaly Airfield', *Sunday Times*, 11.7.2000, http://sundaytimes.lk/000611/sitrep.html (08.07.13).

———— 'Sri Lankan Army Inspects Czech Main Battle Tanks', *Jane's Defence Weekly*, 19.7.2000.

———— 'The Millennium Thrust That Failed', *Sunday Times*, 10.9.2000, http://sundaytimes.lk/000910/sitrep.html (09.07.12).

———— 'How Operation Kinihira Won Chavakachcheri', *Sunday Times*, 24.9.00, http://sundaytimes.lk/000924/sitrep.html (12.12.12).

———— 'Troops on the Road to Elephant Pass', *Sunday Times*, 28.1.01, http://www.sundaytimes.lk/010128/sitrep.html (21.12.13).

———— 'How 'Operation Rod of Iron' Misfired', *Sunday Times*, 29.4.01, http://sundaytimes.lk/010429/sitrep.html (02.11.13).

———— 'Attack on Tiger Ship – a Job Well Done', *Sunday Times*, 13.3.03, http://www.sundaytimes.lk/030316/index.html (11.11.12).

———— 'Navy between Bravery and Brickbats', *Sunday Times*, 22.6.03, http://www.sundaytimes.lk/030622/index.html (04.12.12).

———— 'LTTE in Move to Destabilise East', *Sunday Times*, 30.7.06, http://sundaytimes.lk/060730/index.html (07.09.13).

———— 'Tiger Trap for Trinco Siege', *Sunday Times*, 3.8.03, http://www.sundaytimes.lk/030803/index.html (03.07.13).

———— 'The Ealam War IV: Trinco in Danger', *Sunday Times*, 6.8.06, http://sundaytimes.lk/060806/index.html (12.12.11).

———— 'Ealam War IV Rages on Several Fronts', *Sunday Times*, 13.8.06, http://www.sundaytimes.lk/060813/columns/sitrep.html (03.05.13).

———— 'Heavy Battles in North and East', *Sunday Times*, 13.8.06, http://sundaytimes.lk/060813/index.html (09.12.12).

———— 'LTTE Takes Beating; but a Long Way to Go', *Sunday Times*, 27.8.06, http://sundaytimes.lk/060827/index.html (04.12.12).

Bibliography   243

——— 'LTTE Planning Big Hits', *Sunday Times*, 1.10.06, http://sunday times.lk/061001/Columns/sitreport.html (12.12.12).

——— 'Muhamala Debacle: the Shocking Story', *Sunday Times*, 15.10.06, http://sundaytimes.lk/060910/News/nw3.html (09.07.12).

——— 'Real Heroes and Mock Heroics', *Sunday Times*, 22.10.06, http://sundaytimes.lk/061022/Columns/sitreport.html (03.07.13).

——— 'Charles: LTTE's Prince of Faceless Terror', *Sunday Times*, 8.1.07, http://www.sundaytimes.lk/080113/Columns/sitreport.html (12.08.13).

——— 'Vakarai: the Reality Behind the Euphoria', *Sunday Times*, 21.1.07, http://sundaytimes.lk/070121/Columns/sitreport.html (12.12.13).

——— 'Army Holds Jaya Pirith; Tigers Warn of Bloodbath', *Sunday Times*, 7.3.07, http://sundaytimes.lk/070311/Columns/sitreport.html (25.04.12).

——— 'Tale of Two Wars: Ground Battle and Media Battle', *Sunday Times*, 27.5.07, http://www.sundaytimes.lk/070527/Columns/sitreport.html (08.07.13).

——— 'Heavy Casualties as War Intensifies', *Sunday Times*, 24.6.07 http://www.sundaytimes.lk/070624/Columns/sitreport.html (09.07.12).

——— 'East: the Aftermath', 22.7.07, http://www.sundaytimes.lk/070722/Columns/sitreport.html (02.10.12).

——— '2008 Year of War, Ban on LTTE Likely', *Sunday Times*, 30.12.07, http://www.sundaytimes.lk/071230/Columns/sitreport.html (03.05.13).

——— 'Continued LTTE Resistance Prolongs Sri Lankan Conflict', *Jane's Defence Weekly*, posted on 28.2.08.

——— 'Troops Make Progress but Major Battles Ahead', *Sunday Times*, 9.3.08, http://www.sundaytimes.lk/080309/Columns/sitreport.html (09.07.12).

——— 'Jeyaraj; Probe on Who Failed and What Next', *Sunday Times*, 13.4.08, http://www.sundaytimes.lk/080413/Columns/sitreport.html (24.02.12).

——— 'The Aftermath of Muhamalai Confrontation', *Sunday Times*, 27.4.08, http://www.sundaytimes.lk/080427/Columns/sitreport.html (07.07.13).

——— 'The Significance of the Vidattaltivu Victory', *Sunday Times*, 20.7.08, http://www.sundaytimes.lk/080720/Columns/sitreport.html (24.02.12).

——— 'Vavuniya Attack – How It Happened and Why', *Sunday Times*, 14.9.08, http://sundaytimes.lk/080914/Columns/sitreport.html (08.07.13).

——— 'They Came, They Bombed They Went Away', *Sunday Times*, 2.11.08, http://www.sundaytimes.lk/081102/Columns/sitreport.html (05.11.13).

——— 'Fall Of Pooneryn: Crushing Blow to Tigers', *Sunday Times*, 16.11.08, http://www.sundaytimes.lk/081116/Columns/sitreport.html (05.11.13).

244 Bibliography

———— 'Mortar Monsoon, Fiercest Battles Knee Deep in Mud', *Sunday Times*, 21.12.08, http://www.sundaytimes.lk/081221/Columns/sitre port.html (16.11.12).

———— 'Ealam War IV: Which Way the Last Phase Next Year', *Sunday Times*, 28.12.08, http://www.sundaytimes.lk/081228/Columns/sitre port.html (13.07.13).

———— '2008 Year of War, Ban on LTTE Likely', *Sunday Times*, 30.12.07, http://www.sundaytimes.lk/071230/Columns/sitreport.html (03.04.13).

Baruah, Amit, 'The Killinochchi Stand-Off', *Frontline*, 6.9.96, pp. 130–1.

———— 'Operation Sath Jaya III', *Frontline*, 1.11.96, pp. 59–62.

'Battle for Batticaloa', *Sri Lanka Monitor*, British Refugee Council Newsletter, v. 2, no. 8, November 1989.

'The Battle for Jaffna', *The Sri Lanka Monitor*, British Refugee Council, no. 53, June 1992, p. 1.

'The Battle for Jaffna', *Frontline*, May 27–June 9, 2000, http://www.front lineonnet.com/fl1711/17110120.htm (02.11.13).

'Battle for Thoppigala Erupts Again', *Sunday Times*, 10.6.07, http://www.sundaytimes.lk/070610/News/news4.html (16.11.12).

'Bleeding Statistics', *Saturday Review*, 4.1.86, p. 4.

'A Body Blow', *The Sri Lanka Monitor*, British Refugee Council, no. 44, Sept. '91, p. 2.

Brown, Derek, 'Jaffna Reality – Two Strange Forms', *The Guardian*, 15.6.87, reproduced in the *Saturday Review*, 11.7.87, p. 4.

Bulathsinhala, Srian, 'Troops Smash Tiger Bases in Thoppigala', *The Island*, 21.1.96, Inform Clippings January '96, p. 9.

'Bus Bombing Kills 20 in Sri Lanka', http://www.theage.com.au/news/world/bus-bombing-kills-20-in-sri-lanka/2008/02/03/1201973719546.html (18.11.12).

'Bus Bomb Kills 23 Passengers Near Sri Lanka's Capital', http://www.theage.com.au/news/world/bus-bomb-kills-23-passengers-near-sri-lankas-capital/2008/04/26/1208743266629.html (18.11.12).

'Canada Joins Calls for Ceasefire in Sri Lanka', http://www.nationalpost.com/rss/story.html?id=1252491 (12.01.13).

'Capturing Killinochchi Is a Daydream of the Rajapakses', *Sunday Leader*, 26.10.08, http://www.thesundayleader.lk/archive/20081026/interviews-1.htm (03.02.13).

'Ceasefire Agreement between the Government and the LTTE', http://www.norway.lk/Embassy/Peace-Process/Role-of-Norway/ (12.04.13).

Chandrasekaran, S., 'India in the "Active" Mode', South Asia Analysis Group, Notes and Updates, Sri Lanka: update no. 20, 12.7.00. http://www.southasiaanalysis.org/%5Cnotes2%5Cnote110.html (21.2.12).

Chengappa, Raj and Denish, Roy, 'Return of the Tiger', *India Today*, 22.5.2000, p. 32 (28–32).

Bibliography 245

Cherian, John, 'New Delhi's Dual Approach', *Frontline*, 21.11.08, v. 25, no. 23, http://www.frontlineonnet.com/fl2523/stories/2008112125 2312800.htm (03.03.13).

'Civilians Turn Pawns', *Headlines Today*, 21.4.09, http://indiatoday. intoday.in/story/Civilians+turn+pawns/1/38052.html (12.04.13).

Claiborne, William, 'Tamils Hide in Fear as Troops Take Revenge', *The Age*, 15.8.84.

Colmey, John, 'In the Thick of a Jaffna Battle', *Asiaweek*, 14.8.92, pp. 66–70.

'Colombo's Peace Gesture to Tamils', *The Age*, 1.9.94.

Cooper, Tom, 'Sri Lanka since 1971', 2003, Air Combat information Group, http://www.acig.org/artman/publish/article_336.shtml#top (10.12.12).

'Corporal Nuwan Tharanga: Fallen Hero at Thoppigala', http://www. sundayobserver.lk/2008/03/16/mag04.asp (09.5.13).

'The Crawl to Terminate Sea Tigers', *Sunday Observer*, 15.3.09, http:// www.sundayobserver.lk/2009/03/15/sec10.asp (11.11.13)

'Creeping advantage in Jaffna', *Tamilnet*, 10.2.00, http://www.tamilnet. com/art.html?catid=79&artid=7408 (12.04.13).

Cruez, Dexter, 'Within the Jaws of the Tiger', *Weekend*, 26.10.86, p. 8.

'The Day of the Lions (Jackals?)', *Saturday Review*, 6.6.87, p. 2.

'Death Rains from the Skies', *Saturday Review*, 1.3.86, p. 1.

Defence Correspondent, 'Terror at Sea', *Sunday Times*, 18.10.92, p. 5.

—— 'LTTE's Passage to India', *Sunday Times*, 18.10.92, p. 5.

—— 'Temporary Setback Turns Raw', *Sunday Leader*, 30.4.95, p. 7.

—— 'Of Arms and Men and Machines of War', *Sunday Leader*, 7.5.95, p. 4.

—— 'The Mandaithvu Debacle', *The Island*, 2.7.95, pp. 6, 7.

—— 'Jaffna: Signs of Sunrise', *Sunday Times*, 26.5.96, p. 8.

—— 'Quiet on the N-E Front', *The Island*, 22.9.96, p. 12.

—— 'Black Tigers at Service Funerals', *The Island*, 8.10.96, p. 8.

—— 'Paranthan Death Toll: 171 Soldiers and at Least 171 Tigers', *The Island*, 12.1.97, pp. 10, 12.

—— 'Tigers Counterstrike to Their Edi Bala Shame Goes Wrong', *The Island*, 9.3.97, p. 10.

—— 'Three Pronged Surprise Assault Smashes Tiger Bases', *The Island*, 16.3.97, p. 8.

—— 'Driving a Stake into the Tiger's Heart', *The Island*, 18.5.97, p. 10.

—— 'Tigers in Do-or-Die Stand at Puliyankulam', *The Island*, 4.8.97, p. 10.

—— 'Jubilation as Two Army Divisions Link Up at Puliyankulam', *The Island*, 10.8.97, p. 10.

—— 'On the Road Again, This Time It's the Right One', *The Island*, 4.7.99, p. 8.

—— 'Debacle at Periyamadu', *The Island*, 19.9.99, p. 9.

—— 'Military in Worst Debacle in Nine Years', *The Island*, 7.11.99, p. 9.

Denish, Roy, 'Tamil Rebels Preparing for a Bloody Vendettal', *Weekend*, 15.6.89, p. 1.
—— 'North East Flare Up', *Weekend*, 17.6.90, pp. 6–7.
—— 'The Kokavil Blackout', *Weekend*, 15.7.90, pp. 6–7.
—— 'The Taking of Mankulam', *Weekend*, 22.7.90, p. 6.
—— 'Fort Liberation', *Weekend*, 16.9.90, pp. 6–7.
—— 'Setback at Mankulam', *Weekend*, 2.12.90, pp. 6–7.
—— 'Kumarappa', Tigers' New Grenade, *Weekend*, 9.12.90, p. 6.
—— 'Flying Tigers to Prowl the Skies', *Sunday Leader*, 6.4.97, p. 8.
—— 'The East: Thorn in the Side of Assured Victory', *Sunday Leader*, 29.6.97, p. 4.
—— 'Jayasikurui: 95 n.o', *Sunday Leader*, 17.8.97, p. 9.
—— 'Push and Pull for Puliynkulam', *Sunday Leader*, 31.8.97, p. 9.
—— 'Death at Dark Midnight', *Sunday Leader*, 30.11.97, p. 8.
—— 'Troops Walk into Tiger Trap', *Sunday Leader*, 14.12.97, p. 5.
—— 'Bloodiest Year at the Battlefront', *Sunday Leader*, 28.12.97, p. 9.
—— 'Savage Onslaught on Key Camps', *Sunday Leader*, 8.2.98, p. 4.
—— 'Mirusuvil Massacre', *Sunday Leader*, 22.2.98, p. 7.
—— 'Inching upto Mankulam', *Sunday Leader*, 8.3.98, p. 5.
—— 'Ceaseless waves' swamp 'assured victory', *Sunday Leader*, 11.10.98, p. 8.
—— 'Blackout in the Aftermath of a Fiasco', *Sunday Leader*, 18.10.98, p. 10.
—— 'Desertion and Defection', *Sunday Leader*, 25.10.98, p. 13.
—— 'LTTE Airstrike Power – the Truth Is Out', *Sunday Leader*, 6.12.98, p. 9.
—— 'Tigers Pound Thallady Camp', *Sunday Leader*, 21.3.99, p. 13.
—— ' "Ready Disorder" by Tigers Limits Army Advance', *Sunday Leader*, 4.7.99, p. 7.
—— 'Army, LTTE Suffer Heavy Toll at Periyamadhu', *Sunday Leader*, 19.9.99, p. 11.
—— 'Army in Disarray', *Sunday Leader*, 7.11.99, p. 6.
—— and Hussein, Asgar, 'Vavuniya Turns into Ghost Town', *Sunday Leader*, 14.11.99, p. 1.
—— 'Setback for Tigers at Elephant Pass', *Sunday Leader*, 19.12.1999, p. 7.
—— 'Soldiers in Need of "relief" ', *Sunday Leader*, 23.1.2000, p. 10.
—— 'Red Herring for Independence', *Sunday Leader*, 6.2.2000, p. 10.
—— 'Under Surveillance', *Sunday Leader*, 6.8.2000, p. 13.
—— 'Political Overtones in Military Appointments', *Sunday Leader*, 13.8.2000, p. 4.
—— 'Motives behind the Push', *Sunday Leader*, 17.9.2000, p. 13.
de Silva, Daryl, 'Defence Ministry Confirms Final Tally at 28 Killed, 45 Wounded', *Daily News*, 24.4.95, Insight Clippings, April '95, p. 10.
—— 'Clearing the Eastern Sector', *Weekend Express*, 20.1.96, p. 5.

Bibliography 247

—— 'With Thevanayagam, Pearl, Commandos Battle on to Mulaithivu', *Weekend Express*, 20–21.7.96, p. 1.

De Silva, Janaka, 'Prabhakaran in a Winning Position', *Sunday Leader*, 24.12.2000, p. 7.

—— 'Uncertain Waves and Political Manoeuvres', *Sunday Leader*, 31.12.2000, p. 10.

De Silva, Sergei, 'Good Education – Sri Lankan Military Learns Insurgency Lessons', *Jane's Intelligence Review*, 13.11.09.

Desmond, Edward W., 'A New Kind of Warfare', *Time*, 16.9.91, pp. 30–1.

'Ealam War III Toll: April 19 – May 27', *Sunday Times*, 28.5.95, p. 8.

Edirisinghe, R., 'Sri Lanka Navy Crush Sea Tiger Flotilla: 10 Sea Tiger Boats Sunk, 30 Cadres Killed', *Asian Tribune*, 18.09.08, http://www.asiantribune.com/?q=node/13302 (02.11.13).

'84 Reported Slain as Guerrillas Raid Sri Lanka Farms', *Toronto Star*, 1.12.84.

Eliathamby, Niresh, 'Ferocious Naval Battle Rocks Jaffna Lagoon', *The Island*, 29.8.93, p. 9.

—— 'What Went Wrong?', *The Island*, 21.11.93, p. 9.

Elliott, John, 'Battle for Tamil Hearts, Minds and Stomachs', *Financial Times*, 6.6.87, reproduced in Lanka Guardian, 15.6.87, pp. 8, 11.

Emergency '79, Pamphlet published by the Movement for Inter Religious Justice and Equality, (Kandy, 1980).

'Elephant Pass Troops Stand Firm', *Sunday Times*, 19.12.99, http://sundaytimes.lk/991219/sitrep.html (12.06.13).

'EPS Fall: Reassessing LTTE's Manoeuvre Warfare Prowess', http://www.tamilnet.com/art.html?catid=79&artid=8839 (10.04.12).

'Eravur OIC Bluffed the Terrorists', *Ceylon Daily News*, 7.9.85.

'Extradited Tamil Tigers Arraigned in US Court', http://www.priu.gov.lk/news_update/Current_Affairs/ca201212/20121229extradited_tamil_tigers_arraigned_in_us_federal.htm (10.02.12).

Farrel, Tom, 'Eastern Promise – Sri Lankan Troops Turn Tigers Back into Guerrillas', *Jane's Intelligence Review*, 20.9.07.

—— 'Northern Exposure: the Next Stage in Sri Lanka's War', *Jane's Intelligence Review*, 15.11.07.

Ferdinando, Shamindra, 'Sri Lanka Gets a Wartime Prize', *The Island*, 21.10.90, p. 12.

—— 'The Army's Deadly Wanni Thrust', *The Island*, 17.2.91, p. 9.

—— 'The Importance of Securing the Wanni', *The Island*, 24.3.91, p. 7.

—— 'The Finest Hour of the Armed Forces', *The Island*, 31.3.91, p. 9.

—— 'Army Cuts Off the Peninsula', *The Island*, 27.10.91, pp. 7, 11.

—— 'Operation Sixer', *The Island*, 22.3.92, p. 9.

—— 'Eleventh Year of Ealam War', *The Island*, 27.12.92, p. 7.

—— 'Crucial Battle for Control of Jaffna Lagoon', *The Island*, 21.2.93, p. 9.

248 Bibliography

——— 'Vavuniya Is Calm but. . . .', *The Island*, 26.9.93, p. 9.

——— 'The Battle for Kilali – The Army Fights Back', *The Island*, 3.10.93, p. 13.

——— 'Kilali Offensive a Success Claims Army', *The Island*, 10.10.93, p. 13.

——— 'Tigers Kill 27 Soldiers in Second Attack in East', *The Island*, 24.5.95, Inform Clippings, May '95, p. 8.

——— 'Tigers Vacate Taravikulam Camp', *The Island*, 22.1.96, Inform Clippings, January '96, p. 10.

———, 'Twenty Three STF Men Killed in Terrorist Attack in East', *The Island*, 12.3.96, Inform Clippings March '96, p. 4.

——— with Norman Palihawadan, '47 Terrorists, 29 Soldiers Killed', *The Island*, 24.10.95, Insight Clippings, October '95, p. 5.

——— with Norman Palihawadana, 'Fifteen Soldiers Killed in East', *The Island*, 26.3.96, Inform Clippings, March '96, p. 8.

——— with Norman Palihawadana, 'Eight Army Men Killed', *The Island*, 28.5.96, Inform Clippings, May '96, p. 6.

——— with Norman Palihawadana, 'Nine More Terrorists Killed, Vakarai Town Captured', *The Island*, 13.7.96, reproduced in Insight Newspaper clippings, July 1996, p. 1.

——— 'Fourteen Sailors Killed', *The Island*, 31.3.96, Inform Clippings, March '96, p. 9.

——— 'Two Naval Craft Blown Up', *The Island*, 12.6.96, Inform Clippings, June '96, p. 3.

——— 'Tigers Kill 13 Soldiers', *The Island*, 15.7.96, reproduced in Inform Clippings, July, 1996, p. 2.

——— 'Army Admits Destruction of Long-range Guns', *The Island*, 12.1.97, p. 1.

——— 'Two of LTTE's Frontline Leaders Killed', *The Island*, 10.3.97, Inform Clippings, March '97, p. 7.

——— with Norman Palihawadana, 'Nearly 275 Tigers and Soldiers Killed in Vavunathivu', *The Island*, 8.3.97, Insight clippings, March '97, p. 6.

——— 'Tigers Targeting Tanks in Fierce Battle', *The Island*, 21.8.97, Inform Clippings August '97, p. 3.

——— 'Heavy Tiger Losses in Vanni Offensive', *The Island*, 25.8.97, Inform Clippings, August '97, pp. 4–5.

——— 'Over 200 Tigers, 20 Soldiers Die in Killinochchi battle', *The Island*, 2.2.98, reproduced in Inform Newspaper Clippings, Feb. 1998, p. 1.

——— 'Stiff Resistance Despite Heavy Artillery Bombardment', *The Island*, 7.2.98, reproduced in Inform Newspaper Clippings, Feb. 1998, p. 2.

——— 'Air Force Seeks More Copter Gunships', *The Island*, 15.2.98, p. 1.

——— 'Jayasikurui Operation Kill 1,300 Tigers Admits Prabhakaran', *The Island*, 14.5.98, Insight Clippings, May '98, p. 2.

——— 'Forces Recruit More Men, Criticise Politicians for Hampering the War Effort', *The Island*, 5.9.99, p. 1.

Bibliography 249

—— 'Chava Now a Devastated Town', *The Island,* 22.9.2000, http://www.island.lk/2000/09/22/news09.html (02.09.13).

—— 'Armless Veteran Speaks of War and Peace', *The Island,* 27.10.02, http://www.tamilcanadian.com/page.php?cat=130&id=1311 (02.11.13).

——, 'Army Takes Commanding Position West of A9 . . . Bags Tunukkai, Eyes Mallavi, Mankulam under Threat', *The Island,* 23.8.08, http://www.island.lk/2008/08/23/news2.html (02.08.13).

——, 'Mission Accomplished on Western Flank', 25.11.12, *The Island,* http://www.island.lk/index.php?page_cat=article-details&page=article-details&code_title=66895.

Fernando, Hiranthi, 'Don't Worry Sir, I Will Fight Till I Die', *Sunday Times,* 1.10.00, http://sundaytimes.lk/001001/plus4.html (03.07.13).

Fernando, Romesh, 'North East War Politico-military Dimension', *The Island,* 24.6.90, p. 6.

Fernando, Santush, 'How Thopigala Fell Like Nine Pins', http://www.nation.lk/2007/07/22/militarym.htm (12.07.13).

Fernando, Wimalasena, 'To Serve in Defence of the Realm', *Weekend,* 1.7.90, pp. 7, 49.

'59 Tamils Murdered', *Sun,* 21.5.85.

'Fighting Continues in the North, *The Island,* 12.05.2000, http://www.island.lk/2000/05/12/islnews.html# (12.09.13).

'1st Reconnaissance Regiment Sri Lanka Armoured Corps', *Army Magazine,* thirtieth Anniversary Issue October 10, 1979, p. 23.

Fish, Tim, 'Sri Lanka Learns to Counter Sea Tigers' Swarm Tactics', *Jane's Navy International,* March 2009, pp. 21–3.

'Forces Hit Back Kill 218 Tigers', *Daily News,* 29.7.95, Inform Clippings, July '95, p. 11.

Foster, Peter, 'Tamil Tiger Suicide Squad in Audacious Attack', *The Telegraph,* 22.10.07, http://www.telegraph.co.uk/news/worldnews/1567103/Tamil-Tiger-suicide-squad-in-audacious-strike.html (09.09.12).

Fuard, Asif, 'Final Battle in the Midst of Civilians', *Sunday Times,* 12.4.09, http://www.sundaytimes.lk/090412/News/sundaytimesnews_14.html (12.10.13).

—— 'The Fall of Chalai and the Death Knell of Sea Tigers', *Sunday Times,* 8.2.12, http://www.sundaytimes.lk/090208/News/sundaytimesnews_16.html (12.10.13).

Gamage, Dharmasiri and Senenayake, Tilak, 'Next Ten Days Most Crucial', *Observer,* 22.7.90, pp. 1, 17.

'General: Colombo Can't Defeat Tamils', *Asian Defence Journal,* September 1990, p. 110.

Ghosh, P. A., *Ethnic Conflict in Sri Lanka and Role of the Indian Peace Keeping Force,* http://books.google.com.au/books?id=YZscr75ijq8C&pg=PA131&lpg=PA131&dq=operation+checkmate+IPKF&source=bl&ots=0XZ

250 Bibliography

Jyh-Run&sig=LSoPlhN80q_ayOqT_JmQF2lFVnc&hl=en&sa=X&ei=Ds-pT4S4H8uuiQfcvuWtAw&ved=0CFUQ6AEwAw#v=onepage&q=operation%20checkmate%20IPKF&f=false (10.02.12).

Gopalan, T. N., 'Deadlock at Jaffna Doorstep', Colombo, 12.5.2000, http://www.telegraphindia.com/1000513/front_pa.htm (12.07.13).

Goonetilleke, Harry, 'Operation Edi Bala – a Military or Political Imperative', *Weekend Express*, 9.3.97, p. 4.

Gunaratna, Rohan, 'Tiger Cubs in the Battlefield', *The Island*, 19.7.98, pp. 9–10.

—— 'Tamil Tigers Burning Bright', *Himal*, April 1999, pp. 34–9.

—— 'LTTE Adopts Heavy Artillery', *Jane's Intelligence Review*, 1.6.01.

—— 'A Wake Up Call', *Frontline*, 31.8.01, pp. 52–4.

Gunasekera, Rohan, and Ferdinando, Shamindra, 'Govt. and LTTE Agree on Ceasefire', *The Island*, 17.6.90, p. 1.

—— 'Fighting the Tiger War, *The Island*, 24.6.90, pp. 9, 10.

—— with Ferdinando, Shamindra, 'Hooded Men Identify Tigers', *The Isalnd*, 1.7.90, p. 1.

—— 'Military Modernization in Sri Lanka', *International Defense Review*, February 1991, pp. 107–8.

—— 'Army Halts Rebel Attacks on Camps, *The Island*, 24.3.91, p. 1.

—— 'Tiger Defences Overrun', *The Island*, 23.6.91, p. 7.

—— 'Week-long Army Offensive Makes Tigers Withdraw', *The Island*, 23.6.91, pp. 1, 3.

—— 'A Signal Victory', *The Island*, 29. 9.91, p. 14.

—— 'Arms Trade in South Asia', *The Island*, 12.1.92, p. 6.

—— 'The Battle for Jaffna: Primed for Action', *The Island*, 2.2.92, p. 5.

—— 'Operation Eastern Cut Off', *The Island*, 23.2.92, p. 11.

—— 'Army Captures Five Rebel Camps', *The Island*, 22.03.92, p. 9.

—— 'Tiger Set Up Anti-tank Squads', *The Island*, 22.3.92, p. 1.

—— 'The East Remains a Problem', *The Island*, 10.5.92, p. 9.

—— 'Strangulation of the Jaffna Peninsula', *The Island*, 19.07.92, p. 9.

—— 'Key Sea Tiger Base Captured', *The Island*, 23.7.92, p. 11.

—— 'Army's Dilemma in the East', *The Island*, 27.9.92, p. 13.

—— 'Air Power in Ealam War', *The Island*, 21.2.93, p. 9.

—— 'Army Officers Worried', *The Island*, 29.1.95, p. 1.

—— 'Tigers Lick Their Wounds but Prepare to Hit and Run', *Jane's Intelligence Review*, 1.2.96, v.3, no. 2.

Gupta, Shekar, 'Haven in India for Lankan Guerrillas', *Sydney Morning Herald*, 14.4.84.

—— 'Terror Tactics', *India Today*, 15.10.85, p. 53 (50–56).

'The Guerrilla Chief Emerges from His Jungle Hideout', *Sydney Morning Herald*, 3.4.90.

Hamlyn, Michael, 'Tamils Step Up Attacks on Civilians: The Communal Conflict in Sri Lanka', *The Times*, 11.3.86.

Bibliography   251

—— 'Tiger Guerrillas Step into Rulers Role: Jaffna Tamils Prepare for Post-Settlement Role in Sri Lanka', *The Times*, 18.9.86.

Hanif, Jehan, 'Massacre in Jaffna: TELO Man Tells All', *The Island*, 14.9.86, p. 13.

Hariharan, Col. A. 'LTTE and Ceasefire Violations', http://www.southasia analysis.org/%5Cpapers15%5Cpaper1406.html (4.9.12).

—— 'War after the Fall of Vidatalativu', *The Island*, 23.7.08, http://www.island.lk/2008/07/23/features1.html (12.07.13).

Harris, Paul, 'Sri Lankan Forces Pushed to the Limit', *Jane's International Review*, 1.4.96.

—— 'Asia, Bitter Lessons for the SLA', *Jane's Intelligence Review*, 01.10.96.

—— 'LTTE Turns Up Heat in Sri Lankan Power Struggle', *Jane's Intelligence Review*, 21.8.2000.

Hawkesley, Humphrey, 'Sri Lanka Resumes Air Raids on Tamil Villages', *The Age*, 29.3.86.

—— 'Tamil Guerrillas Kill 7 in Troop Convoy Ambush', *The Age*, 3.4.86.

'Heavy Fighting in Muttur as Death Toll Rises', *Sunday Leader*, 6.8.06, http://www.thesundayleader.lk/archive/20060806/news.htm (4.9.12).

Hoole, Rajan, 'Border Aggression and Civilian Massacres', *Colombo Telegraph*, 7.2.15, https://www.colombotelegraph.com/index.php/the-toll-1983-july-1987/ (15.3.15).

'House to House Fighting Delays Final Victory', *The Nation*, 8.3.09, http://www.nation.lk/2009/03/08/militarym.htm (20.12.12).

'How the Army Was Able to Capture Paranthan by the New Year', *Transcurrents*, http://transcurrents.com/tc/2009/01/post_219.html (27.08.12).

'How the LTTE Destroyed the TELO', Illustrated Weekly of India, reproduced in *The Island*, 18.6.86, p. 6.

'Hundreds Gather for the Funeral of the Slain Tamil Tiger', *Gulf News*, 11.2.05, http://gulfnews.com/news/world/other-world/hundreds-gather-for-funeral-of-slain-tamil-tiger-1.276968 (13.02.13).

'India Asks Sri Lanka, LTTE to Stop Fighting' *Hindustan Times*, 5.2.09, http://www.hindustantimes.com/India-news/NewDelhi/India-asks-Sri-Lanka-LTTE-to-stop-fighting/Article1-375110.aspx (12.07.13).

'India Cracks the Whip', *Asiaweek*, 23.11.86, p. 33.

'India Withdraws Last of Its Troops', *Sydney Morning Herald*, 26.3.90.

'Inside a Tiger Training Camp', *The Island*, 8.7.85.

'Inside Jaffna Fort: Battle of Nerves', *Ceylon Daily News*, 11.9.86, reproduced in *Saturday Review*, 20.9.86, p. 6.

'In Tiger Country', *Asiaweek*, 26.1.90, pp. 35–41.

Ismail, Qadri, 'Military Option and Its Aftermath', *Sunday Times*, 7.6.87, p. 5.

'Israeli, British Agents Helping Lankan Forces', *New Sunday Times*, 12.8.84.

'Is Rajiv Gandhi Being Misled?', *The Island*, 5.10.86, p. 9.

252 Bibliography

Jabbar, Zacki, 'Army Deserters Stand at 5,000', *The Island*, 16.10.98, Inform Clippings, October '98, p. 14.

'Jaffna Bombed', *Saturday Review*, 22.2.86, p. 1.

'Jaffna's Stalemate', *The Sri Lanka Monitor*, British Refugee Council, no. 56, September 1992, p. 1.

Jalaldeen, Rafik, 'Forces Beat Back LTTE Artillery Attack', *Daily News*, 29.1.08, http://www.dailynews.lk/2008/01/29/sec01.asp (13.2.13).

Jansz, Frederica, 'Victory at Vavuniya', *Sunday Times*, 12.5.91, p. 5.

Jayanth, V., 'Talking Peace', *Frontline*, 10.2.95, p. 143.

Jayasinghe, Amal and Malalasekera, S., 'Terrorist Blast Kills Nine at Cold Stores', *Ceylon Daily News*, 30.5.86, http://www.dailynews.lk/2009/06/10/fea09.asp (21.12.13).

Jayasiri, Sunil and Parameshwaran, N., 'Tiger Shellshock Jaffna', *Daily Mirror*, 13.12.99, Inform Clippings, December '99, p. 24.

Jayasooriya, Ranga, 'Tiger Offensive Repuulsed in Kilali', *Observer*, 20.8.06, http://www.sundayobserver.lk/2006/08/20/fea17.asp (03.07.13).

—— 'Tigers Planning Major Attack During Monsoon Season', *Observer*, http://www.sundayobserver.lk/2006/08/27/ (13.02.12).

—— 'Fall of Sampur', *Sunday Observer*, 10.9.06, http://www.sundayobserver.lk/2006/09/10/fea05.asp (02.11.13).

Jayaweera, Neville, 'In to the Turbulence of Jaffna: a Chapter Extracted from the Author's Unpublished Memoirs Titled "Dilemmas"', *The Island*, http://www.island.lk/2008/10/05/features2.html (20.12.13).

Jeyaraj, D.B.S., 'Tigers Leap in Different Directions', *The Island*, 20.9.87, p. 7.

—— 'LTTE Ascendant in the East', *The Island*, '9.3.97, p. 13.

—— 'Birth and Growth of the Black Tiger Suicide Squad', *The Island*, 13.7.97, p. 16.

—— 'Strategic Changes in Wanni', *Frontline*, 23.2.99, p. 59 (57–60).

—— 'LTTE Offensive', *Frontline*, November 27 – December 10 1999, http://www.frontline.in/fl1625/16250040.htm (12.07.13).

—— 'Another LTTE Offensive', *Frontline*, v. 17, no. 8, 15–28.4.2000, http://www.flonnet.com/fl1708/17080520.htm (12.08.13).

—— 'The Taking of Elephant Pass', *Frontline*, 13–26.5.2000, http://frontlineonnet.com/fl1710/17100100.htm (04.09.12).

—— 'The Taking of Elephant Pass', *Frontline*, 13–26.5.2000. http://www.frontlineonnet.com/fl1710/17100100.htm (12.07.13).

—— 'Eastern Cauldron', *Frontline*, 24.8.07, p. 47 (45–8).

—— 'A Deceptive Calm', *Frontline*, v. 17, no. 13, 24.6–7.7.2000, http://www.frontlineonnet.com/fl1713/17130310.htm (03.07.13).

—— 'The Fall of Karuna', *Frontline*, 7.5.04, pp. 122–4.

—— 'Army Seizes Four Villages around Sampur', *Sunday Leader*, 3.9.06, http://www.thesundayleader.lk/archive/20060903/news.htm#Army (27.12.12).

Bibliography   253

———— 'Simmering East Set to Explode', *Sunday Leader*, 10.9.06, http://www.thesundayleader.lk/archive/20060910/issues.htm (03.07.13).

———— 'Talking in Geneva after Taking Elephant Pass', *Sunday Leader*, 8.10.06, http://www.thesundayleader.lk/archive/20061008/spotlight.htm (13.12.12).

———— 'Armed Forces Suffer Debacle as Tigers Fight Back', *Sunday Leader*, 15.10.06, http://www.thesundayleader.lk/archive/20061015/issues.htm (08.07.13).

———— 'Anatomy of Tiger Assault on Anuradhapura Airbase', *Transcurrents*, 27.10.07, http://transcurrents.com/tamiliana/archives/400 (05.11.13).

———— 'Balraj: Legendary Commander of the LTTE', http://dbsjeyaraj.com/dbsj/archives/2177 (5.10.11).

———— 'Civilians Suffer in Battle over Vaharai', *Sunday Leader*, http://www.thesundayleader.lk/archive/20061224/issues.htm (03.04.13).

———— 'Anatomy of the LTTE Military Debacle at Ananthapuram', 5.4.12, http://dbsjeyaraj.com/dbsj/archives/5404 (03.05.13).

———— 'So Near and Yet So Far in the Mannar War Theatre So Far', http://transcurrents.com/tamiliana/archives/555 (03.05.13).

———— 'Frontline Positions Shift Rapidly in Northern Theatre of War', http://transcurrents.com/tc/2008/08/post_18.html (21.12.10).

———— 'Col' Charles: the Tiger Mastermind behind LTTE attacks outside North-East', http://dbsjeyaraj.com/dbsj/archives/14588 (05.11.13).

———— 'Frontline Positions Shift Rapidly in Northern Theatre of War', http://transcurrents.com/tc/2008/08/post_18.html (21.12.10).

———— 'LRRP Infiltration Demolishes Impregnable Tiger terrain Myth', http://transcurrents.com/tamiliana/archives/575 (03.05.13).

'Brigadier' Balraj; the Legendary Commander of the LTTE', *Transcurrents*, http://dbsjeyaraj.com/dbsj/archives/2177 (21.12.13).

———— 'Wretched of the North East Lanka Earth', http://transcurrents.com/tamiliana/page/20?s=jeyaraj (17.12.12).

———— 'Tigers Get Ready to Face the Mechanised Infantry of the Army in the North', *Transcurrents*, 25.3.08, http://transcurrents.com/tamiliana/archives/category/transcurrents-newsfeatures/page/3 (13.12.07).

———— 'The Last Days of Hiruvenkadam Velupilai Prabhakaran', http://dbsjeyaraj.com/dbsj/archives/615 (22.03.12).

Johnson, Robert Craig, 'Tigers and Lions in Paradise: the Enduring Agony of the Civil War in Sri Lanka', 1998, http://worldatwar.net/chandelle/v3/v3n3/articles/srilanka.html (23.10.10).

Joshi, Manoj, 'A Base for All Seasons: How LTTE Used Tamil Nadu', *Frontline*, 3–16.8.91, pp. 21–23.

———— 'The Price of Peace', *Frontline*, March 18–31, 1989, pp. 17–21.

'J.R. Breaks His Silence: I Feared a Military Coup in'87', interview with Vijitha Yapa in *Sunday Times*, 11.2.90, pp. 14–15.

254 Bibliography

Kamalendran, Kris, 'Commander: Army Will Go to Schools', *Sunday Times*, 10.5.98, Insight Clippings, May '98, p. 8.

——'Pre Dawn horror in Ampara: 54 Killed as LTTE Unleashed Terror on Villagers', *Sunday Times*, 19.9.99, Insight Clippings September '99, p. 1.

—— 'Mass Exodus from Wanni', *Sunday Times*, 14.11.99, http://sundaytimes.lk/991114/frontm.html#1LABEL1 (02.11.13).

Karniol, Robert, 'Rocket Boost for Sri Lanka', *Jane's Defence Weekly*, 28.6.2000.

'Kilinochchi Calamity: the Worst Debacle in 17 Years', *Sunday Times*, 4.10.98, http://sundaytimes.lk/981004/sitrep.html (11.11.12).

'Kilinochchi Base Captured – LTTE', *Tamilnet*, 28.9.98, http://www.tamilnet.com/art.html?catid=13&artid=2112 (17.12.12).

'Killed in Action', *Saturday Review*, 23.5.87, p. 1.

Karunakaran, P., 'LTTE Opens All Fronts', *Weekend Express*, 7–8. 2.98, p. 7.

—— 'Battle for Land and Sea Supremacy', *Weekend Express*, 14–15.3.98, p. 7.

—— 'Mullaithivu Debacle, Monsoon to Decide Jayasikurui', *Weekend Express*, 8–9.11.97, p. 1.

——'Jayasikurui and Heroes Week', *Weekend Express*, 22–23.11.97, p. 1.

—— 'Claymore Claims Army and PLOTE Members', *Weekend Express*, 16–17.5.98, p. 6.

—— 'Mi-24 Crashes Killing Crew', *Weekend, Express*, 28.6.98, Inform Clippings, June '98, p. 5.

—— 'LTTE Intensifies Attacks to Coincide with PA's Fifth Year', *Weekend Express*, 14–15.8.99, p. 7.

—— 'Debacle at Oddusudan: Was It the Failure of Intelligence', *Weekend Express*, 6–7.11.99, p. 6.

—— 'Madhu, Periyamadhu Fall to the LTTE', *Weekend Express*, 20–21.11.99, p. 1.

—— 'Unexpected LTTE Resistance Stalls Knihira IX', *Weekend Express*, 21.1.01, p. 5.

—— 'Ealam War III Enters Sixth Year', *Weekend Express*, 23.4.2000, p. 5.

'The Know-How to Combat Terrorism', *Sun*, 26.1.85.

Kulatunga, Aruna and Wijeratne, Premalal, 'The Train Tragedy', *Sun*, 22.1.85.

Kulkarni, V.G., 'The Military Modernises to Meet Rebel Threat', *Far Eastern Economic Review*, 12.6.86, pp. 29–31.

Kumara, Sarath, 'Two Bus Bombs Kill More Than 20 in Sri Lanka, http://www.wsws.org/articles/2007/jan2007/sril-j10.shtml (17.12.12).

'Lalith Assassinated', *Sunday Times*, 25.4.93, p. 1, 'The President Is dead', *Sunday Times*, 2.5.93, p. 1.

'Landmine Monitor Report 2000', *Human Rights Watch*, 2000, p. 534.

'Lankan Forces Capture Two Key LTTE Bastions; 50 Tigers Killed, India Today, 1.1.09, http://indiatoday.intoday.in/story/Lankan+forces+capture+2+key+LTTE+bastions;+50+Tigers+killed/1/24142.html (05.11.13).

'Latest Anti Tamil Violence Claims 56', *The Australian*, 20.5.85.

Bibliography 255

Lieut, Gen, Lionel Piayananda Balagalle's Interview with *Jane's Defence Weekly*, 19.1.01.

'Long Ranger', The Fallacy of the Stalingrad Example', *Sri Lanka Guardian*, http://www.srilankaguardian.org/2009/01/fallacy-of-stalingrad-example.html (15.12.11).

'LTTE Attacks in North Repulsed', *Daily News*, 21.4.95, Insight Clippings April '95, p. 7.

'LTTE Bombing of Central Bank, 31 January 1996', http://www.lanka library.com/phpBB/viewtopic.php?t=1592 (1.11.14).

'LTTE Releases Photographs of Air Mission', *Tamilnet*, 26.3.07, http://www.tamilnet.com/art.html?catid=13&artid=21668 (21.07.13).

'LTTE Had Been Weakened Says Amy Chief', *Sunday Times*, Interview with Army Commander Rohan Daluwate, *Sunday Times*, 2.3.97, p. 7.

'LTTE Resumes Boat Service across Lagoon', *The Island*, 10.10.93, p. 1.

Lyons, John, 'Rebels Use Chemical Warfare on Army', *Sydney Morning Herald*, 29.6.90.

—— 'Cold Blooded Butchery on Paradise Island', *Sydney Morning Herald*, 30.6.90.

Mahindapala, H.L.D., 'The Day When the Tigers Fought and Ran', *Sunday Observer*, 10.10.93, p. 10.

'Manampitiya Police Guard Room Attacked-2 PCs Killed', *Island*, 21.5.85.

'Mannar Tragedy', *Saturday Review*, 22.12.84, p. 3.

Manoharan, N., 'Tigers with Wings – Air Power of the LTTE', paper no. 1720, Institute of Peace and Conflict Studies, http://www.ipcs.org/article/sri-lanka/tigers-with-wings-air-power-of-the-ltte-1720.html (06.11.13).

Manor, James, and Segal, Gerald, 'Causes of Conflict: Sri Lanka and India Ocean Strategy', *Asian Survey*, 25, no. 12 (December 1985), pp. 1165–1185.

Marcan-Markar, Marwaan, 'South West of Batti: State in the Making', *Sunday Leader*, 8.6.97, p. 4.

—— 'Criminals in the East', *Sunday Leader*, 5.4.98, p. 8.

—— 'Troopers Who Refuse to Charge', *Sunday Leader*, 10.5.98, p. 11.

—— 'Sleepwalkers and Slaughtered Sheep', *Sunday Leader*, 11.10.98, p. 8.

—— 'Crossing the Border', *Sunday Leader*, 7.3.99, p. 11.

Marks, Thomas A. 'Winning the War in Sri Lanka', *The Island*, 2.6.86, p. 6.

—— 'Insurgency and Counterinsurgency', *Issues and Studies,* August 1986, pp. 63–102.

—— 'Counterinsurgency in Sri Lanka: Asia's Dirty Little War', *Soldier of Fortune*, Feb. 1987, pp. 38–47.

—— 'Sri Lanka's Special Forces', *Soldier of Fortune*, July 1988, pp. 32–9.

'Martin Calls for Ceasefire in Sri Lanka', http://www.belfasttelegraph.co.uk/breakingnews/breakingnews_ukandireland/martin-calls-for-ceasefire-in-sri-lanka-28465734.html (16.12.11).

256 Bibliography

McDonald, Robert, 'Eyewitness in Jaffna', *Pacific Defense Reporter*, August, 1987.

'Memoirs titled "Dilemmas"', *The Island*, http://www.island.lk/2008/10/05/features2.html (19.05.12).

Menon, Amaranath K., 'No Generals' War, but a Man-to-Man War, *The Island*, 16.8.92, p. 5 (From *India Today*).

Menon, Ramesh, 'Return of the Tigers', *India Today*, 15.4.90, pp. 117–23.

'Military Advances on Paduvankarai LTTE Bases', *Weekend Express*, 14–15.12.96, p. 1.

Military Balance, International Institute for Strategic Studies, 2001, Central and South Asia, p. 159.

Military Balance, International Institute for Strategic Studies, 2002, Central and South Asia, p. 135.

Military Balance, International Institute for Strategic Studies, 2007, Central and South Asia, pp. 324–5.

'Military Training in Tamil Nadu and India', *The Island*, 5.10.86, p. 9.

'Military Ups the Tempo', *The Nation*, 16.3.08, http://www.nation.lk/2008/03/16/militarym.htm (21.07.12).

Miller, Phil, 'Britain's Dirty War against the Tamil People 1979–2009', International Human Rights Association, Bremen, 2015.

'Mini War in Sampoor', *Daily Mirror*, 26.4.06, http://archives.dailymirror.lk/2006/04/28/opinion/04.asp (12.12.12).

Mithuna, Don, 'It Will Only Be a War of Attrition If They Seek a Military Way Out', *Weekend*, 17.11.85, p. 6.

'MoD Issues Casualty Figures', *Tamilnet*, 8.10.98, http://www.tamilnet.com/art.html?catid=13&artid=2153 (05.11.13).

Mohamed, Suresh, 'Troops Poised to Take Jaffna Fort', *The Island*, 26.8.90, p. 1.

——— 'Govt. Forces Pull Out of Jaffna Mandaitivu', *The Island* (International Edition), 3.10.90, p. 1.

'More Sinhalese Civilians Killed', *Saturday Review*, 31.5.86, p. 1.

'More Than 50 Killed in Tamil Violence', *Canberra Times*, 20.4.84

'Muhamalai Attack: LTTE's Defeated Aim', http://www.defence.lk/new.asp?fname=20080426_06 (21.07.12).

'Mulliawalai Terror Bastion under Siege; Terrorists Sustain Heavy Damages', http://www.defence.lk/new.asp?fname=20081226_07 (05.11.13).

Murphy, Martin, 'Maritime Threat: Tactics and Technology of the Sea Tigers', *Jane's Intelligence Review*, 1.6.06.

Nadesan, G., 'LTTE "urmal" Publishes Pulukunawa Captured Arms List', *Weekend Express*, 21–22.12.96, p. 4.

'Navy Chief, Aides, Killed by Suicide Bomber', *Daily News*, 17.11.92, p. 1.

'Navy Firepower Bolstered', *The Island*, 19.7.92, p. 1.

'Nineteen Bodies of Helicopter Crash Victims Washed Ashore', *The Island*, 31.1.96, Insight Clippings, January '96.

Bibliography 257

'No Fire Zone Declared Further Facilitating Civilian Safety', http://www. defence.lk/new.asp?fname=20090212_09 (22.08.11).

'North-East on a Knife-Edge as Tamil Factions Clash', *Sri Lanka Monitor*, British Refugee Council, v. 2, no. 9, December1989, p. 1.

'Now, the Brigadier Speaks', *Saturday Review*, 25.8.84.

Noyahr, Keith, 'The Siege of Kiran', *Sunday Times*, 24.6.90, p. 8.

Obeysekera, Gamini, 'The Long March to Kiran Victory', *Weekend*, 24.6.90, pp. 4–5.

'Operation Blue Star', *Saturday Review*, 30.5.87, p. 1.

'Operation Edibala Enters Its Fourth Day', *Weekend Express*, 8–9.2.97, p. 1.

'Operation Liberation Encircles Key LTTE Post', *Daily News*, 28.5.87, p. 1.

'Operation Search and Destroy Launched', *Weekend*, 9.12.84.

'Operation Sunray', *Sunday Leader*, 22.10.95, p. 4.

'Operation Tiger: the Reasons behind', *The Island*, 7.12.86, p. 9 (courtesy *Amrita Bazaar Patrika*).

'Operations Still on, Says Army', *Sunday Times*, 29.9.91, p. 3.

'Op Jayasikurui the Longest Ever Military Campaign Called Off', *Sunday Times*, 6.12.98, http://sundaytimes.lk/981206/sitrep.html (21.07.13).

Palakidnar, Ananth, 'Tigers Dig-in for 'Last Stand' in Jaffna', *Sunday Observer*, 5.11.95, p. 1.

Palihawadana, Norman, 'Terrorists Get Away with Jeeps from Mahaveli Maduru Oya Schemes', *Island*, 19.7.85.

———— 'Tiger Bullets Greet Journalists', *The Island*, 28.10.90, p. 9.

———— with Shamindra Fernnando, 'Bomb Blast in Colombo Kills 23, Nearly 50 Wounded', *The Island*, 8.8.95, Insight Clippings August '95, p. 1.

———— 'LTTE Cadres Flee Thoppigala Camps', *The Island*, 22.1.96, Insight Clippings January '96.

———— 'Fourteen Soldiers Killed', *The Island*, 10.6.96, Inform Clippings, June '96, p. 2.

———— 'Tiger Attack on Troop Carrier Repulsed, Trinco under LTTE Fire', *The Island*, 2.8.06.

Parthasarathy, Malini, 'A Military and Political Misadventure', *Frontline*, May 31 – June 13 1986, p. 19.

Pathiravithana, Lt. Col Ravi, 'Guerrilla Warfare: Discussing the Use of Sri Lanka's Fleet of APV's and MBT's', http://www.scribd.com/doc/52118278/GUERRILLA-WARFARE-DISCUSSING-THE-USE-OF-SRI-LANKA%E2%80%99S-FLEET-OF-APV%E2%80%99S-AND-MBT%E2%80%99S (20.12.13).

Peiris, Denzil, 'Colombo Rides the Tiger', *Weekend*, 3.3.85, pp. 6, 22.

Perera, Amantha, 'LTTE Regrouping in Jungles', *Sunday Leader*, 28.1.07, http://www.thesundayleader.lk/archive/20070128/news.htm#After (22.08.11).

258 Bibliography

——— 'Beyond Vakarai', *Sunday Leader,* 28.1.07, http://www.thesunday leader.lk/archive/20070128/defence.htm (12.12.12.).

——— 'Tigers Turn Party Poopers', *Sunday Leader,* 6.5.07, http://www.thesundayleader.lk/archive/20070506/defence.htm (16.12.11).

———'War Comes Full Circle', *Sunday Leader,* 15.7.07, http://www.thesundayleader.lk/archive/20070715/defence.htm (16.12.11).

——— 'Govt. Troops Advance beyond Silvathurai', 9.9.07, http://www.thesundayleader.lk/archive/20070909/defence.htm (16.12.11).

——— 'Defensive Tigers Warn of Lethal Days', *Sunday Leader,* 23.9.07, http://www.thesundayleader.lk/archive/20070923/defence.htm (27.08.12).

——— 'Wanni FDLs Heat Up', *Sunday Leader,* 16.12.07, http://www.thesundayleader.lk/archive/20071216/defence-.htm.

——— 'Fighting Intensifies in the North', *Sunday Leader,* 3.2.08, http://www.thesundayleader.lk/archive/20080203/parliament.htm.

——— 'The Battle for Admapan', *Sunday Leader,* 24.2.08, http://www.thesundayleader.lk/archive/20080224/defence.htm (15.12.13).

——— 'Teddy Bears and Flying Gunships Make the Script', *Sunday Leader,* 9.3.08, http://www.thesundayleader.lk/archive/20080309/defence.htm (24.11.11).

——— 'Lull in Battlefield as Focus Shifts to East', *Sunday Leader,* 16.3.08, http://www.thesundayleader.lk/archive/20080316/defence.htm (27.08.12).

——— 'Sea Tigers Strike Again and Again', *Sunday Leader,* 15.6.08, http://www.thesundayleader.lk/archive/20080615/defence.htm (15.12.13).

——— 'Military Engages Tigers on Six Fronts', *Sunday Leader,* 29.6.08, http://www.thesundayleader.lk/archive/20080629/defence.htm (22.08.11).

——— 'Behind the Frontlines', *Sunday Leader,* 13.7.08, http://www.thesundayleader.lk/archive/20080713/defence.htm (15.12.13).

——— 'Troops Gain Strategic Bay', *Sunday Leader,* 20.7.08, http://www.thesundayleader.lk/archive/20080720/defence.htm (16.12.11).

——— 'Heavy Fighting Ahead of Newly Gained Ground', *Sunday Leader,* 10.8.08, http://www.thesundayleader.lk/archive/20080810/defence.htm (15.12.13).

——— 'Wanni Fighting Takes Heavy Toll on Both Sides', *Sunday Leader,* 7.9.08, http://www.thesundayleader.lk/archive/20080907/defence.htm (21.07.13).

——— 'The Battle for Killinochchi', *Sunday Leader,* 28.9.08, http://www.thesundayleader.lk/archive/20080928/defence.htm (21.07.13).

——— 'Tiger Administrative Structure Hit', *Sunday Leader,* 12.10.08, http://www.thesundayleader.lk/archive/20081012/defence.htm (17.9.10).

——— with Wamanan, Arthur, 'Second Food Convoy Delayed', *Sunday Leader,* 12.10.08, http://www.thesundayleader.lk/archive/20081012/defence.htm (18.09.10).

——— 'Army Eyes New Northern Supply Route', *Sunday Leader,* 9.11.08.

—— 'Army Moves to Cut Off Pooneryn', *Sunday Leader*, 16.11.08, http://www.thesundayleader.lk/archive/20081116/defence.htm (27.08.12).

—— 'Floods, Fie and Fury', *Sunday Leader*, 30.11.08, http://www.thesundayleader.lk/archive/20081130/defence.htm (22.08.11).

—— 'Battles after Nisha', *Sunday Leader*, 7.12.08, http://www.thesundayleader.lk/archive/20081207/defence.htm (29.01.11).

—— 'Wanni Battle Takes Its Toll', *Sunday Leader*, 21.12.08, http://www.thesundayleader.lk/archive/20081221/defence.htm (25.06.10).

——, 'Troops Enter Killi with Multi Pronged Attack', *Sunday Leader*, 1.4.09, http://www.thesundayleader.lk/archive/20090104/defence.htm (17.9.10).

—— 'Tiger Air Show as Troops Move Forward', *Sunday Leader*, 2.11.08, http://www.thesundayleader.lk/archive/20081102/defence.htm (27.08.12).

—— 'Mode Shift on the Northern Frontline', *Sunday Leader*, 23.11.08, http://www.thesundayleader.lk/archive/20081123/defence.htm (19.12.10).

—— 'Samthaanms Rain Down on Defence Lines', *Sunday Leader*, 11.5.08, http://www.thesundayleader.lk/archive/20080511/defence.htm (27.08.12).

Perera, Elmo, 'Bloodlust of the brutal Tigers', *Weekend*, 20.03 1987, pp. 8 and 21.

Perera, Tissa Ravindra, 'LTTE Grand Assault Routed', *The Nation*, 15.3.09, http://www.nation.lk/2009/03/15/militarym.htm (16.12.11)

—— 'The Final Battle that Decimated the Tigers', *The Nation*, 12.4.09, http://www.nation.lk/2009/04/12/defence.html (27.08.12)

Perry, Alex, 'If This Is Called Peace. . . .', *Time Magazine World*, 30.4.06, http://www.time.com/time/magazine/article/0,9171,501060508–1189385,00.html (12.12.12).

'Piecing the Puzzle of the Kittu Drama, *Sunday Times*, 24.1.93, p. 5.

'Police Offer One Lakh Reward for Information,' *Daily News*, 14.4.78, p. 1.

Political Correspondent, 'Straining at Ants and Swallowing Elephants', *Sunday Times*, 21.7.91, p. 4.

—— 'DB Sets Stage for Military Thrust', 12.9.93, p. 6.

Political Correspondent, 'The Tiger-EPRLF Power Play over North East', *Weekend*, 8.10.89, p. 5.

—— 'What Went Wrong at Mankulam?', *Sunday Times*, 2.12.90, p. 4.

—— 'Bishop Moves onto the Chess Board', *Sunday Times*, 17.1.93, p. 4.

'Pooneryn as Good as Fallen', *The Nation*, http://www.nation.lk/2008/11/09/militarym.htm (10.02.12).

'Pooneryn or Peace Road', *Sunday Times*, 11.12.94, p. 9.

Povlock, Paul A., 'A Guerrilla War at Sea: The Sri Lankan Civil War', *Small Wars Journal*, 9.9.11, pp. 31–2. http://smallwarsjournal.com/sites/default/files/848-povlock.pdf (19.12.10).

'Prabha Steps on to the Frontline', *Sunday Times*, 19.9.93, p. 7.

260 Bibliography

'Prabha's Jungle Life', *Weekend*, 18.2.90, p. 6.

'Prabha's Tactic; Wait and See', *Sunday Times*, 16.7.95, p. 6.

'Push to Jaffna', *Asiaweek*, 10.7.92, pp. 41–7.

Rajasingham, K.T., '"Sri Lanka" the Untold Story', chapter 50, http://www.atimes.com/atimes/South_Asia/DG27Df02.html (27.08.12).

Raman, B., 'No Crouching Tigers These', *Outlook India*, 23.10.07, http://www.outlookindia.com/article.aspx?235846 (21.07.13).

'Ravana', 'The Black Tiger Phenomena, Its Origins and Their Targets', *The Island*, 14.11.93, p. 11.

———— 'The Assault on Pooneryn and LTTE's Eastern Strategy', *The Island*, 21.11.93, pp. 9, 12.

Raviraj, Franklin, 'Inside Jaffna', *The Island*, 27.1.91, p. 9.

———— 'We Were Taken by Surprise – Wounded Soldier', *The Island*, 21.11.93, p. 3.

———— 'Water War', *Frontline*, 15–25.8.06, v. 23, no. 16, http://www.frontlineonnet.com/fl2316/stories/20060825001405400.htm (10.02.12).

———— 'Cornered Tigers', *Frontline*, 30.1.09, v. 26, no. 2, http://www.frontlineonnet.com/fl2602/stories/20090130260212900.htm (17.9.10).

———— 'Final Hours', *Frontline*, 19.5.09, v. 16, no. 12, http://www.frontlineonnet.com/fl2612/stories/20090619261200900.htm (13.12.13).

———— 'Final Assault', *Frontline*, 5.6.09, v. 26, no. 11, http://www.frontlineonnet.com/fl2611/stories/20090605261102400.htm (19.12.10).

'R.C.', 'Al Quiet on the Northern Front', *Saturday Review*, 30.5.87, p. 4.

Sabaratnam, T., 'Pirapaharan Phenomenon', Chapter 23, http://www.sangam.org/articles/view2/?uid=633 (3.11.13).

'Safe Zone in Sri Lanka Conflict', http://news.bbc.co.uk/2/hi/south_asia/7842612.stm (21.07.13).

Samath, Faizal, 'Terrorist Training Camp at Jaffna', *The Island*, 14.7.85, pp. 1, 2.

Sambandan, V.S., 'The Fall of Elephant Pass', *Frontline*, 12.5.00, pp. 124–6.

———— 'Peace Process in Trouble', *Frontline*, 23.5.03, pp. 128–30.

———— 'A Rebellion in the East', *Frontline*, 26.3.04, pp. 114–16.

———— 'War by Other Means', *Frontline*, 18.6–1.7.05, v. 22, no. 13, http://www.frontlineonnet.com/fl2213/stories/20050701002304200.htm (27.08.12).

'Scribe', 'Carnival and War – For How Long?', *Sunday Times*, 20.6.93, p. 6.

Sebastian, Rita, 'Three Month Battle for Jaffna Fort', *Tamil Times*, 15.9.90, pp. 4, 16.

———— with Lalit Pattajoshi, 'Pull-out Fall-out', *The Week*, 1.4.90, p. 28.

'Security Forces Advance on all Fronts in North and East', *Sunday Observer*, 24.6.90, p. 3.

'Security Forces Secure Large Areas', *Sunday Observer*, 15.02.87, p. 1.

Senadhira, Sugeeswara, 'Navy Cripples LTTE Sea Power', *Sunday Observer*, 12.5.91, p. 1.

Senenayake, Panduka, 'Navy Bombard Sea Tiger Base', *The Evening Observer*, 21.4.95, Inform Clippings April '95, p. 8.

Bibliography 261

'The Siege of Kiran', *Sunday Times*, 24.6.90, p. 5.

'Siva Tells the Hindu – Jaffna Area a Prison', *The Sun*, 21.1.85.

Sivanayagam, S. (ed), 'Tamil Information', (published for private circulation) Madras, v. 1, nos. 4 and 5, 1.9.84.

'SLA advance Thwarted – Vot', 12.9.99, http://tamilnet.com/art.html?catid=13&artid=3916 (13.12.13).

'SLAF Helicopter Carrying 39 Shot Down by Tigers', *The Island*, 23.1.96, Inform Clippings January '96, p. 11.

'South Asia Intelligence Review', http://www.satp.org/satporgtp/detailed_news.asp?date1=12/26/2007&id=1#1 (19.12.10).

Special Correspondent, 'Tigers on the Retreat', *Sunday Times*, 24.6.90, p. 4.

'Special Forces Poised to Capture Thoppigala Jungle', http://www.sundayobserver.lk/2007/06/24/fea02.asp (11.11.13).

'Sri Lanka Army Gains Control over Visvamadu Town', *India Today*, 29.1.09, http://indiatoday.intoday.in/story/Sri+Lankan+army+gains+control+over+Visuamadu+town/1/26672.html (17.01.13).

Sri Lanka: Conflict of June 1990, UTHR(Jaffna), Jaffna Sri Lanka (Typescript)

'Sri Lanka "Forced" to Seek Israeli Help', *The Straits Times*, 3.7.84.

The Sri Lanka Monitor, British Refugee Council Newsletter, no. 38, March 1991.

The Sri Lanka Monitor, no. 93, Oct. 1995, The British Refugee Council, London.

'Sri Lankan Kfir Jets Bomb Mullaithivu; Sampoor under Artillery Attack', *Tamilnet*, 15.6.06, http://www.tamilnet.com/art.html?catid=13&artid=18513 (17.01.13).

'Sri Lankan Troops Kill 92 Tigers in Fresh Offensive', http://archives.dawn.com/2008/02/22/intl.htm (13.2.13).

'Sri Lanka Seals Truce Deal', http://news.bbc.co.uk/2/hi/south_asia/1835737.stm (11.11.13).

'Sri Lanka: the Siege Within', *India Today*, 15.06.89, p. 121.

Sri Lanka Situation Report, Tamil Information Research Unit, Madras, 15.4.86, p. 2, and 15.5.86, p. 5.

'Sri Lanka Suicide Bomber Kills 51', *The Age*, 25.10.94.

Sri Lanka's Eastern Province: Land, Development, Conflict, International Crisis Group, Asia Report no.159, 15.10.08, http://www.genocidewatch.org/images/Sri_Lanka_08_10_15_Sri_Lanka_s_Eastern_Province_Land,_Development,_Conflict.pdf (17.01.13).

'Sri Lanka's War Seen Far from Over', *The Washington Times*, http://www.washingtontimes.com/news/2007/jul/14/sri-lankas-war-seen-far-from-over/?page=2#ixzz2KmptE0gH (13.12.13).

Sriyananda, Shanika, ' LTTE's Waterloo', *Sunday Observer*, 12.4.09, http://www.sundayobserver.lk/2009/04/12/sec04.asp (16.11.12).

———— 'Saved Through Blood, Sweat and Tears', *Sunday Observer*, 12.6.11, http://www.sundayobserver.lk/2011/06/12/fea02.asp (09.12.12).

262 Bibliography

Steinemann, Peter, 'The Sri Lanka Air Force', *Asian Defense Journal*, Feb. 1993, pp. 52–61.

Subramaniam, T.B., 'Adding to the Arsenal', *Frontline*, 3–16.8.91, p. 39.

Subramanyam, Nirupama, 'Fight to the Finish', *India Today*, 30.11.95, p. 68 (inset) (64–69).

—— 'Wounded Yet Ferocious', *India Today*, 15.12.95, pp. 46–55.

—— 'Army Takes Back Ghost Town', *The Hindu*, 21.9.2000, http://hindu.com/2000/09/21/stories/03210007.htm (05.12.13).

—— 'Starting All Over Again', *Frontline*, 25.5.01, p. 57 (57–8).

—— 'Terror at Katunayake', *Frontline*, 17.8.01, pp. 51–3.

Suguro, Suvendrinie, 'More Army Camps Planned', *Daily Observer*, 31.12.84.

Sunday Times Defence Correspondent, 'Pressure on the LTTE Chief', *Sunday Times*, 27.8.95, p. 9.

Sunday Times Defence Correspondent, 'Trigger Temptations and the New Truce', *Sunday Times*, 29.1.95, p. 9.

—— 'Thumpaneveli Flares Up in Midnight Drama', *Sunday Times*, 1.1.95, p. 8.

—— 'Scotch Rumours on LTTE', *Sunday Times*, 21.5.95, p. 7.

—— 'All about the AirForce', *Sunday Times*, 18.6.95, p. 10.

Sunday Times Military Affairs Correspondent, 'Janakapura's Day of the Jackal: Army Suffers Its Worst Defeat in Ealam War as Camp Run Over.' *Sunday Times*, 1.8.93, p. 7.

Sunday Times Military Analyst, 'LTTE Resorts to Cloak and Dagger Exercises', *Sunday Times*, 22.1.95, p. 9.

Sunday Times Military Correspondent, '40 Troops Killed by LTTE in Batti', *Sunday Times*, 24.3.96, Inform Clippings March '96, p. 7.

'Sumedha', 'Road to Mannar and the Key to Peace', *Sunday Times*, 2.3.97, p. 10.

Suryanarayana, P.S., 'The Battle for Killinochchi', *Frontline*, 20.3.98, pp. 59–61.

Suryanarayan, V., 'Land of the Displaced', *Frontline*, 22.6.01, pp. 61–3.

—— 'Stepping Stone to a Separate State', *Frontline*, 21.11.03, pp. 15–16.

Swain, Jon, 'Face to Face with the Guerrilla Commander: Cyanide Martyrs Bar Way to Peace', *Sunday Times*, 10.8.86, reproduced in *Lanka Guardian*, 1.9.86, pp. 11–12.

'Tamil Guerrillas Kill 57 Villagers', *Canberra Times*, 3.12.84.

'Tamil Killings a Reprisal for Earlier Village Deaths', *Australian*, 15.5.85.

'Tamil Terrorists Kill 150, Wound 300 in Sacred City Attack', *Australian*, 15.5.85.

'Tamil Tiger Political Chief Killed in Sri Lanka Air Strike', http://afp.google.com/article/ALeqM5j-TOLA51vP-BoTQDVn2g7JLCjGww (05.12.13).

'Tamil Tigers' Biggest Sea Base Chalai Captured', http://www.lankalibrary.com/phpBB/viewtopic.php?f=2&t=4678 (16.11.12).

'Tamil Tigers Harden Talks Stance', *BBC News*, http://news.bbc.co.uk/2/hi/south_asia/4911554.stm (17.01.13).

'Taraki' (D. Sivaram), 'Why Was the Jaffna Fort Evacuated?', *The Island*, 30.9.90, p.10.
—— 'Silvathurai – Why Did LTTE Do It?', *The Island*, 31.3.91, p. 9.
—— 'Tigers Roam the Seas', *The Island*, 28.6.92, p. 11.
—— 'Tiger Manpower: the Breeding Grounds', *The Island*, 26.7.92, p. 11.
—— 'Recapturing Jaffna: is It Feasible?', *The Island*, 29.8.92, p. 9.
—— 'Tigers' Interest in the Gulf of Mannar', *The Island*, 25.9.12, p. 9.
—— 'Why Are the Tigers Not Opening Elephant Pass?', *The Island*, 14.2.93, p. 9.
—— 'Mainland Mannar under LTTE Control', *The Island*, 22.8.93, p. 5.
—— 'Major Upset for LTTE', *The Island*, 3.10.93, p. 13.
—— 'Jaffna First Policy Dominates Tiger Thinking', *The Island*, 31.10.93, p. 7.
—— 'Pooneryn: Prabha's Strategic Thinking', *The Island*, 14.11.93, p. 11.
—— 'Grads of Tigers Defence College', *The Island*, 3.4.94, p. 7.
—— 'LTTE Outlines Its Demands', *The Island*, 9.4.95, p. 12.
—— 'LTTE Demonstrates Its Sea Power Again', *The Island*, 2.7.95, pp. 6, 18.
—— 'Game Plan for a Grand Slam', *The Sunday Times*, 3.3.96, p. 7.
—— 'Government Clings on Despite Stiff Opposition', *Sunday Times*, 8.9.96, p. 7.
—— 'The Cat a Bell and a Few Strategists', *Sunday Times*, 20.4.97, p. 7.
—— 'The Deepening Theater of Operation', *Sunday Times*, 8.2.98, p. 10.
—— 'Operation Checkmate in Killinochchi – LTTE Style', *Sunday Times*, 15.2.98, http://sundaytimes.lk/980215/taraki.html (05.12.13).
—— 'Changing Strategies and Killinochchi Gamble', *Sunday Times*, 22.2.98, http://sundaytimes.lk/980222/taraki.html (16.11.12).
—— 'Ealam War Growing More Complex', *Sunday Times*, 21.3.99, http://sundaytimes.lk/990321/taraki.html (16.11.12).
'Telecom Soldiers Charred', *Saturday Review*, 6.6.87, p. 8.
'Terrorists Kill Two TULF ex-MPs and Seven Policemen', *Ceylon Daily News*, 4.9.85.
'Thousands Answer Army's Call', *Weekend*, 9.12.84, p. 1.
'Tigers at Bay', *The Economist*, 28.2.87, p. 28.
'Tigers Constructing Strong Defences Around 300 sq, KM in Eastern Wanni', http://transcurrents.com/tc/2008/12/post_203.html (12.12.12)
'Tigers Explode Truce', *The Sri Lanka Monitor*, British refugee Council, no. 87, April 1995, p. 1.
'Tigers Flash War Alert after Leader Death', *The Telegraph*, Calcutta, 23.5.06, http://www.telegraphindia.com/1060523/asp/foreign/story_6258616.asp (17.01.13).
'Tigers Hold Troops as Captive Force', *Weekend* (Reuters Report), 21.6.87, p. 11.

264 Bibliography

'Tigers Say Thallady Forward Defence Overrun', *Tamilnet*, 24.11.99, http://tamilnet.com/art.html?catid=13&artid=4243 (17.01.13).

'Tigers Strike in Waligamam', *The Island*, 27.5.96, Inform Clippings, May '96, p. 6.

'Tigers Urged to Surrender', *Sunday Observer*, 11.4.93, p. 8.

'Top Secret Camp for Terrorists', *The Island*, 5.10.86, pp. 9, 15.

'Trapped and Mistreated', *Human Rights Watch Report*, 15.12.08, http://www.hrw.org/node/77143/section/4 (05.12.13).

Trincomalee group correspondent, 'Troops Destroy Camp, Capture Large Haul of Equipment', *Daily News*, 5.3.96, Inform Clippings, March '96, p. 2.

'Troops Capture LTTE's Last Stronghold in Mannar District', http://www.defence.lk/new.asp?fname=20080802_06 (11.11.13)

'Troops Capture Vakarai', *Daily News*, 23.6.98, Inform Clippings, June '98, p. 4.

'Troops Meet Heavy Resistance as They Advance', *The Island*, 31.5.92, p. 1.

'Troops Overrun Five LTTE Camps', reproduced in Inform Newspaper clippings, July 1996, p. 1.

'Troops Recover LTTE Multi Barrelled Rocket Launcher', http://www.lankalibrary.com/phpBB/viewtopic.php?f=2&t=3650&start=0 (10.02.12).

'Troops Regain Palampiddy', *Daily News*, 19.5.08, http://www.dailynews.lk/2008/05/19/sec01.asp (10.02.12).

'Two Men Who Tried to Acquire Cache of Weapons for Terror Group Extradited', http://www.gsnmagazine.com/node/28137 (10.02.12).

University Teachers for Human Rights (Jaffna) Special Report no. 31, http://www.uthr.org/SpecialReports/spreport31.htm#_Toc212879820 (13.12.13).

University Teachers for Human Rights (UTHR) reports:
http://www.uthr.org/Reports/Report11/appendix2.htm (05.12.13).
http://www.uthr.org/Reports/Report11/appendix2.htm (11.11.13).
http://www.uthr.org/Reports/Report8/chapter5.htm#a (17.01.13).
http://www.uthr.org/SpecialReports/spreport5.htm#_Toc512569422 (05.12.13).

'Vadamarchchi Operation: The Missing Generation', *Saturday Review*, 20.6.87, pp. 3, 4, 9.

'Vaharai Black Tiger Attack', *Sri Lanka Monitor*, no. 139, August 1999, http://brcslproject.gn.apc.org/slmonitor/August99/vaha.html (13.12.13).

'Velvetithurai, a Fishing Village Victim of Pogrom', *Financial Times*, 21.8.84, reproduced in S. Sivanayagam (ed), 'Tamil Information', (published for private circulation) Madras, v. 1, nos. 4 and 5, 1.9.84, p. 12.

Venkatnarayan, S., 'A Visit to Jaffna', *The Island*, 15.2.87, p. 6.

Venkatrramani, S.H., 'Battle Lines', *India Today*, 15.12.84.

—— 'Taming the Tigers', *India Today*, 30.11.86, pp. 22–3.

Bibliography 265

'Victory's Price: 6200 Sri Lankan Troops', http://news.smh.com.au/breaking-news-world/victorys-price-6200-sri-lankan-troops-20090522-bi4f.html (17.01.13).

Vijayasiri, Raj, *A Critical Analysis of the Sri Lankan Government's Counter Insurgency Campaign,* (Master's Thesis, Fort Leavenworth: Texas, 1990).

Wade, Matt, 'Inside Sri Lanka's Devastated Battleground', *Sydney Morning Herald*, 4.5.09, http://www.smh.com.au/news/world/inside-sri-lankas-devastated-battleground/2009/05/03/1241289038787.html (05.12.13).

'Wanni Civilians Denied Relief and Freedom of Movement – Human Rights Watch', http://transcurrents.com/tc/2008/12/post_179.html (17.01.13).

Warusahennedi, Sena, '200 Burnt Bodies Found', *The Island*, 22.7.90, p. 1.

Watawana, Dinesh, 'Troops Sound Victory Trumpet', *Sunday Times*, 4.8.91, p. 1.

——— 'Jaffna Operations Achieve Objectives', *Sunday Times*, 27.10.91, p. 1.

——— 'Batticaloa: One More Sunrise', *Sunday Times*, 16.2.92, p. 5.

Weaver, Maryanne, 'Civil War Looms with Separatists', *The Australian*, 31.1.85.

Weisman, Steven, 'Terror on the Beach in Sri Lanka', *Sydney Morning Herald*, 12.2.85.

Weerakoon, Ruwan, 'LTTE Cornered and Cut Off', http://www.thebottomline.lk/2009/01/28/defence_col.htm (05.07.13).

Weerawarne, Sumadhu, 'An Unlikely Hero', *The Island*, 30.3.97, p. 6.

'Weli Oya Death Toll Rising – 54 Now', *Daily News*, 27.7.93, pp. 1, 16.

West, Julian, 'Passage to Jaffna', *Asiaweek*, 8.3.1991.

'We Will Fight and Go Underground – Mahattaya', D.B.S. Jeyaraj's Interview with Tiger deputy leader Mahattaya, *The Island*, 25.10.87, p. 7.

'Who Is Gunning for Pottu Amman', *Sunday Times*, 17.1.93, p. 5.

Wickremesinghe, Chandima, 'Terrorists Suffer Heavy Casualties; Jaffna Fort Holds Out', *Sunday Times*, 24.6.90, p. 1.

Wijayaratna, Gamini, 'Tigers Overrun East Army Base', *The Island*, 23.4.95, p. 1.

Wijeratne, Premalal and Jayatilake, Rajika, 'Al unquiet on the Eastern Front', *Sunday Leader*, 14.5.95, p. 4.

Wijeratne, Premalal, Hussein, Asgar, Thevanayagam, Pearl and Samarakkody, Sasanka, 'Colombo Crippled by LTTE', *Sunday Leader*, 22.10.95, p. 1.

Wijeratne, Premalal, and Valliere, Winston de, 'Killing Fields of Killinochchi', *Sunday Leader*, 11.8.96, p. 4.

Wijeratne, Premalal and Samarakkody, Sasanka, 'STF Suffers a Severe Setback', *Sunday Leader*, 15.12.96, p. 4.

——— 'The Final Countdown', *Sunday Leader*, 5.11.95, p. 8.

266 Bibliography

———— 'Fish of Fury', *Sunday Leader*, 22.12.96, p. 5.

———— 'Bastion around Batti', *Sunday Leader*, 29.12.96, p. 4.

———— 'Edibala Overshadowed', *Sunday Leader*, 23.2.97, p. 5.

———— 'Edibala: Mission Accomplished', *Sunday Leader*, 2.3.97.

———— 'Saga of CapturingVessels Continues', *Sunday Leader*, 13.7.97, p. 4.

———— 'Tigers Brace for Big Forces Op', *Sunday Leader*, 27.4.97, p. 7.

———— 'Troops Zoom in on Kilinochchi', *Sunday Observer,* 24.8.08, http://www.sundayobserver.lk/2008/08/24/sec03.asp (19.12.12).

———— 'Pudukuduyiruppu Awaits Final Battle', *Sunday Observer,* 8.2.09, http://www.sundayobserver.lk/2009/02/08/sec03.asp (05.07.13).

———— 'Desperate LTTE Attempts to Reverse Security Forces' Victories', http://www.sundayobserver.lk/2009/02/15/sec03.asp (05.07.13).

———— 'Troops Marching on LTTE's Last Terrain', *Sunday Observer,* 8.3.09, http://www.sundayobserver.lk/2009/03/08/sec03.asp, 21.0812).

———— 'Liberating Vakarai', *Sunday Observer,* 20.9.09, http://www.sundayobserver.lk/2009/09/20/sec03.asp (17.01.13).

Wijayapala, Ranil, 'Liberation Thoppigala', *Sunday Observer,* 11.10.09, http://www.sundayobserver.lk/2009/10/11/sec03.asp (22.12.12).

———— 'Muhamalai, Sornapattu and Strategic Elephant Pass Fall in a Row', *Sunday Observer,* 27.12.2009, http://www.sundayobserver.lk/2009/12/27/sec03.asp (13.08.12).

———— 'Crossing of Strategic Earth Bund', *Sunday Observer,* 6.12.09, http://www.sundayobserver.lk/2009/12/06/sec03.asp (11.11.13).

———— 'Gallant Hero Defends Elephant Pass', *Sunday Observer,* 11.1.10, http://www.sundayobserver.lk/2010/07/11/sec03.asp (08.11.12).

———— 'Troops Zoom in on Kilinochchi', *Sunday Observer,* 8.24.12, http://lknewscolumns.blogspot.com.au/2008/08/troops-zoom-in-on-kilinochchi-sunday.html (27.08.12).

Wijesnghe, Geof, 'LTTE Suffers Worst Defeat in Conflict', *Daily News*, 29.7.95, Inform Clippings July '95, pp. 11–12.

Williams, Louise, 'Jaffna Children Brainwashed to Fight', *Sunday Times*, 30.5.93, p. 5, originally appeared in the *Sydney Morning Herald*.

'World Focus on Wanni Civilians', *Sunday Times*, 21.9.08, http://www.sundaytimes.lk/080921/Columns/political.html (27. 08.12).

'Yal-Devi Blast: Death Toll 39', *Sun*, 22.1.85.

Index

air power, double-edged sword 42–4
Ananthapuram 216–17, 226
army camps 13, 19, 31, 58–9, 68, 70, 115, 117, 121, 149, 151, 181
army commandos 108, 161
army patrol 12, 150
assassination 17, 74, 178, 180, 187, 205
assassins 6–24, 168
assault rifles 16, 33, 36, 66, 68–9, 139, 152, 173, 217–18

Balagalle, Lionel 167–8
'barrel bomber' 42, 57, 79, 86, 88, 90
Batticaloa 10, 18, 20, 50, 68, 70, 94–6, 114–15, 133, 149–50, 152, 179–80, 183–5, 196; north of 148, 183
Batticaloa District 21–2, 24, 148, 150, 152, 183
Batticaloa town 22, 95, 150–3, 180
Black Sea Tigers 103, 113, 123
Black Tiger commandos 152, 154
blitzkrieg, Tigers' 70–2

CDF *see* Ceylon Defence Force
ceasefire 13, 52, 113, 175–9, 191, 197, 213, 225
Ceylon 7, 9, 29
Ceylon Defence Force (CDF) 29

Ceylon Light Infantry Volunteers (CLIV) 28–9
Ceylon Rifle Regiment 28
Chalai 123, 152, 202, 216, 219
Chandraprema, C.A. 2, 4
Chavakachcheri 12, 106, 120, 163, 165
civilians 39–41, 43, 53, 55, 57–8, 79, 93–4, 104–5, 107, 115, 120–2, 141, 178, 184, 223–8; attacks on 24; casualties 44
CLIV *see* Ceylon Light Infantry Volunteers
Colombo 12–13, 17, 19–20, 29, 40, 52, 63–4, 69, 73, 105, 114, 122, 179, 220
Colombuthurai 163, 165
commandos 33, 40, 54, 57, 73, 90, 96–7, 132–3, 135, 137, 140, 149, 167–8, 188–9, 203–5

defence lines 128, 132, 134, 136–8, 151, 157–8, 162, 166, 184, 188, 206, 215, 227
Dvoras 86

Ealam People's Revolutionary Liberation Front (EPRLF) 12, 17–18, 67
Ealam Revolutionary Organisation of Students (EROS) 12, 17–18
Ealam War II 75
Ealam War IV 188, 197, 227, 236
Eastern offensive 113–16

268 Index

East, reconquest of 173–92
Elephant Pass 31, 35, 50, 52, 54,
  75–80, 85, 92–3, 104–9, 130–1,
  133, 136, 159–62, 202, 235
enemy frontlines 204–5
EROS *see* Ealam Revolutionary
  Organisation of Students
exodus 223–6

FACs *see* Fast Attack Craft
Fast Attack Craft (FACs) 89,
  181, 191
Fifty-Eighth Division 200–3,
  216, 227
Fifty-Fifth Division 135, 166, 202
Fifty-Seventh Division 200–3, 216
Final Battle 75–6
firepower 32, 36, 57, 77, 79, 118–
  19, 136, 161, 164, 167, 177,
  187–8, 190, 197–8, 235–6
Forward Defence Line (FDL)
  127–30, 134, 138, 140–1, 152,
  168, 182

Gandhi, Rajiv 74
garrison 42, 51, 72–3, 75–7,
  79–80, 100, 103, 109, 132,
  158
Gota's War 2
government troops 178, 189,
  197
guerrillas 6–24
guerrilla war 150–2
Gunaratna, Rohan 68, 69

Indian navy 103
Indian Peace Keeping Force (IPKF)
  2, 63–4, 66–9, 235
Indian troops 65, 67, 74, 220
Interim Self-Government
  Administration (ISGA) 175
IPKF *see* Indian Peace Keeping
  Force
IPKF interlude 63–80

Jaffna: Fort 12, 19, 49–51, 53–4,
  58–9, 71–2, 79; lagoon 6, 103,
  107, 120; Peninsula 6–7, 18, 20,
  48, 50, 52–3, 92, 94, 100,

102–4, 117–18, 127–8, 164,
  166, 233; police stations 12;
  town 43, 53, 57, 59, 68,
  163, 165
Jaffna–Point Pedro Road 119
Janatha Vmukthi Peramuna (JVP)
  31–4, 66, 73, 178

Kilali, battle for 100–9
Kokavil 19, 70, 72–3, 77, 86,
  107, 200
Kokilai army camps 12, 121

landmine attacks 12, 38–9
liberated zone 152–4
Liberation Tigers of Tamil Ealam
  (LTTE) 1–2, 11–12, 15–19,
  56–7, 63–7, 69–70, 106–7,
  112–13, 174–6, 178–9, 183–4,
  196, 212–15, 223–7, 235–6
LTTE *see* Liberation Tigers of
  Tamil Ealam

Mankulam 77
MBRLs 142, 164–5, 167, 179,
  181–2, 186–90, 215
militants 11–20, 23, 34, 39–41,
  43–4, 51, 54, 56, 68; groups
  11, 13, 17–18, 67
military: conflict 2–3, 234;
  modernising of 36–7; operations
  4, 42, 51–2, 60, 106, 114, 127,
  153, 174, 233
missiles, anti-aircraft 116, 189–90
Moorcraft, Paul 2, 4
Mullaithivu 19, 23, 65–6, 70,
  89–92, 120–1, 130–4, 137,
  139, 142, 197, 199–200,
  202–3, 223
munitions 175–6, 190

Nanthikadal 222–3
naval arm 103, 177, 218
NORINCO *see* North Industries
  Corporation
North-east Provincial Council
  68, 70
North Industries Corporation
  (NORINCO) 88

Operation Earthquake 93, 102
Operation Edibala 132–5, 138
Operation Frog 107–9
Operation Jayasikurui 134–8, 153, 168
Operation Liberation 48, 52–6, 59–60, 64, 86, 91, 118
Operation Ranaghosa 138–9
Operation Riviresa 118, 123, 130, 148
Operation Sathbala 90, 92
Operation Seegrapahara 91
Operation Sixer 90
Operation Tiger Hunt 91
Operation Yal Devi 106–7

peace process 51, 112–14, 174–5, 179–80, 183, 191
People's Front of Liberation Tigers (PFLT) 69
People's Liberation Organisation of Thamilealam (PLOTE) 11
Prabhakaran, Velupillai 11, 12, 16, 48, 51, 52, 56, 69, 121, 131, 167, 197, 201, 221, 227, 236
Puccaras 88, 108–9, 152
Puliyankulam 135–6, 140, 158

Rajapaksa, Mahinda and administration 176, 178, 187, 236
rebel: air force 219–22; ambushes 96; army 3, 17, 119; artillery 161, 164–5, 182, 213; attacks 128, 140, 151, 154, 161, 182, 199; cadres 48, 68, 71, 76, 79, 119, 139, 161, 181–2, 202, 227, 234; camps 149, 185, 198, 204; commandos 157, 161; control 49, 130, 152, 165, 180, 186, 224; counter-attacks 139–40; defences 93, 118–19; leaders 178, 226; lines 167, 224; merchant navy 176, 190; navy 101, 218; offensive 73, 163–4, 178; resistance 65, 107, 136, 166; territory 50, 89, 168, 183, 186–8, 215, 219, 221

recruits 14, 16–17, 32, 35, 87, 131, 141
refugee camps 17, 158, 184, 223–4
retreat, last 211–28
rural insurgency 65–7

Saladin armoured cars 32, 36, 86, 90
Sampoor 182–7
Sath Jaya 132–4
Saturday Review 39
Sea Tiger: bases 102, 201, 219; operations 106, 199
Shin Bet 40
Siai Marchettis 42–3, 53, 57, 72, 78–9, 86, 88, 90, 108
siege, of northern army camps 18–20
Silvathurai 71, 74–5, 77, 79, 103; slaughter at 74–5
Sinhala Only Act 30
Sinhalese 6, 8–10, 16, 21–2, 28, 30, 41, 66, 95; settlers 22–3
SIOT *see* Special Infantry Operations Teams
SLFP *see* Sri Lanka Freedom Party
soldiers, embattled 36, 134
Special Infantry Operations Teams (SIOT) 188
Special Task Force (STF) 40, 42, 95, 97, 150–2, 185, 196
Sri Lanka Freedom Party (SLFP) 11
Sri Lankan military: air force 53, 163, 173, 179, 214, 219–22; army 66, 118, 142, 164, 178, 222; navy 64, 101–3, 175, 177, 179, 190, 218–19, 226, 236; Security Forces 1, 3, 12–13, 40, 57–8, 60, 63–4, 69, 71, 100, 164, 166, 225, 227–8, 233–6
Sri Lanka's Eastern Province 187
suicide cadres 59, 73, 103, 136, 151, 225
supply lines, choking of 189–91

Tamil Ealam Liberation Organisation (TELO) 11–12, 17–18, 67

270 Index

Tamil militancy, rise of 10–13
Tamil National Army (TNA)
 67–9
Tamil New Tigers (TNT) 11–12,
 66
Tamil rebellion 6, 60; birth of
 6–24
Tamils in Sri Lanka 6, 13, 15
Tamil United Liberation Front
 (TULF) 11
Taraki 4
TELO *see* Tamil Ealam Liberation
 Organisation
territory, government-controlled
 152–3
terrorist attacks 11, 174, 214
Thondamaru 44, 53–5
Thoppigala 97, 182–7, 189
Tamil Tigers 1, 173, 211–28,
 234, 237; blitzkrieg 70–2;
 cadres 18, 49, 53, 57,
 64, 224; camps 17, 92;
 commandos 157, 222; country
 95, 127, 152, 154, 185–6; last
 retreat of 211–28; leaders 51,
 69; leadership 1, 178; territories
 196, 207
TNA *see* Tamil National Army
TNT *see* Tamil New Tigers
Trincomalee 15, 20–4, 31, 50, 52,
 64, 68, 70–1, 80, 94, 107, 150,
 152, 176, 179–84; north of
 24, 95
Trincomalee District 21, 23–4,
 41, 148
TULF *see* Tamil United Liberation
 Front

Unceasing Waves 132, 157–69
United National Party (UNP) 14,
 112, 174
University Teachers for Human
 Rights (UTHR) 212, 223–4
UNP *see* United National Party
UTHR *see* University Teachers for
 Human Rights

Vadamarachchi 6, 11, 52–60,
 119–20, 160–1
Vakarai 94, 115, 148, 153, 183–5,
 188–90, 196
Valikamam 6, 53–4, 58–9, 118–20,
 122, 160, 163, 166
Vavuniya 19, 38, 41, 65, 73, 89,
 116, 128, 130–1, 134–5, 158,
 200, 215, 223; north of 127,
 131, 138
Vettilakerni 76, 92, 103–4, 123,
 128, 160–1
violence 11–12, 18, 20, 24, 37–9,
 114–15, 179

Wanni 72–5, 85, 87–90, 100,
 127–8, 130–2, 134–6, 138–42,
 151–3, 159–60, 196–8, 200–4,
 206–7, 211–15, 222–5, 233–6;
 and A9 130–1; campaign,
 reflections 139–43; problem of
 127–43; return to, prospects and
 challenges 196–8; rolling up of
 196–207; western 90, 138–40,
 142, 158, 198–200, 205, 211,
 218–19
Weerasooriya, Sri Lal 162
Wijeratne, Ranjan 73–4